*The Unlikely Peace
at Cuchumaquic*

Also by MARTÍN PRECHTEL

Secrets of the Talking Jaguar
Long Life, Honey in the Heart
The Disobedience of the Daughter of the Sun
Stealing Benefacio's Roses

The Unlikely Peace
at Cuchumaquic

The Parallel Lives of People as Plants: Keeping the Seeds Alive

MARTÍN PRECHTEL

North Atlantic Books
Berkeley, Californiaa

Published by
North Atlantic Books
P.O. Box 12327
Berkeley, California 94712

Cover art © 2011 by Martín Prechtel; photographed by
Eric Swanson
All illustrations © by Martín Prechtel
Cover and book design by Suzanne Albertson

Printed in the United States of America

The chapter "Always a Place at the Table" originally appeared in *Sacred Fire Magazine*, issue 9, as "Beautiful Running."
The names of some individuals in this book have been altered in deference to their desire for privacy.

The Unlikely Peace at Cuchumaquic: The Parallel Lives of People as Plants: Keeping the Seeds Alive is sponsored by the Society for the Study of Native Arts and Sciences, a nonprofit educational corporation whose goals are to develop an educational and cross-cultural perspective linking various scientific, social, and artistic fields; to nurture a holistic view of arts, sciences, humanities, and healing; and to publish and distribute literature on the relationship of mind, body, and nature.

North Atlantic Books' publications are available through most bookstores. For further information, visit our website at www.northatlanticbooks.com or call 800-733-3000.

Library of Congress Cataloging-in-Publication Data
Prechtel, Martín.
    The unlikely peace at Cuchumaquic : the parallel lives of people as plants, Keeping the seeds alive / Martín Prechtel.
        p. cm.
    Summary: "A memoir, spiritual adventure story, and ecological fable, this book shares the message that plants and humanity are interconnected, and that the survival of one depends upon the other"—Provided by publisher.
    ISBN-13: 978-1-58394-360-1
    ISBN-10: 1-58394-360-9
    1. Prechtel, Martín. 2. Shamans—United States—Biography. 3. Shamans—Guatemala—Santiago Atitlán—Biography. 4. Human-plant relationships—Guatemala—Santiago Atitlán. 5. Tzutuhil Indians—Religion. 6. Tzutuhil Indians—Rites and ceremonies. 7. Santiago Atitlán (Guatemala)—Religious life and customs. 8. Santiago Atitlán (Guatemala)—Social life and customs. I. Title.
    BF1679.8.P74A3 2011
    299.7'842—dc23 [B]   2011028182

1 2 3 4 5 6 7 8 9 SHERIDAN 17 16 15 14 13 12

B ecause this book is meant as a gift to that thing in original humans, which at one time made them a welcome sound in the symphony of all Nature, this book is dedicated to all those men and women, Keres-speaking, Spanish-speaking New Mexicans and Tzutujil Mayan farmers, who in my early days, against all outside pressures, were still dedicated to keeping alive the seeds of their own tribal shards of the original magic of human culture and beautiful ritual farming.

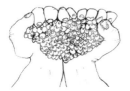

*I*n fond memory of all the plant forms and their people in Europe; the many Asias; Africa; the Middle East; North, Central, and South America; Micronesia; Melanesia; and Polynesia who have been forced into nonsustainable mechanical food production, genetically altered, culturally GMO'd, or who have disappeared altogether.

It is not enough to save heritage seeds.

The culture of those people to whom each seed belongs must be kept alive along with seeds and their cultivation.

Not in freezers or museums

but in their own soil and our daily lives.

CONTENTS

Part IV

Our Agreement with the Holy in Nature 305

PREFACE

In the early seventies when I left the United States, I fled the overwhelming influx of the "modern" Americas crush on what was left of the indigenous and old Hispanic New Mexico of my youth.

Bouncing through Mexico in a seemingly aimless meander like a sowbug rolled up and washed where life's river will wash, I landed like the subject of some forgotten mythology on the shores of Lake Atitlán, blinking and stunned by the depth and beauty of an ancient seed-ritual culture whose heart still beat to pump life into a magical world that was as tangible as my own capacity to see it.

For over a decade, I lived a life of welcome, Indigenous spiritual determination and soul-feeding usefulness to the "germ" of that magic face of the Divine as a full constituent of the hierarchy of Sacred Farmers of the Tzutujil Maya of South Atitlán.

But it wasn't long until the vicious snarl of Guatemala's multi-entity war of the 1980s—funded and promoted by the same mentality both left and right that I had earlier tried to futilely escape by leaving the States—rolled through Guatemala, flattening the indigenous mind and terrorizing all subtle mythic life. Like thousands of Guatemalans, I was harassed by the constant threat of assassination and disappearances, and after not a few close calls and shrapnel wounds, instead of fleeing yet again to another "pristine" place, I came back to New Mexico with my Tzutujil wife and two boys.

Though it took another decade of anonymous, tribeless poverty before I could land square enough to begin living again, it would take another ten years before I could breathe deep enough to know it was all right to live in a country whose people have no idea what the world really is beneath the veneer of global modernity.

Ironically, the telling of all the comedy, terror, struggle and layers of beauty of what we experienced was a story that everybody in the U.S. seemed to want to hear.

Back in the early 1990s, the great American poet Robert Bly and others, after coming across the telling of these tales of ours from a mind so radically "non-European," insisted I teach, not only encouraging me to continue telling my story, but also emphatic that I should publish.

Robert explained to my incredulous and somewhat crestfallen soul that due to the homogenizing entertainment motive of the modern mind from the effects of television, the irreality of the virtual programs of the computer, and a bad public education, the modern public was no longer capable of any quick recognition of tactile reality that had anything to do with the earth or the natural wealth of human emotion.

While the people might be entertained by the grand "things" I spoke into view, they would *never* honor nor accept the legitimacy of who I was and what I taught, if my story were not framed in the format of published pop writing.

This was outrageous to me, for all the beauty I stood for and spoke came from cultures where the grandest of all comprehensions were never, ever, written and only transmitted in osmotic whispers inside the context of hands-on ritual. To write them was to freeze and kill the "germ" of the seed of the knowledge.

But luckily nobody but anthropologists were particularly interested in these "grand" things, or less still in my original thoughts as influenced by a close understanding and service to those grand things. In those days, the publishers didn't want my vision or a manual on how to remake an old culture; they wanted a marketable, entertaining travelogue of the story of my "interesting" life in order to relax the reader with just small wisdoms whispered here and there.

But strategically, I also knew I would never gain a place on any bookstore shelf or make any headway into the hearts of modernity's suffering crowds unless I held back and gave them instead the entertaining story they wanted. Still I refused to compromise or conform by expressing in a hushed tone my feelings about beauty or my politics.

I reckoned that book by book over time, if I was graced with any modicum of public acceptance to my writing, that I might one day speak more freely, not just more of the entertaining story of my life, but the vision of that life.

Because of my upbringing inside of languages not containing the objectifying verb "to be," I had a severe allergy to writing "about" things. I felt that when one wrote, the writing itself should *"be"* what one wrote. The words were not components of a dead vehicle, but live matter. Language written had to be language that, in its speaking, became, in the manner the words were written, the very thing that would otherwise be written about. One did not write about a horse; one wrote a horse into view, and then as the horse charged off the page into the grassy pastures of the reader's soul, one had to stand back, make room, or be trampled.

To me words are real—if they are not real, why bother writing them!

But where I failed from the onset to entertain this notion came in the form of my notoriously long acknowledgment sections.

Toward the end of finishing up my first book, *Secrets of the Talking Jaguar,* unsure of the protocol of tradition and still new to writing, I consulted various authors regarding what an acknowledgments page should contain. Everyone concurred that it should be a simple succinct mention of those people or entities without whose direct involvement the book would not have gone to press.

I'm certain this sound guidance was only intended to impute to the public an appearance of my deeper affiliation with the pale aloofness of "serious authors," a kind of horn-rimmed, wrinkle-browed psychological suit and tie of authorial legitimacy, something that might allow me to slip more easily into the august cadre of East Coast writers, reviewers, and so on, upon whose support every successful book was rumored to rely, but whose intellectual dress code did not admit the likes of me and my writing, which they mocked as over-flamboyant, over-adjectival, renegade and romantic.

So instead of allowing my public image to be rescued from the muck of the misunderstanding of big-city vicious gossip and academic potshots I proceeded to do exactly what everyone hoped I wouldn't.

Long rambling acknowledgments were considered the territory of naïve first-timers who embarrassingly took the fact of their book's existence overly seriously.

But in all honesty and deference to my author friends' advice, when I got thinking about to whom I owed the publishing of my first book, in honor of the very core of what that book and all my subsequent writing advocates, namely the issue of *káslimáal*, the Mayan word meaning "mutual indebtedness" of all life's things to all other things before and after, I proceeded to fail in every way at succinctness.

Like a country-boy high-school quarterback who'd just won his first game, who, when asked on the news, "To whom do you owe it all?" begins by thanking the Creator, then Grandpa who got him his first ball, then Grandma, then Mom who birthed him, and Dad for pushing him into it, little sister Elsa for putting up with it, their dog Diggity who saved him from being run over, his girlfriend, his life on the farm, his best friend Bill, etc., I found it necessary to thank everyone and everything and the spiritual entities that had kept me alive and supported what I did, without whom, of course no book could have ever manifested from my heart.

A lot of people made fun of the size and content of that original acknowledgments section of *Secrets of the Talking Jaguar*. But so many others felt slighted they had been mentioned neither in the book nor in the acknowledgments and so the acknowledgments section of each subsequent book grew bigger still!

This went on and on until four books later, the acknowledgments were getting so long that during book signings and lectures I made predictions that if things kept going on in this way, and I continued to find more and more things to thank, that soon enough the acknowledgments would not only get longer than the actual book, but sooner or later the acknowledgments would end up *being* the book!

But who could've known that this crazy assertion would actually blossom into reality?

For this book, *The Unlikely Peace at Cuchumaquic*, if you really look at it, is nothing more than a 155,000-word love poem of gratitude to all those people, plants, places, cultures, situations, and origins of life's indebtedness to the whole that have so generously given myself both life and inspiration enough to continue courting our spiritual friendship with the Holy in Nature.

The entire book is a small, inadequate, acknowledgments page in which honor for the origins of the contents of all I teach is told as a series of stories within stories, within a bigger story far beyond this book.

All that having been said, there are still some people whose presence didn't find their way into the story and for whom it would be a disgrace for me to leave them unsung. Especially since without them, this book would never have come to print!

The first of these is my wife, little Hanna Keller, and Altai, our daughter. For thirty-five years every morning at three o'clock, ever since the Guatemalan earthquake of February 4, 1976, at 3:00 a.m., I have been startled awake from my dreams, terrified and shaking in a cold sweat. Over the years I fell into so many arms in search of hope and comfort, but it was not until little Hannita held me that I began to live again. And now finally there are solid nights of sleep and a little sunny daughter to plant corn with. She knows it all, Keeping the Seeds Alive. Without them I should never have written. Period.

And then there are those puzzling human wonders who, in this age of numbing sarcasm, still read my books. For my readers don't read books to escape or to feel better, or for travelogues, or to become "initiated"; they read my books for the same reason I write them: because they are in love with what I'm in love with and by reading them we sit side by side, both of us looking out past the world's insanity in hopes of somewhere growing ourselves into roses to feed the hummingbirds of the Holy in Nature.

And then there is the publisher, North Atlantic Books, Richard Grossinger in particular, who in the gnashing maw of the world of North American publishing has deemed that the vision of what I write and do is a seed worth keeping alive against all odds. And Hisae Matsuda, this book's personal editor, who I have to say is the first truly intelligent editor I've been graced with, who not only has taken the time to read and understand, but is also dedicated to getting the world to do the same, a very rare phenomenon these days.

And then there is Mary Dolores Zovich, who has been fifty thousand tent poles holding up the canopy of all we do here at the ranch and in our school. She has not only kept all our animals and people alive with the most timeless dedication, but was the brave and able typist of the initial stages of this and two other upcoming books.

Because I do not write on any kind of machine, neither computers nor typewriters, my handwritten manuscripts have to be typed out on and into machines by others. But this is a veritable feat of divine magic, for my handwriting is an autocultural phenomenon at best, a singular stenography, whose signs change value as the speed of writing increases or the poetry thickens, looking for all the world like worm tracks after a rain.

There are only four known humans on Earth who can be said to be able to decipher my handwriting with any authority: my wife Hanna, Thomas Smith (Robert Bly's secretary), Mary Zovich, and Susannah Hall.

Of these, Susannah Hall is not only one of the best and fastest typists in the world, she also understands and loves my work. To her go one hundred regulation British trainloads of homemade Wanda Butter (Wanda is our supernatural milk cow). And to her best mates Kayode Olafimihan and Hugh Livingstone for all they do, keeping Ms. Hall fed and sane during all those grueling marathons of typing for this book.

To Robert and Ruth Bly, always friends, always grateful.

To Marianne Lust, who, after keeping so many others alive, both worthy and ungrateful, is finally getting used to coming back alive herself. In eternal gratitude for all her help, both obvious and unsung.

To Debra Lubar for keeping Marianne alive and staying well to do it. My best student and smartest friend. All blessings to the whole family.

My full admiration to Inge Hindel, Chandani, and Manoj for their inspiring in-the-city farm of vegetables, medicinal plants, chickens, goats, and bees on the roof, which is not only beautiful but a living example of keeping the seeds of life and culture alive.

And a great wide blessing to all of the Remembrance and Initiation communities in Vermont and Britain, especially those amazing people who keep alive this flower of a ceremony of passage: modern people trying with all their heart to feed the Holy in Nature right under modernity's banal gaze.

To good Reed Larson for all his untiring book searches and research.

To all the students of Bolad's Kitchen who have stuck it out, the Kishigten, New Sprouts, and Shoots and Tendrils in particular, for you have given me a hand to kiss, a heart to break, seeds to crack, and the greatest gift of all by becoming the living vision of the improbable possibility of real culture sprouting back into view out of the lives and bodies of those whose culture has killed and forgotten it. Another seed to you.

And to all these and any others I may have overlooked, please receive a little bit of the magical aroma of the Original Flowering Mountain Jade Water Earth—and jump up and live again.

> *Kix yik ta ja*
> *Kix kás taja*
> Rise up and sprout
> Live, Flower, Flame up again

All Blessings

Martín Prechtel,
Curly Bird Ranch, Acequia del Gavilan,
Ojo Caliente, New Mexico
January 2012

A NOTE ON WRITING WITH
NATIVE WORDS

Any attempt to represent in any established written orthography the music of the sounds of an orally learned, nonwritten traditional language, especially by a writer who speaks both the fettered and the free, is as hilarious and frustrating as trying to rope a big wild pig with a shoestring and a toilet seat, and just about as useful.

For monolingual people with a written language, who have lost any memories of their tribal pasts and of languages learned purely by tribal upbringing with no writing involved, it might seem unimportant to be able to feel the deliciousness of other realities as spoken in a different conformation of tongue, tooth, facial expression, and breath. It might seem elementary that this letter or that character could be used to approximate some similar sound already represented in the writing system they take for granted that was taught to them as children as, say for instance, American English.

But as much as the meaning of a word is important, the musicality of the thought of the word is just as important if we want to live a life that keeps the seeds alive and makes beauty.

Language should be more than a function; it should be an art form whose beauty can feed the Holy in Nature.

After all, our scribbles aren't even worm tracks in wet mutable sand; they mean nothing as they are functionally scribbled today, if nobody agrees that this letter represents this part of that sound, and this can only happen if one has first heard that sound with our ears. There is nothing in the scribbles that has a sound. Therefore trying to "write down" the sound of another people's speech is folly unless the people have heard and remembered the sounds—in which case, why not simply learn the language orally and speak into life the joys, griefs, and marvels all languages carry off the tongue to an ear that knows your tongue?

So, I've resigned myself, on behalf of the few Tzutujil, Nahuat, and Pueblo Indian words in this book to represent them as primitively as possible by approximating as many of the spoken sounds of these native tongues with certain sounds in English and more so with the written Spanish of the Americas who both use "Roman" characters.

Therefore,

- all vowels are basically spoken as in Spanish;
- all dipthongs as well;
- long vowels are doubled;
- the consonants *b, c, ch, d, g, j, m, n, p, q, r, s, t,* and *z* are spoken as in Spanish;
- other consonants *ts, tz, ds, tsch* are explosive and logically pronounced similarly to English;
- if any consonant has a ' over it, this signifies a sound not present in any European tongue. A ' at the end of a word that terminates in a vowel represents a kind of consonant that is an abrupt cutoff of the vowel called a "glottal stop"; it is like a word ending in *p* or *t* or *d* that does not voice the consonant but says it with no sound. For instance, *ba'* (English *baht*): say *bah* and mouth the *t*. *L'* equals an *l* with a *th* and a *d* all lined up together in one sound. *Q'* is a deep throaty tonsil pop, *c'* is a *k* popped in the roof of the mouth.

Well, these are just a few of the examples.

Most important though: I have retained the old-time-honored Spanish colonial use of *x* for what in English is represented by *sh* partly because of its widespread acceptance and more for the principles invoked by remembering its historical "origins." After all, the remembrance of origins is what this book is about.

Before there was a Spain, in the area that would be synthetically and forcefully annexed to "make" Spain, some of the languages spoken therein, namely Aramaic, Syriac, Arabic and Greek, had old writing traditions, whereas Esmalen, Iberian Celtic, Numidian, and Visagothic German, to name only a few, were orally transmitted.

After the Romans forced written Latin down everybody's throats and during the Catholic centuries that followed, when all the local land languages were combined and hammered into Latinic forms to create various types of what is now called Spanish, the official Imperial Spanish, for some quirk of fate, ended up having no *sh* sound, unlike Ladino (Spanish Yiddish), Arabic, Persian, Catalan, and Gallego (Gaelic Spanish), not to mention all the people the "Spanish" ended up overrunning and colonizing.

Because the fundamentalist Catholic nature of the New Spanish enforced national identity (which represented, as always, none of its constituency) all the people who weren't Christians and Catholics were branded as heathens, having in common the nasty old *sh* sound.

During the Conquest, and the Spanish Empire that followed, for all its faults and terrors, Spanish bureaucrats were prodigious chroniclers and took a heck of a lot more interest in the people and places they invaded than any of their northern European competitors.

Therefore, in a fascinating instance of droll medieval bad ritual magic, to represent this "pagan" *sh* sound in their chronicles, reports, and edicts, they took an old "baptized civilized Catholic" *C* facing as it should to the good side: the right, which in a lot of old orthographies represents a *ch* sound, then they added a "backwards pagan reversed" Ɔ and merged them into a ƆC and thus the letter *sh* was born! From Greek they always had an *aquis,* an *x* that had the sound more of a German *ch* or a modern *x*.

Over time this new ƆC letter became a catchall letter to represent this sound in Basque, the *tz's* and *tshch* of the Georgians, and any delicious alien phoneme that was too suggestive to join the Imperial Alphabet!

Mexico comes from the word the colonial Spanish wrote as *Mexica (mesheeka)* for the tribal name the Aztec people called themselves. Therefore Mexico was pronounced *Me'sheéko* for several centuries, as it had before the European interruption. But at some point people again tried to "civilize" the orthography and the country and put a Spanish *j* for the original *x* and it became *Mejico* (pronounced *mehééko*), until more nationalist revolutionaries replaced the *x* and it was written as *Mexico* again but still pronounced as it had with the Spanish *j!* Crazy world.

So let's leave these back-to-back C's, so we can all stay conscious of our own hatred of the "barbarians" we *all* descend from on both sides of the bias.

After all, we should remember that the English word "pagan" comes from old pre-Christian Imperial Roman Latin *paganus,* which means "not cultivated" as in land and people!, i.e., wild!, i.e., unannexed, untaxable, etc., etc.!

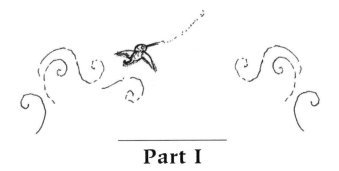

Part I

*The Unlikely Peace
at Cuchumaquic*

Chapter 1

Always a Place at the Table

As young children on the reservation I remember the deep need to run. For all the young Indian people, both girls and boys, running was as great a characteristic of the Indigenous life of Pueblo, Navajo, and Apache people still living in their original beloved homelands of the arid highlands of New Mexico as was their sense of comic joy or the generous ceremonial house-to-house feasting throughout their villages, for which they are still famous.

Like all of the English-speaking public schools in the United States that Native and Spanish-speaking children of our area were forced to attend, there were always kids in the sixth grade old enough to drop out of high school for it was they who were the first generation of minors in their family lines to be enforced by federal law to begin school attendance, no matter what their age. Characterized as arrogant, troublesome, and incapable of learning, they were actually not slow, and certainly no more incorrigible than the rest of us. School for them was an imposed irrelevancy to the reality of their already adultish life they led inside "their" own natural Native territory. They of course felt no compelling responsibility to attend an invader's academy that had so little to teach them in reference to what they already knew and would need to live regarding village planting, hunting, courting, and their constant obligatory communal ceremonial participation upon which old-time Pueblo life has always relied and which was still a going concern in my youth.

The casual special appearances and unauthorized disappearances to and from the classroom of these beautiful, rowdy older teenagers ran pretty much according to how they rated the entertainment value of the few chosen teachers whose method of instruction appealed to them. School authorities learned early on that these students could never be threatened with expulsion for they would have loved nothing better. But there was one aspect of the school that no student ever missed, unless impeded by mandatory village ceremonial obligation, and that was a footrace of any distance scheduled by the coaches.

To be truthful, they couldn't have given a flea's fart for the *racing*. They didn't come to race; what they loved was *running*, running across their own rolling wild homeland, just for the deliciousness of running enormous distances through the sacred itself. Like the feral multicolored horses, wild antelopes, jackrabbits, and swallows that coursed along with them, they too were made of elegant motion and just had to do it. In the same way breezes can't help but sweep the earth, they had to run. It was a delicious ancient inborn itch that paced in the hearts of their Indigenous Souls that would only be calmed by running, and running well and beautifully.

The school sports coaches like most of the world anymore were representatives of that neurotic, competitive-need-to-dominate culture trait that characterizes most large civilizations, and they always felt like they'd failed in life unless they could conquer someone else. They needed to win, needed to cause someone else to lose. That's all they understood. But in our school they lived in a constant tangle of nervous frustration. The source of their consternation was rooted to the unshakeable fact that even though most of these Indian boys over thirteen had running times superior to those of adult Olympians worldwide, they could not be made to compete. They just wanted to run, and run at home over the wild unpopulated land.

Like a lot of teachers in other departments, these tall non-Indian jocks became so infuriated about how they could never get the Pueblos or Navajos to compete in any tournaments that before the inevitable tendering of their resignations, they usually transformed into bitter listless maniac whiners who labeled the Indians as "unconfident, overly shy, or ashamed," or as most of us heard over and over again: "Indians are an unmotivated race lacking the go-getter gene," i.e., competitive "ambition." The coaches couldn't believe the reality that all the young people, like their ancestors forever, just loved running, not racing. This didn't mean they didn't run hard and fast, because they did. However, they didn't do so to beat a peer, but because hard and fast was part of the deliciousness. Though their short-distance times were very good, where the natural peoples of this state of New Mexico excelled was in long-distance running. The young men would run 10,000 meters, or ten miles, or four miles, whatever distance was designated as a "race," sometimes even stopping off somewhere to chat or check something out, always in a group, joking as they ran … and *still* come in well under international times, that is, if the coaches could have convinced them to cross an assigned finish line, instead of just running off to smoke and gossip before they wandered in.

The other problem for civilization's sports teachers and their need to win was the fact that though all the Indian boys ran good and hard they never ran alone, only as a group. If they happened upon a relative or friend along the way, they always urged them to run along with them, no matter how much slower a pace they might have to assume to let their older friend keep up—for such was the grand etiquette of Pueblo Indian togetherness. This meant if one of their group straggled, they would wait or run in circles not to lose momentum until the slower fellow caught up. This was definitely not conducive to an Olympic record, but a normal score for the generosity of the Indigenous Soul.

Even a couple of generations later when so much of the cultural intactness of those times had been successfully undermined and people were thoroughly indoctrinated with the syndrome of modernity's contradictory insistence on an unquestionable superiority while suffering eternally from that hardwired shame of "never being good enough" that fuels civilization's bullet train away from its own indigenous intactness, and after being successfully shamed into becoming as anxious as any Anglo about achievement, certain generations of young Indian men and women who'd been finally coerced into the nervous pride of home-and-away track meets, warm-ups, sweat suits, shorts, numbers, running shoes, trophies, victory dinners at Burger King and, God help us all, recognizing a finish line, would often even then stand jogging just before the finish line after running several miles ahead of everyone if one of their relatives was a participant in the same race and needed more time until he caught up in order to cross the line together. Even after so much assimilation, it still felt awful to do otherwise!

But the best long-distance running I ever saw at that school happened when the heroes of my youth—a group of boys, famous runners all of them, about sixteen years old, several already married, but all of them still in the sixth grade—agreed to run in their first competitive long-distance races. One of our more sneaky and desperately determined coaches secretly marked the finish line with chalk about two hundred yards beyond where it would actually lie by official track standards in order to get the kids running hard across the invisible real line without lagging for the slower ones. But he was outwitted yet again. This had been a 10,000-meter race on the reservation against teams from many other places. When the five boys came leisurely striding in at least a mile and a half ahead of all the visiting runners and while casually sharing their third disqualifying Camel cigarette as they sailed along, they not only technically won a world record that would still hold today if it had been accepted on the basis of time alone, but then after unknowingly having crossed the secret finish line together, in order to avoid what they thought was the marked finish line, these copper-bodied human birds took a collective left and just kept running and coursing the remaining five-and-a-half miles back to their home village through the beautiful high-piled boulder desert hills and sandy arroyos in blossom with the wild parsley and four-petaled yellow mustards of spring to disappear utterly from the white man's world, their school, and its program of achievements, running straight into the initiation kivas where they began their antique lives cloistered again as Pueblo Indians for the rest of their adult lives. Three of them are there to this very day.

Living and running were holy things you were supposed to get good at, not things to use to conquer, win, and get attention for. Running was not meant for taking but for giving gifts to the Holy in Nature. Running was an offering, a feeding of life.

This sometimes humorous but always devastating cultural collision between the need to conquer against the need to feed and give gifts was never more acutely visible to me than it was during ceremonial Pueblo Indian footraces.

These are ritual cross-country races between people born for the powerful gods and goddesses of summer deities and people born for the winter deities. They were run by young men, men newly initiated who of course ran in groups as the champions of the distinct gods they served.

A lot of people always gathered to watch and pray for the well-being of the runners and themselves. In some less traditional, not-so-strict places, non-Indians, non-tribal friends, were invited and fully welcomed to watch. Though this welcome was never extended to any outsiders in my area, there was no ban on our visiting other, more open, villages.

One time while visiting with some friends who had a relative married into a less guarded Pueblo village up the river, a little outside the pueblo we gathered with all their female relatives, sisters and sweethearts, with supporters of each side to encourage them on.

After the fifteen of the Moon side of summer got a strong takeoff running against the forty or so of the winter Sun, the visiting tourists shouted and continued cheering in that adamant well-practiced way as they would at all their competitive events as the painted boys disappeared into the wild. But this was Indian running and therefore cross-country, with long distances; therefore most of it was out of sight. So as soon as the young runners hit the rings of grama and clumps of buffalo grass, the *chollas*, the *sabinas*, and boulders of the uncultivated area and were out of earshot and into the dust-whipping spring wind, the villagers in the supporting crowd walked briskly back to their houses to get on with the traditional feast, leaving the still-cheering tourists alone and baffled as to what had happened.

Some of the good-hearted "white people" made their way with the rest of us to houses where feasts had been prepared, invited there by the parents and godparents of the runners. When the old people were asked by the outsiders what happened to the runners, they were courteously informed that they were probably running—and would the visitors please sit down and eat with them? Such feasting was not only an honor for visitors and one that was expected in the house of the family of the runners, an honor that comes with an obligation to accept whether or not one is hungry; it was a way for the non-running population of the village to magically give strength to the runners. This custom still lives on in every Pueblo to this day.

When further interrogated as to where the finish line was, the people usually said, "Wherever they stop running, I guess." Maybe eventually a more compassionate and patient younger person would tell the visitors the truth. "There is no finish line, they're just running."

"How do they know who wins? How do they know when to stop running? Why do they run at all?"

If someone actually broke the rules of tribal secrecy and told them that the Sun and the Moon and other beings that move in time and give us life are kept strong by the boys who run, and because the Sun annually runs his own race and helps the animals to thrive by doing so, and that the Sun tires, and when he tires, the world and all animal beings begin to flag, and die, and without the animals we would die, and the running of the boys helps the Sun to keep moving and strong and the visible world strong, and that the Moon runs even harder but in a different pulse and by doing so keeps all the waters flowing, the plants growing and maturing, without which we and everything else, especially the animals, die, and because for both the Sun and the Moon in the sky there are no finish lines; they must keep moving or the world dies; for if there were a finish line the universe would cease, so the beauty and strength of the boys' running helped lift again these gods back into their eternal continuum so the world wouldn't die, and though in some ways the boys did compete to outdo the other side in beauty, strength, and dedication, there was still no finish line, just an excellent running as long as it took until the gods had revived enough to do it themselves, so the world revived by the boys' running would be the winner. Then the friendly explainer would be met by a menagerie of Anglo reactions ranging any-where from indifference to contempt to a stirring admiration by those who could feel the terrible heartbreak of the enormous distance their ancestors must have drifted from their own versions of a natural life long ago. Civilization's spiritual fear of being left behind insists that its con-stituents unquestioningly race to survive, running only to ambitiously outstrip their neighbors instead of competing together to sustain Nature, by feeding the beauty of human racing to the Holy.

The running of these young people was a grand thing and they, just like all the weather and every natural phenomenon, animal, plant, river, ocean, air, earth, every natural thing who each run their own races to keep all their own diverse particles of the magnificence of a world made whole and alive by doing so, the running boys would come in to the feast of life when it was time for them to come. And so it was, for when the race had subsided, each boy returned to his home and together we all ate the food that we all knew his running had kept alive.

Everything in Nature ran according to its own nature; the running of grass was in its growing, the running of rivers their flowing, granite bub-bled up, cooled, compressed and crumbled, birds lived, flew, sang and died, everything did what it needed to do, each simultaneously running its own race, each by living according to its own nature together, never leaving any other part of the universe behind. The world's Holy things raced constantly together, not to win anything over the next, but to keep the entire surging diverse motion of the living world from grinding to a halt, which is why there is no end to that race; no finish line. That would be oblivion to all.

For the Indigenous Souls of all people who can still remember how to *be* real cultures, life is a race to be elegantly run, not a race to be com-petitively won. It cannot be won; it is the gift of the world's diverse beau-tiful motion that must be maintained. Because human life has been given the gift of our elegant motion, whether we limp, roll, crawl, stroll, or fly, it is an obligation to engender that elegance of motion in our daily lives in service of maintaining life by moving and living as beautifully as we can. All else has, to me, the familiar taste of that domineering warlike harshness that daily tries to cover its tracks in order to camouflage the deep ruts of some old, sick, grinding, ungainly need to flee away from the elegance of our original Indigenous human souls. Our attempt to avariciously conquer or win a place where there are no problems, whether it be Heaven or a "New Democracy," never mind if it is spiritually ugly and immorally "won" and taken from someone who is already there, has made a citifying world of people who, unconscious of it, have become our own ogreish problem to ourselves, our future, and the world. This is a problem that we cannot continue to attempt to competitively outrun by more and more effectively designed technological approaches to speed away from the past, for the specter of our own earth-wasting reality runs grinning competitively right alongside us. By developing even more effective and entertaining methods of escape that only burn up the earth, the air, animals, plants, and the deeper substance of what it should mean to be a human, by competing to get ahead, we have created a brakeless competition that has outrun our innate beauty and marked out a very definite and imminent *"finish"* line.

Living in and on a sphere, we cannot really outrun ourselves anyway. Therefore, I say, the entire devastating and hideous state of the world and its constant wounding and wrecking of the wild, beautiful, natural, viable and small, only to keep alive an untenable cultural proceedance is truly a spiritual sickness, one that will not be cured by the efficient use of the same thinking that maintains the sickness. Nor can this overly expensive, highly funded illness be symptomatically kept at bay any longer by yet more political, environmental, or social programs.

We must as individuals and communities take the time necessary to learn how to indigenously remember what a sane, original existence for a viable people might look like.

Though there are marvelous things and amazing people doing them, both seen and unseen, these do not resemble in any way the general trend of what is going on now.

To begin remembering our Indigenous belonging on the Earth back to life we must metabolize as individuals the grief of recognition of our lost directions, digest it into a valuable spiritual compost that allows us to learn to stay put without outrunning our strange past, and get small, unarmed, brave, and beautiful.

By trying to feed the Holy in Nature the fruit of beauty from the tree of memory of our Indigenous Souls, grown in the composted failures of our past need to conquer, watered by the tears of cultural grief, we might become ancestors worth descending from and possibly grow a place of hope for a time beyond our own.

Any of us born into the competitive warlike commercial conditions of modern life probably have our heads invaded by the distant gruntings of the scared urgings of civilization's hard-faced-coach screaming, "You're nothing, you're nothing, you've got to win to be something, outrun your nothingness, run, win, be someone, outrun the next guy, outstrip the hungry debts of our cultural past!" But deeper and wider inside the vast wilderness of the territory of our forgotten Indigenous Souls, a place not understood and regarded as nothing by the "Coach," there courses along in its own special way a valuable beautiful runner whose rhythmic puffing and gorgeous able motion keeps the Sun and Moon rolling, our hearts beating, the lizards grinning, the whales dredging the soggy sand of krilly oceans, the world jumping, living, dreaming, flying, whose dusty drumming friendship of feet on natural earth does not run to get ahead or away but to come home again to feast with the rest of our hearts and souls. And strangely enough, even the Coach must eventually straggle in for even he must eat, and of course, when it comes to the thinking of the Indigenous Soul and the generosity of seeds, there is always an empty chair waiting for even him at the feast table.

Chapter 2

Star Arches, the Lurching Earth, and the Seed-eyed God

While it may sound strange to some, the greatest blessing in life is that none of us are born at the beginning of time, not God, not Moses, nor any of them types, not atoms, not light, nor heat, not matter nor antimatter, not seeds, not stories, nobody, nothing, nowhere. Nothing real is born at the beginning of Time.

Nobody dies at the end of time either because, of course, time, being itself, can no more begin than time knows how to end. Everyone and everything comes alive when and where they appear in an already up-and-running continuum of time and disappears later back into the same continuum that of course continues. The only difference being that, hopefully, the fullness of our individual lives while here, makes us into something that feeds and fuels the next thing that is born into this never-ending river. There is no finish line, or heaven-like last act, no glorious arrival. There is only the glorious continuation of things living and dying, appearing and disappearing in staggered layers to keep each other alive in the continuation. However, the rental rate for this gift of being allowed to flourish and reside in this continuum with the rest of the world is that we do everything possible to be indigenously beautiful, promising that we make ourselves spiritually full and delicious so as to feed the next ones to appear in the ongoing river on the occasion of our passing.

What does any of this have to do with seeds? Well . . . this is the very nature of seeds and what it means to keep the seeds alive.

But still this story is not a story "about" seeds, because stories *about* things are like journalistic footraces with comfortable synthesized beginnings and arbitrarily designated finish lines that quickly compete in a commercial world under appropriately named *dead*lines, endings that give the illusion that we can mentally ethically exit any story any time we choose instead of trying to elegantly reside within the matrix of a truly alive story, like a beating heart does a body, dedicating its rhythm to the beauty of keeping its holder alive. I want this story not to be *about* seeds, I want it to *be a seed,* a kind of story that has its own unique running, a story that does like seeds do, starting always in the middle of their own wave pattern of infinite rise and fall, seeds who, like the grandest stories, refuse to stop moving toward life and always hope to come home instead of being genetically and spiritually modified to frenetically race away from life, not vainly pushing to outrun our continuing failures with the Holy ground that feeds us, only to wreck the future we don't think is there for someone we don't know.

But still because a story, like the sun who rolls completely around the globe, is only seen for the first time in the dawn by us somewhere during the ongoing blessing of that never-wavering rotation, a told story must come into view somewhere in its running. This one, however, does not come to us running but squeaking and trudging slowly, climbing up a steep black cindered trail in the moist dawn light of that overly wet spring of 1976, puffing through the mixed fragrances of rotting lake reeds, dank fog, dark logs, and the incalculable melancholy nostalgic aroma of the coffee and corn boiled and patted for the hungry bellies of the people of Santiago Atitlán and cooking-fire smoke fueled by over a hundred different species of trees and shrubs that hung in the hillside cornfields and new growth of pines, oaks, and wild avocadoes that ran up and over the ridge that I too strove to cross and drop deep inside the depths of the next ravine.

In the volcanic highlands of Guatemala a couple of easterly miles behind the large Tzutujil village of Santiago Atitlán, where I'd been living for several years, rose a mysterious volcano straight up off the reeded shores of Lago Atitlán. Called Oxi Q'ajolá, or the Three Youths, by the

Mayans resident at its base, it was up and into this mountain's steep cindery overgrown avenues I strained. Panting, marching, and shouldering my load for an hour and a half, I came upon the unspectacular but very sacred promontory, on whose high spot a ledge presided over a five-hundred-foot drop. It was there, hidden in that ravine, down whose precarious dark sides I would soon descend, shuffling and leaping, that my destination lay: the controversial shrine of Choq'oux Aq'oum, or Medicine Mushroom.

His eyes tiny and bright like a gigantic bristle-headed iridescent dark beetle squinting through the thick drooping vines and large curly slabs of sloughed tree bark that camouflaged the mossy shrine in hopes of keeping it as unseen as the shamans and devout villagers who revered the grand beings that resided here would have it, Chiviliu sat surveying the village below through the clearing mist, and without moving his head glanced up now and again toward the canyon walls opposite for any sign of my agreed upon arrival.

If you weren't looking for the place and hadn't already been shown its location, you would never find it even if you were less than a foot away on the trail that passed it on the way to the volcano top. Chiv was himself invisible here until he wanted to be seen. Everybody knew the shrine was here somewhere, but nobody knew Chiv was here, and even if they had, nobody but shamans would dare enter unless accompanied by the initiated, except of course those enemies of the shrine, Christian converts who'd been ravaging the place for over a century to eradicate what they called "the cult of Holy Boy." This was Holy Boy's original home and it was here I'd come to give Chiviliu a look at my most recent *Qijibaal*, the newest member of my Divination Bundle.

Chiv and I at times practically lived here, making ceremonies for his clients, healing rituals determined through calendric divination. But this particular morning we were obligated again through divination to make a "feast" of delicious songs, sung words, delicious smoke, all delicious offerings for a new "member" of the secret contents of the Divination Bundle I'd earned and been given during my initiatory learning time as an *Ajcun*.

Though wrapped in several layers of the prescribed handwoven white cotton cloth shot through with the purple calendric marker stripes called "sun roads" running from end to end, and much larger and more unique than most of my other traditional inherited *Qijibaal*, the Deity himself was only fist-sized. It must have been the weight of his spiritual worth that felt like a hundred-pound jade cannonball, cramping my neck and shoulders from the tension on the strap of my string bag where he rode.

Riding the invisible, but very present, crisscross warp and woof of the village fabric of gossip that nightly respun the thread of whispered daytime rumors into tightly woven cloth of accepted fact, everyone in the village "knew" the new visitation to my bundle was miraculous for it had eyes made of petrified seeds from way before human beings had been invented. Thrust directly and forcibly into my bleeding hands months before by the Holy Parent Earth Herself during the 3:00 a.m., February 4, 1976, Guatemalan earthquake on the outskirts of the Cakchiquel town of Chimaltenango, for the first and last time in village history the gossip was uncharacteristically unembellished, reflecting reality one hundred percent. It wasn't a large event in anyone's mind other than myself, and I certainly wasn't any kind of a hero, but the most startling aspect of the people's whole scale village-wide collective acceptance of this whispered knowledge of my little seed-eyed God was the fact I'd kept the fact a complete secret. Later when I would come to know the people and myself better, I would come to love and live by the reality of how much consciousness humans are really capable of when their cultured souls are still intact.

I had only just returned back to *ch'jay*, to Santiago Atitlán. Like a lot of others, people of every sort from Central America and all over the world, most of them good, some astoundingly excellent, others not, I would be consumed for some months giving what little assistance my young muscles had to offer to various hands-on relief efforts during the months following the indescribable devastation of that particular Guatemalan earthquake.

The winter past, in what would have been the culminating move in a personal mission to get a friend of mine released from prison after months of telegrams trying to arrange a meeting with the well-fed, fairly congenial, but nonetheless notoriously ruthless police commander who supervised the specter of the crenulated, blue-gray walled-in fortress of the Chimaltenango prison, I'd been finally granted a rare, formal audience set for the morning of February 4, 1976. In pursuit of that cause, the previous afternoon of the third, I headed into the mist of seventy miles of pavement that bored its narrow ribbon of civilization through the forested volcanic ravines and precipices of the middle highland that lay between Chimaltenango and Atitlán. Hairpinning in the little bluebird bus through Pasaqab, Los Robles, Godinez, and all the other little Cakchiquel hamlets in between, I held my breath in the unlikely hope of winning through reason, or the payment of his "fine," or through bribery or all of the above, the release of one Sacrapala being held there, an old Cakchiquel friend of mine from San Martín Jilotepeque. I was swinging around half asleep like a single loose orange in an otherwise already emptied crate unknowingly seeing for the last time the smoke and foggy wonder of the brightly painted Mayanized postcolonial lime-walled Cakchiquel plazas and towns of Tecpán, Patzicia, and Patzun, that led to Chimaltenango. Built by sixteenth-century Spaniards on the site of a pre-European Highland Cakchiquel Maya trading town still known to all highland Mayans thereabouts by its ancient name of *Pa Bocob*, or "place of shields," the town remained the political haunt of the Highland Guatemalan Cakchiquel hierarchy. Years past, the day before I would leave the U.S., I remember retrieving a catalog of the beautiful earth-color paintings of Cakchiquel butcher Andrés Curuchich from a museum trash can. The highland towns and the people of Tecpán, Patzun, Chimaltenango, and his village of Comalapa flowered off those limestone-painted salt sacks in a way photos could never do, and were the added charge of determination that drove me ever south away from New Mexico to central Guatemala. That had been my first glimpse of those amazing ornately carved quiet colonial plazas. The afternoon of February 3, 1976, would be the last anyone would see of them.

But poor Sacrapala ... by the time I was to have sued for his release, his detention had already stretched past four-and-a-half months with no bail or trial date. Deprived of Sacrapala's income from his inherited avocation of driving the little spotted cattle of other rich Jilotepeque Indians overland on foot to Atitlán to the sharpened-down thin blades of Tzutujil butchers some eighty miles away, his wife and three children, whose economic situation had already been hand to mouth, were driven into an even more desperate poverty.

One of his cattle-driving partners, arriving with a little herd just up from my end of Santiago in the last days of January 1976, delivered a spoken message from Sacrapala's wife explaining how her husband had been arrested while completing his once-a-month obligation to the Cofradia. As part of fulfillment to his new appointment serving the entire spiritual hierarchy of his community for the annual feast of San Martín on November 11, Sacrapala had been assigned with several others to help tend the distillation in a schedule of shifts of the corn and fruit mash being brewed into *tzam,* the wickedly strong traditional and indispensable drink of Cakchiquel ceremonies. Uninvolved directly but nevertheless caught as an innocent in some political retaliation in a private war waged between various governmentally connected strongmen, Sacrapala had ridiculously been arrested by the *Guardia de la Hacienda* for moonshining hard liquor for resale, a charge whose conviction brought seven years of prison with forced labor, during which time the state did not feed the prisoner. The family's need to travel to feed him would have put an impossible strain on his relatives, even if he could get a trial.

I came in after dark in one of those busses chauffeured by the orphan Kanche, the scariest but fastest bus driver in the entire country, a kind of Highland bus-driving hero, a well-loved notorious kid not seventeen who always dangerously and thrillingly passed every vehicle at breakneck speeds on any side of the already too narrow and insufficiently paved asphalt, often playing head-on chicken within millimeters of oncoming sugarcane-loaded semis to arrive at all his stops first every time ahead of all competing transport; he was weekly fired to be rehired in the same instant by the next admiring mom-and-pop Bluebird Busline whose business would boom instantly on his reputation alone. The bus still moving, he let me off right at the door of a tiny one-room whitewashed adobe house right off the main ribbon of asphalt that disappeared along with

Kanche into the dusty highlands a mile east of the Chimaltenango plaza. Bordered on one side by a long, clay tile–roofed adobe home of a group of Mayan Mennonites who kept their cattle behind the adjoining old whitewashed walls, the neighbor to the rear of this little adobe house was its owner: a strict, old, unkillable German woman with lace curtains, who lived in an incongruous, giant wooden gingerbread house, with servants, waiters, and original Albrect Dürer woodcuts wrapped in old quilts in her dormered attic. She had been letting me stay here for years whenever I came through, originally thinking because of my Germanic last name that I was some kind of countryman of hers, but being German, her honor forced her to continue tendering me her hospitality when I turned out to be a very different creature than she'd imagined.

Exhausted, and because it was late, without saying hello or checking in, I cleared off the mice and crickets from the small reed-stuffed bed, lit the diesel lantern, and settled back to shuffle through my impressive compilation of assorted official-looking documents with which I had hoped to charm the official in charge into releasing poor Sacrapala. Into the matrix of this randomly gathered, highly embellished, semi-legal stack of heavily stamped, signed, and seal-embossed documents of the normal, very long-winded, superfluously detailed requisite bureaucratic presentation padded with the signatures of famous officials from a hundred irrelevant agencies, I was careful to tuck, hidden but findable, several handsome new Guatemalan fifty quetzal bills engraved with their multicolored portraits of former generals, presidents, flying quetzales, cieba trees, old Mayan temple ruins, and the imagined faces of famous Indian leaders of the past.

I would have felt alone save for the hundreds of baying street dogs. Their wild collective wailing moan should have been earsplitting but was eerily barely audible for having been strangely muffled beneath the atmospheric density of that blanket the Holy Earth always has oozing in Her pre-earthquake stillness; an anxious, devouring kind of restless vacuum that simultaneously instigated and swallowed the endless waves of screaming roosters and the sea of hysterical grating cries of a half a million hens in the darkness every direction for miles.

Tired from my journey and the sleepless life of service I led back at the lake village and failing to notice what was coming, or somehow noticing but so completely lost in the anesthetizing micro focus of my coming heroic moment with all these papers still fanned out heavy on my chest, my mind started to sink from it all like a mercury-stuffed fish dropping into that surging current of thick slumber running heavy with schools of cold dream eels with whom I must have longed to drift into some new perspective or at least into a new day.

Whatever civilization has told us dreams really are, the indigenous heart reveres dreams even more but considers most dream recollection as bad amateurish translations made by our everyday minds of a much deeper speech of the many-dimensional motion of any one of a myriad Divine beings. Dreams have a skin that camouflages with simple, more rememberable forms a much bigger dream beneath. In order to appear more familiar to the waking mind, dreams hide behind things we might see every day but so conspicuously reorganized as to cause us to lift our heads and notice. But the shine of this grand Holy thing of a dream when scratched and dented by the sharp prows of the meandering ships of our hard sleeping heads as they crash into deeper water of those bigger dreams that cruise the oceanic subinfinity of life's primal soup, reveals through these openings through these minor woundings, that primordial subskin brilliance of another world's organic prism, whose uncontrollable light leaks out into us with some small particle beam of life's too-big-to-humanly-comprehend immensity. By daylight this greatness usually wriggles free and is lost to the waking mind. For if the waking mind of a regular human could know this bigness it would either go mad, or have to begin living a spiritual life in order to be able to love the vision without being destroyed by the force of what it loved. But sometimes this great "leak" leaves in the constantly shifting sand of the beaches of our life-beleaguered incapacity to remember, a mysterious track, or a lingering smell, an olfactory trail, a spiritual pheromonal current like the bubbles and rocking wake that a whale's breaching leaves, though having missed the leap or some other sign of their tremendous nature, for its having been here and steamed on ahead, we can still be rocked into life by the tow.

In just such a way, it was that night as I was wafted into some deep trench of bottomless dreams, where a dream, like a seed, caught hold and sprouted and grew out of the rotted humus of who and where I'd ever been. And there it rose: an arch of marble covered with intricate old eleventh-century Iberian Arabesque carving, hanging alone in an otherwise utterly pitch-black sky with no earth or horizon beneath it, the glowing arch spanning at least a third of the heavens. For years I approached it, never stopping until I was close enough to see it was actually some kind of stellar alabaster, which instead of compressed diatoms was made of geologically metamorphized stars that all jittered and sang, forming a gigantic horseshoe-like gateway through which one could seemingly pass to the other side of an even more infinite sky.

But the moment I attempted to go through and under this continent-sized portal, two powerful guards rose on its buttresses and prevented me. Pale, birdlike humans, or human-like birds, gigantic, winged, fierce, and feathered to their feet, they rose from where they had been hiding on the face opposite my side of the arch, coming to roost on either side of the arches, grappling the starry marble with the universe-shaking thuds of their enormous feathered hocks. The size of meteors, crackling sparks showered off the scales of their mile-long talons just from the friction of their motion.

Angry and frenetically shuffling from the farthest point of the sky's arch to the opposite, the stony hackles of their outstretched crocodilian armored backs bristling, they refused to let me pass, screaming, and threatened me with every obscenity, curse, and insult ever spoken in any human or animal tongue, which for some reason I thoroughly understood.

Unhearing, uncaring, unwarnable like a fool, I continued my approach, thinking I could reason with them. But this only sent them into a more concerted campaign to stop me with a more emphatic whipping of the air with their enormous wings stretching out and then extending as if intending to fly from their perch. Then careening forward without loosening their grips, they shot their tongues out at me with rippling words and blinding light, repelling and rejecting every one of my dull-minded efforts to outwit them, accepting only an about-face of the direction back to where I had come.

"It's not for you to come through here, you imbecilic piece of crap," they hissed, raising their scaly hackles and emitting a lot of bad smells. I was refused entrance into my curiosity of that unknown place. Like a gate with no fence, it was a gateway from here to somewhere besides here. But there was no going around either, for their powdery white faces, long, long white hair and human noses scolded with a forcefulness equivalent to some titanic vulture mother protecting her chicks.

Then all of a sudden they didn't want me even loitering around this gate, and determined to do whatever it would take to lift me away from there, the desperation of their verbal pummeling incremented. It came at me like a storm of voices in worldwide languages whose earsplitting shrillness and deep bone-dissolving subsonic roar pumped from their bellowing lungs a relentless gale of such hurricane force that when it caught me, I was pitched light-years away from the arch, like a tree frog blown from his perch by the blast of a cold piston of water from ten thousand fire hoses. I was literally hauled into a waking state, out of the dream flying free and clear of the earth through the dusty air along with my trembling bed which slid and crashed along with me squarely into the northern adobe wall of the little house, knocking me spinning another four feet vertically back into the air to land flat on my back on the convulsing floor, from where, only barely awake, I stared stunned at the cracking walls, at which point the still-quivering, roving, possessed bed made its return journey in less than a second as if pulled on rails sailing into the southern wall over my flattened form not quite clearing the tip of my nose.

The world rippled and bucked from deep beneath, shaking and tossing her head until anything that depended on solid ground was quickly slivered to splinters, shards, and dust.

Knowing in an instant I would be buried alive and unable to take a full breath for all the lung-clogging clouds of dust pouring into the shaking pitch-dark room unless I could get outside, and yet in all my attempts to leave, I was unable to even throw myself out of the now-trapezoidal doorless doorway, for to even regain my legs I was repeatedly tackled by the crazy flying bed and tripped by the rippling world, and forcibly thrown back down to the bucking floor where I joined broken chunks of every imaginable piece of pottery, metal, and wood bubbling together like popcorn popping.

Even the nails of the yet-standing doorway screeched like a train wheel as they violently shivered out of their rusty holes, shooting off like little evicted screwbeans into the darkness, and in the precarious three seconds of such a thorough ground-leveling battering that old house had before its tonnage of earth would come thundering fatally down over me in one final heap, after unsuccessfully wrestling the insane bed, the shaking floor, the unbreathable dust and with no solid ground to push against, I concentrated all the force of my life into my kidneys, sprang from a middle place as deep in me as the quake was in the Holy earth and leapt straight into the opaque soup of choking dust, flying over the bucking ground like a high jumper, up and over the meandering bed, trying to time my motion so as to be assisted, instead of resisted, by the rhythmic arrival of shockwaves that had been knocking me over, by which means I miraculously semi-succeeded into leaping deliberately and forcefully into the soon-to-crash wall opposite the door like the dream arch through which for the love of life I'd desperately wanted passage. Then like a swimmer kicking off the pool wall I thrust out my grasshopper thighs against the cascading wall to sail horizontally, ejected by the wall's collapsing force to fly and fall, rolled up like a sowbug just far enough beyond the door to barely clear the collapsing impact of the thirty-two tons of roof timbers, clay roof tiles, and adobe walls whose careening roar rose insignificant in the collective din of hundreds of towns, cities, mountains, and hamlets of the entire east central highlands avalanching back into a flatter reconfigured earth of tufa and dust.

But I kept rolling and rolling like a hoopsnake biting its tail, becoming a fluid wheel holding my toes rolling on a cam as it was otherwise yet impossible to stand or even stumble to some nonexistent open area. Many families, having escaped their imploding homes, died when entire roofs flying as far as fifty feet from another house crushed them upon landing.

The air unbreathable and hardly moving, I kept rolling until I could go no farther. The world had been pulverized into a thick blanket of fine dry-season powder that rose like goose down into a ten-inch fluffy carpet pile that stretched out in a 250-square-mile radius that was being shaken out like a dusty rug, rippling up and down, in vertical rollers of simultaneously outward-moving ridges and toppling trenches that surged through the earth in a powerful undertow as if it were a sea in a tidal wave of dirt that undulated over and over all the way to the Gulf Coast to disappear under the salty sea. And like the ocean there were also infinite swirls of powerful vortexual eddies of a more local concentration that worked with the general up-and-down waves opening and closing ground everywhere, rerouting rivers, toppling mountains and damming rivers, causing some to flow effortlessly upstream, yet others to utterly disappear for good, in some places forever snapping civilization's arrogant ribbon of pavement. Trusted highways became new cliffs and the rest broken candy brittle.

One hundred-and-a-half miles to the north beyond all this turbulence at the edge of the Petén jungle, the Sayaxche and Uscumacinta rivers had only recently been fettered to pump a powerful electric voltage into a network of overhead cables intended to span the country, but which had so far only run along the same highland highway I'd come in on the previous night.

The deep unstoppable sensual liquid serpents of these turgid rivers had been jammed like pasta through turbines that captured the jungle freedom of the Mother waters and enslaved her motion into a fiery current that bristled in the high wires only recently and very inexpertly strung toward which I, clearing the house that dark early morning, tottered and rolled in slow motion. Utterly demolished only the minute previous, these power lines met me face to face as the tentacles of a vicious demon whose four-foot purple and green jumping arcs of lightning leapt from the ground on every side. The supporting pylons carrying these thick overhead lines had snapped, which in turn broke the high-voltage cables that in their live hissing drop had been caught by the miraculously unbroken slim branches of some tough hybridized sixty-foot eucalyptus trees whose entire length bent down to flagellate the earth without breaking, but whose tips now swept the earth with the fierce tangle of hot wires whose ends whipped wildly in a vicious dance and hissing agony. Like the angry Mother river, in a pain only Deities can know, her water turned to fire, and like a chopped serpent bleeding sparks, she jumped twenty feet into the air, then loudly slapping down while sizzling in flashes of purple and green light made red through the chalk and cinder fog, the wires snaked along the ground farther and farther afield, setting the burnable world on fire, looking for that revenge that all humanly enslaved matter and phenomena must probably seek when their shackles are broken.

But some things, Holy things, the same ones that kept me from being crushed, must have now held me in some special way and kept me from being impaled, roasted, or thrashed in this ruthless, unpredictable, welded frizz of leaping fire. But then there was the suffocation by the dust of the Holy Earth. I was unable to finally breathe in the density of what should have been air; all the adobe walls of the area, pulverized now, were suspended as particles in the air, choking animals, adults, and children to death everywhere. In desperation I pulled my gasping face into my armpit, where I tried to breathe slowly through my torn shirt in hopes of filtering the dust, only to find it clogged as well when salvation came in the form of a single small flying clay roof tile thrown from afar, probably from my neighbor's collapsing cowpen; it hit me in the back of the head and stunned me long enough for me to stop drowning in my desperation, long enough to get some kind of air past the anxiety. How long it lasted I couldn't say; time was gone; but when I began to stir I tried to grab the earth with my beaten hands pushing through a blanket of powder to get to some solid ground.

But my searching hands found themselves wound desperately around what at first seemed like a small hand reaching up toward me out of the dust but which turned out to be a sharp-edged nubbin of stone the size of a twelve-year-old child's fist floating up from inside the earth beneath the bed of powdered earth upon which all the living and the dead now lay.

I had sought to grab the security of what most people rely upon as some kind of solid ground, ground of an unbegrudging daily stability upon which they could depend to be the foundation to their petty conceits and serious enforcements of opinion, but here there was no solid ground. There never really had been anywhere, nor would there ever be again for me. Solid ground turned out to be an illusion maintained by people who live *off* the earth instead of *in* the earth. I would get to know that the earth, its rocks, valleys, ocean floors, mountains, plains, and shorelines were a surging geologic liquid, alive and always moving no matter how slowly. Everything really was.

It was a bad illusion and useless to hope for a firmness in a world that people make on an Earth they don't understand. When trying to photograph a standing deer or sleeping horse at a hundred photos per second, you end up with a hundred poses, because these animals never actually stand utterly still; they are liquid, no matter what the human mind assumes. Every muscle on the earth has a mind, and all the Earth's minds together are only a synapse in the ever-shedding nervous system of the Holy Universe as it runs toward life to make more life. It is about motion, not a racing to arrive at peace, but a motion at peace with Her running.

The trick was not to seek the fantasized comfort, or the falsely anchored dependability that civilization promises. Instead of the illusion of security, it's better to get good at riding out Her motion like a bone cell heaving in the ribs of Her breathing chest—and heaving She was.

Though the sun had not dawned into the dust and I could not see what it was I'd pulled from the earth, when I regained some semblance of breath after being whacked on the head, I held onto this solid piece like a baby monkey holds on to his mother, for I knew that whatever this was I held, it had something inside that was pulling me toward life and away from choking to death into the dust alone. But in my desperation and not knowing the outside nature of what it was I held, I grasped too hard and was of course cut and began to bleed a little, for my fist-sized guardian out of the trembling earth was a ragged, wildly shaped, very sharp chunk of volcanic glass: an obsidian.

I rolled over, put the little thing on my chest, and waited. Then the tremors stopped, and the dust got even thicker and more stagnant.

Broken only by the occasional clanging of some stray broken timbers finally hitting the ground somewhere, an utter silence commenced for maybe as long as it took anyone to believe whether or not they were alive. The duration of the earthquake had been an eternity of probably only forty-five seconds. More than five hours went by waiting for dawn. Then the great orange ball of the father sun came up, and muffled by the dust, the great wailing began.

There is no longer any way to remotely convey to people with enough food and water, the bustle of life, and the illusion of solid ground the unique nature of the particular brand of timelessness that came after that sunrise.

The general consensus among the Indians, Ladinos, rich and poor, farmers and town dwellers alike was that the entire world had simply come to its promised end. Only the rich people were nervous about it, but it was a fact.

Dead lay in small groups everywhere along where people's houses had gone down; people ate up all the dead chickens and dogs; there were no receptacles to cook in or eat in. But most ate right alongside the bodies of their deceased beloved children, parents, or spouses.

Long files of Indian men, sometimes as many as four hundred, returning from their indentured cash jobs on the largely unaffected southern coast with their precious hard-earned cash, walked by us, exhausted and anxious to get home. Though they could not convince our world that only the highlands had been struck, the large body of Mayan men returning to their houses at Balanyá and Saragossa were wishing it had been the end when they arrived to find their villages utterly demolished and not one mother, wife, grandmother, or child left alive.

A friend of mine from Patzun had left his children sleeping in his larger-than-usual adobe house while his wife and he went next door to a clandestine meeting between the sacred Cakchiquel hierarchy and some outsider Quiche leftist guerrilla organization. They were heartbroken when their newly built, big one-room earthen house crashed in over the children, while leaving the entire council untouched. After hours of furious digging, the little rascals, two girls and a three-year-old boy, were found still alive and calm, having resourcefully scurried under a strong table that miraculously held off tons of fallen timber and earth!

The stories were endless, the grief immeasurable, the horror unimaginable, the miracles inexplicable and common, and still everyone knew one way or another the world had ended or was on its way out.

But the living who have lost their world must still dig for their loved ones, and we dug. And we found them and for the majority they were finished.

But a harder thing still was feeding and watering the living. There were for many people many days in those parts where no relief efforts came: no radios, no food, no airdrops, no highways, no trucks, no army, and no doctors save one. For most people, after three days, water became very, very scarce, food nonexistent.

With another fellow, I commandeered half the rations and a large expedition tent from a group of Canadian students on some sort of biological survey on its way to the northern rain forest who were mighty peeved that I had no schedule for returning it. After having pitched it for an indefinite period in a somewhat open field opposite what had been my little house, it became the shelter for a makeshift maternity section of nineteen new mothers and their babies all born from the fright into the dust outside their little houses immediately after the initial series of the three large quakes. Sixteen of the ladies had lost their men in the tremors, and three of the surviving husbands helped me patrol for food, killing, cooking, and eating marauding dogs with the single machete we had between us.

We took turns guarding, sleeping, cooking for, and coaxing and calming the terrified girls during every one of the three thousand tremors that followed, little quakes that demolished in detail what the large earthquakes had left unfinished.

The tent was safe, but in the towns not a few were killed and many others maimed by these multiple aftershocks in the weeks that followed—people unwilling to keep their distance from town fountains or colonial church facades, half-standing town halls, and the like.

After a minor jello-like tremor in Patzicia one afternoon I saw the central one-story tall, beautiful, hand-carved colonial stone *pila,* the colored fountain, tumble to its side and begin rolling with ever increasing speed demonically steering itself on a deliberate mission to crush three Cakchiquel women, who, sprinting as hard as they could for over two hundred yards, finally split up in opposite directions eluding it as if running from a rhino. But the possessed rock continued on to crush a dog to death and break the leg of a toddler, immediately after which the sixteenth-century façade of the three-story Spanish church in front of which a relief worker was giving her speech before distributing food crashed to the ground, dismembered like a dynamited cliff, killing three villagers and the relief worker.

One by one on the eve of the first quake my Mennonite neighbors had been gently roused from sleep by one of their many daughters, a devout, headscarf-wearing, gentle, twelve-year-old who whispered that her favorite cow had told her that God had told the cow to tell the daughter to get the family inside a certain one of their adobe rooms immediately adjacent to my place. Into this Christianity they may have been inspired, but they were Mayans in the bone, and as such would never dismiss dreams or gods in animals, so with the cow in tow they remained awake and prayed the entire night during and after the quakes, suffering not even one scratch and, unlike the rest of the district, had some food left. Every one of them would have surely been killed because all of their other rooms including my place had caved in tremendously like the rest of the world, including the substantial cowshed. Because of the little girl and the cow they were all well, and all of them lamented their having to later kill the old milk cow both for lack of fodder and to feed themselves and their hungry neighbors as the weeks of starvation dragged on, but we all supposed that this was God, indigenous style: a grand being that died to feed the living people that she, God, and the cow had warned.

I'd always considered the general stereotype New Mexicans had about Germans being overly staunch, narrow-minded, bad-tempered people who never missed breakfast to be a little exaggerated, but the old

German woman with the gingerbread house had a bonfire going, warmed feet, and, still complaining about her servants, had breakfast cooked before the sun came up. Taking boards from her now-demolished fancy house she made a fire, dug out dead chickens, plucked them and found, God knows where, bacon, coffee, and cooking receptacles and had it all ready for everyone she could muster for a post-quake breakfast.

Though her housemaid had been killed, her wayward gardeners (who used to steal people's turkeys, pretending opossums had killed them) miraculously survived. The two troublemakers had been on a binge the night before and after dropping dead drunk into the same little bed in their rustic quarters about a half an hour before the quake, three walls and the roof had collapsed harmlessly over them, forming a kind of lean-to under which they had continued to sleep soundly until Greta ordered them to get the fire going and to go looking for people to have over for breakfast, after which we all started digging for survivors.

While digging out her maid's body, a beautiful sixteen-year-old Sacatepequez Mayan girl who had roomed in the old lady's servants' compound east of my little courtyard, I found an ancient Mayan cistern with a precious reserve of about fifty-four gallons of drinkable water under the floor everyone had forgotten about.

This kept the women in the tent with almost enough to make soup of what we could find to keep milk in their breasts. Though one fatherless child did die, the rest made it, I believe.

With the arrival of a few relief groups, some food began to trickle in. Then, sent to supervise the foreign relief groups, the Guatemalan army thundered in, putting martial law into effect, shooting looters daily while eating up the relief food. A little after the Red Cross, the United Nations, Japan, some Balkan countries, India, and other African countries actually set up aid stations, and a bit before the Christians showed up, some of whom would require Indians to convert to Jesus to receive food, blankets, and cash grubstakes for future life, I turned the ladies and babies and three husbands over to better food and care, all of whom continued with two others to live on in the big tent. I shifted my attention to the unrecognizable plaza of Old Chimaltenango, where, under the direction of the great Dr. Carol Bierhorst, I joined a lot of others to help sort the wounded from the critically wounded and helped roving, displaced bands of Cakchiquel families to identify their missing loved ones from the dead stacked in shoulder-to-shoulder rows around the dusty square.

Standing maybe five feet tall, Dr. Bierhorst, originally an American country doctor, married into the Cakchiquel people of that area and ran a "barefoot doctor" clinic there, as well as in Haiti and Papua New Guinea, that included native doctoring methods. For me he was one of the most truly goodhearted, unkillable, heroic, and courageous Americans of all time and a true inspiration to all that knew or even heard of him. Because of him a great deal more got done; a lot more people survived who would not have otherwise. The people loved him. Armed only with his doctor bag and no complaints, his past successful showdowns with armed hitmen sent by crooked pharmaceutical cartels, the ultra right, and other military entities had earned my admiration long before meeting him during this earthquake.

To avoid the outbreak of typhus and other associated epidemics, the dead had to be burned in large fifty-body pyres. Of course the Mayan people didn't agree with that. So we tried to get as many off and buried as quickly before the army in their half-tracks full of the stiff bodies and wrecked house timbers got their pyres going outside the towns with their flamethrowers and jerricans of gasoline.

Everywhere it was the same. Tecpán was the worst I ever saw.

But of all the constant tragedies everywhere pouring in, one cut my heart even deeper than the daily sight of the once-alive and beautiful Colonial Plaza swept to rubble, the dead and dying, the occasional helicopter, and roving bands of soldiers lining up looters and executing them on the spot. For the space opposite the plaza off the southeast corner was now swept clear and flat except for a large pile of steel and concrete where once had sprawled out for several acres the Regional Prison of the Guatemalan National Police from whose hellish bowels I had had such high hopes of rescuing my poor old friend Sacrapala; unlike the local hospital in which the lower floor survived, the entire police building as inescapable as it was had collapsed, killing all the prisoners, wardens, and overnight police officials together. For Sacrapala I had arrived one day too late.

The insatiable ghost of self-hatred that dogged me for my failure drove me harder into an even more feverish intent to do whatever I could to keep people and their cultures alive, which in that immediate situation meant getting broken, starving humans some help. I felt like nothing in that overwhelming time, like a stunned flea trying to save a dying horse. But after several days into this morass of death, doubt, frustration, sickness, killing, remorse, dust, and bad relief food, one morning while carrying on a very pointed dispute in my Tzutujil-accented Cakchiquel with a beautiful, fairly toothless white-haired grandmother in her thick red Comalapa *pōt* and *uq'* who, because she didn't want anyone to hear, insisted we argue as loudly as possible in a whisper about how I really should not be worrying so much about the sharp piece of bone protruding from her tobacco-skinned shin. She just wanted painkillers to die without agony, and that I should actually be treating her sixty-year-old daughter moaning next to her for her broken ribs and quit being an idiot like all doctors, for which she mistook me.

There were a lot of helpers waiting for direction on where to take each prospective "case" as they were sorted by intensity of need. I was leaning over this old-timer listening to her complaints when one fellow standing next to my listening right ear, whose two strong, calloused, scaly, grape-toed bare feet I could see to the side as I kept my attention on the old grandmother, began in a full voice to assist me in her own Cakchiquel dialect adding great force to my viewpoint, and when she finally acquiesced to be airlifted and have that bone set as long as her daughter could come with her, I looked up to thank my timely helper, who with a crooked smile and lifting his sad eyes turned out to be none other than Sacrapala! He was unwounded in body, but like every Indian in Guatemala born wounded in soul in the best of ways. This gave him a boundless indigenous depth that comes only from a largess of cultural grief. But like all the rest of us who have been in times such as these wounded in a way that made living a different thing, clearing the throne of our hearts of superfluous things to make room for the royalty of a more substantial understanding of the Holy, something you could actually hold and try to maintain instead of trying to attain and possess, Sacrapala had lost his need to win and was, in any way he could, out there helping.

The night of the quake, the acting officer in charge of the prison, may he be blessed, rushed to open all the tiny medieval cells with his gigantic iron keys and only got so far as Sacrapala's cage out of which he and two others bolted, tumbling out through the ridged and winged fake marble archway of the front hall just as the entire massive fortress careened to the ground killing every inmate, warden, dog, and fly, including the kind officer who tried to get them all to freedom.

Only Sacrapala had survived in the end, as the other two were later shot and killed for looting. Now loaded up with relief food wrapped in a Red Cross blanket, he was on his way back to his family who had ironically for the fact of their poverty done better than most; living in an unpopulated ravine among the cornfields in the old-time, nail-less, tied-together, thatched-cornstalk hut traditional to the area, which even if it had fallen would've hurt no one; they not only survived but some of their stores of corn had remained as well.

There was no time or way to celebrate his being alive, for being alive was the celebration. But in the course of our brief banter Sacrapala asked if I had any connections that might help alleviate the starving conditions in two or three villages that lay south of Chimaltenango which, on account of the territorial jealousy of a certain army officer, remained off-limits to all aid-giving organizations. Citing some incomprehensibly complicated breach of protocol which just masked the commander's wounded pride, when do-gooders from a certain foreign relief organization stigmatized those people willing to receive their assistance as dirty, uncivilized, ignorant little children who wouldn't need help if they had kept up with the times, developed their country, embraced the modern, and were washed up and squeaky clean like the do-gooders, in one of those ironic, self-defeating acts of revenge, the commanding officer ordered his soldiers not to let anyone through, resulting in several remote, very hard-hit districts being left utterly unattended. Sacrapala's in-laws were there. Everyone knew their situation was dire, but the soldiers would not let anyone pass on the regular approaches until they received orders to the contrary, which probably hinged on an apology from the arrogant, holier-than-thou relief people concerned, which wasn't likely, so of course the army got the bad P.R. and the villagers starved.

But! A heroic plan sprouted in the ever-fertile humus of the ever-present warm compost pile of my past failure to be good enough, in which my Irish imagination sparked a romantic unplausible thought: "What if I could find my way back to South Lake Atitlán, explain the situation, even though they'd already gotten word by other means by now, get some clothing, a little money, my guitar, then row to the north side of the lake into undamaged Panajachel? What if I could raise enough cash there by giving benefit concerts to those temporarily stranded rich gringos to be able to buy up surplus beans, and rice on the equally unquaked southwest coast, somehow cook it all, load up the food in barrels, and then commandeer if need be some heavy army surplus Dodge half-track owned but never used by a certain missionary outfit I knew and clandestinely drive the cooked food, some firewood, water, and metal cooking pots, over the tumbled land as close as possible to those unattended towns, especially Cuchumaquic, and distribute them as best we could, all hopefully without the army seeing us, then maybe wouldn't I have done something worth doing for a change?"

For the first and probably very last time in my life every detail and action I imagined up to Cuchumaquic worked out with a suspicious smoothness untypical of the times, the country, and especially my history.

There was no army watching the southwestern entrance to the little hamlets in question, as these Mayans were nowhere near any highways to begin with except the same one that ran the highlands; a road which for a long time would remain incapacitated. Because of all the rearranged terrain, the back entrances were considered utterly impassable except by helicopter, which would've had to fly over soldier-scrutinized land to get there and thereby risk being shot down, not that anyone had been preparing to fly there anytime soon because every aircraft had been prioritized for day and night emergency work in more densely populated areas.

I thought to do a significant thing for a small place using what creativity I might have to gather any resources I could, instead of just adding more confusion and another mouth to feed to the crowd of people who already needed more than was arriving to those larger semi-urban places. Imagining myself some low-level equivalent of Ignacio Parra, Rob Roy, Robin Hood, or some do-gooder bandit, I would take from the wealthier and more self-preserving caste of gringos, tourists, and resident foreigners, most of whom went about their lives strangely oblivious to the desperate plight around them, and give to other people struggling minute to minute just to live, less than twenty miles away. But then the visitors probably hadn't noticed that behind its beauty and smile, Guatemala was already a desperate place when they arrived, and only a few could see the difference through the dust.

Chapter 3

The Unlikely Peace at Cuchumaquic

It was hard to get to the lake again—the roads were broken, bandits and army everywhere, refugees crowding every landing and market. I only kept saying to myself, "Do what you can in this one little place instead of a lot of failing at helping everyone who needed it and helping no one. Keep your focus." My visit back to Santiago was only part of a day and less of a night spent mostly praying, making offerings with Chiv, visiting home and finding a relative with a canoe willing to help me row the thirteen miles of the lake north to Panajachel.

I kept my little seed-eyed stone with me all the time hidden so his lump and weight would keep me conscious of what I was trying to make happen and to lend courage and perspective to my challenge considering the spoilt and rarified non-Mayan bubble I was about to enter. Something I'd stayed away from. It was a terrifying thought: a town full of self-righteous lazy outsiders.

Aquel and I rowed the seven miles and pulled his old wild-avocado-wood canoe up onto the black beach that curved one quarter mile east of Panajachel proper.

My dismay over what turned out to be the terrifying accuracy with the scenario I had imagined I would find in that tourist town, especially the general lack of emotion, overplayed unoriginal TV sarcasms, and apathetic reaction to my own impassioned pleas on behalf of their troubled Indian neighbors, made it difficult at first for me not to be infected with a quiet bitterness. I proceeded onward anyway, for my pursuit of this small unlikely dream of mine to bring food to unfed people with my art, plaited irony, outrage, beauty, and hilarity into a cable of hope that pulled me beyond my own self-centered expectations toward something bigger and more worthy than my need to be right and important.

In what had once been a beautiful flower-lined village set at the mouth of a heart-soaring river canyon and multilingual trading market for many Mayan groups, Panajachel had become by then an almost suburban American resort town. In certain quarters American and European tourists, semi-resident foreign runaways, and powerful rich families lived on eternal late breakfast coffee discussions served by Indian housemaids, then a reefer, then a swim or motorboat ride in the beautiful lake, a lunch, a hike then a dip in the sacred hot springs, where they found new partners for the moment with whom they shared deep hot-spring spiritual discoveries that generated cool discussions, then a patronizing dinner at the Peace Corp–instigated, Quiche Mayan–owned ribs joint or at the Cakchiquel pizza place, then home, a beer, and, "Let's walk on the beach in the moonlight," to bed with the new partner by 2 a.m., or if alone or married, reading Carlos Castaneda until 4 a.m.

It was innocuous but had nothing to do with the land, the history, the people, or the spiritual integrity of the beauty of the place. Very colonial in a way. The earthquake worried them; it was stressful. "What would happen! Could it come here?" And then one moonlit night not too long after the big earthquake when a tremor dislodged a house-sized boulder from the caprock of the canyon, rolling straight through a house up the road a quarter mile from town leaving two opposite walls standing and two people alive but stunned, eyes wide like a kinkajou, while the boulder continued another quarter mile into the river to plop joyfully into the lake leaving exquisite concentric rings of water muddied by the quaking mountain upstream closing over her, finally sinking to rest contentedly at home in the depths with all her basaltic cousins who had been dropping off the cliff heading to the river by ones and twos for hundreds of thousands of years of volcanic tremors—this of course became cause for two reefers, three beers, a new partner, and plans to return to California until it all blew over.

And into this I dropped, still covered in dust and the smell of the burning bodies of Tecpán, wearing with my youthful suit of self-righteous duty and palpable aura of emergency on behalf of all the world's natural people, especially the demolished east highland Mayans whose deaths, displacements, starvation, grief, and impossible wreckage were bravely borne less than fifteen miles to the immediate north and less to the east of this superficial tourist spot. But fuelled by my heroic need to not let down the people I loved, I was determined to somehow hide my contempt, indignation, impatience, and sense of injustice. Firmly resolved to calmly, unscoldingly, with no preaching, play three pleasant nightly guitar concerts sufficiently entertaining to divert the well-fed inmates of this synthetic bubble of comfort, lawns, croissants, and Italian coffee, away from their stress over the quake, in order to raise enough meager cash to purchase beans and rice in the reputedly untremored Pacific lowland to feed people upon whose ancient backs this entire country relied but who now waited starving for the flower of the present world to formally close, wither, and end as they knew it.

As difficult as such situations can be for the likes of a person like me, when the mountain-like love for something one has is bigger than one's righteous hatred over the unfairness of others to the loved one, it can override our violent need to win and cause a real spiritual intelligence to sprout out of the hard shell of needing to be the one who is right. Like what motivates a mother ocelot in trying to feed her kits to do things alone she'd never try, we in the end can give only the beauty of our grief put to action by the majesty of our love, where it assumes the throne of the needs of the moment, whose priorities become love's motive. But then again, by that point I, unlike the people I was playing my music for and whose money we needed, had worked jobs my whole life just to eat and had also lived long enough among really hardworking people in a hand-to-mouth village who survived without any safety net of cash to bail themselves or me out of any emergency. Life was always a precarious condition. There was never any option of "returning" to the illusion of a safer place. The practicality of my service to what I loved in the village had demanded at this moment that I should remember also that people like myself or the ravaged highlanders would never become grant recipients, receive endowments, or outright gifts of money unless by doing so the donors could be assured of their continued feeling of superiority by their capacity to do so, or received a tax write-off, or could be reassured they would be reciprocated by an equal tax-free donation to their own foundation or family corporation, or a more endowed chair in their academic tenure.

It had become increasingly apparent over the years that the unexpected presence in a room, or the unannounced appearance, in such a neocolonial-type community, of the deep substance of heartbreak and ingenious reality of a person in love whose soul was not whole because it was unwounded but because it was blood kin with the Holy, and therefore wounded, would indigenous or not, always send up a warning flare of instinctual ripples of dreaded uncertainty through the bodies of less solid people mired in civilization's hypocrisies and incapacity with their hands in the earth.

The wide spiritual swath of the rare individual with his or her hat in their hand or its collective presence in tribal peoples, or those untrained in the affectations of civilization's incomprehensible mind-wasting-tail-wagging and unspoken self-trivializing protocols, was perceived as a "come-on," a con to get something for nothing, as something too real to be real since they couldn't be real, a liveliness camouflaging a hidden agenda, and was consistently instinctually sensed as a potential threat to the illusion of security of the would-be donors' well-guarded lifeless ponds of unearned and unrenewable economic equilibrium, or worse yet, conversely regarded as an equally exploitable naïveté, a good business opportunity to get a lot of resellable land or handmade goods for a desperately needed but tiny cash loan "investment."

It has always been a mystery to me why people whose only ability is to give away what they can't physically create will never give what's been given to them to help anybody who doesn't show obeisance to their same lack of substance, leaving anyone who learns the game well enough to be rewarded only by becoming something they are not, so as to appear appropriately and equally damaged in order to fit the donor's definition of legitimate, and lesser than they are. This leaves the game to those social pirates who could act the part with no more conscience than those they would rob who end up taking all the donor's money by appearing as bland as their marks, making their sheltered benefactors feel like flamboyant risk-takers who were being given what their poor minds interpreted as a "real" cultural experience and grateful to the thieves for it all. But I couldn't do that kind of acting. It became a matter of simple common sense to me. For after all, no matter how much an unconscious people deserve a wake-up call, I could still not expect such people to honestly comprehend those with whom they were incapable of identifying, people with whom they could only visit, buy from, and stare at from the other side of the glass, but never actually be one of those solid people. If one of these natural humans stood tall, refused to look pitiful, and asked for a grant, undoubtedly their would-be benefactors would react in fear before thinking it out, acting quickly against anything that threatened their own frail identities as superiors. They perceived any unfamiliar cultural or economic reality other than their own as a personal attack on their entitled territory of comfort and they certainly were not going to reward somebody or a tribe that made them feel "bad" about themselves unless by doing so they were made to look and feel "good" for having done so, and they could assume they could keep on drinking to what they'd "helped" at a safe distance, without having to actually live with them.

By constantly thinking of Chiv, my stone, the mothers and babies in the tent, the starving people in the hills, I hoped to keep these realizations out of the expression struggling in my face. But I must have failed in that, for after arranging the concerts as planned, having played the music, music I hoped would inspire and comfort, trying to speak words of blessing instead of guilt, for all my efforts I received no donations whatsoever, only the pittance cash entry price from the door. Certainly not enough for a heroic foray with cooked beans to starving Mayan towns. Of course as far as they were concerned, the rich had already contributed to this or that tax-deductible charity organization back in the States and Europe, and that got them off the hook with a nice entertaining night during an emergency.

On the other hand a few very good-hearted hippies did come to the concerts and to the rescue. Stranded by the quake, and just as broke as I was, they loaned me the use of their old trucks and with cash from the concerts and our own pockets, together we somehow brought back on credit from the lowland three quarters of a ton of black beans, one-and-a-half tons of white coastal rice, eight cleaned-out topless oil barrels and a beautiful male chachalaca bird who had secretly fallen in love with one of the truck beds on the way up from the hot forested piedmont zone below the Nahualate River.

The hippie moms and two Cakchiquel ladies took the cooking seriously, and when we had three barrels of edible beans and three of rice, with buckets we transferred the precious food to empty barrels already loaded onto the beds of the missionary half-tracks. Along with two barrels of water, some bundles of firewood, cooking pots, matches, and what each time always seemed to me growing up in the long New Mexican distances a very insufficient five extra gallons of gasoline, we headed up the unknown lost route to find Cuchumaquic and villages surrounding not thirty miles away.

Every other day, leaving an interim day for cooking, repairs, and sleep, six or seven of us—mostly idealistic American boys—loaded up before dawn, knowing we were to spend a lot of time lost, creeping along at beetle speed trying to find these places none of us had ever seen, hoping to be able to return in daylight, something which never happened.

The first day was tedious and we didn't get to Cuchumaquic, but where we did end up was a village in great appreciation of the food and so we gave them all we had and lost twelve hours getting back to the next load of cooking beans and bubbling barrels of rice and sleep.

Leaving even earlier on the second attempt it took us more than twelve hours over recently laid plains where once there had risen forested mountains, into unstable rippling seas of tufa and toppled trees whose shaggy roots barely protruded over the newly leveled ground filling what used to be ravines. We banged around recently created hills that further dammed rivers, creating unstable reservoirs that would someday burst and flood out again other towns farther down, Panajachel itself almost washing out a couple of months later. Even so, we had no idea where we were and actually had to stop after having used half the gas. We could see we were south of Patzicia or the Place of the Water Dog (otter) where Chiviliu's mother had been born, east of the Ik Utiu mountain or Black Coyote, and somewhere between there and the big blustering ash-spouting volcano of Fuego and his quieter sisters, Alotenango and Agua farther to the east, but thankfully within a mile of another forgotten starving village.

If the wits sharpened by need and the always exquisite miracle of the natural ability of our inner telegraph had not brought dreams to the hungry people we sought, thereby causing them to have cleared away the exact route where we landed every time, where some little boy or group of hungry youths sent to direct us by running ahead to demonstrate the route through the only viable chutes in order that our vehicle might pass through an otherwise crazy impassable landscape to pull slowly into the midst of throngs waiting together up in the rubble of what had been their hamlets, we should have probably remained lost and stuck with a truckload of soured rotting beans forever.

On the third and last foray, eight days since I'd left Chimaltenango, having cooked the last of the beans and rice, during our final attempt with the little food, money, and gas we had left, to finally get to Cuchumaquic from the directions supplied by people of the other two villages, while moving at our top speed of four miles an hour in the grumbling old half-track listing dangerously to the right as we skirted the side of a deep canyon with a few trees left stripped but standing, we came around a great grey boulder behind which grew a large old *ocuy* tree that sprang suddenly into view on our left from whose thickest branch swung a dead non-Indian man hung by the neck.

Despite all the public executions in Guatemala none of us there had ever seen anyone hung before, and no matter what kind of death it is, it always seems to put a wave of dismay and tense wariness in one's determination, especially in those unsure days.

Having heard about the legendary conservative nature of the people of Cuchumaquic, the lead driver was braking, preparing to back impossibly and turn completely around and head back, taking this hung man as a warning to outsiders not to proceed.

Cuchumaquic, of course, like several other smaller Mayan towns all over the Highlands and Nahuat towns in mountainous west central Mexico, had been a place notoriously off-limits to outsiders. Though a traditional Cakchiquel mountain people, they were not like most of their more adaptive kin.

As all those old kinds of trucks of course had low gear for high, without asking anybody else Grover started grinding down to sub-super-low granny gear preparing to turn, but in that desperate instant through the terrible dust we were raising and in well-accepted Guatemalan road etiquette, I began pounding on the cab for him to halt. From where I was perched in the bed behind the cab with the beans I could see galloping toward us in little clouds of dust puffing up at a pace we could not even imagine in our ghastly steel box of rusty riveted military surplus insanity whose molar-cracking suspension and wheels, hard as we might try, to even match much less outrun even on a paved highway, the approaching shirtless, scraped-up middle-aged Cakchiquel man with ropes crisscrossing his broad bare, ribby chest, his machete case full and hung on his back, astride a skinny but beautiful little sparky red horse. He yelled over and over for us to stop and listen to him.

And listen we did.

And only then after we were already floating in the soup did it occur to my single focused zealous mind how a decommissioned military vehicle like this loaded with non-Guatemalan looking men might appear to the National Army who declared this area off-limits not to even consider what we might have brought to mind to villagers who were already being approached by the initial edge of *guerilleros* intent on a great "liberating" war who would capitalize on economic frustration this earthquake had precipitated, to get the "revolution" going, sometimes through the appearance of relief work. This was exacerbated now by the well-known reality of how several small guerrilla armies who wore tourist clothing, decommissioned uniforms from any army, and fired an odd assortment of captured military weapons would have loved an old Dodge half-track to carry on the movement.

In this man's face I saw what later became those earthquake days for me: something I hadn't expected and something that drove a part of me already immersed into life in deeper still like a seed in service to the Holy in Nature. The man's face and whole being pushed me as far as I could get from any feeling of having to further prove I was not an adherent in any way to the spiritual wreckages that modern whites claim for their superiority.

He hadn't come to turn us around; he hadn't come to kill us, or hang us, warn us, hijack the truck, or give us hell. He had come to introduce himself as Pascual Yac Cumaatz and, after shaking hands with each and every dusty hippie in the truck, announced that he had been following us for an hour to show us how to get to his people. The people of Cuchumaquic.

When one of our crew, still shaking, inquired about the man hung in the tree, Pascual leaned his massive, strong-featured head slightly to the left, staring, then shrugged, and suppressing a tide of rising hilarity, grabbed his horse's mane and smiling said, "Don't worry about him. He won't bother you. That's nothing! He came here to sell us blankets and food that the Red Cross was giving away free in Chimaltenango in trade for our farmland—of course they had to hang him!"

All the boys in the truck, like scared chickens negotiating with a hawk, simultaneously reassured Pascal Yac, who now failed to hold back a rising laugh, that our food was absolutely a gift and his people could have the truck too if they needed it.

Unperturbed, totally at ease, but his mouth now laughing as much as starvation would let him, and leaning forward off to one side like a raptor preparing to lift off a snag, the two wings of this gaunt handsome man's upper lip rolled back showing a mouth full of good white teeth grown from his suffering mother's lime and corn-fed breast milk and years of a good mountain diet, behind which finally rose flapping a full eye-squinting laugh with tears that he couldn't restrain, and wiping his eyes, he rode forward signaling us to follow him.

The beans slopping and sloshing as we bumped nervously along, he explained what had happened in Cuchumaquic; that most of his people had not died directly from the quake though there had been some deaths, but like everywhere in the Highlands, the cookware, water jars, and traditional food storage and preparation utensils had been made of fired Mixco clay, and all had been buried and pulverized: there was nothing to cook with, much less anything to cook, and nothing to haul water in much less to drink as the stream there had also been deeply buried by the collapsing mountainsides.

That there were people sent out here and there to bring back water or food had kept some alive but most hadn't eaten now in seven days, and with no energy to recover from their wounds received in the quake, or to leave in search of relief, many had died as a result and there were more to come.

The once rolling hillsides of cornfields and forests that surrounded the little *cuenca* of Cuchumaquic had been planted when the quake hit. Though before the quake some still had quite a few dry corn ears left purposely ungathered per old custom everywhere, in case of emergency, because most of the hills had either tumbled down or lost all their surfaces, the trees and crops that had been rooted in that rich but always unstable volcanic cinder had slipped into deep unassailable mounds of avalanche scree and deeply buried rubble, a lot of which we were now driving across. They had been patiently starving on top of whatever had been remotely edible.

Pascual had gone out to see if he could find his little horse to bring him in to butcher and share the meat so needed by his starving village.

When, as all animals do, particularly birds, before the imminent occurrence of an earthquake, the horse, feeling the tension of the coming tumult rising, had broken loose that dark morning, disappearing to live unmoving on a tiny patch of still mysteriously grassy ground which had never altered in the quake and from which even a trickle of water yet dribbled.

Pascual had dreamt that the horse was not only alive, but that from where he saw him in the dream he could find water, and the horse would then take him to people bringing food to the village. He'd caught him exactly where the dream had directed, and then seeing us by our dust only a mile from the horse's earthquake dream pasture, brought the horse, us, and news of a small trickle of water in the mountain rubble to his people.

From what I could make out of what Pascual yelled back to us over his shoulders as he rode along on in front, it seemed that over three hundred Cakchiquels were waiting for us, far more than our sloshing barrels could ever come close to fully feeding, for today we had only one truck, the other having lost its *calabaza* (squash), or rear differential, whose mechanism had been ground into filings by all the hastened rough journeys, and we were short of food anyway for having lost some hippies who had headed back to the States and even more stretched for having come to the end of the 1,000 pounds of dry beans and 1,500 pounds of dry rice we'd been able to come up with.

With supplies in such desperate scarcity, we neared this great crowd of starving families, fully expecting to be mobbed by a horde of hunger-crazed people pushing us out of the way, while the strongest individuals elbowed and clubbed their way to get closer to the precious sustenance of the cooked seeds, in the same way I'd seen tragic masses of waving, hunger-driven arms and bodies besieging vehicles and food deliveries in more citified areas and in some cases seriously injuring or even killing one another or those handing out the food.

All of us in the back of the truck concurred that we should all leap away from the bed and get as far away as we could if it came to that, and then wait until we could reclaim the truck and return from where we had set out.

But in that anxious moment of entering what had been Cuchumaquic there were no desperate people running, nor a happily cheering crowd. Only the low, bee-like hum of the murmur of small clusters of sitting humans equally mixed with the little sounds of hundreds of equally hungry yellow warblers twittering in the dead branches of uprooted trees.

Pascual in the lead, we drove directly into what once had been the loosely hut-lined center of the now rubbled little *aldea* of Cuchumaquic. While we ground down into a gear-crunching halt right into the middle of hundreds of sitting people in some seventy family groups, comforting their wounded, broken, and dying, their half-conscious babies, and bewildered old folks lying inside the attentive circle of those who continued a little stronger, not one of the people stirred.

After making some too hurried, overly precipitated imbecilic exhaustion-fueled pronouncement about the beans and the rice, after blessing them and inviting everyone to come get what they could, I delivered a heartfelt apology for our tardiness and the insufficient quantity of the food. A momentary silence landed over our settling dust as everybody looked back at us with six hundred tired, sweet eyes.

Then from every side, in an instant of parallel motion characteristic of a communal mind, an individual man or woman representing their hungry family, their wounded, their young, their old, came gracefully to their feet, each man removing his hat if he still had one, the women with their hands waving to the rhythm of the poetry of their collective response. What they spoke was not a response to us, but to that divine thing that lived in all mother seeds like the beans and rice that fed us all and thereby made us live with the death of Her cooked seeds. They simultaneously prayed for this in a fine old spoken Cakchiquel, adding as well that our families and ourselves be blessed and kept from harm, and that we be able to find in our visit to their proud people, what turned out to be the survivors of not one but five settled villages, a welcome worthy of the effort we'd made to get here.

The inhabitants of this Cuchumaquic and the surrounding valleys had not come together to have a better chance at survival, but rather to die together at the will of Nature which is the Holy's mind, living together peacefully while they waited. They did not see the food we brought as something to save them from the vicissitudes of the aftermath of an earthquake, but as a gift from people outside their area who had themselves come to Cuchumaquic in hopes of being given permission to remain with these proud Mayas and live out our remaining days of the world's end together!

The inhabitants of Cuchumaquic and the surrounding valleys had not united for a better chance at survival. Though they definitely wanted to be close to one another for the solace of dying in the arms of their own people, something all Guatemalan Mayan people, even in less dire times, were always most anxious to be allowed, they had come to pass the world's end at the place all Mayans, every village and tribe, know as their *rumuxux* or the "umbilicus of the world." They wanted the symphony of their thousand years' struggle to live in the arms of the corn seed's earth to end here where it had begun: at the place of their mutual origins. In this way they themselves would become spiritual seeds and their passing become temporal humus from which the Divine could regrow a world beyond their own time. In their parallel understanding of vegetation and human culture, they wanted to be rooted in the Earth's memory of their having been there, even if they as humans had to disappear. After all, all the mythologies said that they as people had themselves sprouted from a time previous to any of our own presence, and like seeds had resprouted themselves from the compost of a world of previous human failures.

They simply thought that we motley unkempt idealistic hippies and half-breeds had come in our funny homely truck to join them for a more noble end! Though wounded, dying, starving, and with their hearts exhausted, their souls in all this dust and misery remained utterly intact. They saw the end not as defeat but accepted it as their graceful and logical usefulness to the bigger mind of Nature who now had other directions to go besides where humans dictate. Humans had obviously outgrown their usefulness; their world had ended; Time was renewing Herself again.

Then, as if in slow motion like something carried out in a dream under water, the men who still had them gave their doffed hats to the senior lady of their nest of seated and wounded relatives. Some limping, every one tired, but in a fashion elegant and in every case courteous, these appointed women came toward us in an orderly file, each one calmly taking turns holding up their old man's hat with both hands into which we dropped one ladleful of cooked black beans and another of still-warm coastal rice.

After thanking us and smiling, shaking our hands, one by one each woman returned to her patiently waiting family; because the earthquake had pulverized or buried all the bowls, gourds, and receptacles of any sort, these hats were commandeered for today's communal eating dishes in each household. In the most calm and unfrantic elegance, the people fed one another as if it had always been this way. An unbelievable calm reigned throughout the hungry throng, especially considering how three more truckloads would have been necessary to even remotely resemble one meal for every person there. There was no mob scene, no angry word, no resentment, no malice or even despair. A lot of suffering but in some strange way, there were no victims.

Though this food was in no fashion anywhere near enough, everyone was given equally from the little there was. We stood staring in amazement, covered in earthquake dust and the muck of dried beans, admiring the unanticipated calm in their suffering, when something even more stunning happened that rewired my entire heart, banishing my cynicism to the compost heap, and was startled into the realization that humans could actually become a noble thing worth descending from when the recipients of this meager meal, the village of Cuchumaquic, again with one collective mind in a simultaneous singular wave of mass approval all looked up toward us before they ate their meager feast, and cheerfully invited us to please come down off the hot truck bed and sit down and rest, and feast with them as their guests!!!

Though most of us in the truck had never actually been chronically starved for food, all of us in that truck on that day were very hungry, but we refused the generosity, not wanting to take even a crumb of food from the mouths of a truly starving crowd. All of us, that was, except myself. After so many years of living inside Tzutujil spirituality and generosity, of those who know the daily reality of starvation's dire and constant possibility, I knew that all foods in their live forms are the bodies of the Divine, whose Diverse forms, in their Deaths, generously fed us, and gave us life. To refuse the bigness of the offer of even the smallest particle of even one plant's or a mineral's Holy Death from a friend was an ignorance that implied a superiority over the Holy in Nature and constituted a condescension to the people and in the end a kind of spiritual violence that not only wounded the grandeur and pride of the Indigenous heart, but worse yet, insulted the Divine bigness of Nature's depth itself. After all, our survival as humans on Earth rests totally in the continued presence of plants that, for the most part, come from seeds. The Diverse Hearts of what is Holy lives in the seed, not in people's mores. That same Holy resident in the seed causes seeds to sprout and make more food in the first place. As small as the face of a seed can seem, it is in this small thing where the most powerful holy beings in the Universe have their homes and govern all life. At least that's what the shamans and village Mayans of my day lived by. And, comprehending this, I was obligated to accept the grandeur of such a gift. Not receiving this kind of gift was a form of stinginess and greed: for instead of feeding the hungry we would be stealing their capacity to give the greatness of the gift of this comprehension back to the gift givers. By refusing we would be impoverishing the nobility of the people we came to feed.

People cannot be made poor if their dignity comes from this comprehension. All people, no matter how wealthy, are living in Hell and poverty when this understanding is lost. They've lost their seeds.

Hoping for food themselves, hungry birds of every color warbled above as I climbed down from the poor tired steel of the old truck to join the people of Cuchumaquic on their wounded ground. Though changed of course, its people were still in love with life, and with the shared generosity of the ground and to everyone there, in just one tablespoon of beans and rice life was a grand deep thing; the world in one way or another actually had ended, at least as any of us had known it, but for those of us feasting, real life on earth had just begun.

Along with most of the other younger men who ate nothing or only very little, I tried to follow their lead by giving the little tablespoons of food apportioned us that day to the hungriest after we pretended to take a bite. A lot of old village stories told how a starving and thirsty, practically dead lost human was handed one tiny acorn lid full of mush or water by a tiny nervous rodent which proved to be undrainable and full of an inexhaustible life-restoring power. The unmeasurable smallness the feeding we did that day has inexhaustibly fueled my own life ever since.

The group of people in Cuchumaquic with whom I was seated and so elegantly feasting had as its hub a family of two little kids, whose mother and father rolled the food into little balls to feed them and several aged starving relatives who lay about us in various degrees of consciousness. One of them laid stretched out on the ground with his hands on his chest had a severely shattered leg and an advanced feverish infection; he kept smiling and kept up a lively conversation with me.

As we conversed, I gave the young father what little help I could, recognizing that he shouldered a great deal of respect and influence among all the people there for his young age, a lot of which came from whatever he kept tightly guarded under his left armpit in an old intricately knotted, cotton, over-the-shoulder-string bag. This rare fancy bag was a little different than the type all Cuchumaquic men in those days usually bore at their sides everywhere they went. Every village in the country had a form: large, small, some colored, black, white, some very fine or others coarse, some cotton, some wool, but you could always know a man or woman's language and village by his bag no matter how non-Indian they were forced to dress, for that never changed.

A few other men walked over after the feast where both Pederucho, as this boy was known, and I "drank delicious words together." Then per universal Mayan custom we visited around a little with the people. In every camp the people greeted me cordially by shaking hands, but Pederucho by kissing his ring finger, then the fringes of his little bag.

A loud banging came thumping from the cab of the old military bean-and-oil-drum-hauling truck accompanying a chorus of exasperated voices yelling in English for me to hurry up and quit "hanging out." Anxious to leave what was for them a mission accomplished, they were uncomfortable with the calm and wanted to leave the spell of what was for them a stressful nightmarish irreality. As amazing as even they could see it was, they wanted to get back to the familiarity of the more anonymous undemanding place in whose more agitated noise of non-starving security they felt more at home. I think they started worrying that maybe the world really had ended. I wasn't listening anyway, concentrating instead on what this man with whom I had been strolling, visiting, and talking was teaching me in Cakchiquel about what his little bag held.

After eating, the entire village made a prayer of thanks to that Mother:

our Food, who had just suckled us. All the crowd concurred with their own ritual interjections at the appropriate joints in the stalk of our mutual liturgies. No one was amazed I could pray in Mayan as well, though very few if any non-Mayans could or would pray in that non-Christian way even if they learned the language. The people were beyond small things now, amazed only at the depth of what followed. For when the little *yaal*, or bag, was opened onto an outstretched shawl, there nestled in the middle of a carefully knotted red silk scarf lay the very last *macaj* of *Yaqui Sac* and *ruxuach ixim;* two good perfect ears of corn; one translucent blue, the other ivory, both of an old-time flint corn that had primordially sustained their people and for which Cuchumaquic had been famous in all the centuries past. This little bundle contained the only seeds that had remained to the people after the ripping turmoil and dust this earthquake wreaked upon their fields and granaries.

Pederucho himself, his family, his entire village, and the surrounding linguistic tribe, no matter how hungry they had grown in the last few weeks of starvation, had faithfully refused to "eat their seeds!" Unanimous and unquestioned, the agreement they had always kept since their origination as a people was to "keep their seeds alive" above and beyond the needs and desires of the present in order to have enough to regenerate another time. The people had always called their seeds "Mothers," and it was to Her they now all prayed, for those two are mothers of all life: the Holy in the sustaining seed. I knew that. He knew that. All corn-growing Indians know it still. It was to these two Mothers that all these grateful, starving people now prayed. Corn seeds, time, human culture, food, and all existence were all the same thing: Time was a plant grown from a seed; human culture was a seed; their food was a seed; all existence came from seeds; they were all seeds, and they were revered collectively as the living Holy. They would of course at all costs "keep the seeds alive," and here they were! We knew what it meant. And we did what all people can only do when confronted with such grandeur: we all had to kiss the Mother seeds and we did.

This ability to understand and tangibly fulfill this vision of keeping the seeds alive made the seeds they guarded not only the seeds of human sustenance, but also the seeds of real culture, the seeds of peace. For this willingness to keep these seeds and such understanding alive not only during such testing conditions, but also in the full awareness that the seeds might *not even* be for them in the end, somehow when seeds are regrown to sustain other people in a time much beyond their own when they themselves may have disappeared, this caused the people, with such understanding in the present, no matter how dusty or materially reduced, to become a culture whose memory would be something spiritually grand. And just like the seeds, such people became something well worth descending from for a long time afterward. This made the village a village of true human beings, to me a far greater people than all the stalemated, earth-, air-, and ocean-wrecking high-rise civilizations operating today.

The big truck tooting its incongruously pitiful little horn was urging me to get going. But Pederucho and I were still passionately expounding to each other, almost simultaneously, more for the beauty of what we were both saying than the need to be understood, how the people, including the Tzutujil, had grown up hearing the old accounts that spoke about how many occasions the fires of time had gone out before our time, the world ending just like now, and how all the seeds that fed all the people and animals, the same ones that feed us now, had been hidden in special places just in case Time and existence after a time of excruciating torpidity and hibernation found a way to "fire themselves" up again. The seeds Pederucho held for the people had descended from seeds replanted over and over from the same ones that were many times in the past hidden, refound, and replanted to bring back to life the entire world. As the earth slowly regained consciousness from those thick nodes of lengthy torpidity, its heat returning after those apocalyptic changes and eons of hibernating ice ages, marked by the Highlanders as "nodes on the ever-growing grassy cane of life," between one node to the next an eon flourished as a growing plant, like our Mother Corn.

But even if, despite all the evidence that the people of Cuchumaquic could see to the contrary, the world did not actually come to an end just yet, then, Pederucho said, all the villagers knew very well that it would take at least ten to fifteen years of concentrated effort of cultivation, good fortune, and no consuming of the harvest, for these two cobs of seeds to recuperate enough seed stock to, even in the best of hands, regrow enough corn to feed the people and reestablish the rituals that accompany all old-time Mayan corn-growing culture. It had happened before in Guatemala, often and even in living memory, and the people, their culture, and their plants had bounced back with equal adaptability and vigor. It happened when given time and room to do so.

But this time, and increasingly worldwide, more insidious and hard-hearted things were at work; something that has seemed to continue devouring the world's seed cultures ever since.

While other places in the Highlands had their own equivalent stories, most would soon wither and disappear; the stories always came along with their seeds, and this is what made culture. The people in flesh and blood might remain after losing their seeds and stories, but they would not be the real people of the seed. The world is populated with them. People who've lost their seeds. They are not bad useless people, but they are not real people until they refind their seeds. The real people they used to be, like the seed, have vanished from this visible dimension to hide in an inner world inside modern citified people. In some small never-looked-at place in the forgotten wilderness of their souls, invisible to the forces that would invade and take over, their indigenous seeds of culture and lifeways live exiled from their everyday consciousness. The entire world is now at this doorway. Seeds and spirits of real culture are things that not only can't be comprehended through television, but don't want to be on camera. This land of the forgotten wilderness cannot be photographed. Together in these times our real souls live a nomadic refugee existence hidden from the modern mind deep inside the wilderness of an unassailable inner dimension, living only in the ecstatic and fleeing all objective study or voyeuristic scrutiny.

In the old stories when it was said the seeds would disappear, everybody knew this would happen. Everybody also knew what this meant: that the consciousness necessary for a real, natural world would end until the original seeds could surface again that could sprout once more in a better social climate more conducive to the true parallel natures of both humans and seeds.

Throughout the Highlands their culture of this kind of seed life and its ritual consciousness could have regenerated itself, and would have, if it had not been for the post-earthquake invasion of petroleum-dependent lifeways and their bankrupting credit systems, that promised "aid" to governments and private institutions operating in countries whose people were neither represented by their government nor understood as worthy by the world business community. So many crops and stores of fairly sustainable food of self-sufficient peoples in their own interdependent cultural groups, spiritual land bases, and ancient regional market systems had been lost, buried, burned, half-grown, or destroyed just enough by that quake so as to leave a vulnerable tear in the age-old fabric of Highland life through which foreign-fueled interests, both left and right, were able to saturate the people with a dependency on a top-heavy unnatural economy, that within only the eight years that followed this invasion of post-earthquake relief scams, practically all the rare squashes, corns, beans, cotton, etc., had literally disappeared from the land, market, and diet along with the stories, rituals, and lifestyle of the people they belonged to.

The great irony of course is that most all of the ancient strains of seeds lost in similarly troubled conditions worldwide were the living ancestors of the overly specialized nutritionally weak, genetically-tinkered-with varieties of seeds pushed onto the people by this modern monster petroleum economy agribusiness travesty. These weaker chemically dependent nonnutritional seeds, like the modern chemically dependent people who unquestionably depend on them, have by their exclusive use banished into extinction both the vitality of all seeds and the vitality of real human cultures. This is what has left modern people without a real origination point, why they never "belong" and are never truly "at home" anywhere, having to export their unrootedness to the rest of the world.

In Guatemala, every Catholic, Protestant, and business "relief" operation opened stores that were touted as cooperatives, providing seeds on credit to create "debts" that could never be paid by manual farming, thereby once again indenturing the indigenous population against their own land. As if that were not enough, along with the "new" seeds came previously unknown pesticides and chemical fertilization techniques that, while initially producing a lot of modified corn that all the people recognized as hollow, tasteless, and unsustaining, also within three years had made the land utterly devoid of any growing vitality. Its natural fallow regeneration capacity gone, the Indians said, "The land can't remember how to remake itself again." This forced anyone who didn't give up in disgust to have to continue to use the chemically dependent seeds and chemicals, falling deeper into a debt to anonymous business interests and religions outside their village circles and story. Those who realized the insanity of pursuing this dependency early on, the farce of going into debt for pseudo food production, found themselves with hungry families to feed, with poisoned land that would now not even regrow its natural bush back in a way that could sustain even the wild greens, and wild animal food whose leaves and flesh comprised forty percent of their diet when in the original way it lay fallow, found themselves forced into buying and selling and hustling merchandise far away from home in the bigger cities. Many, many migrated into a culturally foreign, overpopulated hodgepodge of poverty-ridden shantytowns of unrelated similarly displaced peoples working as grunt workers for a boss in some other place. Two things, both the merchandising and working for nothing, brought their nobility, culture, language, clothing, and self-worth to their knees, and with this of course the dubious promises of the leftwing and its liberation warfare came once again into major prominence.

The 31,000 killed, the 180,000 uprooted, the hundreds of thousands of homes and fields lost were miniscule losses in proportion of damage when compared to the economic and spiritual devastation wreaked upon the country by a so-called "developed" world that continually oozed its neurotic exported depression into those beautiful wounded mountains and people. That terrible decade was fueled by the same economic exigencies during which warring parties representing nothing subtle enough to qualify them as having understood, much less appreciate, the sustainable spiritual and economic value of the real seed peoples' original beauty, ability, and viable lifeways, no matter how far to the left or right these powerfully armed entities leaned in their practically identical claim to be defending the Indigenous, they themselves were nationally defended and funded by a mechanical cynicism from somewhere else. Whether communist, capitalist, or in between, they all worked hard to ruin that world's capacity for a sense of wonder and reverence for the Holy Earth.

But that day as we all sat together in Cuchumaquic, these starving people and this leveled land were for me the first tangible living example of something that had been at the core of everything I and thousands of other 1960s kids, who each in their own multitudinous amateurish directions had been spiritually swimming toward, fleeing their uninspired post–World War II suburban upbringings, something which had historically consumed the efforts and imaginings of uncountable well-meaning, mostly unheeded visionaries trying to change the confusing meander of the ongoing histories of the human-created miseries of war, economic subjugation, and displacement throughout the millennia of civilization's military, nature-killing cultures. Myself having never known or experienced up until then what this much-sought-after-thing might actually look like outside some self-serving cultural bias, or an intellectually overworked theory or an imagined ideal, the realization of what surrounded us on that day only descended upon me slowly. This realization, like a sparkling berylline pebble, sank past my upbringing, my education, my ancestral prejudices, and righteous assumptions, dropping slow and heavy to the bottom of the deep pool of my own Indigenous Soul, where when it finally reached that rich, silty foundation where lay stratified older, forgotten, faraway ways of understanding, I almost fainted as I came to realize that these three hundred dusty people were not a backwards-looking dejected people that needed my help and a revolution, but were the vivid manifestation of the everyday maintenance of the live flowering of what in English I can only call *peace*.

The people of Cuchumaquic had not reacted to the trauma of devastation in the way any of the people from a modern civilization who witnessed it would expect, but also probably didn't recognize the brilliance and great worth such a capacity represented. Modern citizens in other times, in other places, when themselves confronted with similar catastrophic realities, where there was no perceivable hope of a future, were often internally routed in psychological defeat, fleeing blindly to messianic religions or more commonly moving hysterically into a lifestyle of unlimited consumerism that promoted more of the same trauma in the end. The entire post-1947 civilized world, after the global proliferation of nuclear-holocaust weaponry capable of annihilating every thing, animal, plant, and person in the hands of a few unimaginative, politically impounded minds, whose constituencies, after being face to face with the end of the world as an immediate possibility, instead of a courageous unarmed peace of smaller healthy cultures in love with living, have ever since waged a daily competitive war to "gain" personal comfort against their desperation to both forget the horrible ever-present possibility of no future while further annihilating the natural world in the resulting culturally supported amnesia in order to get "everything" they can before it is all over. All of which has since done nothing but further exacerbate the problem they had sought, through their cynical numbness, to flee. For which there are more wars, weapons, and less unmolested earth.

In Cuchumaquic and all the little towns we had visited, on the other hand, all labeled as "backward," "childlike" (i.e., incapable of big thoughts), or the home of simple uneducated good souls, by the same people who made the atom bomb; yet no matter how uncomfortable, they were living a time of courageous peace that made their remaining time on earth into an obligation of ecstasy, nobility, friendship, and memory, becoming in the process the spiritually powerful seeds from which a living future with or without them and beyond them might sprout into view. The modern world cannot claim this.

The unlikely peace of Cuchumaquic was *not* the little peace of physical well-being, it was *not* a painless peace, a peace of no suffering, without typhus or typhoid, or gangrene, or cephalic staph from untended broken skulls or tibias. It was not a peace of having enough to eat, or even anything to eat, or a peace of clean water to drink, much less cook with, and even less to bathe in, or any water at all in many places, in the midst of the cold dry season as it was.

Nor was it a peace of a warm house, home, hut, or any house whatsoever; it was not a peace of families united, or a peace of pleasure, or a peace of going to heaven, or the peace of a mass rapture for the righteous, or a peace of any known future at all. It was not a peace of all evil gone, or any evil gone, or even peace of mind or of any mind, or a peace from a respite from human madness.

There were no houses left, no pots to cook in, no market foods to buy or markets in which to buy them. This was not a peace of people getting their way or a peace of justice achieved or a peace of people obeying laws out of fear of punishment, for in that post-quake era there were no laws in this place, nor was it a peace through anarchy, or whatever came to mind, or if it was a peace of individuals doing whatever they wanted, it was this Peace these individuals wanted to make together. It was not even a peace of peacefulness. Maybe it was not peace at all, but what else could you call it? But I called it Peace.

Instead of individuals running around trying to hoard things and keep them away from the desperate masses of other individuals doing the same thing, as happened in the bigger cities, in these thrashed and flattened little old-time villages they knew if there was nothing left to lose, then what is to be gained by not being happy together, not sharing the little of nothing they still had? They saw the remaining lives their bodies had left as a miraculous gift of ash and water put together and made sentient by the Holy in Nature just long enough to kiss, laugh, and be together on an Earth that obviously did not need humans at all but who had always nonetheless fed us.

As dismal and punishing as it was for those who had been the poorest inside the towns and bigger cities, in those hamlets and smaller villages in the mountainous Mayan cultural areas of corn-growing farmers this odd but irrefutable atmosphere was like the painfully delicious aroma of a never-seen-before flower whose vine inundated this land of dust to create an utter sense of reverent awe of every villager's participation in the ecstatic character of the irrepressible vitality that characterizes the business of the Holy in Nature. That bleak atmosphere of total defeat, interruption, and failure at the hands of Nature's ground-shaking devastation that hung heavy over those urban poor who lost everything having only recently left the villages to crowd Guatemala City and other citified places in search of the security of civilization, at least at the onset, was different for those Indigenous villagers, equally hit in the mountains, becoming for them an ironic feeling of exhilarating hope and peace.

This "disaster" had not been created by people like the human conceit of incessant wars, territory absorption, work, money, scheming, the hatred of the rich for the poor, the poor for the rich, or anything else. Nor was it a retribution sent by any church's god, though a million of the world's evangelical and Protestant Christians, pontificating American Buddhists, and Catholic clerics seemed to have had a lot to say about that.

In most places this peace may not have lasted very long in this, its honeymoon phase, maybe only a moment, in other places two weeks, and in some highly blessed isolated zones as much as six weeks until the "help" that eventually began to show secured again a feeling of anxiety and loss through the delusion of the possibility of solid ground and a secure future through technological advances, eroding the cultural and spiritual integrity of the people until even many of the mountain tribes were drowned in a newly found cynicism imported from the harsh unreal north which would always unconsciously and efficiently find a way to grind the world of small peaceful people into a more familiar clumsy, chain-clanking rank-and-file march of synthetic hand-me-down "modern" development with all its political pettiness, and ugly physical reality.

But the fact that real peace had actually happened here one time for a little while meant peace had probably happened somewhere else just as small and just as real, and probably happened a lot more in times past. Best of all, it could most likely happen again. Did we need disaster to have peace? I know, at least for myself, that even though this peace as we knew it that day may have had to flee and disappear from view on account of those who couldn't see it, coursing back into the magic doorways of the spirit houses of the mountain gods from whence it sprang, it certainly lives on in the shiny eyes of the Indigenous wilderness of all our souls where the everyday civilized mind can neither follow nor see. But even so, more significant still is that the unexpected and positive shock of just the possibility of such a peace existing in such a tangibly experienced conscious reality kicked me awake and all of the convenient mental beach of cynical know-it-all-ness where the disillusioned love to bask, such that a kind of furnace of stars began sparkling in that moment inside the still-impressionable mud of that big tearful oven of my heart of those early years as to not only warm and brighten for me the spiritually cold night of this numb mechanical age we've all been dropped into to live, but to constantly give me a blazing and noble hope whenever I have allowed myself to doubt the reality of this spark of Peace.

I am sure worldwide there are many others like me, and for any of them it has probably not been much different than it has been for myself and the people of the Highlands. But peace like this never meets the criteria for media headlines or historical notoriety, so only rarely do we meet one another. For rather than risk annihilation in the withering gaze of the incoming world's single-minded response of "development," who still to this day see nothing in places like Cuchumaquic other than ignorant Indians in misery who should be taught or forced to become upright participants in civilization's own misguided Earth-draining inability to live at home on this sphere of pulsing water, this unobtrusive peace, like old mythological seeds, always goes to hide again behind the thick hard mantle of petrified human assumptions deep inside the wild mountain wilderness of our Indigenous Souls, unseen and cloaked far from the superficial sarcasm and unidirectional vision of the modern world's over-domesticated cultural mind.

But make no mistake: that peace of Cuchumaquic lives somewhere inside all of us, inside all people, whether awake to it or not, in the form of a powerful tiny magical seed, and there peace lies waiting alive, behind our mental crust, knowing when the day of a more favorable change of spiritual climate occurs in which this seed like peace itself can be openly cultivated and grown again, the peace I knew in Cuchumaquic will come busting again through the sporadic cracks that the Holy causes to quake into the rigid crusts of what in our fear we have rationalized as real.

But for now those who were there or other similar places worldwide in history who, allowed to see this peace during that gloriously strange eternity of some timeless two weeks, had the modern mental barrier softened and composted in its magic, allowing the peace to push not into us but like a warm never-flagging seed of organic life it sprouted out of us from our forgotten core, pushing out with some unseen energy uncovered and recharged, and mitigated forever the motives of any decisions we would ever make.

I don't think it made any of us into more efficient go-getters, or more vehement justice fighters with more juice but only half the story. But something, probably mostly unseen by others, did happen; something slow and untamable, something always waiting just beneath our skins: it filled us with an active longing to be able, like Pederucho and his people, to have the courage to keep such seeds alive no matter what terror and confusion by which we might ever find ourselves surrounded.

We had come to help, some maybe even to save, and at least a few of us, for the romantic thrill of bringing basic unauthorized sustenance to those who were being left unassisted and thereby feel "significant" by our simple defiance of authority, often mistaken by youth as meaningful, yet those we came to help held in their hands, like their seeds, what everybody in the entire world should have wanted most. Peace.

At least the few of us from the truck who could see it knew that both we and the civilization we came from were the starving ones, searching all our lives to be fed by this indescribable thing that the world we were born from could not comprehend, much less maintain. A human world whose constituents have never adjusted to the fact that real peace cannot be obtained, taken, bought, or stolen, nor can it be bestowed. This kind of peace was always there; it just had to be accepted and lived, if even for a few minutes. This peace said that people were not here to succeed in taking over the world; they were here to feed the beauty of being a human to the Holy in Nature. By keeping such seeds alive we become beautiful enough to keep the Holy alive. That was Peace.

As these people from Cuchumaquic after the earthquake understood it, on that day at the end of the world, in a feast of a kind of peace I had never known, and while held stunned in the wounded arms of such a profoundly beautiful people who refused to "eat their seeds," I knew as they knew that above all else in order to keep alive and well anything of what it meant to be a human being on this earth, we all had somehow to "keep the seeds alive" of the small worthy things of life.

As long as there were people, they would always live and die, get hurt; sickness would come and go; but the Holy Mother in the Seed, the seeds themselves not an abstractified concept of a Divine Docile Female, but the tangible Holy Mother who had despite our terrified arrogance and ancestrally charged ignorance as we continue to torture her integrity and magnificence, always held and continues to hold us, now needed us to be like Pederucho, who for his people's village had become a "father" in the biggest sense, trying to keep alive the seeds of the future's mother to replant a world when the time is ripe for us to begin recovering from the absurd physical poisoning and polluting of the world and spiritual malaise of civilization's last era of folly in pursuit of a life of no accountability to Nature.

One very famous old Tzutujil story in Atitlán said that just previous to this most recent cyclic occurrence in time of the present creation, all matter that had served humans had risen up in revolution to destroy the most recent crop of the Divine's overly arrogant experimental humans. Knives, grinding stones, houses, weaving looms, hoes, axes, cooking pots, ropes, domesticated animals, and so on, which no doubt would today include cars, shopping malls, airplanes, high-rises, missiles, tractors, bombs, and so forth had all revolted and destroyed their "enslavers." There were four unsavory, insignificant, unhandsome, lowly regarded, forgotten animals who made it their mission to gather up and hide the "seeds" of every living thing, plant, animal, weather, and light inside an inner dimension within a huge slab of flat rhyolite stone that lay in all irony just southwest of Cuchumaquic. By regrowing themselves over and over again, the seeds were kept magically alive in a kind of tiny submolecular universe, living in cycles of plants and seed inside the matrix of the stone for maybe millennia, until the world had "aired out" and was ready to start up again. The pressure of the diversity of all the world's seeds sprouting in the hardness of the rock then cracked the rock open like a vulva, called the Mother Stone, and from that fissure emerged the sprouts of every living being, from whose eventual flowering and fruiting this world we know today once again organically grew itself back to life. Every coyote, palm tree, algae, *piloy* bean, corn of every color, cotton, tobacco, pumpkin, jungle melon, oak, pine tree, reed, everything, every animal, every being except people, whose newest incarnation would happen in another story from some of these plants.

It was about this slab of stone, the seeds, the end of worlds, the beginnings of plants, the demise of people that Pederucho and I and several old ladies and men were discussing as we were forced to increase our volume of speech, finally yelling with all our grateful lungs to hear each other over the racket of the engine as I was unceremoniously dragged up onto the bed of the already moving truck by the departing hippies. Yelling back, Pederucho said he was sure he knew where this rock was and if, as he surmised, their world was finished either by earthquake or, as I surmised, by global petro banking agribusiness, he promised he would take his seeds into the stone before he himself was finished. But for now as far as I could see through the dust and noisy tumult of our departure, Pederucho himself was the living rock of Cuchumaquic and its living culture of seeds, the venerated source of its peace.

As the truck pulled away, the hot rising dust seemed to gather into a kind of swallow's nest of mud around my newly defined heart, protecting the hatching swallows of new hope and giving me a feeling of long life and sense of delicious friendship with the torn ground over which we lurched.

But away from the villagers in the tired morose silence of the men in the truck, a profound feeling of some new brand of man-made loneliness permeated throughout all of us in the old grinding wreck as night oozed in upon us practically unnoticed. The truck bed was made dangerous by the slippery scum of bean residue and rice that covered the floor and walls of the bed. We slid like hockey pucks from side to side, back to front, and anyone who tried to stand or change position was violently propelled into an involuntary direction, sliding out until they crashed onto others of their companions, jamming knees into mouths and feet into abdomens. Trying to withstand one terrible series of hard lurchings of the truck as it bucked unstoppably down a hill into dusty darkness, one of our members, a long-haired boy from Ohio, bounced clear out of the bed and broke his humerus on a rock.

The irony of young idiot idealists like ourselves was that we who would feed the hungry had not fed ourselves since early the previous day, nor was there any water remaining. We had nothing with us to eat, not to mention that in our exhaustion without the old road or mounted guide we ended up lost in the dark wasting fuel by driving in figure eights for nine hours.

The dawn horizon showed us our folly with heart-sinking reality and the humor of how far we had to go and how similar our condition had become with those we would aid until, far in the distance, one of us picked out a light moving on the skyline that we signaled by flashing our lights.

After twenty minutes a young Sudanese man the same color as the night that was beginning to pass, in a very old Land Rover, bounced up alongside us, his vehicle's grating gearbox competing well with our own impressive bolt-tumbling racket. The engines off, we found he was a UNESCO worker who'd broken the rules, and the lines, and after taking an unauthorized vehicle, was headed to Cuchumaquic in his own unauthorized attempt to bring some food and water and to do a little reporting on the conditions thereabouts without official orders or government sanction.

For sustenance on his very sincere rescue attempt, all he'd been able to sneak off with took up the entire inside of the Land Rover and filled it to the roof with old packaged loaves of Pan Bimbo: a chemicalized, injected, projected, ejected, often rejected, air-filled, wheat paste derivative mixed with various mineral industrial byproducts made in Mexico City in a Latin-American attempt to keep up with even worse versions of similar starch-like substances pushed off as bread in the U.S., but which a lot of people had always known was better suited as a building material than food. The car was full of stale, hardening Bimbo bread, in plastic wrappers.

The Pueblo village I grew up in New Mexico had been famous since ancient times for making hand-drilled bead jewelry of turquoise and shell. But as children some of us were taught to make "poor man's" jewelry, a cheap, lightweight, fairly durable fake version of the magnificent, very expensive real turquoise and coral necklaces worn then by all Indians in the Southwest as regular attire.

We took loaves of the American variety of Pan Bimbo, kneading them down with sugar, glue, and the dust remaining from legitimate drilling and pressed them into wormlike rolls. After it had dried as hard as "rock" in the heat of our Father the Sun we sawed, sanded, and drilled it into beads just like its real cousin but with less than a percent of the effort. It was easily polished, and once strung it was a weightless version of some of the most convincing beautiful rock-like jewels you could imagine which, unless you looked up close, could fool anyone. But, in my opinion, this "bread" was terrible stuff to put into the gastric byways of one's body in any hopes of real nutrition.

But this good man had come to feed the hungry, and we who'd come to feed the hungry were hungry, and after elucidating our plight, showing him our moaning friend whose arm although stabilized needed to be properly set, the Land Rover man, without stepping down, handed us six loaves of the stale bread-like food.

With a new budding capacity for maintaining and bestowing a more noble appreciation rubbed into us osmotically by the example of the truly starving of Cuchumaquic, most of the crew in a clumsy elegance and sincere intended respect expressed their gratitude for the now-precious breads, for which, although we longed to devour them, we waited patiently as much like the admirable people of Cuchumaquic as we could manage, as he gave us each a good long gulp from the closest water can. After letting us have a gallon of gasoline and having exchanged what each lost party's best guess was as to the direction each should take to find his way, that good blue-black man bounced away from us into the orange dust of dawn.

Our breakfast, which proved to our once-unthinking sarcastic selves to be a precious thing, we ingested quietly as it if were a twenty-five course dinner at the French Laundry, all of us giving thanks for the magnificence of such a seed as this wheat even in this ironic enslaved form whose generosity kept fools like us alive today; we the people from the same peoples who invented that strange bread, people who had deliberately tortured all the domesticated seeds and animals with their greed and needs into untenable competitive forms like ourselves. But this tortured wheat tasted as grand as any food ever would, and as well it should to any semblance of a reverent tongue in the head of any person who has spent even five minutes in the land of peace where the seeds of remembrance were still being kept alive.

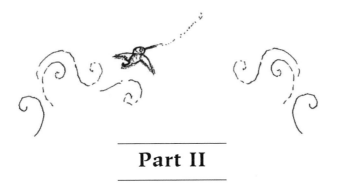

Part II

The Life of People as Plants

Chapter 4

In the Shade of the Fire Flower

It was a common thing in those more vital times for outside visitors to complain sometimes condescendingly, sometimes with love, about how Guatemala's Highland Mayan people, in particular those lakeside Tzutujil of Atitlán, who when forced to actually converse with an outsider, could never seem "to just address anything in a straightforward way. They seem to have an allergy against streamlined description, always talking around the subject, in some endless purposeful abstruse type of florid beating around the bush."

I remember one tired ethnologist blowing off steam about how whenever she asked a "simple" question like, "How old is your daughter?" or "What do you people eat in the spring?" or "Where are you headed?" she would always end up accusing these old tribal talkers of the unpardonable crime of diving into a complex string of incomprehensible multi-references to older stories of other times and places where other outsiders might have asked the same question just like what happened to the mother of what's-her-name to whom such and so happened to her husband and so on going on to describe her life with a million convoluted mixed metaphors, about which you had to understand two million well-known tribal tales to even vaguely have the faintest clue of what they were talking about, if you could wait that long. Their responses looked as if they'd been cleverly designed to both courteously placate the questioner for having asked them a question, while directly avoiding the subject altogether, diverting all attention further and further afield from the central issue for which, as far as the investigator was concerned, seven words should have sufficed.

It was no different than taking on a conversation with an Irish country person, while hoping for directions to a town to which he or she has never been, where after two hours of your patient listening to this person's gorgeous banter, you'll know who made the bricks that "used" to pave the road that no longer goes where you're hoping to get, along with the names, births, demises, griefs, and ways of going of all the attempts to earn a living in these overly wet times that each and every family in living memory who'd ever tried to live between here and where the road you're looking for used to take up ever took on, a place about whose present whereabouts you are now even more uncertain, not to mention pleasantly drunk and with no other recourse than to sleep the night, until this person's cousin Shaugn who is actually due home from the very place you want to go arrives to tell you why you don't really want to go there anyway, and wouldn't you rather like to go where they're going today because it's such a more pleasant place for the likes of a gentle tourist like yourself and so on ... !

To others with PhDs and grants who actually study the speech patterns of such elegant creatures as these Tzutujil, Irish folk, Tribal Svan, Merle, Fulani, Karen, and a million others, this way of responding to outsiders has been broadly analyzed as a simple case of a well-orchestrated cultural avoidance strategy. That in order to keep all native knowledge away from prying outsiders they have obviously adopted the tactics of a mother quail who, feigning the flightless earthbound condition of a broken wing with an exaggerated frantic flapping, loud chirping, and a bumbling scurrying in all directions at once, attempts to draw the attention of any perceived hungry meat-eating threat away from her offspring all the while playing just far enough out of reach of the coyote to skillfully pull him as far away from her unfledged clutch of precious defenseless babies as she is able, flying back to them when the coyote is sufficiently confused and gone far enough afield to be no threat.

All of these ways of reacting to curious and lost outsiders have their manifestations everywhere in the world where there are yet real people at home in their own beloved land. By using such beautiful humorously camouflaged verbal detours, they attempt to keep alive what they hold precious far away from the scalding, culture-wilting gaze of modern people who, having lost their own linguistic seeds of indigenous understanding to civilization's amnesia and being unaware how destructive and discourteous an interruption they are, are themselves only frustrated by the precious tangle of such long-winded linguistic treasure.

While I couldn't say much authoritatively about the rest of the world's antique living cultures, what investigators and other impatient travelers have rarely understood, in the instance of these elderly Tzutujil, was that the questions put to them by the outsiders were not considered by these Mayans to be altogether answerable because they were not questions that could be indigenously asked. To the old people these questions themselves were parentless orphans who like linguistic slaves sweated away for academics, forced to work "extracting," artificially mined isolated facts with tools of pointed words to remove a single idea out of a greater and necessary matrix of a more diverse and immense natural cultural environment.

And these questions were held captive by the outside investigator, and any "native" responses to them were collected like unrefined ore that the investigator then hauled away, processed, and smelted into bare facts at the university, stacked as facts into some obscure book which itself would most likely end up deeply buried in the catalog dungeon of some university library of microfiche. Such questions, if responded to, gathered only dead ideas out of their context; responses, when held far away from their parent culture, remained trapped like baby quail, stuck in category cages shackled into equations. Without their mother cultures and living supporting world, they were like wild animals sold to a zoo where with other such artificially extracted ideas they paced behind bars of rigid objectified bias where they could no longer function as themselves, the words no longer able to make real sense of themselves in such rarified unnatural settings.

When such strange lines of questioning were fired at them, the old people knew they were being unconsciously attacked in the most insidious and violent way by a people who were uneducated in any real art of speech. The worst part is the invaders were ignorant of the fact they were attacking, unaware that they were just big powerful people whose every motion and word was a weapon of objectivity calibrated to aim at capturing a concept, or possessing something "never discovered before." At least not by them. Just like Columbus and the so-called New World.

It was apparent to these old Indians that though the "attacker" was definitely dangerous, ironically he or she usually showed some signs of human goodness and wounded affability and that all of this unconscious violence probably came from the huge and hungry cultural vacuum from which the outsider themselves originated. This seemed to be an origins empty of self-awareness causing the investigator to be "sick"; someone in need of spiritual repair, an illness that caused the investigator to need to constantly mine the world in order to fill with material or intellectual acquisition the spiritual vacuum created by the sickness. Because the visitors had obviously not grown up in a living world where they should have been taught as children to speak in such a fashion as to "feed and sustain" the people, the village, and the world around them with the magic life-giving-eloquence as they conversed with one another, they instead lived by always trying to get something they didn't have, chaining what they "captured" into immobilized ideas of dry prisoners of words, in order to be told by people they didn't like but feared that they were good enough when they hauled their tale back to headquarters.

When these old-time Tzutujil conversed with another Tzutujil, they knew they were speaking with someone who wasn't a hungry vacuum there to suck them dry, but an equal in the everyday experience of life's travails with an indigenous lingual education, whose intention was *not* to get a point across but keep the world alive by the back-and-forth beauty of their expressed understanding about the points they were discussing. This meant that no matter how rich or poor they were, everybody had the ability to feed God just by swimming linguistically inside another person's question. Instead of just answering questions, they fully responded to them with the beauty of the motion of their speech. The Holy, of course, cannot be kept alive by facts but only by beauty.

What the investigators probably never knew was when answering an outsider's query, the old people were not for the first forty minutes or so even talking to the questioner (who by this time they were very much trying to rescue as much as his question!), they were welcoming the question as if it were a tired, hungry, and lost visitor, politely asking the question where he or she was from, his background, while trying to create a house for the question inside their own linguistic village, a home for this unattached, parentless, otherwise homeless enslaved question. It is ridiculous to think they were "beating around the bush"; they were never beating around any bush: they were *describing* the bush, creating a verbal ecology from whence the tangled linguistic vines and forests of a living spiritual and cultural ecozone could spread out around to hide and nestle the subject of the question in a natural nest. Like a fragile egg, the question was too special to be exposed so quickly; they were too superstitious to even mention it at first for fear that while they hatched the question beneath the newly established, thick, cultural, linguistic bush, they might fail the question and its real self would not hatch into what it should really be. By making a kind of visionary nest of words they gave this orphaned, indigenously uneducated question a place to hatch into a form that made the orphan question something that could finally jump out of the flat cultureless vacuum of its past into a new real life where, surrounded by a vibrant anciently connected world, it could start running on its own accord to grow up and develop into a question adult enough to hold its own and to be finally considered by the tribe's own thinkers worth responding to. Any investigator who could stay long enough and actually come to understand this type of cultural response was changed forever, for then their questions could now feed God by their indigenous responses.

All intact natural people and even other intact people not so natural, who live for their land instead of off it or on it, can never begin speaking without first "talking" into a mental field of vision a magnificent empty throne of words so that this one poor, simple, exploited question could seat its newly found regality; for old tribespeople worldwide will never respond to an unregal question without first restoring the nobility of the question and its asker. Nor will they fail to respond regally to a truly regal question no matter how poorly dressed. The Mayans made all questions royal by beating the bush into a mansion of living myth and story inside of which the question and its response could live as the well-appointed royal citizens of spoken eloquence and thereby feed the Holy in the Seed with this now-beautiful, florid story of how they got there.

Efficient, perfunctory, streamlined directness was only reluctantly employed by traditionalists during earthquakes, floods, landslides, and wars. It was considered an unfortunate implementation of a state of linguistic martial law for emergencies only. But in times of everyday life and ritual, abbreviatory, truncated, efficient speech was considered a life-stunting betrayal of what a fully formed human was meant to embody. For after having lived a bit, a person could become a brave wielder of life-feeding eloquence whose words fed the Holy even in the way they died. Blatant simple answers or empty seductive ornateness without a story were the domain of the exhausted, sick, cowardly, and lazy vernacular of civilization's dedication to getting what they wanted without sweating, in which speech was something designed to seduce, compete, win, to conquer or dominate territory. It took away the delicious ornateness of ecstatic humans in love with life. This is a worldwide innate human capacity, but its long-winded ecstatic incapacity to cause the exploitation of the earth, the people, and the future has made it extinct in most modern places, becoming endangered like the seeds in the rest. This is the root of all modern-day depression: the loss of the ability to feed the Divine in Nature by our inborn human beauty of speech and culture. This ability is a seed and endangered. These are seeds we must keep alive.

Like a highway plowed straight through a South American jungle to facilitate the extraction of oil, timber, and the forest-killing produce of industrial farming only to shore up a faraway civilization's hopeless economic flight away from the reality of its own inability to live sustainably on its own previously purloined territory, the impatient insistencies of that same civilization's disconnected facts orphaned by the lack of a viable overview are the standard procedure used to drain the original memory of intact Indigenous citizens caught living under the consumer spell of that same civilization in even what had been their original home-land areas. By firstly killing the Indigenous ornateness of those same people's language, their own worlds gradually became, like the civilization that they adopt, an eternal uncurable emergency.

The germ of any seed of deep Indigenous thinking, whose ornate flowering is its comprehension, has always been frozen by civilization's people, whose TV culture has their children speaking before they've even learned linguistic beauty, a speaking that could make the world jump back to life with words. These are times menaced by a worldwide soul freeze, and it's a wonder these kinds of language seeds have any ground to survive in at all. For that reason I say, in order to find that ground to keep such seeds alive, civilized people must somehow *re-member,* towed by their Indigenous Souls, the integrity of a real life-promoting language.

Some say it is an inefficient and superfluous waste of time to think and speak this way, and indeed it is if it is only an act, with none of the depth, mythology, story, courtesy, and courage that feeds the Holy in so doing, but those that cannot admire such a way of going about life, much less carry it out, are the very ones in charge of the decisions that have wasted the world away, and it is they along with their world that are wasting away.

For in the couch-sitting, drone-minded, comfort-oriented spiritual ignorance of modern life's abhorrence of cultural diligence, and avoidance of the deep work of love both human and natural it takes to have a capacity to see the delicious complexity of the Holy in Nature, much less make it live more by speaking to it, we have become Earth-wrecking refugees of our own unsustainable procedure moving fast into an unnoble oblivion. We are fast becoming a badly educated question with no one left to talk our bush back into life, to hatch us back into something worth responding to.

No dry descriptions, finite comprehension, sound bites, political manipulations, or imperially regulated definition could ever tame, contain, describe, or create the wild delicious vagaries so necessary for humans to speak to the Holy in Nature, to gestate a mind whose speech could talk into life a reality big enough to house a universe.

After all, a kiss between real lovers is not some type of contract, a neatly defined moment of pleasure, something obtained by greedy conquest, or any kind of clear saying of how it is. It is a grief-drenched hatching of two hearts into some ecstatic never-before-seen bird whose new uncategorizable form, unrecognized by the status quo, gives the slip to Death's sure rational deal. For love is a delicious and always messy extension of life that unfrantically outgrows mortality's rigid insistence on precise and efficient definition. Having all the answers means you haven't really ecstatically kissed or lived, thereby declaring the world defined and already finished. Loving all the questions on the other hand is a vitality that makes any length of life worth living. Loving doesn't mean you know all the notes and that you have to play all the notes, it just means you have to play the few notes you have long and beautifully.

Like the sight of a truly beautiful young woman, smooth and gliding, melting hearts at even a distant glimpse, that no words, no matter how capable, can truly describe; a woman whose beauty is only really known by those who take a perch on the vista of time to watch the years of life speak out their long ornate sentences of grooves as they slowly stretch into her smoothness, wrinkling her as she glides struggling, decade by decade, her gait mitigated by a long trail of heavy loads, joys, losses, and suffering whose joint-aching years of traveling into a mastery of her own artistry of living, becomes even more than beauty something about which though we are even now no more capable of addressing than before, our admiration as original Earth-loving human beings should nonetheless never remain silent. And for that beauty we should never sing about, but only sing directly to it. Straightforward, cold, and inornate description in the presence of such living evidence of the flowering speech of the Holy in the Seed would be death of both the beauty and the speaker. Even if we always fail when we speak, we must be willing to fail magnificently, for even an eloquent failure, if in the service of life, feeds the Divine.

Is it not a magical thing, this life, when just a little ash, cinder, and unclear water can arrange themselves into a beautiful old woman who sways, lifts, kisses, loves, sickens, argues, loses, bears up under it all, and, wrinkling, still lives under all that and yet feeds the Holy in Nature by just the way she moves barefoot down the path?

If we can find the hearts, tongues, and the brightness of our original souls, broken or not, then no matter from what mess we might have sprung today, we would be like those old-time speakers of life; every one of us would have it in our nature to feel obligated by such true living beauty as to know we have to say something in its presence if only for our utter feeling of awe. For, finally learning to approach something respectfully in love, slowly with the courtesy of an ornate indirectness, not describing what we see but praising the magnificence of her half-smiles of grief and persistent radiance rolling up from the weight-bearing thumping of her fine, well-oiled dusty old feet shuffling toward the dawn reeds at the edge of her part of the lake to fetch a head-balanced little clay jar of water to cook the family breakfast, we would know why the powerful Father Sun himself hurries to get his daily glimpse of her, only rising early because she does.

The first tooth of his great light, pushing out of the dark egg of night like a baby turtle of fire rising up orange and choking on the fog of volcanic hillsides of *milpas* spewing corn pollen and the now almost rank purple narcotic post-orgasmic smell of wilted *pitaya* flowers whose sweetness had saturated the night, the Sun rose over Lake Atitlán that July morning in 1976 to caress the slowly balding, strongly beguiling seventy-nine-year-old mother of "Chicken Feather," her unmarried, still-at-home, sixty-year-old, already-bald son who caught one small fish every three days and was afraid of the world. Sneaking barefoot over the sand of Tzanjiyam with her water jar, while the lake grebes, teals, mud hens, and gallinules who love being startled found her travel to the water a welcome excuse to widen their yellow eyes and suddenly rise, cutting the air and reeds with their storm of wings screaming up into undulating clouds, until iridescent spray showered down on the single green screen of the mat-makers tule swaying peacefully in the wakes their exodus always created.

Like the water-cutting sound of the spiraling flocks now rushing to settle again hidden back in the reeds, the random echo of paddles, knocking against the hand-carved sides of some ten dozen canoes filled

with farmers pushing across the bay to their terraced fields on the volcano opposite the Elbow of the Universe, disappeared into the light lap-
ping of the otherwise still morning lake, their sounds eaten as food by
the water's ever-hungry soul of the water's reflection, whose grazing fed
the ever-present other side of all things.

I had always been fairly good at noiseless walking, but the crisp
leather of my new sandals and the fresh maguey cords of my load made
my shuffling squeaks seem as loud as a train wreck in that same morning quiet, as I with all the farmers heading up to their volcano-side plantings negotiated the stone ramps and ladder-like boulder terrace that rose
smooth from so many centuries of feet, climbed the steep western slope
of Oxi Qáholá, the volcano of San Lucas where at old Chiv's suggestion
he and I were to meet beneath the old fire-flower tree at Choqoux
Aqóum.

Chiviliu, in the accustomed manner of all village "spirit brokers" and
doctors of those times, had insisted we should formally initiate my little
Holy stone that saw me through the dust and death of the 1976
Guatemalan earthquake five months previous, adding the Seeded Bird,
into my "herd" of divining tools in a setting outside the world of people,
in a place more regal and wild. When a new "member" of any Diviner's
bundle tools showed up there was an already-established ceremony
where shamans reanimated and introduced new members into the "herd"
of their other tools. As the Shrines were known as thrones, Choqóux
Aqóum was the most regal "throne" we knew of, and it was here that
usually shamans reiterated aloud and ritually the stories of how their
new "animals" came and subsequently ceremonially ushered them into
the "herd" of their other Dreamtools. We'd been putting this off for
months on account of the duties with the earthquake and everybody's
strained life with refugees.

Like most of the Mayan villages around the lake, Santiago had been
spared the sweeping devastation, dust, and confusion the central highlands had been forced to bear. For that reason and because of an
anciently established custom descended from both natural instinct and
the nature of the volcanic lakeside climate with its richer presence of food

and water, Santiago Atitlán's population had swollen almost instantly after the earthquake by at least a third again, when many Cakchiquel and Quiche refugee families were taken in from less fortunate areas.

For the months following the quake, families of both related and unrelated Mayan peoples of survivors from little villages that had been overturned or demolished in the tremors that followed were absorbed into the matrix of the town. Almost every household had a couple or more semipermanent visitors at their cooking fires.

In a few months most of them would move back to their destroyed beloved homelands to rebuild, others would find a cultural place in the village and carry on, many of the younger would be adopted, others would marry in, but many who had lost too many of their own, their life and culture, would be driven by grief into a state of eternal unrest, looking for the home they could never be calm enough to rest in, ending up as homeless itinerants drifting as hard laborers from one over-exploited condition on the coastal sugar and cotton plantations to the next.

Our compound was hosting two old southern Cakchiquel fellows. The older of the two had only one incisor left, and it pushed almost horizontally out for which he had been dubbed universally as *rilaj nutuq*, "my cherished old tusk." He was a great friend, ate very little, and could really snore, but he died peacefully nine months later of a combination of old age and the increasing daily burden of a sighing futility of endless grief that people who actually belong to a place instead of "owning it" feel when they lose every one of their living relatives, and the actual physical land to which they belong no longer exists. His village people had not only disappeared, but the entire land it had rested on was actually tossed and washed away by floods during the shaking earth.

The other man, with nervous whiteless eyes like a little weasel's, slightly younger and from a different Cakchiquel hamlet, changed his identity and become a very convincing Quiche Mayan–speaking Momostenango blanket merchant, traveling town to town as they all do, with compact loads of beautiful folded handwoven wool blankets towering cube-like over their bent-over backs. He continued to stay with us whenever he came to Santiago to sell. At least he did so until later, when the big killing time of the following war came in on us and he disappeared, hopefully to live on somewhere else.

All of this displacement had the village more heavily taxed for food, and their everyday lives were reconfigured into a strange hybrid existence in which certain normal work cycles and activities were suspended or altered as to give life a character caught somewhere between a great festival of friendship, food, and conversation, and a pending economic disaster. As with everyone who had taken in displaced families, Chiv and I were both overly occupied with things in our own ends of the village to assist each other ritually as much as was normal.

Left to its own devices the rich cultural soil of the supple but stubbornly Indian soul of Atiteco people of Santiago Atitlán, though less than a decade from losing it, was still in those times capable of an age-old cyclic tradition of absorbing customs and populations of different people while growing themselves into a collectively mutated, always fresh and renewed, still-integral Tzutujil village.

It was as if some exuberant digestive organ of the village inner life, instead of affording their new homeless family additions a place to gradually forget their past and start anew, forced the stories of hardship and loss to be even more fully remembered and even embellished until by constant repetition they blurred, merged, and mutated into a vibrant mythology whose spurious attributions and glorious exaggerations were highlights known to everyone from four to ninety to the point that within six months, the people's stories of personal grief, earth rumbling, death, and displacement had magically merged with the already-existing body of Atiteco traditional knowledge to the point no one could tell them apart. The stories of the homeless had been given a home just like the people.

All of this, strangely enough, caused the mutual grief of all tribes and parties to metabolize in some natural uncalculated way so as to grow an even more vitally alive Tzutujil people.

Like the seven active volcanoes whose inevitable staggered eruptions devastated and burnt millions of acres of hand-tended crops, wildland, and villages, but whose ash fertilized in the most needed ways the same ground it razed, the old village had actually been repeatedly culturally revitalized by various disasters of the past by influxes of refugees of other tribes.

But this ability to not reject the burden of the visitor's grief and nutritional needs was an organic thing and was charged the price of their tales. It couldn't be rushed and had to be given its natural time. Like a molting animal, usually fairly strong and self-preserving in their regular life, but unprotected during the necessary altered time of delicate waiting, the entire Indigenous population after the earthquake was in a vulnerable cultural molt that could have revitalized itself according to its own natural form if not opposed and interrupted by outside interests, all of which left them unarmored to the nerveless claws of modernity's most inferior expansionist function, eventually resulting in years of violent warfare and a rapid vicious invasion of outside business economics, religiosities, architectural imperialism that boiled up and reworked Indigenous Guatemala into a spiritually flattened unrecognizable place. But four years before all the terrible wars and loss of culture, and five months and eighteen days after the Guatemalan earthquake of February 4, 1976, two days short of the Big Old Feast of Santiago, when most refugee Mayans had decided on their lives and the old canyon village of Santiago Atitlán settled back into its renewed form, Chiviliu and I finally found the ceremonial circumstances we had hoped for to meet and address my stone with the depth he felt it most demanded. The ceremony to add a *Qijibaal* to one's bundle could only happen as an amendment to a curing ritual, the latter carrying the former on its back like a horse to the Holy.

The opportunity for this occurred when Chiv agreed to *nruyikamá r bey,* "take up the road," or spiritually advocate the cause of a recently arrived sad group of what had been once wealthy Sacatepequez merchant Mayans, who after having survived the loss of all their buildings, clay works, and corn stores in the quake had traveled the one hundred miles to Atitlán to find old Chiv.

Arriving beautifully attired, they courted him with gifts and the appropriate length of bush beating, explaining en masse how much faith they had in that old prayer maker. They convincingly petitioned Chiv to do his best to develop some previously untried way to restore the mind of one of their adolescent daughters who since the earthquake had been seeing and speaking with beings other people couldn't see, constantly fleeing the sounds of military helicopters while trying to board invisible trains in the night. They'd already been to every doctor and shaman thereabouts, and she was coming more and more dangerously close to the edge of her own extinction.

That morning before I showed up on the mountain, Chiviliu, on behalf of this girl, had already put into motion a large private ceremony of flowers and deity gifts to regenerate the displaced elements of the spirits of all the mechanical inventions that had mysteriously hit and entered the unhappy girl since the quake. The fright of the earthquake had released the souls of ritually unfed modern inventions who upon their destruction had entered the girl, displacing her own soul out of her body and into the mechanical devices. By exchanging the extravagant offerings he insisted on—several live turkeys, candles, *pōm*, tobacco, liquors, jewels, songs, beguiling liturgy, and shaman-created prayer—Chiv, in five separate rituals, was already well in the midst of bargaining for the girl's intact and original soul in return for sending the souls of the poor unstoried, unfed, modern inventions back to their rightful mechanical domain.

Chiviliu had summoned me with a messenger to join him at Choqóux Aqóum, where together we would try to carry the heart of this a much more dangerous and subtle part of the concluding ritual.

To describe what came about there, however grand, indifferent, incredible, subtle, useful, powerful, or weak, for those who may have been there, would be the same as us stealing food from the mouths of the spirits whose hearts of chance make possible the happenstance of living hope beyond the calculated limitations of human imagination, and would by telling, photographing, or recording, create a new debt of insult to the past beyond the dismal spiritual back taxes we already owe on account of our spiritually disrespectful and invasive times. Let it simply stand to say what happened was not for humans to feel, enjoy, or understand, but its breadth of significance happened in the unseen for the Holy Diversity on behalf of that girl.

Chiv sent his life's last adopted orphan to lead the exhausted family back down the volcano when we'd finished their part of the ritual day, back to the courtyard of old Ma Xuan Chamjay, the famous one-time jaguar hunter, braggart, and big-hearted man who, like he had for so many others, had taken them in. The girl gazed back at the mountain shrine one last time with eyes that, though they would never be again altogether her own, were happy again with a looking that saw and smelt life-giving things instead of the unfed tortured souls of helicopters.

With the burden of the bite of the ceremony and wild glow of those wild beings Chiv and I had to turn into in order to survive those realms we had to go into still champing heavily down upon us, Chiv and I began to address my little stone before we normalized again.

His head tied up in his favorite flowery Chinese scarf of silk, Chiviliu held the little seed-eyed stone with both hands lifting him up an arm's length off. The old man's blue glazed monkey eyes seemed to be gazing more around, over and into the flowering afternoon canopy of trees than into the stone which he kept turning around and around. What was inside the rock was the unseen world outside, a version Chiv could see about us.

After the time it took for him to puff away at least two stone pipefuls, and after he'd called for the smoking incense pot, Chiviliu rolled off his haunches to sit on the stone shrine's smooth rock seat in front of all the fires, and began a prayer of rare words, the kind used to feed life-giving deities which this newcomer to my little rolled-up sack drank as it rode the smoke of the *po⁻m*, carrying our prayer to the other world, arriving like a majestic packhorse of really fragrant mist loaded up with a feast of precious words.

When you looked into this little Holy being born out of the earthquake dust, you seemed to be looking into a handheld maze of black glass in which tiny portals meandered as if eaten into it there by tiny sea worms, whose hard black sponge of obsidian as a whole appeared for all the world like a little pygmy owl with razor-sharp eye sockets, horns, and a glass beak and whose arrogant little body even sat up like one. Saturated and embedded in the lining of the glass at every turn, hole, cranny, and bladed ridge were petrified seeds of every size, shape, and plant. One perfectly round but veined, another fennel-shaped, others like grass seeds, iris seeds, strange five-sided bristly cones, others caltrop-like, while still others were flat and wispy, looking as if they'd just blown in from some liquid infinity inside the glass and frozen in motion like a school of tiny squid. The little raptor's eyes were especially sharp and filled as well with hundreds of diverse little seeds.

"He yá! Tzrá at itzabula atet ruauch rijaatz cht chay Tziqin"—"Heyá, there you sit little seed-eyed bird of black glass," and turning to me, Chiv gurgled, clearing his throat from the smoke, "You had better not misplace him, A Martín, this is a piece of all our old seeds that were hidden in the stone in that world before this one, the last time the sun was finished. This is the living throne of one of those four thrown-away despised forgotten unwanted animals, who kept the possibility of making another world alive by hiding the seeds deep beneath the known world, inside the rock of Cuchumaquic from which they envisioned once again the possibility of our world resprouting in a time beyond their own, and, look! Here we are! Our world: this world we live in, this world that suckles us all, with her firewood, cotton fibers, avocadoes, corn, animal and fish, meat, and everything that feeds everything else, everything that is the "Flowering-Mountain-Jade-Water-Earth" was resprouted from these very same seeds!

"This world has been regenerated then lost again many times over, either ground to dust, burnt to ash, drowned by flooding water and more, but every time the seeds were hidden, to resprout Time all over again. They are the *rumuxux sacriq*, 'the belly buttons of dawn,' that which collectively sprouts a place called the Fruit of Soil from which this earth grows back alive all over again, making a place where all plants in turn can resprout and all things can jump back to life."

Chiv, in an unexpected breathy hiss, began to whisper, something he did so rarely that because he was always so notoriously loud, no one even knew he knew how to whisper, "Don't lose this Brother-Father, keep him with your 'Sun Tools,' your Divining kit, this one is the mistress-master of all the growing of Time and all divination: the Seed Lords and Seed Ladies. Now that you're one of us, you will always feel lonely and betrayed by what humans value, but loved by the echoing Holies. Get used to it."

Even Chiviliu's whisper echoed, and like his more usual trademark baby elephant call, Old Chiv's breathy admonition echoed down through the forest ravines, percolating into the heart of this holy mountain. And into this fine road of echoes opened by his windy sound the two of us poured our own compositions of delicious symphonic words, our *kilaj nimlaj tzij,* hoping that the Holy being now sitting in the seed-eyed obsidian bird would find his new home a delicious and worthy palace of words; words which we'd wrapped this gift of Earthquake in the form of a *sac zuut,* a sacred cloth woven by the women for this moment. When we finished speaking and wrapping and Chiv had placed this precious piece of the old seed-hiding stone from the beginning of human time into what was then my still immature version of what would later divide into several powerful Diviner's Bundles, the canyons still echoed their own prayers back to us.

Chapter 5

The Fiery Speech of Seeds as Time

Most shaman diviners had at least a couple of their own precious Holy things as part of their divining kit like my seed-eyed bird. Though these might look to the untutored more like some ancient pre-European pottery God images of clay or stone, clay whistles, jade ear spools, or amber lip plugs, obsidian cores or concretions, to the diviners they were called *chkat* or thrones.

Like my seed-eyed bird, some were inherited directly from the spirits, others from a teacher upon initiation, or from an ancestor, or combinations of these. Though deified, they were not "gods" so much as Holy shapes. Like material nouns in the sentences of a prayer, whose physical forms were also "thrones," both had shapes that would seat only the literal presence of a specific one of a myriad Time Deities. These deities during a divination might sometimes rush into their "chairs" like a mob of little kids entering a candy store, causing a breeze with sufficient force to tumble and scatter their thrones, much to the terror of one's clients, who could see nothing to cause it. Some famous diviners made careers divining by this phenomenon alone.

On the other hand, like a lot of the village's numerous non-divining *Ajcuná* or "shaman healers," Chiv was nonetheless responsible for a number of these deity thrones as well held in trust for deceased shamans waiting for a posthumous successor. There were also a lot of *Aj Qij*, or Diviners, who were responsible for bundles in which there might reside a great number of deity-sitting places of whose rituals and prayers they were utterly ignorant, but whom to the best of their abilities they ritually fed, to fulfill a promise to their owners. And of course there were some really good Diviners who had no thrones at all, and others with no bundles even!

Divination bundles were basically handheld portable abbreviations of Temples of Time, where certain gifted *Ajcuná* and all *Aj Qijá*, both men and women, simply said, could "see" and "converse" back and forth with Time as a Deified vital spiritual force, a force whose own speech and sight sprouted their "words" and "vision" into a Fruit, which is what the Tzutujil called the World: *Ruachuleu* or Earth Fruit.

This type of Time divination can be understood as a kind of culturally sophisticated, non-invasive, non-toxic oral and mental ritual back-and-forth spiritual ultrasound that allowed the diviner to see and dialogue with the spiritual origination of all matter and the goings-on of that matter in whatever was taking place in the world—especially, of course, in people's lives in present time. In a very unique fashion it allowed the diviner to "see" from the perspective of some of the specific diverse parts of Time Deified themselves, something not visible to the everyday life-chasing minds of the present breed of humans. Traditional Tzutujil considered themselves dull-sighted, hard of hearing, numb-nerved, and thick-skulled when it came to the spiritual perception of the great beauty and goings-on of the world and Earth, and like a lot of the world's people they would do nothing without consulting, through Time divination, the speech of those diverse, temporally-relegated-always-flowering-Holies whose unfolding blossoms gave the world both its physical form and life-moving soul.

People in the village commonly reminded one another how in our earlier form all humans had the full capacity of this understanding as an innate gift, as most wild creatures still do. But due to a greedy massive misuse of this ability by us humans, who of all natural beings are the only ones to be able to efficiently survive though unhappily with no wisdom, we threatened the stability of the entire net of Time as the living world. To remedy this as a species we had the deities, the Mist of spiritual myopia and Fog of amnesia, breathed into our minds by the Holies themselves giving us short-distance vision and limited comprehension. The intention of the Holy Diversity was to cause humans ever since to be continually baffled with the twists and turns of life with only a limited capacity to remain whole and make useful decisions for the welfare of all things. It was hoped by *suuts muyev,* the powers of Mist and Fog, the most-revered gods of the Tzutujil, that this new limitation put upon us would force future generations to establish a need for slow development and gradual initiation, causing a deeper remembrance of our non-human origins, where we could keep conscious and alive the learning humans need, to know how to ritually feed the world in a time-articulated existence. This made us more beautiful and spiritually useful to the universe. As we grew older we would become more deeply aware of what ritual things needed doing to bring the young into the same grace with Nature. Because people would no longer be able to think well enough on their own without the assistance of the divine mind of Nature, Time Divination was given to us to force us to approach Deified Time with respect. Understanding that divination was the voice of the Divine in Nature, we had to consult with it in order to make any serious choices.

This kind of Tzutujil Divination became a kind of bureaucracy of Gods: a roll call of calendric Time, blossoming just like a plant the ages and eras flowering on different parts of the vine of life. Over time, individuals began to be born in succeeding generations a little "less foggy" than the rest. They were always a little strange to the mass population as they lacked the insecure avaricious nature of regular humans. They would in every era become that generation's shaman-thinkers who, chosen by Time, would be the official translators of the language of Time. These *Aj Qijá* would then help the people in supplying to them some percentage of the unseen missing half of the always incomplete puzzle of life in which humans, trying to think and act unassisted by the Divine spirit of the Earth, made the people lose reverence and true spiritual intelligence and become only clever wreckers of the future. By forcing the people through divination to "remember" the Beauty and privilege of being allowed to live, humans could regain their lost place in the scheme of the Holy in Nature. These diviners were called "those who kept the seeds of Time as existence alive."

Everywhere in the village you could find the usual small-time so-called "diviners" with whom for fifty cents desperate people could ascertain which party had purloined their fishing nets in the night from the lake; or whether or not an estranged woman's husband had a girlfriend on the coast; or if some villageman's wife were seen chewing gum and blowing bubbles in public, meaning she had a secret lover; or what a dead ancestor might think about any of their descendants when they sold off their inherited lands and so on, but these weren't really calendar diviners, but simple seers. These kinds of sideline careers were a common predilection for Mayans, and they existed everywhere and of course had a very real tribal function.

On top of those there were, in every village, a great many fortune-tellers of every sort, some who held what could be described as Mayan versions of the Victorian-style English séances; or others who had trained warblers who, after listening to your troubles, waddled over to a huge stack of folded papers and picked out one of a million very fascinating written fortunes and waddled back to present them to the askers; or, on every street corner there operated serious-faced interpreters of the future in iron-filing patterns made on leaves and paper by meteoritic lodestones held beneath, and of course palm readers, most of whom interpreted their own palms, as they touched you with the other hand. I loved all of them, and never missed an opportunity to hear what they had to tell me.

But shamans, once initiated, pretty much shied away from employing fortune-tellers when it came to any important approach to the Holy. Strictly speaking, serious calendric Time diviners were actually totally unconcerned about the future and the petty folly of everyday human frailty. Being wound up about such things was seen by them as a kind of spiritual license, part of the delicious frail blessing that followed us in our lives as funny old human animals. *Aj Qijá* on the other hand were occupied principally with diagnosing the unseen and unaddressed aspects of spiritual conditions of the *present* in order to find out what was needed to heal an individual, or a family, or an entire village from the negative effect of their bad record with the Divine in Nature in the immediate past. As indicated by Time divination, rituals would be suggested that would "feed" and thereby heal the tattered holes we left in the Holy Net of Time, reestablishing some hope for an integral series of future "nows," which made up everyday existence, and thereby heal both the "body" of the present and the bodies of those living in the present.

Looking into the future was a fairly irrelevant activity anyway, for in the Tzutujil language there is no real future tense, nor a noun that signifies the future. Divination was about the hidden life of the present.

In the same way that hospital technicians work for surgeons and MDs, good diviners were usually limited to diagnosing sicknesses for non-divining shamans. The difference being, in order to heal individuals of sicknesses or a village from a sick situation that arose as a result of unthinking Earth-destroying spiritual detours that damaged the Holy, shamans that employed such diviners were spiritual nutritionists instead of aggressive surgeons. Shamans were preoccupied with the spiritual nutritional needs of Time. Like ritual chefs, they tried to make delicious feasts of prescribed ritual beauty according to the discovery of what Time needed to eat as determined through divination. Shamans in any attempt to feed, reanimate, and heal a Deified Segment of Time who'd been wounded or spiritually weakened and malnourished through some human trespass, rip-off, or unconscious spiritual interruption of what it was that Time needed to survive and to continue flourishing as whatever matter or everyday life proceedance his or her piece of the animate Diversity of all existence might be, had at their disposal a minimum of 260 ceremonial possibilities to put into motion.

The way this type of medicine worked came from the ancient Tzutujil knowledge that every human body is the Earth, and that all the Earth's geographic particulars are deified places and phenomena. All of these rains, rivers, seas, lakes, caves, mountains, weathers, climates, and animals, plants, star clusters, Moon, Sun, Venus are themselves specific segments of Deified Time that like all the things of the world were tied together by a symphony of Time "singing" its lyrical notes into a musical sentence. The physical manifestation of this spoken reality was the human body as an Earth with a symphonic arrangement of blood (water), flesh (plants), bone (stone), lungs/heart (wind), gall bladder (morning star), intestines (the Milky Way), etc. By healing and giving ritual nutritional strength to that segment of Time in question as a human organ, the corresponding part of the universe's body would be simultaneously bolstered and realigned. All past eras of time would heal, and in the Earth the corresponding part of the person in question simultaneously revived into a whole body, geographically speaking. Shamans were doing this by use of an orally transmitted spiritual "map" called *Nq'ijij*, or Divination, that revealed the places on this Earth Body where we humans had wounded Time ... a great deal more than simple fortune-telling.

In all Mayan ritual, shamanic and not shamanic, the Tzutujil people called all their rituals Feedings: Feeding God, Feeding the Divine. Food was everything for the villagers who knew that the ultimate origins of our own human body and all life's organic substance at some point down the line came one hundred percent from plants. But plants, the world that grew them, and the spiritual body of Deified Time had to eat as well to stay alive. But Time didn't eat plants for they *were* plants. The spiritual munificence that gave the whole Earth, water, and atmosphere its ongoing renewable life and reality was called the "Flowering Mountain Jade-Water Heart-Earth Navel," *Kotzejal rax juyu, rumuxux, Ruk'ux Ruchuleu.* And that complexity as a Flowering whole needed to be "fed" or the bigness of life would wither and die.

This entire spirit system as a whole was also Deified but not as a singular Deity nor a set number of many deities, for it was made of Time as a diverse phenomenon in eternal motion and mutation. As far as the part of this system for which we human beings were responsible, it was the creations of beauty that our unique hands and speech could make by which Time was nourished. In order to stay intact, the world had to eat the beauty we made. In order to keep up with the debt we humans incurred against the Net of Time for the displacement and death of living plants, places, and animals of the Earth we caused in just feeding ourselves, clothing ourselves, appropriating our living space, and the power to make more of ourselves in pursuit of the top-heavy folly of human reality, the Tzutujil had rituals that required the expenditure of a large percentage of the "time" of our everyday existence to make Beauty, and be beautiful in every occasion. Everyday Beauty was an obligation of remembering that even in just how we walked, we fed God.

All the natural things of the world also addressed the "debt" they too caused the natural world, because of course they too needed to eat, fly, swim, live, flower, and take cover. But because the natural things of the world were the diverse manifestations of Holy Time itself, they could feed the Holy "whole" of Nature by just being themselves. A falcon's life was a ritual, and all falcons followed the ritual obligation of what it took to be a falcon and thereby fed the Holy in Nature by being falcons to the best degree. Every willow, cloud, or water snake did the same. In other words, the Holy natural things fed all the other Holy natural things: animals, plants, winds, rains, canyons, lakes, etc., in the way they lived and by dying to feed one another in staggered units of naturally played-out schedules of deaths, births, and periods in which they thrived. Everything was fed and supported by the next thing that died to feed it by living according to its nature.

Only humans had a greater debt, because for all their ingenuity they made demands beyond their already overly heavy debt for the multifaceted gift of human complication. The human capacity to damage and interrupt the proceedance of all natural life and matter with their clever ability to exploit nature to not only feed themselves, but "get" what they wanted, was tallied by the Holy in Nature as a debt of such immensity as to be unpayable to this Holy Diversity in a natural fashion. While we humans, like all other beings, had to live and die, having agreed that our natural deaths should let our bodies become food for all the matter that gave life to us, the "extra" burden of the human magnificence and the strangely unique overload of human cleverness made the debt that humans caused to the Net of Time to be something about which the Tzutujil spiritual specialists, Diviners and Shamans, were eternally trying to address by way of the unique phenomenon of human ritual. While our debt could never become even, addressing this eternal debt as best we could in the most beautiful, determined, and patient way was the Tzutujil definition of what made a real adult person. A "real" person was an initiated person who tried to maintain Time by feeding this Holy system the "fruit," as the people called it, of the same creative hands, delicious creative language, rich generously long rituals, and cleverness of humans whose Earth-wrecking cleverness also did the wounding. People became real humans when they learned how to stay in debt beautifully instead of getting away with ripping Nature off and deferring the debt to future generations.

These fruits of our unique minds, thumbs, and voices flowered ritually on the trunk of ancestral knowledge of how to go about this a long "time" ago when the original treaty agreement between the Divine nature of Time in Nature and the people had been ratified. Thus *ritual* actually meant an organized spiritual application that employed the same unique mind that in everyday life caused humans to wound and mine the world with their agriculture and human-centered demands. With these same mental tools, instead of blenders, phones, shopping malls, airplanes, war, and overcrowded pharmaceutical-dependent cities, people made what the Holy as Deified Time needed for food and clothing, which did not resemble what people wanted; what the Deified Time as all Matter needed was a specific type of beauty of which only humans are capable: a Ritual Beauty that took a lot of time, know-how, and non-returning gift-giving that was not a stock investment in the future, but a late payment for the grace of living. This was maintained through certain given rituals of human beauty without trying to benefit from the gift as a human. These rituals were given to the Holy at certain "nodes" or junctures in Time to feed the new growth of Time, or otherwise the effects of our top-heavy physical taking out of the land and the price of spiritual equilibrium would suck the trunk of the Time tree dry.

Time, to speak colloquially, like all living things and people themselves, was known as an organic thing, a growing thing with a plantlike nature. To all Mayans everything in the world was understood according to the nature of plants. People, Time, and the Holy in Nature were all plantlike. The so-called Mayan day names were the officially designated names of what lived and died during each of those days, and were called flowerings. To keep the world flowering meant to keep the blossoms on the trunks and branches of Time flowering so the flowers could again make "seeds" in hopes of replanting the continuing Eras of Time and the physical things that occurred during them.

Time did not exist; it spoke. And when it spoke, it spoke in flowers. And when it sang its story, these flowers turned to fruit whose seeds sprouted the physical reality of our living world. It lived, grew, flowered like nodes on a grass, fruiting then dying back to seed again the next cycle back into view. Thus time had to be fed and fertilized for reality to grow.

For this reason, all real Mayan diviners of this serious type have always used some kinds of seeds to count the specific flowerings growing on the branch of the trunk of Time.

Because it was known that any group of seeds was the "speech" of their own diverse sector of flowering plant time, all kinds of seeds were used for counting Time. Some people divined with a large handful of corn seeds, others with spotted beans, some with big beautiful squash seeds, and some with all kinds of wild iris seeds mixed together. This was no doubt the reason that seeds of all types were used by eccentric diviners as well as untrained, uninitiated diviners while still perfecting their art.

But the only seeds that fully "made" official calendar diviners, received at the time of their initiation, were the dangerously poisonous, beautiful, shiny, vermillion red beans from the pods of the tzejtel tree. For the rest of their lives the *Aj Qijá* had only four hundred of these same Fire Flower Tree beans to make their more expert counting of Time as its manifest flowerings on the trunk of the world as a tree.

As a group the magic contents of a Diviner's kit were known endearingly as *nu muk,* or "my herd," and no matter what God images, thrones, charms, dice, spinners, or other magic made up the "herd" of a Diviner's bundles, *all* Highland Maya Time-divining bundles were literally sacks of seeds! Because calendric diviners were in charge of keeping Time alive, this meant literally keeping the seeds alive! Seeds were everything. Seeds!

Calendric divination bundles were tightly packed, very carefully guarded, beautifully handwoven, heart-sized cotton sacks of a preciously regarded particular type of *seed*. Sometimes exquisitely decorated but always extravagantly meaningful, these little bundles of seeds are what a Mayan Calendar actually still looks like to the living Highland Mayan. The calendar was a living thing: a magnificent sack of seeds. It was not and never had been represented through any form of writing. The so-called "written calendars" of the old Maya were not actually calendars. The old Mayan hieroglyphic notations from Yucatán and other parts of the Mayan world touted as Mayan calendars were actually calendrically divined almanacs that recorded what the seeds had shown during given time sequences of the past in hopes of determining analogous cycles in a projected future. There were a lot of those writings, especially among the imperialist eras of Mayan culture, but before, during, and after, the calendars themselves were unwritten things, existing only as living, active, speaking things in a sack of Red Fire Flower Seeds. These little sacks of the Seeds of Time were and are still called in most dialects, *r cholic 'Qij,* "the talk of the sun," or *chol'qij,* "the speech of Days," or more exuberantly in Tzutujil as *ruqan Sac ruqan Qíj,* "the legs of dawn," "the legs of the sun," meaning in the same sense the walking of dawns, the walking of days. When a diviner set up to divine it was called *n Qijij:* to make it Day, i.e., to make it clear and visible.

Chiviliu and I had been waiting several months to be able to ritualize purposefully there at the shrine of Choqóux Aqóum exactly where we sat on that day, on this specific calendric day for it was then that the particular tzejtel tree for which this shrine was so famous should be in the wild glory of its full fiery blossom.

It was only at the site of this one specific unprepossessing mountain temple, at this shrine of Choqóux Aqóum, that Chiviliu had insisted we make today's ritual. No other time, no other shrine. This was on account of the immense spiritual worth and place in the universe this particular shrine had for anyone who knew the story of how it was at this singular spot that divination and divination bundles for the tribes had originated.

All of this momentous spiritual treasure of the place was dependent not on a hundred-foot fir or a massive thirty-foot-diameter cieba but on a very scraggly common-looking crown of insubstantial bushy shoots that rose immediately to our west, under whose dappled afternoon shade both Chiv and I, having been in a segment of the ritual where we could finally slide out of prayer position to rest our cramping knees and let the blood back into our painfully tingling feet, lounged freely on our sore tails like two tired old coatimundis.

Facetiously and collectively nicknamed Los Cabildos or the Government Offices, all of these mountain temples were where most old-style shamans maintained their ritual lives, nourishing, charming, others probably even "bribing" the hierarchal spiritual bureaucracy of Deified Time manifest as all Diverse existence that listened and feasted there. At each of these mountain temples or shrines different Deities had an "ear" that listened and a "mouth" that consumed the prescribed ritual gifts of each of their unique body and Earth functions. Some were rain, others rivers, growth, stone, clouds, seas, animals, plants of every valley, and every mountain. All the manifest flowerings of nature as time into matter could be fed at these shrines with the beauty and intoxication of the private rituals of shamans and some bigger non-shamanic village rituals as well. These mountain temples were better known to the people as *kósbal q´ aq´*, "a place for fire to commence," or *palimaal*, "where they stand up," which was a coded abbreviation for a much larger sacred meaning.

While *palimaal* and *kósbal q´ aq´* referred directly to the overall operating principle of all Tzutujil ceremonialism and ritual thinking, these two coded terms for the mountain shrines were not the only couplets that represented such knowledge. Though two of the most prominent of several hundred others, even these terms the lay villager understood one way, the ceremonialist in another more complex fashion; everyone knew the bigness of it all.

Kósbal q´ aq´, for instance, a place for fires to get going, meant to most people the obvious: an altar or "mouth" or "door" (being the same word *chi*) in the mountains where a shaman ritualist could set up their great blocks of hundreds of brightly burning tallow candles whose fat and flicker fed various Time Deities to keep some particular organ or segment of the "body" of annual and centurial Time "fat" and nourished. These myriad shrines were always in some part of the *Kotzejal Juyu Ruchiuleu* or Flowering Mountain Earth, which is Tzutujil for the uncultivated wilderness of the geoanatomy of the Natural Earth. Deities such as these only lived in the natural unpopulated Earth. There were thirteen sacred houses in the village, serviced by the village hierarchy of ceremonialists who also fed natural Wild Time from inside the village, but their function was to keep Time fed in the wild through "altars/doors/mouths" that fed directly in conduits of a spiritual neural system of the village directly into the wild from the sacred houses.

Though located right in the grumbling noisy village belly, each sacred house was nonetheless a small sacred bubble of inner space that contained an entire ecosystem of a section of Annual Time that resided in the wild. When you stepped past the reed-covered doorways of these sacred houses, you left the village and entered straight into mansions of Deified Time; inside mountain forests, oceans, the Sun, into Thunders, ravines and caverns, and the entire Flowering Earth.

But outside the village, held altogether, the mountain shrines themselves were understood as a kind of delicate net called *K'at*. Like arteries and capillaries in the cardiovascular system of the geoanatomy of time, this "net" pulsed with corpuscles of living time recharged with the fat of newly supplied beauty from the world's rituals, coursing through the body of the hungry universe to keep it walking, playing, unfolding, and dreaming the next layer of reality alive. A Time shaman could "feed" a particular "day" directly at one specific shrine of 260 of these *kósbal q´ aq´*, the one corresponding in the Body of the Earth universe to that parallel place in the client's body. The world, earth, body, and universe were concentric versions of each other, held in tangible layers one inside the next by the net of time like infinite nestings of matryoshka dolls.

The word *q´ aq´* or "fire" was an equally large flower of Mayan thought as well. For the hot, food-cooking, night-lighting, iron-smelting fire, this world in which we live considers the tangible reality of flame as something felt, something seen, or consumed; the Holy on the other side understand our fires as blossoms, flowers, and the fruit of Time as sent to them from us on our own side of the dimension of life. To the eyes of the Holy Time when any knowledgeable ceremonialist set up large blocks of eight hundred candles of "burning fat" to make his or her grand prayers, they were not only making Fire, but as far as Holy Time was concerned, they were causing their shamanic words to bud, then blossom, then hopefully Fruit. Thus our ritual Fires flowered into something that made Time "mature" into *ruach* or visible life-giving things peculiar to that particular segment of time.

When any segment of Annual and Bigger Time cycles "came alive," they were said to "spark." The Tzutujil word for *Life* and the word for *spark* is *Kás*. Any segment of Annual Time when coming alive made all the things that happened at the time come into tangible existence, i.e., the birth of all wild ungulates, the maturation of kinds of wild fruit, the beginning of the spring heat and rain, the flowering of the red stone cactus, the wind of the season, etc. These things were Time become matter and tangible life. When the previous segment of Annual time, i.e., the previous twenty days, comes to "fruition," it does so 260 days after its previous "blossomings," a gestation of some nine months earlier. Therefore the blossoming of the next section of time immediately after is given life by the "universe-feeding death and decay" of the "composting" of the previous segment seen by the ceremonialists as "fat" of the earth, which became the Fuel that makes the Fire (or Flower) burn and live; the past is burnt for a bright burning (flowering) present. This means the fat of our time must ceremonially fuel the next time. These fire-fueled rituals were called Flowerings.

When the spirits, i.e., Time Deified, of certain twenty-day segments of Time make the world live with whatever that time "blossoms" with, the Deity in question "sets up Fire" in their dimensional existence inside the "Mansion," i.e., the wild uncultivated body of the natural universe, of Time as a whole; their Fires, of course, are the Blossom, Flowers, and Fruiting that we see in this world: the Fruiting of all plants and animals that Feeds us, clothes us, gives us joy, and a place to develop into the beings we must become. To maintain this we give the Time Deities our Flowers of Fire, flowering words grown from our composted past, and they give us the Flowers and Fruit of the blessing of everyday life.

For this reason each mountain shrine had to have a distinct tree to

Flower, ideally as one of 260 species of organic Time! For each tree was itself a segment of continuous time that developed, grew, thrived, blossomed, and so on as a tree in an annual cycle of Time's life-giving and dormancy. Another way of calling the Mountain Shrine Temples was *Chuach Che, Chuach Abaj.*

> At the Face of Trees, the Face of Stones
> or alternately
> In Front of Wood, in Front of Rock

Every little temple had differing forms according to what kind of "government" of Deities each segment of Time had. The Stones were the Mansions, the Trees the growth; the stones made the ozone fires, the wood was the fuel. In other words by these terms it was clearly understood that for anything to give life to another thing or being, it had to be involved in combustion as it fueled what "ate" it.

So not only did Time, like a tree, blossom, flower, fertilize fruit, feed, and reseed, but it also refueled or "caused to Flower" the Flame of which this consuming-eating reality we live in consists. Flowers were what gave all things their food. Ask the Bees. Any plant that feeds an animal that feeds us or another animal depends on "seeds" to regenerate and animals to pollinate them. In order to keep those seeds alive, to keep the plants alive, to keep the world of eating things alive, the oxygen air alive, we humans alive, the plants too must eat, and what they eat are the more gradually combusted forms of all living beings. The composting of previous things that lived in the "previous cycle of time" was and is understood by the shaman as the same as a burning of the fat to cause the Flowering of the present, i.e., the Flowering of Time. The Flowering of the Time in its annual tree cycles was caused by the burning into the humus of nutrition the previous cycle of time.

Ritual of course was a human version of the same. A great culture-composting feast of human ornateness to keep Time from starving to death. And it was at these mountain shrines where these "Times"—as the Earth, as matter, as God/Goddesses—were maintained by humans to account for the *over*consumption we accrued to the surrounding

Flowering of Time, above and beyond the original agreement we had with the Holy in the Seed.

Time and the annual ritual obligation to Feed to Time and ceremonies to keep Time as the flowering earth alive were called Blossomings, by which was meant simultaneously "ignitings." Because Mayans didn't just count time, but reckoned Time in Diverse Blossomings, each of these mountain shrines had one of a great diversity of species of large and small trees of the tropical Highlands of Guatemala. Pines, spruces, oaks, guanacastes, mahoganies, hormigo, aropa, wild avocado, jocote, atzaal, nanze, zapotes, mulberry, tzan tzuy, choreques, mimosas, and ciebas, to name only a very few. These specific, magnificently healthy, towering pines, *ocuy, lamát,* or *canoj,* were usually accompanied by spacious stone benches, Deity forms, and petroglyphs and enclosed in mostly horseshoe shapes facing any number of directions depending on which ways the local rivers or streams flowed, sometimes toward a village, or where certain planets rose. But all of them had to have their particular tree. Each one of the trees was the plant form of a specific deity of the natural world and a specific type of Time manifested as some particular living microclimate in the world. A story belonged to each of these live Growing Gods as trees or bushes, stories that were the oldest stories of the world's origins wherein each story was itself only a tributary dribble flowing to an even bigger artery of mythic depth in which the fire-flower tree held the most unique and indispensable position.

The Tzutujil, and I venture to say most intact indigenous people, don't have Corn Gods, Rock Gods, Fertility Goddesses, River Goddesses, or any Gods of this or that, that sit enthroned at a distance directing the corn or the river. Each of the things of the world was the physical living flesh and blood of the Deity as she or he stood before you. There was no "Corn Goddess" or "Corn God." Rather, a corn plant was a God, we ate him, and he lived on in resprouted seeds as the possibility of himself as corn regrown from his mother the stalk. All the "Gods" were manifestations of segments of time. Not symbols of Gods but Deified Time whose motion became matter: matter we consumed, wore, cooked, exploited, and built with, and upon which we depended one hundred percent. They had voices, lives, long novels of their lives, appearing and reappearing in the very real nontheatrical drama of which all life consists.

Of all the living God beings, the fire-flower tree, also known as the coral bean tree, the tzejtel was considered the least incredible, the weakest, totally lazy, and as more of a comical weed by the uninitiated who heard his story. Yet in all the "big" stories and rituals of all the most powerful, beautiful, able, and responsible systems of other segments of Deified Time as trees, the tzejtel was however admittedly atypical, equally overlooked and the smallest integer of the deified universe; it was evident by all the old mythologies that the universe cannot move without him because he *is* Time. Time and all that happens in time put together as one flow.

While this Holy plant had a lot of wonderful secrets for an initiated ritualist, some of the best things about it were easily seen and common knowledge to all. Never uncommon, never hard to find, not universally loved or even noticed, its wood overly soft to build with and never used for fire for being basically toxic, called in the story an unemployed lazy boy because nobody used him, save as living fence posts or occasional convenient boundary markers. What everybody did know was that the most famous trait of fire-flower trees was their inability to be annihilated by any force, natural or man-made. They were the definition of unkillable. Not immortal for they could die, but they would always revive.

This atypical tree's notable position came not only from its commonness, or the personified comedy of stories about his undomesticatable uselessness, or of course for his unkillable vitality, but along with all of that it was the fact that the tzejtel has always been revered by all Mesoamericans as a living calendar for both settled farmers and wandering hunters. This is not to mention his prominence to the ritualists who serve them both. It would require an entire solar year for an individual to watch this tree to learn how this might be, but once you did, you could easily see how this tree was dedicated to marking Time and why that was his lazy "work," just hanging around being a calendar by being himself.

To start with, for three months of the year the trunk and branches are practically invisible for the profusion of crisply cut heart-shaped leaves that flutter and handsomely quake, shimmering in the wind. Then one day all of a sudden every single leaf drops to the ground, and in moments a million indescribably red machete-like flowers pierce the bark everywhere until all over again the branches are smothered out of view by rows and rows of brilliant standing blades of petaled flame. Once the hummingbirds have fertilized this fiery tree, in three months, the flowers will have all dropped just like the leaves. With neither leaves nor flowers, he once again covers himself with pithy pods, which after the next three months at some coordinated appointed moment all open up like dragonfly wings, and in double opposite twists they forcibly scatter a literal rain of very hard vermillion orange beans across the earth into the trees' shadow below.

Now for the last three months of the year, no leaf, flower, nor pod grows on his bare bark, and he often looks dead or on his way, and naked he stands for three months until he leafs out again on exactly the same moment every year, no matter the rainfall or the temperature. The tree is a living marker of seasons, a farmer's living calendar.

If that were not enough, the tree himself is a dreamer and a creative being that is in no way threatened by having to adapt, but is actually invigorated by any adversity thrown his way. Addicted to changing his shape, but in such a very particular way that what really matters to such a plant is never lost to him in that he remains a perfect calendric measure, while given to flights of peaceful defiance of all that would destroy him.

For years, without knowing I had assumed that the giant, spiky-trunked coral bean trees I saw in the coastal rain forests and the common slim smooth-barked birch-like tzejtel saplings growing at 1,500 feet, the dense short-trunked twisty branches up at 5,000 feet, and the uncommon meandering scrubby vine at 8,000 feet were all different subspecies of *Erythrina*, or coral bean, the tzejtel.

But by taking seeds from all these plants from every altitude and climate and replanting them in these differing zones, I watched each grow up to act and look just like the ones already thriving in that neighborhood so as to be indistinguishable. Never a refugee and always at home!

The thornless high mountain vines grew massive spiky-trunked coral bean trees at sea level, the spiky-trunked monsters' seeds grew as modest unkillable highland flowering fence posts, and so on!

But in every instance, the leaves and timing were identical, the flowers burst forth in exactly the same way the pods, the beans, and the three months of nakedness never disappeared.

This plant could mutate like people stuck in situations of harsh exile, who appear like the locals but still retain their own self-culture. The tzejtel knew exactly how to "keep her seeds alive" by changing and adapting while still able to "count" time under all conditions. This is one of the manifestations of the Holy in Nature that Diviners and time-feeding Priests revered about the tree. But then, as far as the seeds of this plant themselves were concerned, there lay hidden even more amazing things besides the capacity of the brilliant red seeds of the tzejtel to not only sprout themselves and adapt to all conditions: if done in just the right way, by grinding the rock-hard seeds against a certain type of stone, the seed would ignite into fire like a match! And from just one bright red bean with a blue and yellow flame a deadly smoke rose whose airborne alkaloid was strong enough to kill a hut full of bedbugs! If you know anything about bedbugs, then you know that's a really powerful poison.

Because of the red flame-shaped blossoms, the trees when in flower, if seen growing bunched together, made the hills look as if they themselves had caught fire, and, in fact, his seeds could actually light fires. This is why the tree was called the *tzejtel,* for *tzej* means simultaneously "makes Fire come forth" and also "makes the Flowering come forth."

For while *tzej* means "to blossom" and equally means "to ignite" as far as Tzutujil thinking goes, you can cause a fire to "blossom" in the morning to cook breakfast, as much as you can watch an orchard burst into a "flame" of flowers. Fires are flowers and flowers are fires. As simple as this sounds, it really comes from something that needs to never be forgotten.

When a ceremony is made to "feed" a portion of Time Deified, a Goddess, or God whose body is the things that flower, harvest, or come to life during its reign, then that ritual is called a "blossoming." But the blossom that the tribe is making always begins and continues with the presence of fire, either in bonfires, candle fire, incense fire, fat fires, alcohol fires, with even more or all of the above.

The procedures for making the fires were not arbitrary and always accompanied by "flowering" words and handmade offerings. When the words have all been "consumed," the incense all burned, the alcohol burnt, the firewood gone, the fat candles all burned, the ritual dances, songs, and complex, expansive offering houses have disintegrated and returned back into the ground, the segment of Deified Time that lives in that place is said to have "eaten." For the Holy to eat, the "sustenance" we feed them must disappear, consumed, taken by the Divine away from the present into the other world. However, when the Holy Matter as the Fruit of Deified Time receives our rituals as their food, the Deities don't see the flames of our candles, our incense, and our bonfires as Fire but as "blossoms" on the Flowering Tree of Human existence. They drink in the beautiful smells of the ritualists, beguiling ceremonial gifts, actions, and words as the aromatic perfume of the ritual's blossom, the blossom of human deliciousness.

We humans in an equally parallel way receive our food from the Holy in Nature where each Deified Segment of Time blossoms into the tangible life-forms we consume to live on, causing them as well to disappear in the forms we humans see ... but which is flame to the Holy who from the unseen inside of things makes their own constant life-giving fire rituals, as those Flowers and Fruit, conception and births of all the thriving, to thrive here as plants, animals, and blessing instead of Flame.

Not confined to simply "sniffing" the Holy's beauty, our eating and consumption of the very substantial and real deliciousness of the Holy in Nature is very literal and causes us to make disappear the beauty of the gift that the Holies pumped into reality. We must then use the vitality we are afforded by this meal to feed again the source of what we caused to disappear. This is ritual.

In the tropics we can easily see all the exuberant and distinct flowerings that burst forth in their appointed hours on all the trees and plants to make happen the annual cycle of the ecstasy of pollen, aroma, nectar, and beauty that causes the fertilization of each layer of flowering plants in order that the flower dropping her petals swells into a fruit, that in turn develops in "Time" to become one of a diverse form of viable seeds that regenerates more of itself. This is the sustenance of all the world. This sustenance is caused by the Flowering of Time Rituals sent by the Holy. All fruits as such are called *ruach* by the Tzutujil.

The word *ruach*, for instance, while for the Tzutujil it means the fruit of any kind of plant, does also simultaneously and not as a homonym signify the "fruit" or outcome of any action, direction of travel, idea, day, place, mood, etc. For all things and their functions are understood in a plant way. The phrase *"Naqs ruach jaura?"* "What fruit does it carry?" can also mean "What kind of plant is this?" or "What does this earth here grow?" It can equally mean "This new idea: how will it turn out in the end?" or "That person's strange actions—what unseen possibility are they headed toward?" and so on. Everything is about plants and plant natures, with trunks, branches, and Time flowers fruiting into what develops in time. This is why Time is understood as having a gradual plantlike nature: it grows and develops, plants, dies, and is reborn.

With all of these meanings in the word *ruach* and none understood exclusively of the other, this word for *fruit* is the usual word meaning "a person's *face*." The apparent natural form of anything in the world, any being, or any person is said to be called his or her face as a unique individual instead of a species or type; therefore all faces are "fruit." The Earth is even called *Ruachuleu*: the Face/Fruit of Soil! When saying hello to anyone you always politely enquire *"L'utz a wach?"* "Your face is well?" which is an abbreviation from the much more ceremonial, "Does your 'fruit/face' hang well on your ancestral trunk?" With a language like that actively spoken, you cannot easily forget what your life should be aiming toward. It's all about plants.

But these "faces" of ours can speak, and if delicious enough, our amazing human capacity for speech whose content can sing, praise, and make delicious images can then be a great blossoming with the ability to "feed" Life. These words are known in Tzutujil as the "seeds" of our Fruit, i.e., our Faces; word seeds, if delicious enough, replant the great blossoming whose own fruit can be ritually renewed to feed Life itself as the Hungry Mother Holy in Nature. While these oral ritual gifts are generally translated into English, as the simply dry inaccurate term of prayers, these kinds of speaking don't beg, but make life live.

In like manner Time as a plant, a tree, when it flowers, speaks, in delicious flowers of speech which call in the unpredictable ecstatic Holy Agents of Fertilization like pollen-filled bumblebees who cause these speech flowers from the divine desire to fruit into plants and animals, whose flesh feeds the world.

Old-time Tzutujil initiation taught that we as humans are required to speak and flower the world into life, and taught us how our beauty fruited into edible gifts of spiritually energized sound that, like a tortilla, wrapped a delicious center of polyvalent beauty; that along with the "speech" of our hands that also flowered through the beauty we carved, painted, braided, built, and wore whose fruit became the beautiful offerings, we were obligated to ever feed the always speaking "flowering" Deities of Time as matter and all life manifest. These types of gifts we as people did not consume. They were for the long-suffering Holy Earth; we consumed the simultaneous gift of their own bodies, this world, so we gave our existence to them.

Every single day on the calendar and every sunrise cycle as a flowering of the fires of Holy Time were the cycles of these days on a flowering tree and vine upon which centuries of days come to physical view from a world that bubbled very real but invisible to us, inside the trunk of Time and the Holy ground.

For every day of existence don't we humans have to keep Time alive, doing our part to keep the next day blossoming and fruiting into view? To keep the sun rising? To keep the seasons rocking back and forth, our ceremonial offering fires and poetry lit so that each distinct Flowering day can itself go to feed the next sunrise to keep the plants, animals, and each day alive with the adventures each contain, keeping life up and running, jumping, vital and blossoming just as the ceremonial blossoming of the other world keeps us alive enough to return to them our small equivalency of that same echo of the beauty they afford us?

While the Tzutujil word designating that something is alive is *kás,* meaning a "spark," the word *spark* is also how one says "debt." This makes the word for "life," *káslimaal,* meaning "mutual enspark-ed-ness," to mean simultaneously "mutual indebtedness": one and the same thing.

The ability for every person to learn, to retain big ideas, is also called *xin k'asé pnwá,* "It lives in my head," meaning both simultaneously, "It sparks in my head" or "My head has a debt," implying "What I know about life I owe to the lives of those who live it."

So this plant, fuel, fire, blossom, Time, matter, mutual feeding of that great diversity of the Holy in Nature as Deified Time that feeds us with our literal existence is one of the grand understandings of the word for "life," *káslimaal,* mutual indebtedness. Our mutual back-and-forth debt, a kind of "You are the reason the other one lives," between this living Blossom of Now and what makes it is also a "mutual insparkedness," a mutual fire sparking.

The spark needed to start the ritual fire in every ceremony, no matter when or where, is seen as the initial spark that begins Time and life all over, fresh in every case, the rising sun of that day being the "roaring fire child" of all Fire himself.

For this reason in times more grand and natural when humans didn't need divination to have the greater conscious existence that could directly dance naturally with the world, Time as cyclic chunks that needed bolstering by humans did not yet exist. Because humans weren't stealing, overusing, forgetting who and how it came from, their "debt" was instantly addressed as it is for plants and animals, by the way original humans went about just being original humans. This is no longer possible for humans. Something big and forgotten happened. People became uncourageous, fearful, and dedicated to self-survival. Human life was forced to change. Time was no longer an ongoing changing thing; it became a planted cyclic thing, a surging pulse whose vitality was suddenly divided into ongoing notations of an ecstatically choreographed infinity of seasons, years, and eons as seen from a single settled spot.

To the Tzutujil this big change was the instance of the very first tzejtel tree. This tree now brought the people the ability and responsibility to have a life of cyclic Time-feeding ritual whose individual rituals through-out the year are called Fire Blossoms. Time no longer lived here where people lived, but still from a distance caused this place we live to flourish. We humans can no longer live where Time lives either, but we cause the continent where Time lives to flourish and thrive. Like lovers who can't see each other or touch, the two live by the gifts each gives the other, sent by sound and ritual. Our life is the kiss Holy Time sends on to us in his song.

Chapter 6

The Miraculous Return of the Tree of Time

The light itself was pollen-yellow and the shadows violet, late that one afternoon as Chiv and I, beneath that exuberant new growth of incorrigible blunt-nosed tzejtel shoots at the volcano-side shrine of Choqóux Aqóum, sat reiterating, reanimating, reigniting, reflowering our own hearts with the remembrance of all these grand understandings when all of a sudden Chiviliu in his exuberance leaned sideways and kicked my bare anklebone with a gnarly old toe that looked more like a petrified grape with a yellow claw. Handing me his pipe so I could reload it from my famous cache of Coban tobacco, he lit it from a ritual ember left over from our earlier Fire, then through the misty blue fragrance of his puffing he went on to remind me of the biggest thing of all: that the very same little unassuming ratty example of a tzejtel tree, almost too small to shade us, was none other than that very first tzejtel to ever appear on earth eons ago. This was the very same tree, he said, not a descendant of the most Holy original one, but the very same one: the ancient parent of all other tzejtel trees in the entire wide earth.

When this tree first sprouted into view, Time as a plant began right here where we sat! I knew that, he knew that, most people knew it, but it was always stunning and new every time we knew it again! People had come and gone and yet this original Plant of all Time was here for us fragile mortal beings to sit under and remember. This tree, a lazy dreamer at first, slowly dreamt the first days, which all flowered, coming into view on the tree, then these fruited and further matured, each day dreamt into his hard red Fire beans, beans that for the first time fell to the earth and replanted Time everywhere that Time felt like growing. The beans each contained the power to regrow another entire tree of life, just as every day contains a spark that could restart a mental vision, just like in every atom there is enough of all that is needed to explode a brand new universe back into life. Chiviliu and I reeled and laughed ecstatically with the thought, a knowledge not achieved but a knowledge in whose joy we rolled like a couple of old derelict alley cats with enough to eat caught in a patch of catnip.

But in those days there in the seventies in Atitlán there were already villagers both young and middle-aged, advocates of the new Christians and their new cash-based non-earth-oriented, non-seed awareness lifestyle, who thought the fact that this tzejtel was the same tree as the original was a load of frog farts. There were others like some outsiders who liked the idea but took the idea as the machinations of the uneducated who needed such a belief for a metaphorical idea to help the principal of Tzutujil Time to be understood better. The heavy ritualist, though, knew that tzejtel tree much better and didn't care what the others thought. This Tzejtel was the first one.

Even a dull rationalist would have believed once he or she witnessed what that grand old rootstock had endured on account of the age-old reverence, in which all the village people originally held the miraculous tree and his mountain shrine. Even those who didn't fully comprehend still held dear both the tree and those villagers who did know the depth of what lived in the Tzejtel. The genuine affection and lavish ritual gifts the villagers originally bestowed upon all Time as this Tree and his feeding place: the shrine, was akin to the love all people have for their children.

Generations and even centuries of various European, Mestizo, and North American religious officials, missionaries, and civil officers, assuming their uninvited control over Indian towns and lives totally unable to comprehend not only the beauty and brilliance of Holy Time and reality as the Flaming Flowering of Time, missed the reason why the people were so entranced and their reverence so deep. They became viciously jealous of the loyalty all the villagers showed the shrine in their willingness in offering expenditures, time, effort, and punctuality to the native priest-hood in carrying on what everyone knew was nothing less than an obli-gation to ritually feed Deified Time as the Holy in Nature, to ensure life continuing on as the gift it already was to us. This deity's popularity and seemingly unkillable nature frustrated and threatened every outside con-queror, missionary, and political authority in history who'd ever tried to control Atitlán. For four centuries the story never changed, the complaint the same.

Unable to hardly convince anyone to attend church, pay the *decima,* or stop being "savages," those outsiders, mostly Eurocentric types, couldn't fathom that their "simple" Indians might actually have a sophis-ticated culture. The outsiders lived in an experiment of their God to test the loyalty of its creation in a dead world where Time didn't speak, ani-mals didn't dream, nothing seemed to feel, and humans couldn't give life. Along with their boring God the outsiders were depressives, so all the outsiders could ever see from the sixteenth century to the 1980s was idol-worshipping, not the feeding of Time to address human's spiritual ecosystem debt. Seeing all things dead they stupidly thought by "remov-ing the cause of their idolatry," i.e., the Tzejtel tree, they would in effect "kill" their church's and culture's nonreal competition. How this was sup-posed to stimulate "native" consideration for their uninteresting baffling presentation of neurotic Christianity, I have never understood.

But instead of succeeding in eradicating the local spiritual life of the traditional Tzutujil, the People of Time Seeds, like the durable Tzejtel tree himself, their rituals were simply driven even further underground, the "seeds" kept even more preciously secret and hidden, and life went on in a whisper.

Though not alone as victims of these attacks, this single tzejtel tree, the Tree of Time at Choqóux Aqóum, has to have been the most contin-uously tortured and persecuted tree in the history of all human cruelty to living beings.

Three and four centuries ago during Spanish colonial times, the campaign of the clergy against what had been the original very large spiky-barked giant of a tree, which in these times was covered in hanging offerings, was confined to forcing Christian converts into sawing the Tree of Time off at its trunk, after which there were fifty years of cholera, yellow fever, endless rain, floods, volcanic eruptions, and a series of devastating earthquakes nationwide, reducing the Indians to a tenth of their already reduced post-conquest populations and ironically physically removing all Europeans from most of the Mayan highlands. But by then the Tzejtel springing from the old root trunk was already right back to size and life went on. This was the pattern off and on for three centuries.

But this changed sometime in the mid-twentieth century, when different waves of mostly North American Protestant Christian religions came dribbling in on Atitlán missionizing in opposition to their traditional enemy: the now-Indianized copacetic post-colonial Catholicism. It didn't take long for them as well to begrudge the prominent place in the people's spiritual life of the brilliant complexity of what this tzejtel tree had that caused the villagers to ignore the missions of all Christians. But not willing to take the time, nor having the spiritual intellect to understand the Beauty of what the people so deeply loved, they saw only ignorant natives worshipping the "False God" of a Tree.

As Chiviliu always said, "The beloved original Tree of Time was bothering *no* one, with no unkind words of his own, while minding his own business, dreaming and flowering our living earth into life," these new Christians, like their old Catholic enemies over the earlier three-and-a-half centuries, once again forced the few converts they'd recruited to fell this same Tzejtel who had already regained his former luxurious glory.

Then before, during, and for a dozen years after World War II, when the first North American evangelical zealots, Mormons, Pentecostals, and Adventists poured into the whole of Central America, turbulently competing among themselves for which of them could corral the greater congregation of converted Indians in the villages on the shores all around Lake Atitlán, they too came to hate the tree for what they called its presence, "a tenacious symbol of the failure of the Christian religion to fully stamp out paganism" among the ornery Atiteco Mayans.

Once again, unwilling to even imagine that "ignorant" poor Indians could have any thoughts worth saving, and apparently not intelligent enough to comprehend the more intact spiritual depth and beauty of why the Tzutujil revered the tree at Choqóux Aqóum, all these missions along with the first non-Spanish Catholic clergy, German and American, vied against each other, taking turns to repeatedly be that "one named by Christ" to be the first to finally extinguish this "presence of evil and ignorance" up on the side of the volcano, and continued with machetes, saws, and axes to make salad and sawdust out of what was left of the Tree of Time.

But they only discovered how animated the tree became with such adamant pruning, when the following season the tree pushed back into view with even more vigorous shoots, growing as much as six inches a day, continuing to be covered successively by leaves and flowers and undauntedly showering down his rain of Time-counting red beans!

One German Catholic priest, a feared persecutor of Atiteco traditionalists one day wearing his ever-present black frock, in a fit of temper stomped up to the shrine with a sharp handmade German broadax and a German shovel, and all by his sweaty self cut the Tree of Time down when it was in full flower, and dug the roots out for three consecutive days only to himself die drowning a week later crossing the Lake in a motorboat during a storm.

The villagers just shrugged their shoulders whenever anybody brought it up: "What do you expect if you try so hard to assassinate Time?"

Not to be frightened off, and realizing the tree had once again returned from the dead, one evangelical preacher with an approach more like the modern warfare he'd just come through as an infantry chaplain in World War II cut down the Tree of Time, then poured gallons of gasoline into the trunk, set it all on fire and kept it going for five days straight. When he was done he "salted" the remaining rootstalk and "rooted out" the evil fire-flower tree. The tree, who the shamans said deified Time as an organic thing, must have interpreted this fiery treatment as some form of ritual "fire feeding," for the next season anybody passing near the shrine could see the happy tribe of at least a hundred strong tropical saplings, so enormously stimulated by the abuse as to make a more prodigious showing of flowers and seeds there than had ever been seen or heard of in the past century. Baffled by anyone who spent all their waking hours haranguing the public about how theirs was the only single God and all the others didn't exist, who would deliberately and with such persistence insist on eliminating a supposedly nonexistent god by persecuting that nonexistent god's living manifestation as an unkillable tree, the body of traditionalists didn't do anything much to fight back. The shamans among them kept visiting whatever bits were left. After all, Time didn't die because some idiots killed a tree. They went on feeding Time with the same rituals and words, maintaining the health of the big Holy understanding that resided there and whose origins still originated there an understanding that kept the world a viable living breathing thing.

Then a more modernized sect of Catholicism was assigned to Atitlán, and a right-wing branch of this, with a kind of more rationalist American education, hauled several cases of dynamite up the mountainside in the very early seventies.

Intending to blow up not only the tree and the roots of the Holy Tzejtel out of existence, these fellows were going to even exterminate the shrine Temple and eradicate its location as a place to have a shrine once and for all.

The blasts left several thirty-foot craters, revealing a network of more distant rootstock of the Tree of Time stretching beyond sight. But all of this they assiduously excavated, piece by piece.

While these pagan-purging religious types were still celebrating this event at an embassy party they organized for outside officials and clergy in Guatemala City, passing around other images ripped the same day from sacred houses, drinking, toasting their supposed success to this their "final solution," and the definite end of any evidence of Indigenous spiritual life in Atitlán, several shamans worked at filling in a few of the holes, gathering up splintered stones, and bringing others from higher up. They rebuilt the table part of the once-extensive shrine about forty feet to the west of where it used to sprawl. Other than the missing ancient images that had been already purloined from the shrine before the explosion and sold by evangelicals to collectors and the absence of the old tree himself, this major part of the stone part of the shrine at Choqóux Aqóum looked exactly as it always had.

This is how it appeared when I first accompanied Chiviliu to Choqóux Aqóum in the early seventies: little knots and queues of seated shamans and clients waiting for their turn to make their delicious words and fire rituals at the "table" of the reconstructed stone shrine, no tzejtel trees, and a lot of craters filled with a thick camouflage of regrown underbrush.

Less than two years later, however, when I began taking my own sick or suffering clients up to the hill shrines, searching for their health with my barely initiated capacity with rituals and words, everyone began noticing that the shrine table itself began to bulge up as if some gigantic gopher were trying to surface. Over the next months a five-foot mound of cindery volcanic mountain earth totally swelled the stones of the shrine table up and out, so as to topple most of them to the side and burying the rest until one day at least forty thick, robust, asparagus-like happy shoots of tzejtel rose to take over the spot once again!

A new stone table and throne was built even farther to the west, and the tree that originally flowered the earth into life by its Dream of Fire as Time in Flower grew profusely into several great spreading forty-foot beauties.

In the decades to come the Fire-Flower tree would be further tortured by the machine-gun fire and grenade blasts by idle or vindictive soldiers stationed there during the killing years of the 1980s. Even more saws and axes would come. But so far, the same ancient rootstock of the Tree of Time reaching far beyond the grasp of the modern human has always returned annually, its living calendar never missing a season, to set a profusion of flowers and later leave a jeweled storm of elegant, smooth, vermillion-colored beans strewn over the tortured, rearranged rock shrine's still-visited surface, maintaining his promise of keeping the seeds of Time alive.

And that's how it was and how Choqóux Aqóum looked that one late afternoon in July, when Chiviliu and I sat remembering out loud how this very tree in whose generous shadow we sat was the very same one and only original Time Flowering Tree, from which Time originated, radiating concentrically forever out right from here into the universe and from whom all the other tzejtel trees of the world had descended.

Though there are thousand upon thousand of tzejtel trees all over Central America, some with red beans, others with cream-colored beans, others with a very appealing canary yellow bean, all the tzejtel trees of this world were considered to be descendants of this single miraculously living original tree at Choqóux Aqóum. And while all the others would live and eventually die, Time, like this tree because it was Time, would not die. For this reason all the calendar diviners of our area wanted only the red beans from the Holy Tzejtel of Choqóux Aqóum as the calendric Time counters in their *Chol qij Qijibaal* or Divination Bundles.

Most calendric diviners had new bundles put together ritually for them by their teachers at the culmination of being novice diviners, serving as a kind of diploma signifying a fairly full capacity and knowledge. Thus every diviner had four hundred new tzejtel beans in his sack that would grow old with him or her.

On our side of the Lake, diviners often inherited a portion, as much as half, of his or her teacher's bundle. In this way, a kind of cell mitosis took place, said by the Tzutujil midwife shamans to be identical to that experienced by pregnant mothers whose "hearts" at conception divided into two halves from where one half a baby was grown by adding the father's seed which "sparked" the missing half into being, the mother growing spontaneously another half to complete herself into a new kind of woman. This made women into more and greater individuals with each pregnancy as "Time" went on, causing her inherited heart to increment more and more according to a woman's own nature. The divining teacher was understood as a mother who gestated his or her student, and by giving the student half their own inherited beans of the Heart of Time, the student was rooted in the human history of those diviners who'd been keeping the Walking of the Sun, the Walking of Dawns alive, i.e., Time. But the student also received two hundred *new* beans from the Old Tree at Choqóux Aqóum to give half the bundle a fresh presence in the present, just like the tree did, who no matter how anciently rooted, still annually flowered and put out brand new beans.

The teacher was renewed as well, for when he or she appropriately lost half of his authoritative perch, he gained a renewed youthful second half.

Ideally students were supposed to mature into able diviners who eventually took on an apprentice of their own. In turn, they themselves upon "graduation" would receive half their beans from the teacher and the other half from Choqóux Aqóum, directly from Holy Time . . . and on and on it went. But it was always remembered that every single bean in all the bundles had come from Choqóux Aqóum at the base of the generous unkillable original Tzejtel tree from one time or the next.

Other bundles, however, remained undivided for lack of a student, in which case the diviner on his death bed usually bequeathed his bundle directly to an already established diviner, leaving some living *Aj Qij* with as many as five or ten bundles to feed, i.e., ritually maintain.

I myself inherited three bundles from dying diviners, each of which I religiously "fed" and regularly employed.

Whether directly inherited or earned through apprenticeship, the sacred counting seeds inside all Divination Bundles had descended directly from the same Tzejtel at Choqóux Aqóum, but they did so only after having passed through the hands of anywhere between twenty to sixty generations of previous diviners to the present. Though the diviners and the people they served were dead and long gone decades and even centuries past, every bean added into the original matrix of four hundred beans at differing intervals throughout Time had been used identically to keep Time and the Time-dependent tangible world alive. But the old Bundle of each inheriting generation of their respective era would also have brand new red beans added into the bundles upon termination of their instruction, every bean having been shed by this very tree who invented Time at Choqóux Aqóum. Time was renewed, the people renewed, the culture renewed, but the beans always stayed.

Before each divination, while preparing myself to "count" and listen to what Holy Time had to say, while holding one of these heart-sized hand-woven sacks of Time seeds, I could always feel how strongly the seeds held all the stories of all that had ever happened to the people and the tree they came from through ages and ages of time up to this present transient moment. You could literally hold and feel on a daily basis all the layers of people who'd been dedicated to the same thing you were, still bubbling in the bag; those who had held them and who must have felt the same weighty spiritual largesse as well; beans from the origination tree, still original and still here.

For those Mayans I knew then, the past had never been something that could find a way to depart. The past was more like something that feasted on the beauty the present could make and was then renewed, bursting into flower and fruit again, becoming the new present Time. This meant people were eternally occupied with the maintenance of the present natural world. Renewing the viable present meant people must live all the way and grow old, while concentrating their decisions and way of life to becoming more beautiful and incrementally more spiritually weighty so that especially our deaths during that never-ending present were sufficiently delicious to the Holy as to also feed Time. This kept the whole big picture alive. In this manner, our deaths made the past something that could never exist as forgotten and lost territory but always remain as the living Foundation of Time as the tangible present.

But people being people wobbled, lost their way, tossing this immense understanding under the wheels of the strange detours they made out of fear and spiritual amnesia. The divining bundles were there for this reason to help the people determine more specifically where, when, what, and how the combination of decision-motivating thought and ritual direction might more adequately move any of us better toward helping to restore the necessary organic motion of the Tree of Time, or House of the World as it is simultaneously known. Our unconscious inadvertent wounding of the Natural Universe was considered to be a constant characteristic of human striving, and the Divination Bundles were there to help us remember again how to be real people.

It is easily visible to any of us how indicative it was of the general incapacity of civilizations to want what is truly best in humans, when we considered the irony of how deliciously this single tree himself was abused up on that hillside overlooking Atitlán, where he was so many times deliberately attacked by the same mind-set of civilizations whose millennia of dissociated unnatural policies are still hard at work wrecking the world we live in today.

While that Holy Tree of Time was a fixed place on the earth, a belly button that had to stand still, in the inner workings of the village our Divination Bundles were quite nomadic spiritual treasures. In our bundles, we hauled around the tree in the form of his beans and the Time they contained, this goodness in our hands going right along with us wherever we went. Wherever we found ourselves, because of the way the bundles were always actively at work and never regarded as dead metaphysical religious relics left over from the past, but as living and *full* of still viable seeds, we felt we were little branches on the Tree of Time carrying the Tzejtel along with us. These were seeds filled with Time, but also they were viable plant seeds as well with the organic ability to quite literally regrow another tzejtel tree anywhere they might get planted! This was an amazing defiance of science and probability for seeds that old to be capable of sprouting a new tree: a tree of Time no less!

You could even tell which of the beans in the bundles belonged to which past era in their long history by the colors they took on as they grew older.

Since these kinds of divination bundles, once earned or bestowed, stayed with the Calendar Diviner his entire life, they could not be sold or loaned out. Passed only to a successor, the seeds would therefore have been in the possession of a diviner anywhere from twenty to seventy years, during which period they were every day counted, ritually fed, and touched. Like Catholic priests who did mass every day for themselves, old-time Calendar Time Diviners lived by daily conversing with the Diverse Deified Time by means of the beans. The ecstatic pitchy aroma of the vanishing smoke of the ever-present *pōm* that daily filtered through the cloth of the bundle, combined with the natural skin oils in the Diviner's deft counting hands, rubbed in as they caressed the beans during the counting and arranging, burnishing the beans until their colors deepened into distinctly recognizable shades that corresponded to their particular era as Time went on.

Always a bright solid vermillion-orange color with no black when fresh from the old tree, fifty years of divination burnished them into the color of toasted orange peels; fifty more years and they would deepen into a coral red; fifty years later they became the color of a shiny blood-bay horse; and every fifty years after into deeper shades of burnt bone until they looked like smooth black obsidian pebbles with a red ocherish sun-glazed overtone in a couple of centuries.

Depending on the energy and quickness of a diviner's teacher, and the sharpness of his or her memory and that of all the teachers before, a student could learn the name and life of each person behind each color of bean. This student of course would pass this on to his own student who'd add his own name and notoriety as associated with his own color. And from one life to the next death, on and on it went. The Tzutujil linguistic classification of all people and life as plants and their cycles were powerfully obvious to the diviner, for all the old and ancient generations of *Aj Qij* were known to us tangibly not by having seen them alive in human form, but only as living seeds in our bundles and their time-deepened colors. Though dead, they weren't gone either for all the seeds still spoke in terms of Divination as seeds of time that insist on sprouting. The ancient ones were layers of Time whose Distance, like the geologic layers upon which we all live, cooperated, mixed in with the fresh ones as a life-directing team to keep present Time alive and in motion through divination to help alleviate human suffering in the present.

The old shamans, priests, and diviners, men and women, thought that this kind of thinking was the general mind-set of the inborn natural human, but that mostly everywhere it had been eroded by some strange force, reduced into the dust of amnesia, and forgotten. Fully aware that people afflicted with that kind of amnesia and bringing with them an era of profoundly wounded, unaddressed, and unfed Time were soon to explode in upon us, Chiviliu and I maintained a steady stream of sacred remembering to better bolster our own hearts against the shock of its inevitability.

But we did so even more for the benefit of the Tree himself and the bundles who need these tales to keep strong. Told in such a fashion, stories of these types were considered the "sprouting" of seeds, and not only necessary to keep the understandings but also the Tree of Time himself and the world alive and viable. Understandings must hear their own tales from us for them to know we understand their gift. All things live and listen by sprouting into view as remembered Beauty told into reality.

But this old-time ramble opened up a flood of even more delicious memories. We were simultaneously reminded of yet another bit of the majesty regarding the diviner's seeds: that not only were all the tzejtel seeds in the bundles, from all the eons of generations, from the same exact tree and location, but unlike most of the other more fragile seeds of the world, these tzejtel seeds were still all viable, able to resprout in the right condition no matter how antique they may have been. For this fact we both recalled that something even grander was still occurring.

Though divination in other forms would probably always be around, due to the culturally erosive effects that the "non-seed" mind-set of modern industrial culture has when it succeeds in infecting a people such as the Tzutujil with its conceptual virus of matter as a dead soulless resource, something with whom you needn't negotiate for permission to exploit, the subtle complex art of Calendric Divination though very much alive in a slightly differing avatar and climate in other parts of Quiche Mayan Highlands, was already in the process of extinction in South Lake Atitlán.

Diviners found it increasingly rare to have a real student, with sufficient lifelong dedication, to receive the necessary knowledge and training. As "Time" went on, many diviners had no one at all to even formally bequeath their bundles and divining kits.

Some diviners, having divined that a few generations down the line a true successor would be born into their line, would ask their own families, in the event of the diviner's death, to ritually feed their bundles on special altars, teaching them the rudiments of the ritual despite the fact that none of his or her present family had the actual gift or "permission" of the soul of the bundles to even handle them.

No one ever touched a bundle unless directed to do so by the Diviner or shaman. That was a law extended to all Holy things and places; to do so was a kind of rape, which might cause the spirit of the bundle or the place to flee and never return. But it was also idiotically dangerous, like putting your hands in a sleeping jaguar's mouth, or diving intentionally into a boiling river of molten stone.

To the Diviner, a Divining Bundle was a kind of spirit wife or husband. After a diviner passed away, it was considered pretty dicey to trust one's relations to take care of and feed one's wife, much less a spirit wife they could not touch and from whom they received no material benefit. It did happen and sometimes came out well, but mostly the bundles were just passed to other diviners, or even non-divining shamans who knew how to "feed" the bundle without expecting any personal increase in power or fortune.

The worst thing of all was if a divining bundle was forgotten in some corner of a house, or in a museum, left unfed, unritualized, and stared at, thereby starving the seeds of Time, leaving them to drift into oblivion. For a diviner this was the same as killing the flowering of Time. Chiviliu and I gurgled and laughed to remember how the present Tzutujil response to this bad situation came to resemble a similar condition in the past when sixteenth-century Spanish Catholic clergy ironically enforced on the villagers the common old European ordinances that prohibited any confirmed "pagans" to be interred on the so-called "blessed ground" of their Christian cemeteries alongside the baptized dead.

Like the present situation with the onslaught of modernity's disinterest in viable culture, these stern colonial Catholics and their old rules ended up inadvertently reestablishing certain Mayan pre-invasion burial customs, customs they had already vehemently banished a century past. The first wave of Spanish ecclesia, in their zeal, had mandated that all Indians convert, receiving baptism, and at least accept last rites and a Christian-style burial in a Catholic consecrated cemetery. The Tzutujil did not have only one single burial custom for the many strata of population in their complex pre-European culture. Every stratum was interred to bolster a different stratum of the universe upon death. Shamans were usually buried in faraway places in their beloved undomesticated wilds.

But centuries of foreign domination failed to wipe out what even in the twentieth century the church designated as "Pagan Cabalistic practices" of the Tzutujil, which included divination, so the church denied "uncorrected" shamans and diviners from permission to be buried in a Christian cemetery. So again following in the most antique traditions previous to the sixteenth century, diviners and shamans, even those with no successors, were secretly buried away from the village back in those wild natural places out in the forests and valleys with their little sacks of treasured divining seeds and bundles placed squarely on their chests.

The ancient red, mauve, orange, and black beans of the bundles would eventually sprout, and just like at Choqóux Aqóum, sending their persistent roots right down into the dead diviner's composting heart until one day bursting vigorously out of the grave like a weedy thicket of fire-flower shoots they continued growing until one shoot prevailed who, after several years, became a powerful massive spiky tzejtel tree, making ornate, fire-colored, machete-like flowers, red divination beans, and shade!

The beans of course had all been descendants of this very one at Choqóux Aqóum but were now rooted directly in the great diviner's body out in the wild. As far as the people were concerned, the diviner had disappeared as a person and had now become a tangible, quite alive, literal ancestral tree, visible in all reality.

Living shamans were addicted to sitting in the "shade" of a deceased ancient diviner, under his grand tree. We always stopped to rest whenever we came to one we knew. We sang songs, prayed to the whole idea, the tree, Choqóux Aqóum, the calendar, and the old diviner who now spilt his beans all over us as a living tributary tree of persecuted time in all his glory.

Shamans and all hardworking men and women in those days were connoisseurs of shade, and the shade of diviner trees was of the very best kind; it was Holy and a kind of energizing food for us, and we were instantly renewed by the shadow of its canopy. The brave could sleep in its shade and make divinations without beans by learning things from the dreams the old tree pumped directly into one's heart. But for most people such dreams and Time's speech were too strong and dangerous. Only shamans and the like even considered sleeping under those trees.

All Tzutujil called their children *tzej jutay,* "flowers and sprouts," and every adult was known as a tree shading their children's shoots sprouting at their base, keeping them from harm and teaching them and cultivating their developing strength under their parental protection. In this way when seated like a new living sprout of a human tree of time in the life-giving shade of an old diviner's Tree of Time, we were all protected from the brash rattle of the harsh reality of modernity's distant ogreish clang by the tangible growing and flourishing of the old calendar as a living parent. It comforted the hell out of us.

Like real societies of people worldwide, who even if they are not totally blessed with the capacity to comprehend the depth and details of all that others do, regular Tzutujil men and women not having the initiation as shamans or diviners still loved, fed, and respected both the diviners and what they served. For this reason any everyday farmer, fisherman, weaver, mother, or laborer, even if not grasping all the depth of the Fire-Flower tree and the flowering of Calendric Time, would still feel "counted back to life" and restored spiritually by simply taking their ease and drying their sweat in the shade of some old diviner's newly flowering body under the spreading tree.

But fire-flower trees of every type, height, and dimension were very common all over the highlands, the mountain lowlands, in villages, and on the coast. It didn't take long before people began suspecting every substantial tzejtel tree of having sprouted out of some forgotten diviner or shaman heart in the distant past. Because the trees were everywhere and they were all potentially magical and good for renewing life, magic was everywhere.

If even a gifted unfoggy child for whom it was indicated by divination at birth that he or she had to become a diviner, especially if the child had sprouted into a family descended from a well-known, ancient, long-gone diviner, even if hundreds of years had gone by and there had been no divination bundle left behind for the child to inherit, then that child, it was said, would know exactly what to do, where, when, and how, magically already "taught" by reason of being the blood relative to the one specific tzejtel tree sprouted out of his distant ancestor's heart long ago.

This young man or woman could freely take the necessary beans off the forest floor that gathered lying in the shade of his or her great ancestor. To this budding new diviner these seeds were said to actually speak in an "echo" of flowering Time from the great ocean of both past and future, echoing a profound life-giving surf-like pulse that overlaps the shores of this flower of the present time and the unkillable tree of life. Some of these innately endowed diviners didn't even bother "counting" with the beans but just held the sack and knew things. Such diviners were rare, anomalous, gifted, different from regular people, but they were life-restoring people and considered to be the greatest of all diviners because they were blood relatives to the very tree at Choqóux Aqóum in whose "fire" Time was dreamt into the flowering of matter and everyday reality. These diviners were Trees, not people.

There seems to always be a way and deep desire for these kinds of seeds of understanding to keep alive their meanings and what they grow. They keep themselves living through the ecstatic nature of the Indigenous Soul that resides deep inside all people. Visibly evident in some people beyond modern society's incapacity to even want them, the seeds seemed to always find a way to return, ornately thriving even in the most spiritually depleted ground and cultural surroundings.

Our hearts finally quiet with thinking, Chiv and I watched the afternoon shade walk toward the old tzejtel tree newly returned as a youth from the body of his own self at Choqóux Aqóum until it covered us all and stars hung in his branches overhead and the incense embers glowed their last.

An entire night of sleepless, foodless ritual lay before us down in the *cofradias* of the village, whose scattered smoking diesel-oil lamps flared orange and bare electric bulbs stretched out twinkling beneath us like the Milky Way above. We rose, stretching and standing up into the fragrant layer of cooking fire smoke and food, creeping up the hill, our stomachs rumbling as we picked our silhouetted way through the murky humid air of the highland evening, back to the murmur of the ever-restless human world and away from the timeless Time-dreaming tree of Choqóux Aqóum.

Chapter 7

The Frenchman Gets "Everything"

When the last candle had burned itself to the floor, our last wafer of *pōm* resin had smoldered into the last of the night's embers, and its smoke in spirals and puffs had carried our final prayer off into the face of the Father Sun just sprouting into dawn, Old Chiviliu and I trudged the remaining up-and-down trails that crisscrossed the steep viny basaltic cliffs of the ravine behind Pch'ijul, the more arduous shortcut from the north quarter of Xechivoy bypassing the main village so as to avoid the inevitable string of good-hearted chatty ambushes from ever-interested friends and family heading toward their canoes to paddle off to work or blinking fishermen returning from a night on the water. It was well past midmorning when the two of us, swollen-eyed, dry-mouthed, fatigued, and more than hungry, slumped onto the deep-colored, use-burnished benches that lined the west wall of the old man's Sacred House.

After three days of tramping back into cave shrines, up into hill shrines, and back down into the town to await our turn in shaman-crowded Cofradias and Sacred Houses, the promise of toasted dried *cúljá* fish broken into a sauce of ground tomatoes with black chiles, *tújá* corn cakes, and the welcome familiarity of the hard benches, the smoky darkness, the pine-needled floor, the orchid-covered altar, and the huge old toothy dried fish swimming in figure eights as it swung suspended under the ceiling beams in the cool morning breeze felt like a flight clean through heaven.

Happy for food and knowing by our noses that the granddaughters were bringing it carefully from Yakix's side-house kitchen, we were not daring to budge until they came through so as not to endanger any remaining spark of energy we would need for chewing, when an impatient human chatter, an uproar in a language neither Mayan nor Spanish, was heard loudly making its way past the main compound entrance.

Still kneeling over the last tortilla on the griddle of her cooking fire, Yakix moved up and out to drive off the intruders with the able diplomacy of courteous pleading for which she was known and one that had become a daily custom for her when dealing with the next set of never-ending clients hoping for Chiviliu's famous spiritual ability to feed whatever Holy Being needed feeding in order to alleviate a sickness or some misfortune in their lives.

In her eternal dedication to protect her old man from death by the inevitable overwork that went with his career on behalf of the people, Yakix's very convincing iron-gripped insistence and sweet tongue usually worked well enough to get the old man at least one meal and a short nap before the hordes worked their way in to drag him off again. Though in his early nineties, it was by his constant motion in ritual on behalf of the suffering that had made him famous, wealthy, and well loved, but rest would forever be a foreign luxury for him. Nonetheless most Indians would wait patiently for days if need be, once Yakix had explained how they had to let him recover from his superhuman efforts.

But this noisy bunch out in the courtyard, whoever they were, still unseen by us, forcibly swam through her net of sensible suggestions, completely disregarding her courteous petitions to return the following morning.

And soon enough in they barged, Yakix indignantly chattering into the middle of their gigantic backs, like a desperate mother squirrel whose children were about to be eaten by an avaricious team of unimpressed weasels.

And there they stood: big, pale, and steaming, five tourists in their mid-twenties with almost matching tee shirts with very serious meaningful looks on their faces.

The three boys all had their hands in their pockets except for one big long-haired fellow who kept a flattened French cigarette fiercely puffing with his right hand, while the two girls stood sideways with long hair and angry eyes. In the otherwise relaxing incense smoke and cool murky candlelight of the windowless room, they swayed there in a bare three seconds of long, hard-faced, blinking silence. The old fish swayed with them over their heads in the rush of air they brought in with their rude intrusion.

Since they obviously hadn't understood Yakix, and Chiv himself couldn't figure out what they were saying, the old lady and Chiv, in accord with the accepted village opinion that maintained all pale, non-Spanish speaking outsiders probably spoke one dialect or another of the same language worldwide, both looked at me hopefully, implying that I should step in and convince these people in their own native jargon to come back later so we could finally eat and get some sleep. While I was too exhausted and hungry to play games with spoiled overfed white kids, I was also too exhausted to properly despise them as much as I should have, and definitely way too tired to care if they watched us eat.

In that instant Old Chiv, understanding my reluctance, proceeded in what I initially mistook for an application of the old adage upon which a lot of natural peoples worldwide still rely, "Well, if you can't drive 'em off, and can't kill 'em, then sell 'em something!" and comforting Yakix only gradually succeeded in convincing her to leave it all to us. Then giving the invaders a quick once-over he rose up like the old glaze-eyed gorilla he was, greeted them all one by one in his very best antiquated Spanish with an eerie overacted tone that too accurately imitated a "white" man's phony business-meeting enthusiasm, with the requisite shaking of hands and all. He refused our "guests" the great organic depth and eloquent language of his customary dignity, which I would grow to discover during my years with him was something reserved for the dignified.

Yakix, muttering and shaking her head in disgust over her rare defeat, was finally humored as well, especially when Chiv began arranging five tiny hand-carved man stools in a semicircle in front of our bench as if these people were visiting relatives preparing to eat with us, which I know we were both hoping they would accept and follow so *we* could eat.

Most of these tall people were good enough to try sitting on the tiny stools, which pretty much disappeared under their luxurious non-Indian bottoms. Even seated they were still at eye level with Chiv standing. All of which set up a loud giggling from the ever-present peanut gallery of incurably curious little Tzutujil kids piled on top of each other to peer around the door, who, unable to contain themselves, finally tumbled to the ground rolling and writhing in a loud surge of liquid mirth that forced Chiv to keep lighting his empty pipe, biting down hard on the stem to divert the hilarity rising in all our bellies from maturing into a general uncontrollable belly laugh—all of which sent Yakix grinning back to her cooking hut.

To keep us all from laughing ourselves to death the old bluffer feigned great indignity at the increasing mob of kids swarming to the door to get a glimpse of what the others found so funny, and with a wave of his impressive hand ordered the urchins to scatter, which had hardly any effect at all.

The biggest visitor, the man with the long thick chestnut hair loosely fastened down his back with a rubber band, sideburns, jowls, a decent nose, and some serious grudge it seemed, wouldn't sit. He just stood and smoked, avoiding all eye contact with me, which I took for good Tzutujil manners but which panned out to be his own brand of hatred. Alain, as he was called, was a big French boy, and he was their spokesman and was not prepared to present his case sitting down.

The air was tense, and these people wanted us to give them our undivided attention, but in a village like this one you always fed the people before you talked, and we were really hungry.

Of the other two boys, one was a Belgian South African, and the other fellow and girls were all English-speaking Americans. Yakix and Chiv's granddaughters had begun to bring in clay coffee mugs of Chiv's homegrown coffee for the "guests," but they didn't want coffee, and they didn't want beer, which Chiv also offered personally; they just wanted what they wanted.

Since they would neither eat nor drink what Chiv's household was offering, this meant neither Chiv nor I could, in any stretch of Tzutujil etiquette, proceed to eat alone without them. That would have been an unthinkable breach of our own dignity, so we stayed hungry.

Realizing we would just have to push through for a while longer on empty stomachs, I acquiesced to translate for Chiv, knowing this detour was probably the shortest distance between them leaving and us eating. Because their Spanish was worse than their manners, and my mother's French was overly thick with Canadian *patois* and unacceptable to the six-and-a-half-foot French giant, I translated Chiv's Tzutujil into American English for them and their English into Tzutujil for Chiv.

What Alain and his seated companions had come for, as he explained with a lot of hound-dog-like eyebrow liftings and such, was instruction from Chiviliu in order to complete their already extensive training as shamans!

"We want to learn everything this Martín person has gotten from you," he said, and then went on to mentally read off a long list of credentials, teachers, trainers, shamans, and contemporary authors whose names were intended to impress Chiviliu and convince him of the "advanced" eligibility of each of them on their own and to show how this fellow Martín was really second-rate and definitely not as prepared as they were to receive the bounty of what Chiv, obviously for lack of better students, was wasting on the likes of me.

Their "credentials" were in short a lengthy roster of how many huts, tents, houses, and conferences they had sat in with Khosas, Zulus, Guaranis, Shapibos, Ayamaras, Koreans, Dayaks, Navajos, Hopi, and others, but especially a Huichol shaman with whom they had repeatedly "sat in" taking peyote, not to mention all of the mushroom and ayahuasca rituals in which they had ever participated worldwide.

Nodding in great admiration as usual, Chiv could not, actually, recall ever having heard of any of these places, people or "rituals," or substances, but he nonetheless listened, smoking, patient and hungry, while I, starving, slit-eyed, exhausted, disgusted, and befuddled as to why we needed to humor these spoiled children, nonetheless mumbled my best translations into his more enduring ear.

These strange pushy young people were in search of a place they could buy or mine supernatural power as if it were a fuel source instead of a burden of responsibility that was divinely bestowed on those with the grace and bearing strong enough to not disappoint the powers they served. They were precursors of what would become over the next two decades a veritable part of the New Age and eco-tourist industry for tribes and villages throughout the world, where certain individuals less scrupulous than Chiviliu could make a good cash living turning out very serious bundle-toting "student" shamans from modern city suburbs, with none of the cultural and natural context in their bones. Atitlán would certainly get its share of these types later on once the self-sufficiency and renewability of their own antique ritual methods of farming and fishing, regional inter-village marketing, and traditional ritual feeding of the Holy in the Seeds that made them sprout and the animals to multiply and stay healthy had been successfully undermined by the outside world, and people dependent on the new imported money accumulation credit economy of every type of invader had taken over; people desperately needing cash to survive in that confusion would sell anything including empty performances of spiritual traditions they no longer maintained or truly comprehended.

But then this was something new to us and the first time either Chiviliu or I had come face to face with these types of people. Apparently vacationing around Atitlán for a time, they had been startled to see a singular blond person like myself suddenly appearing in the crowd of annually appointed Mayan men and women, all of us dressed with the finery of our various appointed positions in service to feeding the Holy in the Seed. The village hierarchy of men and women were a magnificent sight to be true. But these visitors mistook their fleeting glimpse of my semi-cloistered presence in this ceremonial beauty for some kind of shamanistic training course for which they could just sign up!

Most certainly these people and others like them were attracted to some very real indigenous intactness for which their own souls achingly yearned, but their overly domesticated mind's spoiled personalities and spiritually starved upbringings did not serve their aching souls. And in their jealous desire they damaged the very thing they desired by desiring it. Instead of courting what their real being loved, their untamed conquering minds would simply take it. But like a woman abducted who cannot be made to love her kidnapper, the great beauty they desired would die if dragged away by force.

Like jealous suburban house terriers longing again to become wolves from a legitimate motivation of ancestral memory, who could only tragically end up killing everything natural and each other in this untutored feral attempt, these children could not see the immensity of the even bigger cultural beauty to which the small fraction they perceived one afternoon belonged. But what they couldn't know was that immensity did not actually get to parade around much in beautiful clothing. It was a life of hard, mostly unseen service. But the villagers were always beautiful, and in that they did so to feed the Holy. What villagers did in just living was where the real beauty of life kept itself: how even people with no finery at all walked, or how they spoke their antique magnificent seed speech to the ground, each other, and the plants that fed them, or even the unseen everyday things they did in service to that grand event of Divine Time in motion that had given them their corn and short hard lives. What these outsiders had perceived one day while I happened to be marching flute-playing was just the smallest whiff of a people in love with something that the world those children came from was in full outward flight away from. But shamanism in this town didn't have any fancy clothes, and was actually even meaningless and useless without the regular planting, fishing, and baby-chasing of everyday people whose ornate comprehensions gave real gifts to the Holy. These youths' Indigenous Souls were aching for life, tribe, and meaning, but without the grief-filled remembrance of an intact Indigenous Soul and mind they approached this longing with an inherited mind-set not their own, a mind-set responsible for the demise of the very intactness they desired, a mind-set not capable of seeing that its "wanting" was a type of greed through conquest. Nonetheless these poor, would-be dangerous, power-desiring children were intent, very demanding, and totally oblivious to the incredible mental and physical endurances one needed to keep a sense of humor in the face of our daily failures as shamans when constantly trying to very faithfully but not always successfully heal one condition or the next. They were especially numb to any evidence of the stress we experienced by their presence, in particular our saggy sleep-deprived faces and the rumbling of our very hungry bellies.

But Chiv, of course, inhabited by something bigger than his human self, would never pass up an opportunity to serve his Gods, and after listening politely for the third time to my translation of what this humorless bunch wanted—"To learn what Martín knows. We want everything!"—Chiv finally sat back, relit his reeking deer-headed pipe with the glowing eyes, pursed his big old monkey lips, and traveled off into the wild rainy thicket of his mercurial mind. Then suddenly, staring off to the left toward his flowery altar heavily populated with covered deities, stiffened in a gaze fierce like an elf owl just before snatching a bird three times his size and weight, Chiv clicked his lips and, relaxing, looked down,

"Well, I guess we have to give it to them!" he said to me in a quiet resigned tone.

"Give them what, Father?" I mumbled back, staring in amazement. Grinning at my newly animated face changing from boredom and contempt into a sudden wide-eyed baffled new interest, Chiviliu declared even more emphatically:

"Just look at the size of that *mos;* aren't you scared of him? He scares me. I think we'd be better off giving him *Everything!*" I gaped incredulously at the old man, "Everything?!"

"Heya, yep, Everything. What can you do? We have no other choice. Let's give them Everything."

And while I sat there tingling awake, dumbfounded and forgetting to breathe, Chiv, like a tapir pushing himself to his sturdy legs out of a favorite mud wallow, his grand old-time sacred headcloth dangling loose around his tough, ninety-one-year-old, iguana-like neck, rose and shuffled off past the reed-covered doorway, ducking under its low beam at the south end of the hall which led into his famous oversized granary.

Alain asked me what Chiv and I had been discussing and why Chiv had left to the other chamber. "He says we have to give you what you asked for, we have to give you Everything."

A lot of animal-like snuffing, grunting, and rustling around resembling the thrashing of a giant raccoon who after hissing, romping, and thumping about, let out some minor expletives, then the telltale grinding sound of somebody shifting big pottery cooking tubs, too heavy for a single human to safely budge, came echoing into the Sacred House to warm a little the cold, well-trained stiffness and silence these spiritually hungry shaman tourists kept up.

After hearing Chiviliu's victory trumpet, always a lot like the sound of a happy baby elephant, Alain, unable to contain himself, blurted out, "You know, you really have no right to be in this village. You're messing up their traditions!"

The Americans concurred, nodding knowingly.

I was finally old enough to know better than try to catch a cannonball fired straight at you, and just like Chiv probably would have done, I nodded in complete agreement. When the intended heat of his comment had settled back a bit, I replied in good Prechtelian form,

"Maybe if you got around to telling Chiviliu about this, he will finally let me go back to painting like I was when he found me, and I wouldn't have to carry all his stuff around all the time."

But Old Chiv saved us from our quarrel, reappearing brandishing a fat opalescent kernel-filled-ear of corn of the type called *tújá*. From the sound he must have laboriously retrieved this live jewel of seed corn from thousands of ears in the matrix of the granary mosaic, the kind old-timers always used to lay the corn in to keep the Mother happy by arranging the different colored butts of full ears in a wall of stacked corns of varying type and colors until there were four walls of corn-ear mosaic adorning all four sides. Their Seed House! These rooms were sacred, and no arguing was allowed in there for fear of terrifying the Mother corn's "placental" heart, which would flee terrified and abused by the sound. Arguing sterilized the viability of the seeds to sprout and removed the nutrition of the ears who are of course her body's children and our lives and food.

Holding the then rare but now extinct ear in both hands, he kissed Her and held Her up to me. I did the same, making the incantation everybody always says to the ear, "*Utz nkatzä a chi, Utz nkatzä a wach tie,*" "It's good to see your mouth, good to see your face, Mother."

Then turning on his heels, almost falling over, Chiv pressed the beautiful full ear to the still-standing Frenchman's lips, hoping he'd put his breath on Her and kiss Her as we always do; and when he didn't, he pushed Her into his big soft hands.

"Does this mean you accept me as your student?" the Frenchman, sounding almost friendly for the first time, asked Chiv.

"No, we're giving you Everything you asked for instead," Chiv replied, sitting again, motioning for me to translate.

"What does the corn mean?"

"It doesn't *mean* anything. It's Everything!" Chiv spoke leaning back, lighting up his pipe again.

"I don't understand," one of the girls finally spoke, jumping up to join the huddle of tourists staring at the corn around Alain, "What's Everything?"

"That's Everything!" Chiv replied again, this time spitting on the floor after blowing out a blue smoke ring.

"This is corn, what's that have to do with Everything?"

"That's the trouble with 'Everything,'" Chiv apologized, "You can't 'know' Everything much less understand its mind. Our heads are not big enough for it to lie there by itself, but that doesn't mean just because you don't understand Everything that you can't hold Everything in your hands."

"Look, Old Man, we didn't come here for your riddles—we can get corn anywhere. We came here to learn to become shamans like you! We want to learn everything you can teach us like Martín is doing," Alain explained.

"For that reason exactly, and you already have a good hold on it," Chiv explained back to him as I sought to keep up translating while engrossed. "Everything this poor orphan Martín knows and what he still needs to learn is in your hand right there. Thank you for coming, send your relations my blessing—would you like some coffee, a beer, or maybe something to eat before you go?"

"What do you mean?" Ignoring the food offer, Alain ploughed forward, "Is this how you begin teaching? What do I have a hold of?"

Finally looking disgusted, Chiv took the ear back out of the French-man's hand, kissed Her, and put Her into one of the million pockets of his old *paquan*. He sat up, took a couple of breaths, and pointing with his long old tobacco-stained fingers and nails, began in a little fiercer tonality:

"All right then, listen now, man! What you need to do if you would court me, to convince me, Nicolas Chiviliu Tacaxoy, to even want to teach you in the first place, was just a moment ago in your hand, which I will give back to you if you want to try.

"Everything is in the seeds. Everything! Listen! Take the seeds off the cob; rent some land after asking around our village what side of which volcano this kind of Mother Corn could be planted in order for her to thrive, and ask around the village what time of year this particular old-time corn needs planting. Get your *maxuina*, your foot-plow, your hoe, your *icaj,* the big ax, your machete, your heavy rope, your forehead tumpline strap; clear the land properly; learn which trees to leave in the corners for the field guardians to sit in their cloud thrones; stack and slash, burn it without killing the volcano forest or yourself; carry down on your back the bigger wood, branched and peeled, to make corner trees for your new hut; cut the branches for firewood; haul it already split and tied on your back with your tumpline. Learn to pray for this, and where to pray for that. Make rope from maguey fiber by cutting the blades, washing the fiber in the Mother Lake; split it with glass spikes; scrape it; tie the fibers to your big toe, and make strong cord of maybe thirteen arm-lengths; measure the field in fourths with this; learn to tie string bags of corn sacks made from the measuring string in a size that fits only you.

"Pray like all the regular people; learn from farmers how to ask the seeds that one special evening at just the right time of year if the seeds are willing to 'perish' by being planted, dying for the appearance of humans, to die for your dreams of eating again; wait for a dream in which She, the Mother of Life, comes to you weeping and says it's okay to pro-ceed, then go plant like the men show you but only after making the offer-ings in all the corners, the right offerings! Any regular person can tell you this. Learn from the other people who plant, anyone can show you what to give the sprouts when their little heads first "dawn" out of the Holy Earth. Because of course, the Father Sun at dawn is a corn sprout. That's a big thing right there; it's the same as when the sun rose for the first time, or the first time you ever saw the sunrise, or the first day the child of a mother crowns her baby's head into view. The Sun Father, the children, the sprouting of the corn, are all the same thing. Learn to live in your little field, guarding it against hungry coatimundis, peccaries, parrots, *quel* birds, all birds, monkeys, deer, rabbits, squirrels, gophers, tepesquintles, marauding bad human neighbors, hard wind, hail, too-hard rain, or no rain; pray for rain; if still no rain comes, haul water on your back to the plants; don't let them die.

"Learn to cut the last leaves at the unripe cornstalk's base without damaging the plant, give them to women so they can wrap their *subáán tamalitos*. Watch, worry, and then break each stalk back below the last fully formed ears.

"Don't eat any green ears until you have a big enough cornfield to have the luxury, for you need to make seeds.

"When the ears are dry, the stalks dead and drooping, pull the ears and put them gently into your string net bag, tie your tumpline on, lift it to your back with the tumpline over your forehead, start trotting home bent forward, never stop, watch ahead for snakes, have your women and children swing their incense burners under the net to welcome the corn's ten-mile return, and welcome Her new face back into Her freshly swept and blessed granary, which you will have already built.

"Go back the following year, use the same seed, the same methods, the same prayers, but in a new spot—and plant all the corn from the seeds you now have and do this for three years or more of annual replanting until you have enough of this very corn to bring back to my family, sufficient corn to feed myself, my wife, and my last orphan grandson for just six months. We usually eat and share at our fire at least thirty to fifty pounds of dry corn a week to make *joq' subáán, patin, lej, gór aj, buaq'*. To feed us six months, return ten *quintales* [1,000 pounds], that you alone have grown from this beautiful little corn ear.

"If you, Sir, can take this little Holy cob of *tújá* corn and convince Her with ritual, hard work, more hard work, learning from the regular farming Tzutujil and with patience learn to grow and multiply them into 1,000 pounds of corn for my family, then I will teach you whatever you want. But let me tell you, if you have been able to do this the way I say without once bothering me about it, then you will know Everything that this Martín knows already. So, what more could I teach you?

"If you don't do this then don't come around here any more."

And retrieving the pretty little ear of corn from his bottomless pocket, Chiv shook the French boy's hand with both of his, leaving the man's hand holding the corn again.

"So, we thank you for your visit. When you've finished growing enough, please come again; otherwise do well with whatever you do in life. *Adiós.*"

Chiv, already seated again when I'd finished translating, watched Alain who, not comprehending and feeling mocked instead of honored, and unaccustomed to not getting what he wanted by force of his parent-taught superiority, clenched his molars and in a silent shaking lip-curling rage hurled the ear of amber corn square into the north wall of Chiv's Sacred House. He stomped off, his broad shoulders swaying like a Jamaican model, head moving side to side, one arm gesticulating, swearing in French, his unsure partners in tow; he took to the sharp cinder-covered basaltic shelves and cobbles of Pch'ijul never to be seen again, at least not by us.

Though notoriously hard, and therefore prized for being practically impenetrable to the greedy gnashing teeth of rodents and any number of weevils, moths, grubs, or worms that annually reduced people's corn stores to dust, the kernels of this rare famous corn, once dried, were set very loosely on this mother cob, and when this one hit the wall it exploded like amber shrapnel, bouncing from one wall to the next, until its life-giving kernels settled chittering and rattling throughout the Sacred House, restless like a rainstorm on the roof, until finally calmed and counseled they all lay still, spread evenly throughout the old mud and lime floor.

We all wanted to laugh really hard, but there was nothing really happy about it, excepting maybe we would finally get to eat.

Besides the huge insult of treating any corn that way, the anxiety all villagers felt about leaving the kernels of the heart of the Holy Mother "whose ears are Everything" lying about neglected, unfed, with no special place, position or intentional function, forced us to postpone our eating again until Chiv and I with all the little giggling children got on our hands and knees and gathered up every Holy grain, excepting a couple that Chiv's roaming chickens swallowed before we could rescue them.

Then in a huddle, Old Chiv, the little kids, and myself poured all our grains into his outspread headcloth, which he in turn transferred to and knotted into a little bundle into one of the tasseled corners of my own headcloth. He gave them to me and said, "Plant them whenever you get around to it, because they are Everything and you have a lot to learn about that! *Jo' nko wa'a*, let's eat!!"

Chiv trumpeted that the coast was clear. Yakix and Chiv's great-granddaughters, who had been waiting at the doorway all along, instantly appeared bearing food and with us ate till we could laugh again.

I replanted and replanted that knot of seeds over and again and held them as long as the world would let me. Though all those seeds were later lost to the village, in one way or another, with the reverence of both hands I hold them still.

Chapter 8

Checkmated by My Love

The greatest and most renown Tzutujil *Ajcun* shaman of his time, Nicolas "A Clash" Chiviliu Tacaxoy's life had spanned pretty much an entire century, wherein he had served twelve times as priest of Holy Boy, ten times as village headman for the entire Hierarchy council, and at least eight times as Headman of seven different Sacred Houses; he was prominently remembered by both allies and enemies for his infamous struggle in various non-sympathetic religious and political ages and climates to keep legal and alive Tzutujil spiritual custom in service to the complex ritual cycle upon which all traditional life depended.

At those strange junctures of difficult times experienced by the village when either powerful outside religious figures, anti-Indian government policies, or bizarre combinations of them all purloined or commandeered at gunpoint various Sacred "objects," Chiv was in the middle of it all. In the 1950s, when soldiers of Arbenz confiscated Holy Boy and his representatives, imprisoning both the God and his priests, ordering the people to desist from their "backward-looking" customs, Chiviliu would mysteriously gain a reprieve for the village through some unlikely friendships and allies that, unbeknownst to the people, he'd made in certain government circles and among some normally unsympathetic Protestant converts who, though they also thoroughly detested the same "harmful misguided Native ritual beliefs," hated the Catholics even more. Chiv somehow secured higher-up governmental reprieve for freedom of religious activity from the new socialist regime that was soon to tumble. Except in two cases, even the sacred "objects" in question were secretly returned or released back to the village hierarchy.

Although recognized for his clout with both the spirits and the political forces of his day, his legendary creative fire and cleverness had backfired in more than a couple of instances, causing in one case the eighteen-month imprisonment of all the shamans of the Lake Atitlán region, some one hundred and forty individuals.

But then on his own he mysteriously secured the release of all his colleagues by some magical ruse, in which according to a thousand versions of the legend, his imprisoned form was assumed by "Holy Boy" who himself remained in the prison grounds as an alternate appearance of Chiv's presence, making it possible for the real Chiv to meanwhile reportedly drive back alone eighty beef cows to the old medieval-looking Solola prison facility to feed his peers and the guards, accompanied by an "official" writ from Guatemala's president of the day exonerating the entire body of shamans accused of "mass witchcraft against the State."

But even then while incarcerated, huge losses had occurred to the great "Heart of Food and Water Bundle" in the form of many seed fetishes that were never found again and for whose most important loss Chiviliu never stopped grieving, pursuing every vague clue of their whereabouts for the remainder of his days. Till the day he died, Chiviliu never gave up hope and charged me with following up on any leads or rumors regarding the whereabouts of those "objects" that had disappeared decades earlier about whose loss he felt strangely responsible. As he'd been the presiding leader of those particular Sacred Houses at the time they were stolen, there were foolish converts who spun rumors that Chiv himself had sold them to collectors.

Despite my heroic pursuit to find the "objects" in my desperate desire to redeem Chiv's innocence before his death by coming up with any or all of these revered tribal "Seed Hearts" as they were called, except in the case of one ridiculously complicated return of what turned out to be a practically insignificant stolen "relic" from a European museum, I utterly failed to vindicate the old man in the end.

But in keeping with the inborn flash of his unkillable heart he also made sure I understood that what he grieved even more than that was not so much the losses of those "Holy Objects" but the loss of people wanting what these so-called objects meant; their spiritual understanding of the incredible mythological epics that their tangible presence embodied as delicious ritual abbreviations to feed the Divine in the Seed, as these ritual ceremonies unfolded through their annual staggered "flowerings" of Time.

Like all the other women and men of his type and generation, he sighed eternally for the loss of these stolen beings' place in the cyclic regeneration of the power of growth of plants and animals, upon whose generous deaths at the harvests and butchering all human existence has always been utterly dependent. Though the things stolen were sacred, they were not deities in themselves but "thrones" like my seed-eyed beings, only that they were tribal, not private. These thrones were the "sitting place" for Time Deities: complex details of each year's ritual, Deified, where the other half of reality made the half we live in with all its plants, animals, earth, suns, moons, stars, water, and so on, continually revived. They were the same beings as in the big mythological stories, but through the presence of the thrones they could be directly addressed like ancient relatives, given Feasts of offerings, tangibly danced with and adorned. The people bemoaned their loss more as a sign that as a people they were, as they put it, "finally losing their seeds." Because what had been stolen were the seeds of their way of being: small things that held big life-giving knowledge whose presence was a ritual antidote to the ever-present threat of the village's spiritual amnesia. They were a kind of visible rosary that helped us to not forget how to do all those ancient things, a kind of memory device that made what those "Holy Things" were sprout again ritually into view every year, a complex of rituals that fed the powers behind our food-growing plants. They were the spiritual DNA of the village that made the Divine in the Seed of all food live by being "re-membered." Spiritual forgetting killed the possibilities of the Food growing. "Losing the seeds" meant losing the ritual and the way of life of living by and as seeds.

The knowledge of "what came next" ceremonially in the annual ritual embodiment of that old mythology had always been the highly respected burden of the village hierarchy of village men and women who had spent their entire lives over and over, annually learning by doing under the previous hierarchy until all the sequences needed for the ceremonial feeding of life were involuntarily pulsing in their bones. They knew whatever divine understanding these stolen "objects" housed on their ritual thrones need not disappear with the "thrones," but they seemed to have fled right along with them.

What Chiv and the entire body of village hierarchy, men and women, mourned so deeply was not so much that these deified tools of anti-amnesia had been stolen, or even that the people at large, the regular people they had always served by themselves serving what sat on these thrones that caused everyone in the village and things that fed them to flourish, but that these villagers had apparently succumbed to the outside amnesia of modernity. Every villager's former unanimous respect for this immense ritual understanding even though they didn't one hundred percent comprehend it all, leaving that long learning to the ritual specialists, it was the reality that these "thrones" *could be* stolen that devastated the old people. Not what was stolen.

Though very secreted and cleverly guarded and rarely described except during the deepest ritual context, the opportunity to steal them had always been there, but it had never been an issue. Only people who had no comprehension of the magnificent, however delicate, net of interdependency this Tzutujil method of "keeping the seeds alive" contained for the world and their people would even want such a thing. Anyone who would want to steal them, to sell them to a collection somewhere, removing the ritual throne for the Divine Seed of Time away from the people's ceremonial feast, was heedless of the fact they were shredding and unanchoring the entire universe that gave even the thief life. That there might actually exist people who were antipathetic to "keeping the seeds alive" was like a devastating earthquake in the souls of the traditionalists.

When this first happened, of course, all the old people and younger traditionalists bitterly surmised, since what they considered human culture was ritually "keeping the seeds alive," that these events signified their own culture might be on its way out. With no one to continue living it, it would become something objectively surveyed instead of actually lived. It would only be a matter of time before the husk of the ritual life: its "material culture," the clothing and paraphernalia, would be appropriated and dribble away into meaningless frozen forms in collectors' cases, documentary films in the vaults of museums or books on the conjectured past, no longer capable of understanding time and the earth in its living "sprouted seed" form of the annual ceremonialism within everyday farming Mayan life.

After I had been his ritual helper for several years, and by the time he came visiting my two little stone huts precariously embedded in the orchid-covered cliff overlooking the fisherman's canoe bay of Xechívoy, to announce he would die the following day, Chiviliu no longer had any doubts that the spiritual culture he had spent his life living, the culture that served and ritually fed the Holy Mother in the Seed and her tree of visionary time of the flowering earth's own annual complex cycles, renewable seasons, their fruits, deaths, and rebirths, had already been virtually strangled by an insidious invasion of a non-comprehending mentality that looked *at* things, collected them, but could never *be* what they saw. Like the seeds in previous creations spiritually heading away from present time to cloister themselves back into the "Rock," the cultural knowledge seeds of this spiritual culture were already preparing to wait out this next node of "dead time" on the stalk of life. Until a renewed earth could relight and reflower itself alive again, our capacity with this spiritual brilliance would live inside all of us as a living earth, but out of reach of the modern mind in the refugeed existence of the depth of our Indigenous Soul.

In other words, what "religious things" had been stolen could never have been stolen in the past because they were not stealable objects but "deified comprehensions": comprehensions that lived inside us and all around us. As soon as the commercial minds of Euro-American civilization came from an outside world ruled by its own pain of having lost their seeds a long time back, the stunned existence they were living infected the mind on contact, causing the indigenous part to evacuate. What was for a traditional Tzutujil mind an impossible thing to even think or say, a thought introduced through the increased presence of missionaries of modern life methods, business, and business-oriented one-God religions, the objectification of "matter" as a thing, including plants, food, animals, clothing, and so forth, made all these living beings into exploitable soulless objects instead of powerfully necessary tangible spiritual synapses in the spinal chord of the Human position as part of all nature. A real Human of this sort was not unwelcome on the Earth. But the strange-stare-of-the-dead-matter-mind that was now coming in on them made the people into enemies with their own personal Indigenous Souls.

Chiv mourned his culture's growing inability to make more of its natural self and keep the seeds alive no matter how many "objects" went missing. On the other hand, if they *could* be stolen and stayed stolen, and the living mythic story disappeared unstruggling as it left along with the "object," then the comprehensions the objects held no longer existed as a renewable viable seed! The stolen thrones were not symbols either, but tangible, living, literal, ritually alive places where these deified comprehensions, as life-giving Time, could live, feast, rest, and flourish.

He didn't order me to merely "carry" a bundle to safety, or just retrieve lost relics. What he wanted me to do was swear I would "keep the seeds alive" after he died; to keep alive these comprehensions as "seeds," and comprehensions of the seed nature of Time and the Divine in its diversity. He hoped he had planted it all deep enough in my heart for me to continue "cultivating" the seeds and plants without the Tzutujil culture somehow, bundles or no bundles. He wanted me to keep the "spiritual" *Ruk'ux,* or Heart, the spiritual DNA, alive in these cultural seeds and so as to possibly regrow real Human culture again in an unspecified time from those "seeds" but certainly well beyond either of our eras. The idea was to continue replanting the "seeds" in the land that brought that mind of discomprehension. Since for shamans the bodies of people were the Earth Herself, we should replant the Earth Bodies of those who'd "lost their seeds" and couldn't remember how to be on the Earth, or in their Earth Bodies anymore. Their land, the territory of their culture, he surmised must have suffered the same effects that they now promoted from their own experience of some earlier invasion of their own ancient village mind by some other harsh forgetful culture. My job was to live with these people but not lose my capacity to keep the seeds alive with no people of the village to back me up. This meant returning to the U.S., he said. How could I possibly keep it all alive in that environment?

"Do not be prejudiced against the form these seeds end up having to assume, Ma Martín. As all seeds, plants, and people do, they may have to alter their forms to survive the climate in which both of you find yourselves," he said.

Instead of sending the "seeds" into the Rock at Cuchumaquic, Chiv wanted to see if we could keep these seeds alive in a more nomadic, non-static way: by planting them inside the living heart of people living in a destructive culture. This way no matter how far the "seeds" wandered, a person could carry the seeds to replant them wherever that heart might land. Wherever they grew, however they grew, something would survive the spiritual destruction at hand.

Real spiritual treasures could not be actually stolen, but they most certainly can be forgotten, and in the case of seeds being equal to a people's culture, this would cause them to lose their vitality unless someone could somehow remember them back to life in some new living way. Knowledge and culture, like seeds, lose their viability after a while and must be recultivated, or they will disappear. The "seeds," like the comprehensions, were nothing if not kept alive by continual cyclic replanting to grow into adult seed-making plants of comprehensions. They could not be kept alive by simply storing them away indefinitely like preserved objects in a museum. People are always saying they write things down so as to remember them, but in reality, they do so only to ensure they themselves don't have to remember. When knowledge is lost as a culture lived and exists only in written form, it has an identical fate with seeds kept unplanted in a jar: someday they will forget how to be the living thing they're meant to be, even if planted; they both lose their viability.

The core principles of how to feed the Holy that Chiv worried so much about and wanted me to keep alive, as implausible as that was, were the organic tangible fruitings on the stalk of living Time called life, and would become as useless as more sacred texts without teachers and the living cultural context of their origins unless physically planted and lived out. But how could that be done by anyone without a village who knew, without an established Hierarchy, without the generations and regenerations it took to slowly maintain such comprehensions? Even a life lived in a village to feed one's family, the village and the Holy who feed us all with the sprouted seed, is a long, multigenerational, mostly limping effort that takes every square inch of heart, every extra calorie, and every human to even remotely maintain. How could I do it alone? It was impossible. But the old man was going to die, and he was that crazy old wild man, and it was a wonderful vision.

Chiv and I climbed up to the little summit behind my little cliff house and called to the last fingernail sliver of the sinking orange Father Sun to address him: "Don't forget about me, Old Chiviliu, and when you travel tomorrow morning, don't forget to gather up my *Ruk'ux*, my Seed Heart, my spirit at midday tomorrow and haul my *Ruk'ux* up into your string bag of time knotted with stars, take me to your Home and put me to good use." Sixteen hours before he died, Nicolas Chiviliu Tacaxoy told me that he had no idea how I would "keep the seeds alive" when he was gone. It was a total mystery to him, but to try anyway! Sitting together as the evening darkened over us together for the last time, he said over and over as if repetition would make it take better hold and make it happen that he was sure with what resourcefulness and knowledge that I already had tied "under my belt," that if anybody could figure out how to keep these seeds alive in the times coming it would be me. But then after a silence, he added as an afterthought in his rare whisper, "I know how you are, you are a purist, but watch out not to judge too narrowly the appearance of the fruit of the seed on its return, do not hate the seed for looking odd or different, or having a strange accent when it returns to you each time. Your only job is to figure out with the old-minded words and understandings how to keep the seeds alive. But don't do it here in Atitlán, because that will have equally disintegrated. Do it in the USA, in the modern world, in the place you came from! You have to promise to plant the seeds in the land that sent us the trouble. Then if the seeds take root there, then someday bring them back here, or if you too are gone, have your student deliver them to this place. Maybe the last generations living here to come can resprout themselves back into a village with the seed mind intact, maybe not. But now that this village has almost totally forgotten how to be its original self, what's to be lost by trying?"

The village was already starting to forget, looking and acting like rootless money-oriented, gizmo-dependent Americans, avaricious merchants, Ladinos, and other outside civilized people who could no longer see the world as anything but a resource, a prop for recreation, or an uncooperative headache of natural laws that needed taming to make it obey. But this, as bad as it seemed, would be nothing compared to the common experience of village death, violence, and rag-tag hand-me-down TV culture that would ensue at the onset of the nineties.

Well ... his last request was a dying man's last orders to me, and as absolutely impossible, grandiose, and unrealistic as it all was, I was checkmated by my love of him and our mutual love of the Divine in the Seed, and of course like the life-loving idiot I'd always been I promised to do everything I could, which I was certain would be very little.

Chapter 9

People as Seeds, Their Youth as Chocolate, the Dead Echoing Back to Life

On the afternoon of April 21, 1981, from the same floor, off the exact spot, where kneeling five years earlier Chiv and I had gathered up all the kernels of that rare yellow corn scattered by the angry Frenchman, Chiviliu himself was carefully retrieved like a heavy sack of precious seed by kneeling officials of the village hierarchy.

As he himself had predicted the previous day, around eleven o'clock the following morning during his daily ritual while he danced, his own seed bundle held always close to his chest like a swaddling baby, after spinning wildly around, one knee raised to his chin, the grand old man died in midair at the apex of a leap, crashing suddenly to the floor like a big felled tree in just the dramatic and blessed style he had always boasted he would leave.

From off that same tallow-encrusted, liquor-stained earthen floor of his own Sacred House beneath the swinging stuffed prehistoric toothy fish in front of his extensive altar, their sacred headcloths dangling long from their necks, misty eyed and in tandem, the younger members of the Ajauá raised him up like the heavy seed of life-giving echoes that he was, grunting from the spiritual weight of his increasing post-death worth. They placed him as a hub around which all the officials, holding the reed mat bed of *po⁻p*, gathered like a spoked wheel. For six hours the entire body of the men and women of the spiritual council waited, tightly crowding the hall around Old Chiv's inert body. Laying stretched and torqued a little sideways, his hand still clamped onto his bundle, like a dead hawk ground-wrecked by a deadly wind shear, his talons still locked onto a dead pigeon, the old people were unwilling to touch him or alter his position for fear of disturbing the deathlike trance from which he'd notoriously returned back to life off and on several times over the years.

It was dangerous to touch or move an unconscious person whose soul was traveling far into time, for then if even the tiniest detail were disturbed the traveler would be unable to find home again and would die, eternally searching for themselves.

But the people must have known that this time Old Chiv had really flown, for as the hours stretched on most of the women priestesses and half the men began weeping and wailing to help their colleague and friend into the open arms of the lords and ladies of Time, their equivalent hierarchy in the Universe. Chiv had finally died.

The initial mire of helplessness, confusion, heartbreak, desperation, rage, and unbearable bone-aching loneliness that one trips and falls into upon seeing what or who we love lying inert and dead oozed through the bodies and minds of that royal company, and every member eventually let loose an ocean of moans and wails; a gale of personal lament rose and fell in a concert that concentrically rippled out in waves throughout the hut-lined stone byways of the whole village and surrounding hamlets until the entire Tzutujil world was a murmuring symphony of genuine synchronized remembrance, tears, and praise. Because he'd been a passionate creative force, an outspoken living home for the voice of the Holies in Nature, often stating wild but necessary whimsies to be well-established tradition, and for having lived to the fullest, he had terrible unmoving enemies his entire life, but their silence or poisonous reviews at the news of his death were drowned out in the sound of the village grinding to a halt in an emotional tribute. It was not altogether a spontaneous untutored reaction but an ever-latent function of an ancient indigenous spiritual organ still intact inside the body of the tribe as a whole, whose obligatory function during these difficult nodes of life change and losses was to digest the substance of our loss fueled by the force of an ever-deepening grief, gradually and concertedly metabolically converting the vacuum of the space caused by a loss of such an incalculable worth into even more concentrated life-giving spiritual nutrition that renewed the everyday existence of the living world upon which the village future always depended. The dead who were admirable in life fed the living in their deaths.

The people knew that not only were they dependent on the generosity of animals and plants that regularly died to sustain them but that their own life cycles were relegated thereby to the same rules as followed by plants. Therefore when a person died they were known to have "fruited" and turned into seeds, to plant more of their worth in a time beyond their own, not in heaven, but as seeds to renew a continuation of the glory of the vitality of the living earth right here but in a time beyond their own, right now for the living. Sometimes when all went well, when any of us having lived faithful to the human obligation of becoming ritually and spiritually beautiful in a way that fed the Holy by our very living even in our beautiful failures, then the living world was actually bolstered by the ecstatic shape of an ecstatic echo caused by our passing.

Just as when a plant dies and sends her seed into the wind, the ground "eats" it and up sprouts the "echo" of the parent plant fresh and renewed to make more seeds and echoes. Thus a plant's life speaks its future back into life in echoes. The people would say, when any plants sown into the ground sprout after being planted, that *x él ki bi,* or "their sound returns." As far as the farming Tzutujil were concerned, when a person was lowered into the ground at their funeral, they were being sown by the village just like a corn seed in hopes that the person's spiritual *ruk'ux* or "germ" would sprout and echo life force back into the world. This echoing was not necessarily a reincarnation back into human form, for when a person's seed-worth sprouted or echoed, it would more likely become a great storm fish or a bank of cumulus clouds, rain, or winds or some kind of life-giving weather, not to mention whole ecosystems! This was not a metaphor but understood as the literal obligation of humans to make beautiful seed echoes by a kind of seed consciousness, a kind of sacred living that carried life farther along in a plant way. This made funerals into a kind of ritual gardening where deceased villagers very dramatically and simply could continue giving life to the world as a parallel plant person. Mayans have always been this.

Births and deaths were obviously dependent on each other; it was simply that they were on opposite sides of the echoing, and their rituals corresponded accordingly.

At the core of the ritual obligations of Birth and Death there were particular women who knew what to do. During pregnancy and birth, of course, it was the midwives and their associates who administrated, coaching not only the mother and catching the newborn baby, but also directing a radiating tangle of the baby's relations and honored villagers who always helped the mother and child by their positive presence, directing them in all the details of what the family's ritual obligations should be before, during, and after a birth. The welfare of mother and baby depended on the ornate nature of the beauty of the diverse rituals known only by the midwife that Humans supplied and the Holy demanded that during birth needed doing by different age sets, kinship, and genders in the family.

Likewise, ritual direction at the time of a death in a family was in the hands of a guild of mostly older women who after being properly "courted and called in" by the relatives led the campaign for the beauty during the funeral. Functioning for all intents and purposes as nothing less than midwives for the dead, these women made sure the full weight and power of the deceased's echo was fully received on the "other side."

Both types of midwives had to be women, one to bring the echo sprout in, the other to send its beauty echoing to feed the Holy. Both of their ritual careers depended largely on simple things: a special type of corn seed and a particular type of hand-spun native cotton thread, originally both very common and also very Holy.

The baby was called *jutay*, a "sprout," issuing from a seed heart, inside the Earth womb of the mother. The baby was the live effect of an echo returning back to this world sent by the Holy in Nature after bouncing off creative cliffs of the shores of Time. A baby born was a sound, a song, responding in the most wonderful tangible way back out of the ground from a place the human eye couldn't see.

Though the valuable substance of a dead person's body remained to feed and compost the welfare of the present, meeting with the divine digestion of the Lords and Ladies of Time—whose teeth of change are Holy Decay and whose eating gives life to the life-giving soil—the great beauty and energy of the soul released from the compost-bound body by Death was a power-filled echo, a responding Death-freshened echo, that returned the audial shape of its innate worth and authority back to the cliffs of the Mind of the Holy in nature, who added to and returned that same echo as the living sound in the shape of a new life sprouting back into our world.

To ensure to the best of Tzutujil ability that all of their people's magnified echoing and sprouting happened in a way that continued giving life to the world and the people, both birthing midwives and death midwives depended on three things equally. Because tangible life was understood ritually and the general ritual mind of the tribe understood tangibly lived life as the "clothing of time," something that gives Time a manifest physical form and a place to play itself out, by tribally "dressing" it, the ritual profession of both birthing midwives and the midwives for the dead depended on a type of hand-spun thread made of a native cotton, that technically speaking should never have been touched by metal during its cultivation or preparation into thread.

And because funerals were plantings and births were sproutings, human life lived was understood in terms of what plant sustained them most. Therefore both types of midwives depended equally on the seeds of a specific type of corn that every traditional family kept tucked up in the smoky rafters of their thatched huts for both births and deaths in the family.

And both also had to possess an equal capacity of memory of mythological tribal history, in which roll calls of ancestral descendants bottomed out attached to the Sun, Moon, the Earth, the clouds, and all the trees. This capacity of recall had to be carried on in an equal capacity for both types of midwives to eloquently speak all of this ancient continuum in such a seamless water-like flow that it could merge into the spinning of the cotton thread of the past into the cotton of now so as to ritually draw from the "fluffy matrix of the present" a thread that could "weave the cloth" that hung on the shoulders of Time and gave form to creation. The sparkling birds chattering, green grass growing, lake rippling, and wooded hills are all the living embroidery of the clothing that hangs on the soul's echo that gives Time a form. People at birth, during life, and especially at death had to become functional participants in all of this so as to ritually remake the world when anyone was born, or anyone died. These amazing old women were the ones that led it all. To the people none of this was a bench-sitting poetic metaphor, but an active doing thing, a spiritual technology that was physically carried out and, as such, was an obligation to Holy life.

The main goal of these rituals of births and funerals was to make sure people became seeds. And while there were experts who led them, the rituals were a thing of the people, made by regular people for regular people, and were in no way an esoteric function for the elite, nor carried out by a trained hierarchy of priests or shamans.

For the ritual to happen, regular people had to sincerely weep, not because someone had "died" but because they missed this once-living friend. This was subtle but at the core of seed life. They wept similarly when planting a corn seed, for the seed was leaving. But because all beings in their death replanted the earth back into life by their echoing seed, death was not the issue for weeping; loss was the issue. Grief of course is about loss, not the fear of dying. Fear of death comes from not resprouting as an echo. Fear of Death ironically causes violence and war. Grief causes life.

Therefore traditional funerals were approached in the same way as the planting of a cornfield, or should it be better said, that corn planting was carried out like a funeral!

When you missed the deceased people who'd been there a minute ago, who now disappeared into the ground never to return as companions or speaking individuals, but whose life force like an echo returned to this world as a baby's head "sprouting" forth from the wombs of birthing women, from birds' eggs, from echo-fertilized eggs of all the world's female creatures and plants to sprout young things back into the living day, you knew this next generation of the world's new life was the collective symphony of the world's dead and dying echoing back to life. Life was loss's happy echo. This was the return of the seed sprouting, the purpose of a funeral. What energized that sprouting was a ritual that had to be carried out by the living. It was not automatic; it didn't necessarily happen without the dedication and help of the living. Likewise, seeds whose plant and corn ears that only a moment previous had been held in our arms, but who disappear to us when planted, under the earth, when they hopefully sprout, they reappear in an utterly different form: green, tender, and not the same thing we had piled in the granary. These sprouted plants were the "echoes" of the long-gone seeds who grew and continued to change for the next 260 days to return to us again as new seeds that fed us who could die and grow once more.

Ethnologists might say the villagers and corn had parallel lives, but the reality of it was for the Tzutujil that corn and the people were right and left halves of the same organism, and that organism lived by the principles of seeds as maintained ritually by both halves to keep it whole.

Because of this complete human-corn existence, all births and deaths required a highly revered type of food, whose presence was considered absolutely indispensable. This ritual sustenance in both births and deaths could be prepared from only one specific race of ancient corn and no other. No other kind of corn would work, they said.

Long before any type of the villager's present daily bread had been invented, one hundred percent of which were made from various ancient breeds of corn long before the various styles of the ubiquitous *wai* or delicious tortillas now dry cooked on clay griddles, before *sa'coc'*, or thin *lej*, or leaf-steamed *buaq'*, or corn-leaf steamed *subáán*, or thickly stewed smoked waterbird and corn *patin*, or green corn and new bean *xep* had made their way into ninety percent of Tzutujil daily sustenance, this ritual food was the only known way to eat dried corn. Unlike all their other corn-derived foods, it was made without first cooking it soft with lime to remove the dermis. Called *maatz*, this food was consumed as a paste-like drink that had been prepared the same way in an unbroken thread for millennia, and was considered the original human food that made the Tzutujil into Tzutujil.

This single ancient strain of corn that made up this ritual drink for which no other could be used was considered the literal very-much-alive carbon-bearing life-form of the vegetal memory of all their ancestral life and the very substance of the never-ending physical body of their collective tribal people. It was not the gorgeous translucent varieties of flint corn from which most of the above foods were made, nor the corn Chiv had given the angry Frenchman, but a shorter, fatter-eared flour flint corn, ivory-colored, opaque and smooth.

Nobody ever ate this corn at meals or prepared it for any everyday consumption; nor could it be sold or commercially marketed. And it was not even planted just to have it, for even its cultivation had to be part of the ceremonial for a birth or a death. That's how we know that ancient agriculture was all a ritual, filled with beauty and gratitude. Every field was a temple. Indeed all cornfields had miniature temples, little versions of big ones called *warambal jai,* special little resting houses made to feed the Deities of the Holy in Nature displaced by the aggressive presence of corn farming to feed ourselves.

While this sacred corn, because of the nature of the rituals of both Birth and Death, was the same breed for every family, just like the human genetics of every family line, each family had a correspondingly unique genetic sub-strain of the same corn that nobody else had. When families became related because a boy married a girl, the genetics of their families' corn strains would mix in just the same way as the newlyweds once their "mixed" genes showed up as a beautiful baby when both of their bloodlines, just like the corn, married: revitalized by crossing only through births and deaths.

In keeping with old tradition, by the time the story-telling, bellybutton- and crotch-binding midwives of the dead had washed Chiv's dead body and began "tying him up" with the threads of the "long story," every person of the three hundred present was drunk and weeping, grief-drenched, as they "paddled" his echoing soul to the other side with a "canoe made of tears and paddles of old songs."

Peripatetically wandering from guest to guest, and alternately pounding on Chiv's old chest and pulling her skirt back up, Yakix, Chiv's youngest widow, pointing through the soot-encrusted cobwebs and smoke-glazed rafters of her expansive cooking hut, had no problem directing the younger women of the household to reach beneath the steep roof comb while balancing on each other's shoulders to where the family bundle of Birth and Death corn hung, snugly tied up and hidden from casual view. They found it coated and camouflaged in the shellac of centuries of cooking smoke right in the place everyone designated as the Belly Button of the Home: every family's personal version of sky's Belly Button of the Universe. As the center of all remembered origins of life as our own belly buttons are for us, their position in the House and Sky was the memory of the family, and deified. We always addressed the *Rumuxux Jai* in all our prayers.

Carefully lowering the bundle down, they first passed it to Yakix and all the other administrating matrons. Each of them kissed the smoky package and passed it out to the men, and when the bundle had completed its circuit of kisses and tears it received throughout the entire ground-sitting entourage of the wake, it was returned to the women.

Unfolding the bundle, they selected five ears, two perfect, two crooked and odd, and one regular. After shelling the corn into a basket that rested on Chiv's old bristling white-haired chest that breathed no more, every male in the room of any blood relation and life friendship to the old man was given a small *puño* of ivory seeds.

Without being told, these men knew that they must plant these Birth and Death corn seeds out in their terraced mountain cornfields. Unlike the large fields of life-sustaining corn of other strains that comprised over eighty percent of most Mayans' diets, these few seeds were planted in a special spot and diligently doted on when they sprouted, and hopefully grew, for the destiny of the plants that came from the special kernels was not only the destiny of the living echo-soul of the dead person, as that person developed into new forms after death in a fresh initiation on the "other side" of life, but also the part of an individual's literal life body substance that never actually left the collective body and life experience of the people as a continued tribe.

If all the Gods allowed it, for a lot of disasters can happen to cultivated plants—birds, wild herd animals, hail, windstorms, hurricanes, fires, cold, sunless days, rain, rot, and so on—when the limited number of corn ears that could be grown from such a modest quantity of seed had matured and dried, the people, like the seeds themselves and with time newly renewed seeds of the dead, gathered together again the corn ears in hand. These farmers were the same people who'd been at the "wake" and given the seeds of the deceased who now returned almost nine months after the funeral of weeping. But today they were happy: the "return" of the corn meant the dead person had successfully "echoed" into a new life-generating force, reseeded, and was sprouting again into life from the unseen depths of Time rooted in the Holy Ground of the present. The world and the living could now go on.

The paste-like gruel, nutty-smelling and smooth, the ritual drink called *maatz*, was then prepared from some of this "returned" seed and formally offered to all the people there in this second funeral. This was not a memorial but a life-restoring funeral. The remainder of the dry ivory-colored seeds, stored back under the roof comb into the dark smoky rafter world of the hut's thatchworks would remain there to await either the next family birth or another death to once again restore themselves, renewed, regrown, and eaten again back into the belly of the people. Both people and plant were restored by the ritual for the dead.

When they consumed the *maatz* it would always be about 260 days after the funeral, as this is how long that variety of corn took to mature. This was the pregnancy, the gestation time of the Mother Corn to rebirth the life substance of the Dead back to life. This is what the Mayan "calendar" was really about. This was the resprouting and renewing of Time as a plant. The resprouting and renewing of people as plants.

Drinking in all the *maatz*—for all of it had to be ingested; you couldn't leave a single drop undrunk of this nine-month renewal of the dead, of the people's grief over their loss—was known to renew the people of the deceased by returning the living "plant" of the life substance of their genetic dead back directly into the genetic body of the deceased's living relatives. In other words, we drank the dead back into our bodies, and when we did so as a group, the body of the entire tribe was very literally healed of its natural annual atrophy and revitalized.

Everyone always commented on how powerfully restorative the drink had been for them, having cured all forms of physical and mental loss of vitality, restoring ailing memory capacity, and rebounding physical strength, all of which raised the daily conviction to live on. This *maatz* of regrown seeds of Birth and Death was a general tonic to maintain the Indigenous intactness of life. Though no one would ever admit it, and there were those who didn't really relish the drink as its taste was simple and primal, everyone was always eager to take in this original corn food, knowing that this elemental plant ritual from the transformed dead was the most powerful and central of all village ceremonies. For by this, the Dead actually sustained the living, just as the living had replanted, recultivated, and reincarnated the Dead as a seed.

The evening of the day Old Chiv died, that group of women whose specialty was preparing the dead as a seed to be "unwound" in the other world so as to resprout him as a life-giving force led the mourning of the attending grievers whose presence, songs, sounds, and sincere grief lent force to the "sacred farming" of the funeral which would "plant" and bury the dead as a seed to resprout as the force of the next day.

While the mourners were wailing, to make Chiv, now dead, into a "sproutable" seed, one or two women from this proletariat guild of women washed the body, then placed an ancient bead and one small seed of corn in the belly button topped with a cotton plug, and with a ball of white cotton hand-spun thread these great women began to narrate out loud in great detail the events of worth and service to the great Holy Diversity that feeds us all that had been accomplished by the deceased when he was alive. While one spoke, another very slowly, deliberately, and tightly wrapped the midriff of the dead until a precise and tidy girdle a hand's-width circled the belly and lower back like a dazzling white band that bound the jeweled navel hidden beneath.

The events of the dead person's life recounted in a chronology from birth to death, and to the moment the women were speaking, became the threads themselves and were known as the *Sac Bey Q'an Bey*, "white road, yellow road," the ritual term for any umbilical cord, and it was upon such roads that all stories were carried and all lives were lived.

When they came to the end of that living story, hopefully without breaking any threads, a difficult accomplishment to say the least because of the fineness of the filament, they commenced making the *liix*. These were the genital bindings made first by padding raw fluffed cotton throughout the crotch area; then, over this, they again bound the crotch and thighs in such a way as to make the whole with the girdle into a kind of wrapped underclothing made by a single unbroken string. This genital binding was where the sprouting of the dead as a seed into day would spiritually take place the following day: the crotch being the human equivalent of the procreative germ and cotyledons of the corn seed from where its leaves issue forth as they rise hopefully from the womb of the ground to lick the Face of the Sky.

In this way the old women "tied and spoke" the body of the deceased into a seed, while the mourners sung and wept in grief to put a "crack" in everyday reality into which they could drop this newly prepared "seed" to resprout the world, while others were simultaneously very tangibly excavating a burial hole in which to lower the body, which was now a seed.

Humans are amazing ritual animals, and it must be understood that the Tzutujil, nor any other real intact people, do not "practice" rituals. Just as a bear must turn over stumps searching for beetles, real humans can only live life spiritually. Birth itself was a ritual: there was not a ritual for birth, or a ritual for death, or a ritual for marriage, for death was a ritual, life a ritual, cooking a ritual, and eating were all rituals with ceremonial guidelines, all of which fed life. Sleeping was a ritual, lovemaking was a ritual, sowing, cultivating, harvesting, storing food were rituals, even sweeping, insulting, fighting were rituals, everything human was a ritual, and to all Tzutujil, ritual was plant-oriented and based on feeding some big Holy ongoing vine-like, tree-like, proceedance that fed us its fruit.

This seed ritual of death was also part of ritual childbirth. Because the birthing mother throughout her pregnancy and during labor was reincarnating a plant substance echoing in from another layer of time, births themselves were always called the "sprouting of Dawns, sprouting of

Suns." Just as when any kernel of corn was sown it was regarded as a funeral, because the seed had to die, be buried, lose its original form, likewise all births returned the rooted "sprout" of that planted seed into the possibility of new corn through the seed obligation of living again. When the sprouted seed began to poke his little pointed crown through the cracking earth into the present, it was called *awex* or "dawning" of the earth or being born as an echo of light. When the Sun came up, he was even colloquially said to have had his "seed sprouted into day" after having died the previous evening. Likewise when a baby boy or girl was born, they were literally a seed sprouting out of their mother's earthen womb: a vegetative sunrise made of the echo of a past being, sprouting by crowning out of the mother's vulva just as a seed, like the sun from the earth, appeared as the fruit, or face, on the tree trunk of Time's daily growth.

Modern people of good mind would call this poetry, but for intact people this is not a special or creative thought. It is how everyone spoke every day and scientifically participated in a mythology made tangible that is the cycle of all life as a plant.

Like the deceased, who had the dried cobs of the Holy corn of Birth and Death shelled over that personal place of all our origins—his or her navel—newborns and mothers after all their deep and dedicated warrior struggles to bring the children live into this world had as an inalienable part of birth this exact same corn, that had been grown either at the previous clan birth or death, placed under the umbilical cord just before the umbilical cord is parted by the midwife and the baby is officially separated from the mother.

At the time of birth at the appropriate moment, after all the blood had gotten into the newborn through the umbilical cord that had fed the child for what the Tzutujil consider the previous 260 days or a Mayan nine months, the attending midwife or midwives separated the cord from the child, leaving a little stem which they always tied with a bright red cotton string.

While the red color protected the child from any bad spiritual negativity entering through the navel stump when the belly-button stump finally did its job and shriveled up into a tiny little chip and dropped wherever it pleased, the red thread helped the people make sure they could find it in the village dust or the baby's poop. It was a sacred thing and jealously guarded until the harvest of birth corn began to come in from the men 260 days later.

The juices of birth would unavoidably anoint the kernels when the cord was parted, after which the cob was shelled and the kernels tenderly distributed by the midwife to all the male relatives of the child present at the birthing. After receiving the same corn in a way practically identical to that carried out over the body of the deceased as did the midwives of Death in a Funeral, and needing no reminders, with a feeling of honor and vigilance these men soon after planted and tended the corn plants in a way no different to plants grown for the deceased. They knew full well that like the soul of the dead, the child's well-being and capacity to hardiness in this harsh windy world for the next 260 days utterly depended on the fate of the resulting corn plants in their charge. If the corn flourished at the hands of the ritual farmer, so would the child; if it did not, the men were probably at fault for negligent cultivation of the soil and lack of respect for the great female Holy in Nature.

As each particular family's magical priest farmers, full of prayers and offerings, these hardworking men cared for the child's "plant" soul just as the mother took care of the child's animal soul. As in the wild, plants without animals cannot thrive. One without the other is worse than death. Tended together, an intact human child developed. Those 260 days after the initial birth were seen as a man's pregnancy, another gestation of a baby as Plant Time in the future fields to become a thriving member of a Tribe of Plant People, the Tzutujil. The word Tzutujil comes from *tzutuj* or corn tassel.

After thanking their much-relieved farming men folk for taking such diligent care of the child's plant substance and soul just as they would've in the case of a death, the birthing Midwife and ladies of the household then sorted this newly renewed Birth/Death corn. The young unmarried girls chose first, picking out the most brilliant, straight, even, and appealing ears like the husbands and resulting children they hoped for. But then the old grandmothers retrieved the most extreme, oddest looking, unique, crooked, multi-headed, and creative ears of what they called the "miraculous prophet child" corn and, combining these with what the young girls had selected, both types were tied, mixed together high up into the middle of highest part of the hut's sooty "Sacred Sky" inside under the roof comb into the "Belly Button of the House." The remaining, more "Joe six-pack" ears, regular-people-type ears, not too crooked, not too inventive, were then ceremoniously toasted for the sacred *maatz* drink on the *xot*, the clay griddle, until they parched and popped, the delicious smell impossible to resist as it permeated the air of the chosen day of naming the nine-month-old child and presenting him or her into the first stages of little kidhood.

The toasted kernels were then ground dry into a coarse meal on the *cá*, the grinding stone, the molar of the house, by one of the young women. Unlike natives of Northern Mexico and the American southwest who still grind their corn dry, this occasion is the one and only time dry toasted corn is ground by Highland Mayans.

A sieve of loosely woven grass or palm leaves was placed over a clay pot, the ground meal put into the sieve, and fresh cold water strained through the meal, dripping a thin, delicious-smelling, milky-looking liquid into the pot.

Invoking two major deified smells, *r sumsjil, r poqjil,* 'the smell of dry toasted cornmeal," "the smell of rain on dust," the moistened corn was returned to the *cá*, the grinding stone, more water added, and "ears" or wooden hand-carved troughs, added around the sides and bottom of the grinding stone to catch the juice as the strongest girl reground the remaining marc to force any leftover substance out of the skins of the ground-up seeds. This liquid was poured back into the first of the original milky corn liquid and was then carefully poured back through the corn marc back through the sieve and the whole repoured over and over until deemed ready.

The liquid was then slowly reduced in the clay pot in the most cautious way with prayers over the open flame. The great red pot concentrated it into the familiar pasty liquid of the ubiquitous sacred drink of *maatz*.

When all the guests had arrived, the baby was anointed with this regenerated Birth and Death corn drink on all the major joints, the bottom of his or her feet, cheeks, and forehead by the midwife who had attended to the Birth. In the same spiritual fashion as when the deceased had their belly button bound up by the Death midwives, the Birthing midwives then began slowly winding up the little red string–bound belly-button stump shed months earlier by the nine-month-old child, attaching a white cotton hand-spun thread to the initial tail of red thread binding the stump. With this they very slowly bound it up while the midwife told the story of "all" that had happened up to the birth, beginning with the tribal version of the world's origination up and up until she arrived at the baby's ancestors, then the parents, then the mother's pregnancy, then the birth, then the baby's life in this world of the last 260 days until the very moment of the winding, and then the winding was halted.

The result was a little one-and-one-half inch ball of thread. This was the most precious fetish of a person's beginnings. With great prayer this little ball of DNA and stories was then placed inside the family bundle by the eldest woman of the clan. Inside the bundle, every ancestor of the child had their belly-button stump and "thread story" sitting there in a huge pile like a nest of ancient turtle eggs going back for thousands of years!

This bundle of all ancestral belly-button stumps and tales of their lives was the "Belly Button of the Home" and presided equally over all Births as it did in death residing right next to the package of the corn of Birth and Death. After adding the child's "origins" in the form of the belly-button fetish into the Bundle, the bundle was danced by the father, while the midwife holding the baby danced in front of him. Then the father gave the bundle to the mother of the child, who danced it for a while, then greedily exchanged it for her baby, with whom very happily both Mom and Dad danced, while the midwife proceeded to dance the bundle of thousands of years of ancestral story umbilical stumps, with the person that had named the child, usually with their own namesake. Because each belly-button stump had given birth to the next ones, the entire ancestry of our life danced along with us as well.

Finally all the oldest and greatest guests danced the bundle, after which the baby was officially named.

The same belly-button-anointed corn regrown and renewed by the baby's birth would also be the same corn renewed at the next birth, or more probably the next death. In either case the thread story would be told and "tied" automatically to the last generation in the case of the child, and tied to the next generation in the case of the dead. And in both cases the corn made into *maatz* was also consumed back into the live "body" of the village. All people at birth were brought in to this village world and absorbed back into the collective village body in this same way. The seeds of this particular breed of maize were also themselves kept alive *only* by being renewed as crops planted at both births and deaths and at no other times. In this way they were always alive, always present, always new and life-giving. This corn was the people themselves as plants. Though the people came and went, seasons lived and died, the corn plants grew and withered, but the World Time and corn as people were always there. It was this that was the basic substance of ritual intelligence of all life renewed. It's no wonder the Tzutujil word for mind was *atas gor,* "corn dough that remembers"! In such a ritual life, one never tried to escape one's daily participation in the holy precedence of everyday things being functionally important to Divine Time, for then every event in a day was part of a living mythology, not a thing studied.

Feeling its weight close to your chest, you could not be anything but overwhelmed by the tangible reality of the multiple millennia of story-wound belly-button stumps of over thousands of actual people born; people long since gone but who together were in the bundle tied together as the sequential ancestral thread to which every person in the hut was tied.

Holding one of the ivory-kerneled cobs of Birthing/Dying corn, you felt the same way, if you could recognize the majesty of the same fact that the ancestors of these kernels had been sequentially planted in exactly twice as many generations as had been born, for those whose belly buttons were in the bundle the corn had been not only renewed by all their deaths as well, but also consumed as ceremonial food by every single individual along the way. Yet here you were today in this small moment in the infinity of time holding a simple ear of corn that held all those stories, lifetimes, births, deaths, planting and replantings, to rest right here in your hands. But it was not a relic, a dry preserved symbolizing something; they were live seeds, a living holy being that would grow again through Birth, through Death.

And of course it always followed that after a while you realized that you yourself at this never-to-return-again moment were living magically, for like the corn you were a little sack of carbony ash and water supernaturally organized into a sentient, burping, farting, talking, dreaming, hungering, grief-stricken, sometimes confused, animate ritual being, who could and should feed the world by having been here, and being so short a visit of ash and water in the form that could kiss, cry, try, fear, feel loneliness, and still live, could plant this corn and like the corn die to renew the world in your having been here but then no more, but maybe still remember as a vital indispensable link in the time continuum of this sack of belly buttons. It's no wonder then that the sacred corn was always housed beside this collective family "belly button" up in the smoky eaves, in the "Heart of the Sky," because each was just half of a grander completeness of life that the other shared.

It was as if everything in the world, even seemingly complete beings, were born missing one small vital component that someone or something else had in their possession and that everything and everyone had something, without which someone or something else could never even happen. Something unique for each, but who universally was incomplete without. To be whole we had to "court" the "other," not boss, commandeer, force, or seduce, the other to "obtain" what we as incomplete beings required to truly live. The grass needed the carbon dioxide of the swamp, and the sea turtle the vital sea oils of the eel, the hermit crab the shell of the moon snail; the atmosphere needed the fertile crossfire of the lightning serpent's scales of ozone. This was the definition of the Tzutujil word for life: mutual indebtedness. The whole world was a ritual of a million component rituals in which every being kept alive another being by courting them by the beauty of their innate natures in order to be graced with the gift the other held of what each was missing.

This worked in every direction in every way especially in Time, and especially in the age groups of the tribe. Just as our babies who were carried from basalt-lined family compound to family compound suckling at the great milky breast of their mother tucked beneath her beautiful clothing were called and known to be "flowers and sprouts," by the time these little girls and boys could meander from one family's cooking fire to another cooking fire on their own little fat feet, they knew full well that fact themselves and even called themselves the *kixeli* or the "replacements" of one or more of their grandparents, who everyone called the "Big tree, Big vine," *Nim ché Nim caam* grandparents who had drunk birth corn *maatz* at their grandchildren's coming, who would have the same corn planted for them when they died, whose corn after they died, these *kixeli,* replacement grandkids, would drink back into their own bodies to retain the echo of their grandparents' never-dying vegetal sound for the next generations, until they too became "big trees, big vines."

But even then as they grew from the life of a sprout among sprouts, from a rascally herd of short pot-bellied geniuses forever thundering across the paths, ridges, shorelines, mouths bulging as they dropped to the ground from pilfering fully ripe fruit trees, raising hilarity and kid culture village-wide to weigh in only too soon, overloaded with firewood or water, hard on the heels of their fathers or mothers, carrying their own weight straight into the fire-blooded weirdness of the teenage brain. But even then they were plants: corn plants. But something even more seed-like started to appear on the eve of adolescence for these children, born as corn in their lives as Tzutujil, now became cacao. Young people ceased being corn and became sacred chocolate.

Whereas the corn plant was mother sustenance herself, the wild cacao, the chocolate seed, secreted the ecstatic life of erotic dreams whose desire was what made all things make love, pollinate, mate, fight, to make more of themselves. Cacao was the undisputed traditional patroness, the enchantress of pubescent time of what drove all things to break the suburban, plebeian, humdrum regulation of everyday life pushing into and "out of time" the fertilization of flowers for seeds, souls, earth, animal, and all time to rebirth all existence. In other words the teenagerness of the Tzutujil was not just corn, but also cacao.

While we were all flowers and sprouts, infants born into this world as corn, from corn, suckled on mother's milk made of corn, from mothers fed with corn, like corn plants cultivated by corn culture to have plantlike minds, by the time adolescence crept in on us a new plant and Her dreams would marry corn. This was ever present ritually, for in the complex teenage rites of passage, various cacaos were added to the drink of *maatz* to make what was called *q'atouj*, a drink that turned this regular corn life into an ecstatic wild pollination of life, something confusing, emotional, and unruly like all teenagers, but utterly necessary for the continuance of Time, the Earth, the people, and her culture.

During the gigantic simultaneous ceremonies of Spring, when the next season was being ceremonially courted out of unseen time into the visible blessing of Holy Rain, after five months of dry maturing wind, the annual gathering of the new "harvest of days," *Hun Huná* as a year's time was called, teenagers on fire and ripe for initiation were pushed, pulled, chased, caught, cajoled, and otherwise forced into their ceremonial place vital in the maintenance of Holy Time. They would become new beings, neither adults nor children but young heroes and heroines whose efforts under the tutelage of only slightly older men and women and truly old people would go toward reanimating the world by teaching these young people how to wrestle death with their beauty, courage, and learned cultural ritual language, hoping in the initiating showdown to inspire the Death Lords into making their rot and decay compost the past time where the Earth could have her Divine erotic night of ecstatic love from which new earth, the new life, the renewed raining, plant-growing, food-filled blessing of being alive would burst forth.

The youth had to control all their urges for a year of endless complex ritual education and strenuous participation that culminated in the drinking of a powerful ritual drink that was none other than the same Birth/Death corn drink, made from corn donated from all the families of the initiates mixed together. The difference being that other holy plants were part of the drink as well. Not hallucinogens, because only amateurs use those, not substances exactly but plant seeds of truly magical ritual food substance that, due to their opened souls and readiness from initiation of a more conscious vision, came to the youth from the magical food.

One of these was none other than the real unprocessed *ch'qijya* , or chocolate. The word chocolate in English was a Nahuat word whose real meaning was identical to the Tzutujil *ch'qijya* . Both words mean "dry water." Before the European Spanish colonial time, all chocolate plants were prized as the deep ecstatic side of plants unlike the workaday side of plants like corn, who could be shown to lose her puritanical water by fermentation into a native liquor that had been used for millennia in all ceremonies since the invention of corn.

Chocolate beans of the old domesticated type contained the Heat of Male Fire, with the gushing desire of Female water, which made ceremonial steam, which among the Gods was their main holy being. This "Dry Water" prepared as a drink in the old way had never become something casually imbibed for any individual's personal preference but reserved one hundred percent for the last days of initiation as one of the five plants seeds needed to make *q'atouj*. In the pre-European times chocolate was drunk in a couple of other ritual circumstances, but if anyone was caught drinking chocolate out of collective ritual context, they were executed on the spot. Chocolate was not the casual recreational habit it has become today.

The only other crime known to be addressed in the same drastic fashion by the original Highland Tzutujil Maya was the killing of the male quetzal bird to take his long iridescent green tail-feathers instead of following the normal method of live-trapping this beautiful bright-red-chested fruit-eating bird after he had mated and molted his tail feathers naturally, then releasing him.

Anyway, besides the grand ingredients of domesticated "Dry Water" chocolate and Birth/Death corn, *q'atouj* had to also have the giant aromatic bean of the unruly deep-veined pod of a variety of wild practically uncultivable jungle cacao called *peq'*. This seed, when toasted and fermented identically to its sweetheart cousin, did not taste like chocolate but like a super-delicious unearthly fragrant almond that contained more than just the theobromine of cacao but twenty-four other only semi-identified alkaloids. An incredible plant that the young men received directly from the Lords of Death under the earth during their initiation, it was understood by them as the very Heart of the Goddess of their own teenage heart's empty throne longing for love, and whose symbiotic presence in the drink with the regular chocolate made both act differently in the body and soul than either separately.

When drunk in the context of the complex ritual, drunk into one's brand-new initiate body in exactly three gourdfuls only, at that momentous moment when all male and female initiates were literally set loose from their year-long ritual separation and obligations, this became a ritual explosion of earth-planting human seeds. By some grand rewiring of their human souls there was no way they could sit or rest, no matter how exhausted the body or fatigued the mind, for the powerful combination of the holy mythic stories of each ingredient, literally ingested suddenly and ecstatically, caused them all to collectively see and bodily understand in their very bones how they had become those very plants whose seeds they drank with all the same primal intelligence, ingenuity, and desire of the natural forest.

Their souls became a growing field of innate plant knowing. For this both new men and women danced together; these little heroes and heroines of the village swayed ecstatically all afternoon, all night, and most of the next day, until everybody, their euphoric initiators included, all dropped eventually onto the ground into a sleep of planted seeds, in whose dreams "everything was known." But luckily, enough of these visions were forgotten upon waking for the people to go on happily as regular humans. Otherwise the knowledge would have overwhelmed them, the experience overly Holy and powerful to be able to live normally in this tangible world as a useful villager.

But now renewed, regrown, molted out of childhood, and ready as young adult "plants" to make their own "Flowers and Sprouts," their own families, until they too grew old and "thickly barked" with age and with any luck developed into respected old trees and old vines themselves, so that the next generation of flowers and sprouts would kiss them on the belly button, until they too would die and in their death have those same belly buttons bound and be made into seeds to plant back again into the temporal ecosphere, regrown as birth corn and drunk back into the Belly of the World that continued organically sprouting, birthing, running around playing, flowering, ecstatically in love with their fruited sweethearts, kissing belly buttons and replanted jumping up and living again.

This was what was meant as living as People of the Seed. The spiritual expertise of how to maintain this with all its ceremonial and practical know-how was a veritable college, a natural Indigenous school, a sophisticated brother and sisterhood of seeds, dedicated to "keeping the seeds" of all this knowledge and the actual doing of it alive, and thereby keeping Time Fed and Alive, the world fed and alive. The deliberate generational furtherance of this made the people who were dedicated to it into humans who grew into more indigenously, organically worthy forms of people as they attempted to keep it all alive.

When you consider the subtlety of this it would seem a miracle that any of this life could have survived any of the centuries of European invasion and colonial presence that so relentlessly battered all Native American culture and this Earth in such a titanically ugly and thoroughly clumsy way. But what little of that grand thing that could survive, wanted to survive, and what wanted to survive did survive and was very much alive until not so very long ago, in that village along the shores of the "Belly Button of the Earth," when an invasion of a very different frequency disrupted even that resilient symphony of life-giving echoes in the continuum of Time.

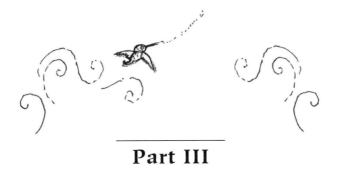

Part III

Keeping the Seeds Alive

Chapter 10

Burning Up the Memory

In the Highlands, the old-time Mayans of Guatemala never carried on wars for deliberate annihilation of a neighboring tribe. If theirs was a warrior class, groups of singular warriors, well appointed, dressed like rich wild birds, and accompanied by supporting teams of noncombatants would skirmish with fancy warriors for territorial claims, but to neither side of these flare-ups would it have ever occurred to burn their opposition's crops or gardens, or to kill the farmers that worked them. Their goal was to have an elaborate and impressive human cockfight, one in which each fighter sought to capture the other alive so as to drag him, finery and all, trussed up in a corn-harvesting netted bag on the victor's back to his family compound, where the captive was feasted as an honored guest, given all he desired, and killed in a sacrificial warrior's ritual a year later, turning the captive into a Holy gift of beauty to the powers that give all people life.

It was an unthinkable thought to kill what fed people, for it was that which their beautiful fighting sought to feed by its ritual beauty. Why would you destroy the manifestation of the very Holy Food and Plant kingdom you were trying to capture for your own? The plants were what the people would fight for, if they fought at all, and the plants were the Holiest of all beings, so why wreck them? If you captured a people, you captured their plants and were proud of it; you didn't destroy the plants or the ground they grew on to destroy an enemy. They would capture their plants, their people, and their Gods and maintain them, continuing the enemy's rituals for them so that they flourished for the captors, and for this they needed the people, their rituals, and their Deities. Whomever, wherever, whatever you captured you were responsible for. That was Highland Mayan warfare.

But utter annihilation, subjection, then putting your own in charge over an enslaved enemy was an odd unthinkable thought. Like a puma or a jaguar, the Mayan warrior class didn't hate what fed them.

So it was overwhelming and sickening to them when they were attacked from without by an enemy with one Imperial God, no revered plants, who would rather level a people and salt their water, burn crops off the land to cause surrender, than live with the Tao of an intact conquest where the flowers, chocolate, beautiful girls, music, and ritual were left alive.

In the spring of 1524, Pedro Alvarado, with Ramirez, Mendoza,and several others with an entourage of a couple of hundred European soldiery, swollen to several thousand by native Tlaxcalan mercenary warriors from eastern Mexico after dividing troops with Cortez as he headed north across the Peten to Honduras, commenced his "reduction" of Guatemala. After seeing 24,000 Quiché men killed in one day, then shortly after the same with the Mam, then with only the Cakchiquel Maya between them and the Europeans, the tiny Tzutujil tribe knew that their turn was next. They began hurriedly dismantling the legendary causeway that once connected the point of Tzanjiyam on the north point of the Bay of Atitlán to the shore of the Tzutujil mountaintop ceremonial center of Chitinimit.

Located on the summit of a steep hill surrounded for 300 degrees by deep blue lake water out of which it pushed like a gigantic head, Chitinimit was a beautiful carved stone ritual place and ball court ringed by buildings where no one actually lived, save a small group of the priestly class. While it was there the people did their rituals of feeding time and the land, it was on the skirts of this mini volcano covered in the finely made palatial huts of many Tzutujil clans where the royalty resided.

The bulk of the Tzutujil population lived in a score of ceremonial hamlets on the opposite shore, and when the Spaniards approached, they all withdrew to the summit and shores of Chitinimit.

A beautifully carved wonder—for a few of its serpents and jaguars still remain hidden and revered—the stone causeway bridging the bay was torn apart and all the stones rolled back into the deep Lake Atitlán. At the base of the huge Volcano of Chichuc, the "elbow of the universe," Chitinimit was unassailable from the rear because the extreme steepness of the volcanic grade was practically impossible to scale militarily, and unapproachable from any other direction except by water in canoes. Having had a monopoly on all the canoes throughout the lake, by the time Alvarado and his forces arrived, the Tzutujil had of course the entire fleet beached out of their enemies' reach on the shores of Chitinimit.

For the few watercraft the Spaniards could commandeer from other lake Indians, they were literally sitting ducks for Tzutujil warriors with their stone slings, knocking armored Europeans *kerplunk* into the "Mother waters" to drown, and unarmored they were all too easily picked off with powerful Tzutujil arrows.

Well stocked with corn, fish, honey, water, turkeys, enough for three years under the legendary leadership of Hun Q'iq'—"One Northwind"—the Tzutujil hierarchy frustrated the invasion force in their every attempt. Stymied militarily for the first time, after a couple of futile weeks camped at Tzanjiyam, Don Pedro Alvarado had decided to pull out and head toward Tecpán in hopes of "reducing" a bigger, more powerful people in the more attackable landlocked mountain town of Iximche, "corn tree," the capital, so to speak, of the Tecpán Cakchiquels.

But on the eve of their would-be departure, a captive Cakchiquel man, having lost his love of life after seeing his own neighboring tribal branch of Tecpán flattened, plundered, murdered, the girls raped, and all bound in irons to be sold in slavery to Pizarro to cross the Andes to crush the tribes of Peru, and bitter at the seeming pending success of their old rivals the Tzutujil at repelling the foreigners' initial vicious assault, asked to speak directly to the Adelantado. To Alvarado and his officers he gave the secret that would without a doubt bring the Tzutujil paddling across the bay from their perfect unkillable perch to voluntarily submit to the Spaniards without a fight . . .

All the invaders would have to do is send three separate parties. The first to the immediate Pacific slope south of the hills fencing in the bay should commence chopping down the extensive Tzutujil cacao plantations that ran to the lowlands. The second group should burn all the stacks of log honey-hives that studded the hillsides that rimmed the south bay shore, while the third should simultaneously commit to flames all of the unharvested late-April cornfields all around the cultivated mountain ravines surrounding the bay. "The Tzutujil," he told them, "care as much for these three things as they do their people, because to them these things are the people. Burn and destroy their corn and chocolate plants, and the bees and the people will have been conquered!"

So the Spaniard, not letting one day go by, did as the vengeful Cakchiquel suggested, and the Tzutujil, having a tremendous intelligence network of runners and sentinels who signaled with their now-extinct but still-legendary long wooden Alphorn-like trumpets that could be heard for miles, signaled from volcano top to ridgetop to the hierarchy in Chitinimit and back in less than fifteen minutes, a distance of over sixty miles; they immediately realized what was ensuing when the first chocolate trees began to cry out, and the bees swarmed in terror through the smoke as the corn began to roar up in dry season flame.

Just as the captive had predicted, the entire Tzutujil royal family and the hierarchical heads of every strata and clan of the tribe paddled across in their gorgeously carved long canoes unarmed, but dressed, perfumed, as the great plant royalty they were, and beached their canoes at the feet of the Spaniards in a mysterious tone of utter friendship.

They not only submitted to the "King of Spain," wanting instantly to become Spanish citizens so as not to be enslaved like their neighbors, for somehow they were aware of Spain's law that did not allow enslavement of Spanish citizens, but they also made the curious, but what turned out to be brilliantly thought-out, request to have themselves, the entire hierarchy, immediately baptized as Spanish Catholics, stating definitively through a Tlaxcalan translator that each male member of the

Tzutujil hierarchy was anxious to change their given native names and be baptized, each according to their present rank with exactly the same name, in keeping with his elite position, as what they perceived were their equivalent among their conquerors.

In other words Hun Q'iq', "One North Wind," the so-called Tzutujil High King, was to be baptized and renamed "Pedro Alvarado" and Don Pedro would then be his "Padrasto" or godparent for life! His second noble would be named Ramirez, the third Mendoza, etc., and so on until the entire Tzutujil upper class had taken on the names and importance of those who'd overrun them and had them as relatives of a sort. The invading Catholic priest accompanying the army was delirious to comply, while Pedro Alvarado, under the guise of wanting more proof of their loyalty, would only allow the Tzutujil to retain their land and give the native "newly baptized" hierarchy continued sovereignty over their own people if they, to show good faith, would turn over three thousand Indians as pledges to the Spaniards to work as slave laborers for Pizarro, and agree to have a church built, gather all their people on the more accessible side of the bay opposite Chitinimit, and establish the "capital" of the lake area now known as Santiago Atitlán. They were to agree to levy and pay the legal tribute all Spanish colonial holdings did to the crown, which in their case would be levied according to *ecomienda* census ever after, a tax henceforth no longer in slaves, but in cotton cloth, cacao, quetzal tail feathers, honey, and corn.

The Tzutujil complied, capturing three thousand poor enemy Pipil Indians immediately to their south and turning them over as "their own" people. (All the highland people sent to cross the Andes perished, frozen to death en route.) Nonetheless, outside of the Sacatepequez Cakchiquels who immediately after had a successful twelve-year guerrilla war against Spain, the people of Saqualpa, some of the Qekchi and the Lacandones, the lakeside Tzutujil with no real fighting came out light-years in better shape than all of the area's Mayan tribes, at least in that time and that sense.

The people are corn, their ecstatic relation with the Holy in the Seed of adolescent time is cacao, and the ecstatic pollinator of all, the biggest gods of them all, the bees, were the Patron Gods of Highland Mayan royal clans. The people and the plants and the fertilizing power of the Bee were inseparable. Devastate the bees, the cacao, or the corn and you have destroyed what makes them human. When you were happy you said *"ki nu kux,"* "the sweetness of honey in my heart." Those old-time people had made the quick, difficult decision to keep the seeds alive, and they did, though they must have known it would mean the end of a myriad native institutions. But to survive, they developed an incredible array of deliberate reconfigurations of old ritual ways secreted craftily right inside foreign European institutions, but without their overlords' awareness. These hidden rituals and lifeways would admirably withstand in an amazingly detailed way the next 450 difficult years.

During that long period of devastating earthquakes, volcanic eruptions, massive flooding, a myriad nightmarish political realities and their accompanying unnatural reconfiguration of overcrowded settlement patterns, double taxing, and European-introduced mutated viral epidemics that left in their wake rampant poverty and mass suicides where estimates of sixty to eighty percent of the entire population both native and invader utterly disappeared, the Tzutujil were able to "keep their seeds" and their core ritual life of seeds very much alive. At least until around the time when Chiv died and that time that was upon us now, the time that he'd warned us about.

When Chiviliu died, crashing to the ground like a fruit-laden tree articulated with life-giving echoes, those preparing him for burial tying up his belly button and his genitals like cotyledons for his resprouting from this layer of the womb of time into the next layer of earth as the great plant his life here had made him the seed, nobody's relatives who died in that year had any problem finding seeds of that special Birth/Death corn to grow more to make *maatz,* to replant their earthly substance, to resprout day out of the next ground of night.

But ten years later, almost to the day, not even one kernel of any kind of native Tzutujil corn containing the original *Ruk'ux,* seed heart, the original DNA of the old types, could be found in any house, anywhere in the village.

Because of the constant terror and violent death that characterized that horrid decade of the 1980s, there wasn't even any food corn, the corn that had unendingly sustained the people for millennia, much less the old ritual birth, death corn, which totally disappeared for any of the births, and the initiations. The initiations themselves went extinct because of it. Babies were still born and named, but they were no longer sprouts from seeds, and the dead were simply bound for Christian heaven, their seed echo forgotten for the earth.

Eight years or so after the 1976 earthquake, during the famous terror of the internal wars between established U.S.-supported corrupt government and various left-leaning modern-thinking would-be liberators, a regiment of some four hundred conscripted National Guatemalan army soldiers were ordered to take up permanent residence in a soldier camp immediately southeast of Santiago. Ostensibly bivouacked there by the Government to contend with so-called armed leftist insurgents, who of course were left-leaning nationalist Indian villagers from all over the region living as citizens right in the village, most of these "guerillas" were themselves former Guatemalan government soldiers who learned their craft and hatred of the government from their new enemy through their notorious illegal enforced conscriptions.

The rest of the people just held their breath and tried to carry on while soldiers roamed the town at will, demanding free food and the "company" of the Tzutujil women who were forced to deliver themselves to their camp, while soldiers ransacked dwindling family granaries of anyone refusing. People were hungry. Everything was eaten up.

The military in those days, as in so many other countries of the world and in other times in world history, did not have the use of tax dollars to feed its conscripts. When out on their so-called internal "protection missions" like these, the burden of feeding the soldiers was always carried on the backs of the local farmers and fishermen and housewives who were supposed to be grateful for the "protection" they received from the military in confronting the confusing issue of the "enemy," who were more often than not the peaceful seed people's own scattered disillusioned warlike relatives, some who demanded food as well. The people were really stretched.

To make things worse, the men were for the most part unable to renew the corn because of the army patrols who fired on the villagers tending their mountain fields, unable to distinguish between a villager and a suspected guerrilla, or suspecting villagers of transporting food to the guerrillas. Soon enough the traditional arable mountain land where most all the varieties of corn, beans, squashes, avocadoes, *tajpal, jocotes,* and so on were cultivated, not to mention the birth corn, was declared by the Joint Command as off-limits to all people under penalty of death, which effectively caused half the village to give up their seed way of life and move toward some kind of cash-earning commerce usually in Guatemala's famous city markets far away. Even the few that succeeded in this were often searched and robbed of their earnings on their return by soldiers enforcing a curfew, which now required all people traveling in or out of their own village region to be in possession of a type of internal passport.

After over four years of food depletion, the people developed a lot of schemes to hide food, especially their corn. Soon, of course, because there was hardly any food—little imported from the surrounding country, and in a situation where none could be sown—nobody was willing to feed the daily marauding military.

Hungry bands of angry renegade army patrols began pillaging suspected caches of hidden food, eating up all of the sacks of Birth/Death corn, commandeering any other stores of corn when they found them, using the rationale that the corn had been illegally hidden by villagers secretly trying to support relatives involved in the "left-wing insurgency." Sometimes the rightful owners of the Holy Corn would be arrested, and sometimes they would never be seen again. Finally a small outlaw band of younger soldiers "raided" an overlooked but well-stocked granary cleverly hidden underground. The young evangelical Christian Tzutujil man whose wife and small children owned it resisted the bandits; the man was killed right there, dragged off with the corn and quartered into pieces. At the edge of starvation, the village had nothing left to lose, and a furious raging crowd rose up, gathering numbers as it closed in on the soldier's encampment.

Four thousand outraged, unarmed men, women, and children (or seven thousand, depending on whose account you heard) marched that same night to the soldier camp and demanded the dead man's remains to bury him in a proper Christian way.

Terrified, the soldiers fired randomly on the crowd, killing twelve on the spot, wounding seventy critically, and hitting at least a couple hundred, a large number of whom were maimed for life.

Miraculously and uncharacteristically, an unprecedented international uproar ensued. There had been hundreds of ghastly massacres and disappearances and wagonloads of brutal Indian killings to an estimated national death toll of 180,000 to 280,000 in less than eight years, but they hardly ever made the news outside of Guatemala and Mexico, only rarely being reported by the BBC. But this time a mysterious series of conditions ensued that made this very small massacre into a big international event.

A national election campaign for president of Guatemala had been in full swing, and at the time of the massacre, per Guatemalan custom, the runoff for the two candidates with the most votes in the first round of elections were vying with one another to reinstate the monetary aid, agricultural, military, and business, that had been officially cut off by the U.S. Congress for quite real human rights transgressions.

These non-Indian presidential would-bes, each with their own private sections of the military, who, under the "normal" operating conditions of the twentieth century, could have cared less than a clam's fart for the plight of any amount of murdered "Indians," simultaneously declared publicly this same-as-ever atrocity to be Guatemala's worse-than-ever massacre: an "international travesty" characteristic of the heartless status quo thinking of the corroded and corrupt present Guatemalan government, for which the battling candidates promised independently but synonymously that each of their refreshing modernized presence in the presidency would root out and change everything for the better!

The overwhelming majority of the conscripted soldiers of Guatemala's standing army of that time were young Mayan men from hundreds of villages from all over the country. Most were illegally extorted or shanghaied into "service," beaten, and trained to obey an elite cadre of solidly non-Indian career officers from the families of the aristocracy of the country's oligarchy of various wealthy landowners who of course had since independence from Spain depended on the steady source of cheap labor supplied by the poorer population of the country, both Indian and non-Indian.

The typical result of such a choreographed hypocritical farce occurred when entities sympathetic to one of the party candidates inside the government, in order to quell international outcry over this particular incident in Atitlán, with unprecedented swiftness, ordered a dozen of these conscripted Indian soldiers, none of whom was directly involved in this particular bout of shooting, to be militarily executed in public, while not one of the white officers who ordered them to fire was punished. In an unprecedented compliance to the frustrated villagers' adamant request and the possibility of renewed international aid if carried out, the army was ordered out of the southern Lake Atitlán region altogether. This was heavily documented and paraded by the new hopefuls as an example to the civilized world they so deeply hoped to impress that this was a New Guatemala with a sense of "equal treatment and justice" for their precious Indigenous population that defined Guatemala as a nation ... !

Smarting from the bad P.R., feeling scapegoated and betrayed by what they saw as a conniving cabal of treasonous business-oriented politicians looking for outside capital whose dirty work and bidding they had been in the service of anyway, the military having lost all face and their "honor," like all their types worldwide, reacted by punishing yet once again the innocent pawns of the game: the corn-eating village Indians the government was hypocritically claiming to defend.

With nothing left to lose before they made their bitter exits into self-enforced civilian exile, the renegade officers formed their Indian soldiers into squads and ordered them out with flame throwers, flaming gel, and gasoline to fan through every ravine of the surrounding Holy mountains and set fire to every last stick of the few standing cornfields of that meager pre-spring harvest they could find.

Because this was the dry season, the entire mountain region, arable or not, whether cultivated or wild, indiscriminately whirled up crackling into flames. Wild animals fled in all directions, some drowning in the lake; others, running too close to hungry humans, were killed and eaten. Hovering just an inch above the lake water, the smoke drove off all the grebes and ducks and rolled through all the starving villagers' huts and houses, blanketing the piedmont hill to the south, creeping up and over like an atmospheric sea of disappearing memories and dreams burning off and heading back home away from human folly. Rolling west to cover the ocean, pulling back into the withering bud of unmanifested, unfed time, the smoke drifted heavily and low over the waves right into the setting Father Sun who, filled to capacity with all that was lost, swelled into a sad gigantic orange shield for weeks on end.

Because most families had already been reduced to eating up all their seeds or starving, with these flames the old Tzutujil seeds of life and deaths unique to Santiago Atitlán completely disappeared just like Chiv said they would. Not one indigenously cultivated seed remained to carry on. There were no seeds to replant the following seasons after the smoke settled down. The Birth/Death corn hidden in the ceilings had all been eaten.

But at least the soldiers were gone for the meantime and the people given for the first time in centuries Home Rule. The people had won, but this time there was no one to surrender to, to keep on planting the seeds of time. It was all too little too late. This, unlike the Spanish Conquest, was the beginning of what Chiv always said would be: the original Tzutujil, the real people of seeds, were ending. A new people of amnesia, cash-dependent and seedless, would take their place even though they were the same people.

International seed companies, supplying religious cooperatives with their chemical fertilizers, pesticides, hormones, and standardized hybrid "machine" seeds, as the Mayans called the seeds that had to be repurchased every year and didn't grow right if saved and replanted, took good advantage of this new branch of the disaster which had in any real overview to be understood to have developed directly out of the international corporation-run politics of the post-earthquake era of the 1980s.

This policy that backed politically sympathetic governments economically worked hard to rig things especially in the aftermath of colonialism, wars, and disasters to rid the entire world of self-sustaining, small regional market people, whose renewable seeds and cultural spiritual seed ways had made them generationally fairly peaceful, happy at home in their annual cycles of intense labor, indolent feasting and physical recovery, celebration and ritual, smiling, passionately in love with being together. Away from the anxious cash dependency of the efforts of the lower echelon of corporate business policy, they made no tax money for any governments or profits for any big businesses. Ever since "civilizations" and empires have existed, self-sustaining seed people have always been the express target of oppression and assimilation.

With the soldiers went the seeds. With the seeds went the rituals of the seeds. Without these seed rituals the culture virtually melted away. With the culture went the language, and with the language went the stories. Without the big mythic stories, people's faith in the ground and their centuries-long largesse of understanding how the ground, the water, the air, and growing old functioned, the tribal memory disappeared; even the personal memories of the old became a quaint, disjointed, unconnected irrelevancy of a forgotten past, and with that went the architecture, the beautiful clothing, and with that the sanity and the peace of being a person whose death was the planting of an echo in a seed that could plant the world back to life. It was the death of turning grief into beauty into life and into food for the living. It was the beginning of the kind of empty Death whose broken elliptical cycle and finality that modern civilization so terribly fears but utterly promotes by its own flight away from it in an eternal search for youth and Shangri-La. It was the beginning of living the unthinkable thought: the end of the villagers living without their seed souls and rituals.

For people like me, both in and outside, the village of Atitlán would seem to have turned in those short ten years into a strange, hard, money-dependent, unhappy, overcrowded town of avaricious Guatemalan citizens, with cell phones, televisions, Methodists, gas stoves, fridges, purchased food, polyester, pets, motorboats, pharmaceuticals, drug abuse, and suburban minds where their pride in being "Mayans" was a fundamentalist type of mental tax shelter to avoid the spiritual back taxes they owed to their once intact past. These were not the Indigenous seed people of before. But I will never judge them amiss, for it was not their doing.

Just like Chiv predicted, his people's lives slid effortlessly right into a mask of form that was at first a clumsy imitation but which soon enough quite efficiently mirrored the very culture that overran their own. This was why he had wanted me to go to the States to somehow "keep the seeds alive" inside the very core of the land originating this spiritual amnesia, where this kind of cultural loss was enshrined as a desirable modus operandi. He wanted me to jump right into that gigantic roller mill of depressing flatness that daily and eagerly ground into mediocre dust all its own indigenous plants, animals, and people, that its dull, desperate imperial mind had invaded a couple of centuries past. How could I ever do it? I mean "keep the seeds alive" in such a place?

Well, no matter how bad the people of the world get, one can never underestimate the capacity of the Holy in a Seed.

Seeds have a greater sense of humor and bravery than humans. They obey long, long, drawn-out plans, plans beyond the minds of men, that come down written inside the seeds, by their having to adapt to every kind of ice age, drought, wind, climatic cycles, the impacts of ice-tailed comets, deep serpentine primordial strata of earlier underground seas, cloudbursts, hurricanes, and more; mutating together and obeying the roll of the dice of the knee bones of the Grand Female of chaos whose womb's offspring is Time. Until I learned to flow with that, the ride was going to be hard.

Chapter 11

The Seeds Come Back Riding
"Little Bald Gourd"

I wouldn't be able to bring myself to depart from the beautiful ornery village where I'd come alive and been given a real place, at least not on the prompt schedule Chiv had insisted on before he died. But with my Tzutujil wife of the time and our two young boys, we did leave only when the hellish uncertainty of Guatemala's constant secret death patrols, and the presence of government soldiers everywhere, made it impossible to even appear without being killed or captured and disappeared. After a long soul-wringing struggle of two years living hidden inside different parts of Guatemala, we finally found a way to the States, where for several years before the Hills and Seeds of Atitlán were burnt and the soldiers left, we eventually settled as much as we could back into the matrix of my beloved New Mexico, close to where I'd been raised and from where I'd originally departed south to land in Atitlán as a younger man years in the past.

Ironically, the U.S. was as hard for me as it was terrible for the wife. We spent so much of our waking existence trying to not succumb to the ever-present and seemingly irresistible tractor beam of the modern world's mass trance that powerfully insisted that everyone merge into the seedless trappings of synthetic comfort and security of the suburban alloy of modern life that masked rootless, absent cultural origins.

Assimilation seemed imperative if you didn't want to live lonely. But to keep the seeds alive I was like a culturally lonely misplaced grasshopper who kept jumping out of that steep mental punch bowl that the general populace in the U.S. thought constituted the only possibility of life.

Eventually as the boys grew, they and their mother found it less painful to let go of what I painfully wanted to keep alive. It was impossible, herculean, and unfair to ask children who'd not really been old enough to really see it to keep at least a little bit of the fine aroma of the Flowering Mountain Earth, the ways of seeds alive in a place that no longer had anything comparable and which wouldn't applaud them for trying. The family, without the village, understandably didn't want to sustain the mockery and sneers of the only peers that life in the modern condition offered them. The children hid my spiritual professions from their friends and teachers. They just wanted everyone to accept them no matter what the terms. It took a lot of strength and a strong initiated vision of what we'd originally been to keep going under the everyday pressures of cultural rejection.

In the original seed way of the old-time Tzutujil village, my work as a shaman and village official was my small part of "keeping the seeds alive," and it was not a lonely thing. I was simply one of many like myself. But it was respected and honorable, for the magic we maintained was a vital component of the great organic engine of the heart of that Grand Female being upon whose generous breasts everyone knew they were sustained. She gave us our corn, fish, cotton clothing, know-how, and even our ecstatic voices to eloquently sing Her earth back to life. But in the States, or probably any part of the modern world that had a long time back lost any capacity for this, whatever I did could not be truly comprehended and therefore had to be maintained in a quiet, non-communal, personal way, which had no resemblance to a real keeping alive of seeds and only brewed superstitious judgment from the populace.

Most people are very social and want to be part of the big party going on around them, and my little family missed their home "herd" if you will. Shamans are never known for hanging out in coffee shops or small talk, so while I ended up as something revered, singular and outstanding to some Americans, I was seen by most of the people as something weird, backwards, dangerous, and superstitious.

In all the strange routes I attempted in order to keep alive somehow the "seeds" of the vision, a vision these people didn't seem to see, or even desire, my family drifted farther and farther from their friendship with my direction until we broke away from each other under the pressure of my distance from accepted American culture.

What had eroded us, day by day, was partly the belligerent unblinking stare of modern life's superficiality, whose synthetic carpets, clean bathrooms, pharmaceutically induced sleep, drug-induced wakeups, drug-controlled moods and appearances, chemicalized food, and television-directed accents and opinions left no hint as to their organic indigenous origins, spiritual or otherwise. Among the old-time Americans, as strange, ethnocentric, and arrogant as they could be—especially the farmers and ranching families—they still had a little bit of some ground-rooted originality and zest. But here we were lost among a people who didn't know or even care where any of their own disposable junk that they relied on came from. Who grew the cotton? Who wove it? Where was the petroleum from, from what shells, fish from what ocean, where drilled, who drilled it, who cooked it into polymers, what polymers, to be further emulsified by whom, where, into this quiet ugly appropriate non-tribal storyless sweater that somebody on TV had worn but did nothing other than jeopardize your health by its off-gassing acrylates? Where was their strange food from? Whose seeds did what individual use to plant these gigantic, inedible, soccer-ball hydroponic tomatoes whose real ancestors Highland Mayans cultivated first? There were some very good-hearted and generous families and individuals to whom we certainly owed our physical survival. But we could not live here and stay as the Tzutujil we had been if we were surrounded totally by people, plants, toy dogs, houses, pots, pans, cars, values, tools, concrete, asphalt, airplanes, glass, pistons, exhaust, medicines, telephones, TV, radios, flattened accents, clothing, and food for which we had no story of where they originated. In the original villages and tribes of the world, all of this would have to be known to be included into the village soul and daily life; otherwise people left it alone or invented one. Those who didn't, lost their culture and their seeds, swallowed by the monster of empty origins.

For a truly Indigenous Mind to live without knowing the stories and origins of everything and every human was an insanity; this disregard for the world's natural spiritual origins was tantamount to whales living without their inborn sonar. Without the origins you weren't living where you were. You were not anywhere. In the States this was an enforced state of affairs, no doubt the primary source of their mass depressions. Modern people had no choice to be utterly synthetic if their own origins were lost, so the populace as a whole seemed to abbreviate their own origins into a category of "less fortunate times" from which their present state of unconnected amnesia was proclaimed to be a triumph of freedom over an oppressive past: freedom from Origins. There was no mutual indebtedness, no *káslimáal,* nothing was counted or intertwined, it was just there, taken for granted or completely forgotten while they plodded on to a more "comfortable" future!

The Mayan villagers and all intact "seed" type people in the world, whether animal people or vegetation people, who see themselves in terms of what feeds them, know deeply the literal and spiritual origins of all the animals and plants as heavily as they know their own origins, because they are twined interdependently. They truly knew in a non-corny way that a people really are what they eat. The story of the origins of all that fed us made up our physical presence.

And what were the people in this modern world eating? They ate fast-food amnesia cakes, conforming to not remembering the origination of themselves, rewriting the story of anything they consumed as their own invention in service to the mediocre, synthetic, storyless, empty present disguised as a triumph of comfort.

Our family was not of course unique: all immigrants, and intact village people invaded by the same from without, have had to negotiate this. But very few ever survived as themselves. Eventually, one generation without vision of a full cultural initiation would be seduced into the mouth of this synthetic culture of no origins. We were not driven apart by how the people in the States saw us or how poor they thought we looked, or how much sympathy they had or didn't have for all the war losses we daily wept about; we were undermined by the fact that no one could see what we could see: how our babies were literally corn sprouts to us, and how all human mothers were corn plants, not metaphorical corn mothers, or some flat psychological symbols of a spiritual concept, but the literal seed life whose ritual magnificence we were tribally obligated to physically, anatomically, geographically, spiritually, and temporally made of and fed with our lives.

They were for the most part not bad people, but still they could not sit beside us and look out and see what we saw and help us to keep seeing. Instead they looked *at* us without seeing that we were seeing something else. While we tried valiantly to be accepted by a people crowding around us who gave no value to the story of all the things that served them and fed them, we grew lonelier and lonelier.

Loneliness motivates all humans and animals, but it is the hardest for tribal people. The family wanted the freedom of being loved by the Americans they were surrounded by even if they had to discard their seed and who they had been to get it. But I stubbornly accepted the slavery of keeping the seeds alive. Both would end up mistaken routes to take, but the desperation of our hearts had me fast becoming a fundamentalist Mayan and the family quickly drifting into good wasteful American consumers with a lot more friends than I would ever have for over two decades.

After dipping diligently in and out of a million different approaches and ideas to try and keep Chiviliu's seeds of comprehension alive, it would be a while before I would realize that instead of "keeping the seeds alive" I had been idiotically trying to keep the ghost of a long-gone village alive as I had known and loved it. I just couldn't surgically remove what all the old people and I had done there for these grand years together from my heart. Unable to really let the tears flow and accept that the village I had been a part of was definitely dead and gone, that it would never be that way again, and neither would I, in the States, I couldn't seem to stand still long enough to let that be a living reality for me. That ancient seed cycle was too deeply rooted in all I'd become in Atitlán. It would take a long time for me to grow big enough through negotiating that grief of the tragedy of the cycle broken to become the more realistic able person Chiviliu knew could fruit inside me right on that vine of sorrow.

Real villages cannot really be created by people who will follow a single individual no matter how visionary. Such synthetic beginnings lack true origins and are as bound to fail as they are well meaning. Real villages can only come from listening to the Holy in the "seeds," as the Tzutujil would say, not a person. Like people, ecosystems, cultures of interrelated animals, plants, winds, oceans, and people, villages must organically grow from the mind of the Holy in the Seed and ground. Old Chiv knew that villages came from the big understanding of the seeds themselves, seeds he wanted me not to keep hidden like some esoteric secret, but seeds kept alive by communal reverence, hard work, and replanting against all odds. But that was all yet to come. For in those years all my attempts to "keep the seeds alive" were more of the nature of a hopeless unnoticed assault on the well-armored numb monster of modern life, more like spitting a determined barrage of overcooked peas at an oncoming Sherman tank than having any resemblance to cultivation.

It was just then that the solders' fire and smoke billowing over the lakeside mountains surrounding Atitlán converted the villagers' last corn seeds into vaporous ash that rose into the stratosphere to join company with the jaded haze of the civilized world's automobile, industrial, and energy factories' exhaust, the material grief of modernity's self-destructing stage play, whose combustion from the bottom up burnt the fat layer of the earth's own memory in the form of crude oil, the remembrance of the earth's own oceanic Placenta Heart time in the womb. When we received the news that the soldiers were gone, we decided to return to the village.

Even with the absence of a military presence, and the new reality that Santiago Atitlán was now not so dangerous as it had been, getting there alive, at least for the likes of me, would be still a difficult affair with all of the military checkpoints, guerrillas ambushes, imitation *cuatero* guerrilla shakedowns, real and just plain well-armed bandits everywhere unexpectedly waylaying Indian travelers or anybody in random roadblocks, where mass gunpoint robberies, arrests, executions, and disappearances were still the order of the day.

I and many others exiled for years into lives and places a million unhappy miles away because of the dangerous presence of the soldiers, each by our own methods felt our ways back to the lakeshore to kiss again the tearstained cheeks of that unruly beauty of Siwaan Tinamit, the Canyon Village, at least one more time.

Any exile returning to the village felt triumphant just by the fact of having actually arrived, even though it was fairly safe ground now compared to before. But getting there was always a thing done under cover and at night, no matter who you were. I finally managed to catch up with the family who'd been sent by a different route and time on account of I was more "wanted" by warring parties than they, and therefore they had a better chance of being undetected and surviving without me if I were caught.

The night I arrived the village was still full of the remaining multifaceted rituals of the ever-beautiful Tzutujilized Catholic Holy Week. It had not yet succumbed to what would come in a few short years later, when all of the last old generation fell back into the Holy earth along with their extensive memory and their seeds, their echoes muffled by the village and adoption of modern life.

In the middle of those two tearful tiny weeks that followed, both the saddest and most spiritually exhilarating I had ever experienced, an immense miracle of the more common kind that goes largely unnoticed by the world, the kind I love the most, came puffing and trudging along the cindery byways of what would become my former home forever.

During my exile in the States many children of Tzutujil friends and relations in Atitlán came sprouting their dawning light into this world out of their hungry mother's struggling bellies to give birth to almost an exact number of the portion of the population that had been lost: hideously starved to death, shot down, gone mad, tortured, or disappeared in the violence! A truly alarming number of these kids had been kept waiting for names, the parents holding out for my return so that I could personally, per old tradition, bestow my own name and with it my spiritual worth on each child, both boys and girls. Part of my "worth" probably came from the fact that everybody knew I could gulp down a lot of *maatz*.

Every month for years the parents had waited, hoping someday we could all drink the great *maatz* together from the skull-like gourds, name their children, tickle their feet with live mother crabs for agility and somehow in the process cause the Seed spirituality to resprout again in such a way as to make the village reflower after the massive cultural blight of uncomprehending outsiders, Christians, politics, business soldiers, and war that had wilted the traditional life everywhere you looked. Before all that, life had never been easy, but it had been good. Not because it was traditional, but because it was delicious and everyone had been inseparably part of the village, at home feeding that Holy thing in the seed by just the way they lived.

While I knew we could not risk messianically trying to give new life to the Old Ways, because no doubt even more people would be killed, inner dissension would escalate, their spirituality would become a religion, its capacity to keep alive the Holy in the Seeds reduced to dry, mechanical, and liturgical techniques instead of being a living knowledge of a people "at home." Sects would arise; people claiming they had the "right" ways and the others the "wrong" ways would take over. No matter what happened, most certainly the governmental minds of both left and right, sanctioned and unsanctioned, would suspect it all equally. Nonetheless I still thought naming babies would be fine, and it did in some way keep that small bit of the seeds alive, for the moment anyway.

The families counseled together, rushing to get their naming rituals scheduled in such a staggered way that I could go from one compound to the next nonstop! Tragically, however, because the real birth corn of the original unbroken line could *not* be found in any household anywhere for having been either burnt or confiscated by the former soldiery or previously consumed by the starving villagers themselves, a tasteless, dull, whitish hybrid dent corn, a pesticide- and chemical fertilizer–dependent cattle feed, sent by the U.S. in starvation relief, was all there was to be had. With the ritual mastery of the old Tzutujil style, the familiar ritual capacity of the people to give dignity to a rejected thing, the matrons of the naming ritual raised the corn's anonymous homeless status by talking fondly and nobly to this poor dejected corn, praising its forgotten, magnificent ancestry and holy capacity of life, thereby ritually converting this corn's slave-like past as a servant of unconscious humans into the true nobility from which all indigenous maize descended before Europeans mechanically expropriated the corn "seeds" from natives taking away the names, rituals, and Placental Hearts of the people, the land, and the plants. Seeds are slaves to modern people, there to serve them, not Goddesses who suckle us into life. The ritual language released the poor slave and gave her throne back.

But just as the people were talking their unhappy, mechanically grown refugee seeds into a status worthy of naming and identifying with their children, the unexpected miracle came waddling in.

I think the animals must have known it first, for all the village dogs started wagging their wails, momentarily calling off their feuds, lining up quietly side by side along the stone walls staring at what no people could see. The loose village chickens and turkeys stopped scratching and commenting; the wind held his breath; the Mother Lake flattened into a waveless mottled mirror of breezeless jade anticipation waiting for what was Holy to look into her water, to reflect back to a forgetting world the deep wonder of the face of what had become invisible to most. Even the leaves on the lime trees forgot to rustle, and the birds stood still.

It was on that day, just a little before the first naming was to get under way for a big-toothed six-year-old cousin of my children, when a faint rustling and breathy murmur, like the sound of the vanguard of rolling foam of the first fan of water that announces an imminent flash flood in a dry valley, gradually became the roar of a crowd of loud, happy people who began drifting into and over the walls of the meager compound of our family huts, in a chaotic symphony of reports that brought us news of something coming whose message for all their entangled sound we couldn't make out.

At first we were alarmed, worried that yet another violent incident might be in motion, but after running out from under our shady thatch up to the black stone walls to have a look, we could see a quarter mile down, and for a quarter mile in every direction in the hub of a swelling crowd of thousands of joyful chattering women, shrieking children, and yelling teenage boys standing on walls and each other's shoulders and looking over the surging press of the crowd moving toward us, a little man only four foot five if that, with a face too big for his body from forty years of malnutrition, but a face full of jokes and those kinds of hard-earned forehead wrinkles that make some of these patient, astute men dedicated to feeding their children at all costs more handsome every year. Struggling under a maguey net full of ivory-colored ears of dried corn, so large and heavy over his tough little back that it seemed as if his two sinewy copper legs and bare gnarled feet with toenails already work-swallowed back into the horn of his calloused toes were actually a large netted package with its own two legs that walked along on its own.

His cargo no doubt was creaking in that old characteristic way of everyone else hauling the things they'd grown out of the mountains, but we couldn't hear it, where he came thumping and shuffling under his weight through the blue-gray volcanic sand of the paths between his tiny house of stone, corn stalk, and corrugated tin that hung off the cliff edge of Panuul through the middle of the village to our place, for the boisterous racket of the flood of amazed, unsolicited, admiring villagers, that oozed along with him swelling its ranks along the way.

By the time he had arrived at our house, his progress was so hindered by the people's joy that a few taller unburdened Tzutujil men took hold of some part of the man's load and escorted him like a king, laughing and weeping in amazement with one another, raising to fervent procession what would have otherwise been on any other day in the recent past the more usual, smaller, lonely creaking of one person's everyday heroic miracle of bringing home the seed to feed their family.

He had birth corn.

The original *Yaki Sac*, ivory corn, the real kind, the assumed dead, extinct, gone-away corn; more than one hundred pounds of what had been everywhere else burnt to ash or eaten.

The corn was alive and entering the town, returning from the dead after a hard war, and the people gave the returning corn of birth and death a returning hero's welcome; wildly amazed, intrigued, and unable to guess where little Ma Buxtol, not an old man, but the funny, clever, raggedy father to a family of six live children and a healthy wife, had come up with this unexpected pile of the living Holy Face of who the people had always known themselves to be.

When he assumed the rough basaltic steps into our old compound in Panaj, half the world tried to join him, knocking over half of the walls, inside of which the crowd of course still didn't fit. For as far as you could see in every direction regardless of neighbors, boundaries, paths, and walls, on top of the walls, straddling roof beams, and perched on sweathouse roofs, people crowded and relayed to those behind them in concentric waves the news of Buxtol's triumphant entrance with the even more heroic live seeds of a Holy Corn that had already been universally spoken of in past tense.

It was just like the last time, ten years before, when the entire village had gathered to welcome the last-ever ecstatic return of the initiate boys, who were to annually reemerge from their deeply coordinated underworld journeys heavily loaded with the Holy seed fruit of their own souls from the hot coast; the people came together, but only this time the crowd was spontaneous and all for the lost corn.

Before climbing up into the courtyard, Buxtol, whose playful nickname meant "little bald gourd," stopped walking with the precious heavy load on his back strapped over his sweating forehead and remained standing, swaying in place. The people knew he wanted silence, and the crowd quieted in waves, taking a long moment to achieve this all the way back.

Then yelling so all might hear, Bux in his rather high joking voice asked for permission to enter with the courteous old ritual question, meaning simultaneously, "Are all of you there?" and "Are we welcome?" "*Ex kola aii,*" he called out.

A question heard and replied to a thousand times an hour anywhere in town, a question always asked by harvested corn spoken through the voices of men on whose back they return from the fields, this time the question was made big by these being the only seeds of the corn of life and death left for them on earth, returning home.

Like a landslide careening down a ravine, the whole world let loose a deafening welcoming reply, each according to age, gender, and village rank while stretching their necks back and forth like gathered cranes to get a look.

"*Ex kola,*" he yelled again.

"*Ok kola joj ta' ket tok pa alè.*" "We're present father, come over the threshold into us, Bux," we yelled back, and into the packed courtyard he struggled, and in front of the door with the young men holding his load he pulled his tumpline from out beneath his little straw hat, while turning to help let the load settle gently onto the cindery ground in front of what had been my old family hut. Then turning to look around he spoke, pretending as always that everything was news to him,

"*Nix kola rilaj a* Martín *wavie'.*" "Could it be that 'old' Martín is present here somewhere?"

"*Jie in kola anen ta', lutz a wach rilaj ala', bajni'qíj majun xkaston kruachbal ki'?*" "Yes, I'm present father; how well does your fruit (face), old son, how many days since we haven't seen each other's faces (fruit)?"

"*Utz nwach ta', majun xinwutkij a wach pok at nim!*" "My face (fruit) is well; I didn't know your face (fruit) anymore—you're so tall I couldn't see all of you at once!"

Then grabbing the net with his small strong hand, he looked at me and spoke while the crowd whispered everything we did, and said sounding all the world like a giant meadow of crickets,

"*Nkamompa ke'e' ru wach ctit'ral rilaj vinaaq chawa ta'.*" "I brought a couple of faces (fruit) of the children of the old woman for you, father," by which he meant the corn herself, speaking as all people always did when referring to Mother Corn.

And after speaking this way for several minutes, the ever-bigger village crowd held its collective breath as I asked the question all of them had been asking each other.

"*Ba tzra xa' vil ju jala ashnaaq rilaj taq kásbal ruchiulew, xatet a* Bux?*" "Where did you discover these beautiful and venerated makers of earthly life, Little Gourd?" which in the old Tzutujil courteous ritual speech that all adults employed when present in some situation regarding the Holy or the Grand meant, "Where did you find this beautiful rare corn, Little Gourd?"

Like a dam of traditional restraint holding back a river of human curiosity, all courtesy broke down in the crowd who'd been listening so quietly you could hear their hearts beating—now began yelling, entreating Bux to explain where he found this long-lost corn.

Superficially, when measured by appearances and possessions, Bux might have been considered by those who had never known want to be, if not the poorest, one of the poorest men in the town, whose family lived in the most diminutive, rickety, cornstalk hut, perched like an osprey nest on a canyon cliff far from the lake and the famous town market, and whose children ran about in clothing of patches on top of patches as did he. But neither he nor his plump, tired, beautiful, simple wife, nor any of their children were ever hungry, and only one child out of seven had perished, both miraculous oddities for most families of those times, no matter how well off; this was a constant source of curiosity for the entire village and his neighbors in particular. He was my children's grandmother's brother, and I had always been close with his family. Though he and his wife were practically landless, no one could ever determine the secret behind his ability to bring in so much food, no matter how trying the times. He was always everywhere in the mountains, the coast, always working like a regular pedestrian Tzutujil farmer, a friend to all, never secretive or evasive, eternally a joker but always a magical kind of regular guy.

Except in ritual contexts, everything he had to say was on the back of a joke, a harmless prank, or a fictitious tale whose endless creativity was his trademark.

He always joked about how wealthy he was as he swung his hoe like a demon, about his quadrilles of unruly workers on his coastal plantations, talking like a Ladino *latifundista*, wiping his brow about how exhausted he was from reviewing his vast land holdings by helicopter, the problem with keeping good bodyguards, the boring overfilling dinners with the President, or how he'd just lost three truckloads of women's fancy skirt material over a cliff somewhere as if he were also a wealthy merchant, or cows as if he were a cattleman, bananas or coffee as a plantation owner, but no matter what, Bux would always make everyone laugh every time, but never at him because in the end everybody else was only two steps richer than he and the vicissitudes of being a people on the earth there in those times was a shared knowledge.

And of course, with several thousand villagers listening and looking on, that morning was no different when great, strong old Ma Yé from Panabaj, one knee up on our *koxtun,* demanded somewhat condescendingly:

"Naks chiej atet xatquin xa mul jaura?" "By what opening of luck was the likes of you able to gather up this impossible thing in these impossible times?"

Tiny Ma Bux, forever undaunted by the "rich" farmers, started off apologetically: "Well, everybody here knows how many of my thousands of acres I have the workers plant every year, and I knew I wanted Old Martín, when he came back, to name my boy, but Martín had to go and check the crops of his aging father in his father's land. Of course to make the *maatz* drink for the naming I had to keep the seeds alive until Martín came back. So I, without the help of my lazy workers who everybody knows you can't trust with such serious things, personally planted this Old Lady corn six years ago up there on my very best land."

The crowd laughed, squinted their eyes, and hissed a little, for everybody between the age of six and one hundred knew his only land was a rock wall on the north shadow side of an unassailable ravine of decaying tufa rocks about five hundred feet straight up the vertical drop beneath the southern overhang off the side of the Chichuc volcano, the elbow of the earth, the volcano of San Pedro.

Swallows loved the place, and even wild goats sometimes visited it, but no one except a swallow could descend that narrow aerial hole without ropes and pitons, much less try farming in there. It was inaccessible, out of the sun and rain, and soil-less. The people just laughed. But Bux continued.

"So, I tied my sash to the rope of my helicopter and had my driver fly me up over the bay and hold me over that hole while I hoed my excellent land and planted and tended these children of the Face of the 'Old Woman,' the corn of birth, over and over again for over six years. I planted it up there so all you greedy people wouldn't steal my corn!"

The crowd scoffed less, for outside of the helicopter and the driver, it started to sound more and more familiar.

Then they stopped laughing altogether and grew silent as Bux continued: "When the soldiers came, I knew it was going to be bad after they killed and quartered up Ma Tziná; we were going to lose it all, especially our food, and I had to keep the seeds of Death and Birth alive so I could name my children when Old Martín came back. I knew they would eat it all or kill it all or all of us so I lowered myself by my *coló*, my handmade rope, over the cliff every year in chosen spots where the sun hit and planted that cliff in hopes none of the soldiers would find it or me, hiding the seeds in a cave up there.

"When the army set fire to the Old Woman's Mansion (the wild mountains!) they tried to burn this corn too. They put a big old fire at the bottom with firewood and gasoline, and it rose angrily burning up the hole like a pitch fire in a Ladino chimney, but it was only hot enough to wither the leaves, leaving the stalks and faces (ears) undisturbed, actually giving it the last little heat that sunless side needed to fully dry out and mature! I told nobody because when the world began to go looking for food, starving, going crazy eating all their seeds, I knew up in the cliff they had a chance if the birds allowed it, and they did.

"So when I saw Old Martín the other day come back playing his little flute again with the old people, I had my driver fly me up there again and harvested that venerable cliff by helicopter, and here are the seeds, the faces of the children of the Old Woman Corn."

There was not a sound other than the renewed breeze, the singing of some birds, and the sound of a couple of babies fussing when Bux, like everyone else staring at the holy ground in a deep remembering, lifted his oversized, teary-eyed head and triumphantly added,

"*X ul ruwach rilaj ilie camic.*" "The face of venerable 'Mrs. You Know Who' has returned today."

The whole world yelled, cheering in war cries, shrieking in pride at his triumph, at the triumph of the seeds, and commenced running in every direction ostensibly to tell anybody who hadn't been there but mostly because they had to do something with the emotion of the thought and the energy of something old and magical going right for once.

In the days that came I drank a lot of that rare, hard-fought-for *maatz*, delicious poor-farmer *maatz* of the most precious pearl-like ivory-colored *Yakii Sac* corn that had ever been *maatz*, and I tried as hard as I would ever try to not disgrace any child's future by finishing every drop I was asked to take in, and hoping by doing so to do honor to the grandest of all my heroes ever, Ma Buxtol, a small unknown man who against all odds would keep the seeds alive.

In an emotionally charged welcome of old friends, relations, and a string of aged colleagues and comrades retired from the formal hierarchy, who like Chiv ten years earlier would soon pass on, hordes of people, hopeful my arrival meant that somehow the old ways of life and holy struggle would magically resprout again, came in and out of the massive series of child namings bearing gifts of food and smiles to watch me prayerfully consume one after the next, three full tree gourds of the Holy *Maatz*.

Even with the fortune of the presence of the real sacred corn instead of what would've been gourdful after gourdful of a horrible, tasteless paste of commercial hybrid cattle corn, each gourd still held a minimum of a quart of the thick gruel, making my obligation to drink in succession the equivalent of three quarters of a gallon to as much as a gallon and a half in one quaff so one's namesake would grow to live healthily and well, into a ritual challenge bordering on a gastronomic marathon of Olympic proportions.

Always known for my inborn capacity to drink *maatz* in the many ceremonial contexts we were required, the loud sound of my uninterrupted *glub, glub, glub* a cause for great admiration and hilarity, this time the long string of little kids of every age from newborns to six-year-olds who'd been waiting all that time for a name, for which I was expected to drink a gallon of *maatz* for each and every one, was more than a daunting task; one that had never occurred in the village before and which would probably take a couple of months of nonending gulping and naming ceremonies before we could all catch up on all the namings for these lively pot-bellied little creatures.

But just then a journalist vacationing on the opposite side of the lake, hearing of my heretofore unreported, hushed-up presence on the lake, unthinkingly wrote a newspaper article announcing it, and what I had hoped might have been months or maybe even years was reduced to only two weeks.

Rumors of known right-wing hit men asking questions of my where-abouts on the north side of the lake still bearing a competitive grudge after all that time, and knowing nothing else but keeping score, like old-time safari trophy hunters who tried to fill their lists of what they "bagged," anxious to complete an obsolete list of suspected revolution-aries or uncooperative free-thinking radicals considered "dangerous" by the right wing ten years previous, began drifting into the village on the scared banter of some of my younger friends recently turned merchants. Returning from their selling and buying expedition throughout the coun-try looking for cash instead of farming or fishing, in order to feed their children in the "new" economy, they heard and saw everything and luck-ily came around to warn us.

I would really learn to comprehend the depth of what Chiv had known would come in on his people after his death, knowing as he did that I would never be able to stay or return to visit ever after.

Though no one pushed it, it became apparent to everyone that to remain meant death. Even then, unnoticed I would have to somehow arrange to make a slow, quiet break for it and hope to get to the U.S. without being detected.

The only thing on my behalf was that I was not being looked for by any official authority left or right, only scary clandestine right-wing enti-ties left over from the previous decade.

The wife wouldn't leave, choosing to live back in the village come what may after the confusion of our life in the States. I would go back to New Mexico and try to raise my two adolescent sons, sent stateside by a different route. Though I loved the American West, especially my native New Mexico, the United States as a cultural phenomenon was the epitome of a cultural avoidance system and probably as oppressive for me as it had been for her, but my staying in Atitlán was guaranteed death or worse. But ironically for me at that time, though keeping the seeds alive was near impossible in the States, it was now utterly impossible in Atitlán. I got ready to leave, avoiding a send-off so as not to alert my adversaries.

I fell as ill as I could get, mostly from a strong infusion of the deepest sorrow, outrage, terror, apprehension, shigellosis, bad war-era *psiwanyá*, possibly too much *maatz*, and the feeling of having all that hopeful possibility of the tribal beauty returned crushed again. But I refused to leave without at least a handful of those ancient reborn seeds of Ma Buxtol; the little ivory Seeds of Life and Death he'd brought through the fire. Maybe with those seeds I could better remember who I was supposed to be when I wasn't there, what I was meant to serve a little clearer if only that little bit was left me, so every day in the land that seemed to have forgotten, I could gaze upon a little of what life had been and could be: each kernel like a translucent bead on a rosary of indigenous remembrance.

Chapter 12

Swimming Past the Dogs of Amnesia,
the Seeds Disappear into the Redwoods

L ive, open-pollinated seeds of any kind were highly restricted and very difficult to carry through U.S. customs without their being confiscated, destroyed, quarantined, or sprayed with various poisons in those days and probably remain so today.

Only certain biology, genetics, and agriculture departments of universities serving that strange, incongruously unfair alliance among government agricultural agencies, global corporations, banks, and world "development" had the required documents and permission of the U.S. government to import live seeds, enjoying basically a one hundred percent monopoly over the world's natural seeds in which they claim exclusive legal patent over the genes of nature that the world's indigenous and village cultures had developed and gracefully kept viable. While the vastly endowed agroscience business racket could fiddle with the seeds, hybridizing, even genetically altering and obscenely exploiting them for chemical large-scale commercial agriculture, a single farming villager from any part of the rural world would never be allowed to bring in the country so much as fifty kernels of corn, wheat, beans, or rice any more than he would ten kilos of opium.

While I have always disliked the use of addictive recreational drugs, their subculture, or business, for as things stand today they are yet more unhealthy accoutrements of civilization's failure and represent its people's inability to live with the frantic effects of their own inventions. But wars waged against plants are absurdities when carried out by the very cultures that are addicted to them. All food and seeds should belong to the people who belong to the plants. Any real tribal people never need drugs to feel the Holy; all intact people receive visionary understanding just from the power of the food they eat for dinner! That's the real magic of the Indigenous Soul. Food is the vision. People who can't see the Holy in the Seed need substances to feel alive.

But be that as it may, the chances of the likes of me talking a United States customs agent into letting me past their podiums in possession of a short cob of Mayan corn were as slim as the shadow of a mouse whisker at noon.

It wasn't simply my appearance that usually found me searched, or that my blondness didn't fit my natural New Mexico Indian accent that in their generalist minds they took to be an act, something fake and therefore suspect of something hidden, unusual, or amiss, nor was it the generalized widespread Northern New Mexican male way of walking derived from the fact that no Northern New Mexican man has any buttocks and therefore his pants hang vaguely cooperatively off a silver buckled belt in a certain telltale curtain-like way that always raises suspicions of something non-American, the resulting walk interpreted in their training manuals as attitudinal, instead of what it took to hold up jeans without a waistline, or was it the overcompensating chin-forward pride, or the friendly but quiet independent demeanor, that made it so I had to get to airports before the rest of the passengers to ensure I got through the searches in time to catch my flight, or take an extra day in either direction in the likelihood I was detained.

What probably cursed me so I knew personally a large gamut of all the agents in so many American airports was my uncharacteristic disregard for certain details of the synthetic comfort on which so much of modern techno-life depends. Details accepted as what is considered the gold standard of normal and safe, and neurotically defended by big-city and suburban Euro-Americans. I pridefully knew such people could no more survive as they were, not physically, spiritually, or culturally away from their phones, cars, lawn mowers, TVs, financial plans, coffee shops, or malls, in the broad severity and rugged deliciousness of the ever-changing one-hundred-degree heat, sub-zero cold, one-hundred-mile-per-hour winds, flooding, pollen haze, and dusty harshness of my beloved New Mexico much less the hard insecurity of the Guatemala I was leaving. This arrogance must have been indelibly written all over me, the likes of which the loyal servants of that governmentally enforced standardization of behavior in the form of immigration and customs people who were trained to bristle up their hackles, sniff out as suspect, and subsequently search and restrain such a person until determined fineable or ineffectual, would cause me to be singled out.

For a more definite capacity of alarm, of brainwashed instinctual back-bristling, sniffing, and searching out of unhomogenized individuals, these human trainees were supplied with funny little beagles, Chihuahuas, and Alsatian dogs that the agents held leashed, surveying the incoming passengers entering "U.S. soil," sniffing bags, butts, crotches, shoes, and purses in the customs hall, all of which made it fairly clear that if I actually succeeded in flying from Central America into the Houston airport to make my Albuquerque connecting flight in my efforts to find my way back to my home in Northern New Mexico, I would be very likely pulled out of the crowd for my seeds in customs as with hundreds of others I gathered up my baggage to effect the plane change after the port of entry. Here the dogs would, no doubt, easily sense my seeds and, raising the alarm, cause my bags to be searched for contraband and the seeds confiscated and probably destroyed. I would lose my Rosary of Remembrance, the seeds of Bald Gourd, the only handful left to me from the old days in the village.

So even before I departed Atitlán for the last time, at the juncture of heartbreak, outrage, and no small degree of delirious creativity approximating a shamanic inspiration due to an intense fever, I prayed, then shelled one cob of the corn of Birth and Death that Bux had saved for me: about two fistfuls, every kernel of which I then carefully and painfully hid everywhere I could imagine, remembering that to the old-time Tzutujil, the Earth is our body, and in the body of the Earth I knew I was in some way hiding the seeds again back into the Earth to keep the seeds alive for a later time. I hid them between my toes, under my toes, under my this, in my that, and other places of the "earth body" even stranger, including my meager bags, in hopes at least a couple of the still-alive, beautiful naming corn, so tenuously and diligently struggled for, might somehow slip past the dogs and authorities to keep my aching heart company.

Through the early morning dark under the protection of that great Mother Bird of night who quietly hatches all possibilities, with a couple of the same brave young fellows with whom I'd arrived, but this time in a different, more dented, tiny yellow Japanese truck, we twisted and turned out of the lake for my last starlit glimpse of that dwindling world, swinging in the dust of back routes I'd learned during the earthquake relief of 1976. In this way we avoided all but one of the gauntlet of road checks that crossed all the much quicker, main asphalted thoroughfares on the way to the planes. The only one we hit was just outside Guatemala City, and it was still dark and early enough that the underpaid police had yet to man it, and we passed unhindered.

Sick, saturated in grief and loneliness, I landed with a crowd of business travelers in Houston, but every time I began to lose perspective if not hope, I would peek in the little space between my obsolete wedding band and the finger it spun on, and seeing a single little brilliant kernel shimmering back, my shoulders would drop and I would remember again in the airport milieu who I was and what I was meant for, and how big such small things are for little people like me with big invisible ideas.

After being stamped in through immigration and herded in and out of what seemed to me, due to my fever and my having already slipped back into the Mayan aesthetic of the tiny and well-made, a series of gigantic purposeless halls of dull drywall, upon entering the circling baggage carousel of the corral-like parlor of customs, where hundreds of muttering frenetic people, barely able to drag their luggage from the tilted conveyor belt, plopped them on little carts that only slightly cooperated as they moved toward customs document inspectors in the slots in another hall, three soldier-brained, monofocused little dogs beelined straight for me and my gear, dragging three well-fed, cheerless, uniformed humans by their leashes.

During certain illnesses, feverish ones in particular, there are sometimes layers of presences, presentiments, and capacities that bubble out of the depth of our natural souls, who normally, like a pod of whales, keep their distance and out of sight of the plodding everyday mind but which under certain conditions become less shy and even flamboyantly daring. Running through me from brainpan to toe like a warm rod of sight was the recognition, in the split second before the mechanical-brained dogs' arrival, that none of these people would ever care about what I cared about, not because they were nasty ill-willed people, but because they could no longer comprehend what having these kinds of "seeds" meant to a person like me, having themselves lost their own cultural seeds probably centuries before. I would never make it understood to anyone in that airport in short order what my little seeds meant to all past people and plants, living in other dimensions, who were not really dead, as long as we kept their seeds alive, or what they might mean to myself, or to a village disappeared, and, not to mention, to Old Chiviliu. Therefore on behalf of this collective remembrance, I made that afternoon an unorthodox and for me uncharacteristic decision, the likes of which I'd never done before or since.

What most people think is their mind is but a cluttered closet hidden in a sprawling Italian mansion, an ornate villa whose every room they've never really fully visited. The one room closest to the front door of the waking state is the one we always seem to dream of. With my own mansion wholly rented out and overloaded with the temporary purveyors of a rampant fever of pneumonia, my real being, from a place beyond that mansion of sequential time, somewhere in the surrounding wild open forests of the Indigenous Soul, began to move to the surface like a mother animal to protect the seeds.

Aiming without sights or estimation, as natural as a playful jaguar gripping a giant river carp, or a dry rattler delicately licking up the electric yellow pollen of a desert primrose, or the geologic speed of the beeline of a mantis rocking her way towards some particular crack to lay eggs for children she will never see, I pulled way past the jade horizons of my kidneys, drawing up from a deeper well the same magic that makes birds suddenly swarm and migrate, or old male elk to run together in long sub-alpine lines to dance for hours in hidden mountain breaches just before the first snow, and tossed it around me like a throw net of protective superficial smiles and musky animal enchanting breezes that spread out away from me straight to those closet-minded dogs. This stopped them in a place beyond all their training, in a place in the geography of ancient instinct for which their trainers had no maps and naturalists had no knowledge for lack of a measurable generality for the habits of the bigger cycles of animal ritual.

The short and long of it was that the dogs, when they hit the boundary of the dream field around me that my renegade feverish mind had made overly accessible, at about fifteen inches off from the intended trajectory of each dog's pointy snout—my knees, my bags, my butt crack—they simultaneously forgot, stiffened in their tracks, and dropped purposeless to the floor, panting with big, perfectly dumb, contented smiles. The hor-rified handlers, after a minute of hopeless leash jerking and the strange yelling, hisses, and squeaks of emphatic secret voice commands intended to mechanically catapult the dogs out of this uncharacteristic insubordi-nation that they attributed wholly to what in their minds could have only been the dogs' faulty training, finally got the mutts out of their trance. But when the dogs jumped to their feet, they pricked their ears, bristled their backs, and stared slowly and bizarrely in an eerie unison to their collective left, then hit the ends of their leashes of the unprepared agents so hard that they vehemently dragged them with a mission straight to a nice older Welsh couple coming in from Gatwick and busted them both for the terrible crime of a forgotten but nonetheless undeclared illegal half-eaten steak and kidney pie, for which they were mildly corrected but forced to relinquish to the agents and dogs who completely forgot about my existence, as I and the seeds moved sick and tottering toward my next flight.

There seems to be an unfenced boundary, a kind of nonspatial hori-zon within which an Earth and its people live, think, speak, and die mythologically intact in a universe of story in whose tangible pro-ceedance even human failures, mediocrities, and detours seem to have a purposeful position. Crossing this line into the dimension of the distracted urban meander of modern civilization's entertainment-centered mind, the horizon seems to become invisible, the other side unseeable.

Once this line is crossed over, one enters a territory that makes the mythic person's "magical" proportion retreat back across the line, fleeing this place, knowing that once allowed inside one's heart, out of loneliness, to be embraced as a "normal" citizen of unconscious everyday, then one gradually forgets the grand gift of the significance of one's own magical smallness in the majesty but humanly unpopulated vastness of nature's magical bigness. Depression and self-hatred are the outcome of that.

Modernity's seemingly bottomless addiction to an endless pursuit of recreation, substances (legal or not), TV, or religious or scientific promises of another more anesthetized world, of having to constantly "escape" or "get away" from an everyday life of dead, demythologized stuff, and a daily insignificance in a schemeless, unstoried whole is fast creating an anti-existence based on forgetting instead of re-membering, which, if it doesn't first kill the viability of the holy ground we need to live on by compromising the diverse "Seed Heart" in its flight of escape, we will someday not have enough reality left here on earth in our bodies to remember, much less anything to remember it with; the muscle and its reason for existing would atrophy simultaneously.

Any one natural person's intentionally crossing that boundary from the spiritual intactness of an indigenous mythological seed existence would need to have a very long, resilient spiritual umbilical cord into the "old country" of a meaningful life; otherwise they would be turned loose to scramble for a nonexistent shore of solid reality in modernity's hodgepodge and most likely become out of necessity rather hard, brittle, and thin, or worse yet a fundamentalist native person: a genetic descendant of what he or she can no longer be but vehemently insists upon identifying.

It takes little cleverness to inspire forgetfulness and disregard in a people who have lost the memory of the aboriginal vision and are already masters of this unfortunate art. What is difficult and worthy of praise is to be able to bring alive again a "real" memory instead of the poisoned memory of the recent past: the memory like that of a seed who can again grow itself into a plant of marvelous character and more imaginative notions, even in bad conditions.

To further immerse the mechanically specialized minds of dogs and soldiers into a trance against which they are undefended by calling up something ancient in them for which neither their manuals nor their people's last millennia of experience had any calibration was no proud feat; a real accomplishment might have been to find a way for those minds to begin serving the remembrance of their weeping hearts long enough for them to long for a real existence at home naturally on an indigenous earth. So I wasn't that proud of my manipulation of that phenomenon, but nonetheless the seeds and I were heading home to the only home I now had.

In that Santa Fe room I rented in the district of Las Animas, a beautiful beat-up old adobe left over from the late Spanish era of the early nineteenth century, I was like a lizard molting in what he thought was a dark dry hole that turned out to be a ceramic downspout. The Holy Sky rained as hard under the aged, bowed *vigas* as it did above the leaky roof that habitually pooled late summer rain and winter snowmelt sufficiently to stock with fish but which, no matter how many times we patched it, picked a fresh place to burst back down into the room, usually two inches from where I slept.

Like that same lizard, I was shedding very slowly, only one painful scale at a time, the scales of the grief-thickened skin that had naturally grown over me to cope with the constant pain and heartbreak of the tribeless existence I was now forced to lead in the U.S. People shrank away from me, sure I was some grim, flinty, well-dressed attitudinal dragon. Only people with the most experience with life, and therefore the most courageous, recognized that my armor was really a chrysalis protecting the bud of a changed, reionized man, hoping desperately to crack out of this hard surface into the clear New Mexico air.

Two unsure frozen winters had blown in, liked the place, and stayed longer than usual, the last one thawing into a cold vise of spring gales that got through my toughness, driving a nostalgic memory of pain into every fence post, smell, and twitter of beast as I passed, making it exhausting to go anywhere.

After trudging through the bleak territory of trying to raise two unsure teenage sons without their mother, in a land where they only wanted to conform, themselves aghast at my own unwillingness to follow suit, my own desperation over my dwindling capacity to keep culturally alive the village mood and knowledge I could no longer physically see nor hold up, my little sack of seeds swelled up to my consciousness in importance until it practically assumed the status of a Saint canonized into a single Being I could pray to, something more accessible, an abbreviation that didn't really address their complexity that their cultural origins really demanded.

Their story, the whole story of those seeds, when I could stop rushing about fielding the unhappy thrashing about I had to endure in making a living for children who thrashed even more in the middle of it all, long enough to remember, helped rescue a little my true form from the toppled rubble of the now-petrified, unmoving, unreal vision of what life in the village had been. Emerging beneath it all my tender skin from all this change needed time to adjust to the new harsh surroundings, but it was time I never got. But the seeds got me through because they became a single, simple tight beacon of something whose deeper meaning I couldn't always conjure for the focus of attention the onslaught of modern life demands; but knowing that this deeper meaning existed, I could always keep moving toward it, waiting for that point in the trail of exile where one could sit and remember long enough the depth the modern world wanted me to lose.

But seeds are words, really, the speech of nature as plants, and they have big ideas far beyond the melodramas of men, and are not in any way supporters of purity or spiritual petrification. For in my own instance, after being kept hidden under the stone slab that I was molting off, events began to move without the permission of my isolationist stance in what would develop into a strong convoluted tangle, toward a new life as a public person, all for the seeds to carry out what Chiviliu had wanted.

An unsolicited telephone message arrived, inquiring if I would agree to be one of the teachers accompanying Robert Bly, the poet, in one of his notorious "men's conferences" in the Mendocino area of northern California.

He and I hadn't really gotten that deeply acquainted yet, at least not in the deep-friend kind of way we would later on. We had only just met. Some busybody name-dropper had recorded my voice somewhere without my knowledge and, supposing I would just disappear back into the "jungle," made a commercially available bootleg recording that he sold in alternative conferences all over. Someone gave one to Mr. Bly, who, liking what he heard, came looking for me while he was in Northern New Mexico giving one of his moving, well-attended poetry readings.

Just as tribes and village people the world over love gossiping, there is a breed of Americans who are no slackers in this capacity for malicious rumor creation. The only thing I'd ever heard about this tall, imposing, Norwegian-descended, farm-raised, Minnesotan, war-protesting poet with hair just like the back fur of a 150-pound Great Pyrenees dog, came in on the acrid tongues of people with pet-store parakeet minds who only repeated things that got them more heady beverages at cocktail gatherings, or overcooked yuppie-siphoned media that told venomous tales of spoiled middle-class white men searching for a male liberation equivalent to the women's so-called liberation of a decade previous, in which men ran around disturbing the peace in Southern California in varying states of nudity, with "caveman" eating styles, a lot of bad drumming, and mock rituals.

So distant was I from any aspect of what these kinds of people thought was important, never forgetting that these people all lived and accepted their part in a culture that had essentially killed the one whose death I was grieving, that for my pride and, I must admit, basic timid disposition, I was reluctant to stand up in front of a couple of hundred "white guys" and pretend to have something that they might remotely ever accept or want to hear, and I refused the offer.

But after a little slower, more human-like back-and-forth discussion, it became clearer to me that what the man actually wanted was someone who could not only teach from "both sides of the line" drawn between the Indigenous Mind and the modern Euro-American, but also concretely protect him physically and spiritually from effects of what he called the "psychic bombardment" of his soul by the media and people jealous of his unprecedented popularity and literary success. He needed a spiritual doorman. I must have looked fierce. Guarding and serving someone who, even if they didn't comprehend the Holy complexity of what I lived and served, still respected and held my capacity high enough to ask for help, seemed suddenly more appealing, village-like and less compromising. Not to mention I was a desperately struggling parent and my children needed me to take the job, for the pay was respectable.

Robert Bly's incorrigible and predictable liquidity, with which he almost always, at the last minute, changed both the subject matter and personnel, adding on people and ideas he'd only just come across in conferences already billed, replacing them for some more relevant theme, not only never startled or aggravated me like it did the rest but also made me feel more at home in the fair number of conferences and public events I was fortunate enough to work with him in all the many years that followed. Unlike most of the other teachers and attendees, I found the fluidity of change was very much like the demands of Mayan rituals, and that kind of challenge had been my forte as Chiviliu's favorite assistant. Though it was all non-village going, it was still giving some of my abilities a place to land in a land in which I was otherwise out of place, a basic refugee, a gypsy without a band.

Months later, while preparing for that first conference, maybe less than two days before I was due to fly, the first time since I'd left Guatemala, Mr. Bly called and said he'd changed his mind and now wanted me to teach "indigenous initiation to the guys" and "initiate" them in the redwoods outside of Mendocino, California. I had a "whole week and three days to do it" at one hour a day!!!

Rolling my spiritual eyeballs completely around at least a couple hundred times, I laughed hard, then audibly groaned like an overloaded donkey on an overloaded swinging bridge, knowing full well any legitimate initiation was no casual thing and could not be taught anyway, like some kind of remedial technique, outside its natural cultural context, any more than nutrition can be afforded to the chronically starved by giving them a lecture on how to make biscuits. Not to mention, what I knew initiation to be, in Atitlán and other places, was not a tool, something wielded by "people who know" to fix a broken society. You had to have an intact culture to initiate one's young people into. How could you initiate someone out of the cultural vacuum of the modern world back into the same vacuum and hope for initiation? Of course the idea of male initiation was at the time in America and Europe yet another popular quick passing talk show fad that a lot of groups of attitudinal soft males were cashing in on.

While I had already agreed and been contracted to teach, I knew I couldn't even accomplish what his words actually meant to the likes of me, so instead I asked politely what he thought I should bring along with me, to do what he requested, what kind of gear.

"Bring everything," he said.

So I did.

When my plane arrived in San Francisco and I'd retrieved my bags, the men sent to fetch me began to pale and complain for I'd brought seven footlockers of ritual equipment to make sure I'd complied with Bly's demand I bring "everything."

But my drivers' actions and the looks on their faces were nothing compared to the looks of terror and dismay I met, even without my baggage, which had been sent on ahead to the designated conference site, when I arrived at the pre-conference teachers' meeting in the Bay Area somewhere.

I must admit, in those days, when I still smoked Chiviliu-style, big handmade cigars, with my farming machete at the back, small knife and string bag, straight posture, and the old-time protocol of respect that meant standing forever silent until invited to sit, I might have inadvertently intimidated the mild-mannered, literature-minded, psychologist panel of soft American males who couldn't find their way to realizing I was real. And I had nothing I could offer to get me into their "club" while they continually patronized me as the "Guard" and kept me out of any decision making!

Only one Guatemalan teacher invited me in, and together we wept and recalled the old life and the homes neither of us would see anymore, for the changes and the ongoing violence.

Happily the next day the crowd at the conference turned out totally different than I'd imagined, much friendlier and more diverse than the panel of famous teachers.

Beside the easily bruised flock of bearded Rumi-reading white lawyers, self-help pop-psychology addicts, and psychotherapists who frequented these conferences, this particular gathering, as it unfolded, while at least half fit that description, the other half represented a fairly well-attended, spread-out cross section of north American male leaders, mayors, community organizers, cause fighters, heads of alternative schools from various Spanish-speaking city barrios countrywide, many African American leaders of all types, very few Indians, Japanese, Americans, Southeast Asians, not too many Chinese, but mostly city men of every color and group, if not every language.

Charmed, pleasantly surprised, and in a funny way relieved by the emotional sincerity of their reasons for gathering to somehow rediscover a viable way of going about being men in a modern condition in which maleness had been mostly defined as a need for a ruthless ability to get ahead, never leaving yourself open to failure, leaving the rest to work beneath them to trudge back and forth from work, to arrive dead and featureless at home. They said out loud, if not with total comprehension of what the real ramifications would mean if actually put into action, that they wanted to develop a new way of being men that did not simply lead the world where it had always been headed, into the complete, nature-killing tailspin of economic ruin and suicidal annihilation of the human soul that conforming to the status quo of modern life seemed to endorse.

So inspired by this first exposure to people in present-day American culture saying things that were so grand and different than the modern age I'd been wrestling, I automatically fell to serving the men in all the ways I might be useful. One of my famous "seven footlockers" had a large powerful array of hand-gathered plant medicine. People were getting sick, some from not being used to strong real emotion, others from the side effects of the normal epidemics of male guilt and shame, allergies to plants, bugs, etc., and the effects of viruses that all diverse people, plants, animals experience when they first come together. I doctored these fellows day and night, headed off a couple of suicides, some negative traumas, and the dangerous results of certain individuals' untutored naïve miscomprehension of ritual that had one Vietnam vet throwing live ammunition into a big fire with another boy, the cork pulled off his repressions, jumping naked into the same bonfire. I *was* a guard, guarding white men from their own bad rituals.

But when the psychologists who weren't so "hands on" and physical with life were unable to revive catatonic men when I did it unthinkingly as a matter of normal village shamanic action, the panel of other teachers started getting nervous. Feeling envious and to make sure I didn't get underfoot in all the serious presentations of "real teachers," quoting my lack of PhD training, and with no book or a talk show to back me up, having never met a person like me whose knowledge didn't come just from books and celebrity ladder-climbing, the board of teachers instantly reduced the morning talk Mr. Bly wanted me to "present" daily for ten days to a single thirty-five-minute stint right after lunch on a Tuesday, when most of the men were normally back at their bunks, burping and taking naps or secretly calling home. The teachers in all of Bly's conferences always reminded me of twenty-five newborn piglets scrambling for milk on only eight nipples, where every "teacher" whined and squealed, ruthlessly elbowing their insecure, desperate way to be scheduled to be on stage with old Mr. Bly. It was a comical sight and the accepted competitive order of the culture they claimed to be changing. I couldn't even compete, nor would I. I was basically swept under the rug.

Instead, to do my best for Bly, with whom I became good friends, I spent my time holding weeping men, lost men, scared men, doctoring nausea, diarrhea, fevers, and all the sundry troubles to which all humans are prone at all hours of night and day. As a result my single after-lunchtime slot was packed beyond capacity, with even groundskeepers, cooks, and drivers who weren't in the conference showing up. Like passengers on a Calcutta bus trying to get a seat, hammering their bottoms into seats where no more could fit, all the men jammed in squirming hip to hip, and after three hours of my non-stop rap refused to let me go. Of course, running on Mayan Time, Seed Time, I thought I'd just begun and had only been talking some ten minutes. My everyday lectures were reinstated, and the rivalries got even more petty and ridiculous, but I didn't care. I was in hog heaven, so to speak.

Utterly stunned by what they were trying to do there, I hadn't wanted to let them down. I was even more amazed that they were listening to what I said, and not less in a state of wonder that I could speak in such a public way and that I had something to say worth hearing.

It wasn't that people in the past had never stood still and listened attentively to me talk. Thousands of Tzutujil Mayans and coastal Guatemalan Indians had certainly done so many times, but always in ritual context and, strictly speaking, they weren't listening to me talk; they were simply listening to the great horde of old images and magic eloquence that whoever was running said ritual needed to know how to conjure in order to make the world come back to life. It could have been any one of a number of people and had been thus throughout Tzutujil history.

But here I was standing in front of seated attentive representatives of a culture whose very syndrome of existence and running rules not only never listened to what some incongruous half-breed like me had to say, but didn't think we had anything to say to them. I always heard, "Haven't we outgrown all that village stuff a long time ago?"

But that day I was respected, and people listened. Unfortunately, inexperienced in the modern world and culturally lonely as I really was, I erroneously interpreted this listening as a sign of friendship, the kind of village-together friendship that I'd lost when I lost Atitlán. Not having yet learned, like a lot of people never do, that once on stage one should never confuse the attention one receives as a bona fide affection, and it would certainly be a soul-eroding experience to mistake public attention, no matter how positive it seems, for love and friendship. These things are a cultivation of a very gradual and deeply rooting tree. The momentary exhilaration of an objectified crowd is not the same thing.

But what I really failed to comprehend was how little I was comprehended, yet how satisfied they were with the simpler things they thought they were hearing. My unseeing heart, hoping I'd found a new home, was swept away by how deeply I was affected with this first instance of even a slight acceptance by a people who couldn't see they were very distant from what my presence there represented, people who, my entire life, had represented the mind of those whose arrogant unconscious hand had sown the mega-culture mind-set that was proving to be the nemesis for all original places, animals, plants, and natural humans, including the Mayans, the very ones whom I had always served and who were now sucked into the same malaise.

I was so hopeful at being heard by even just a portion of what I took to be an apologetic enemy that I subsequently assumed that this meant clear evidence of some glimmer of hope for the possibility of a spiritual peace where the conquering need of the civilized mind could stop persecuting and exploiting the hidden vitality of all people's inner Indigenous Soul.

This same Indigenous Soul all people had hidden somewhere could cause culture to sprout, making the civilized conqueror into real people who became inveterate givers of gifts, heroic potlatchers, romantic, alive, proud, and ever eloquent for God and the Holy in Nature.

But I was already one of those inefficient romantics and, overcome by one of those ecstatic fits of generosity to which such people are prone, in front of everyone I decided to give all the conference men the very thing I had that my indigenous heart knew was the most valuable gift I had to offer: my corn.

I well knew how ungenerous a culture based on commerce is by definition, and that like it or not, all these people, when they weren't here in the rarefied atmosphere of a retreat in a Mendocino forest, lived and followed without much awareness of it the mores of a commerce society. I also knew, if any kind of peace were to ever develop on this Earth, it was going to have to begin with people who had it economically the easiest, and who were going to have to relearn the legendary generosity of the proud small farmers, nomadic pastoralists, and tribal ritualists their own forgotten, wild, indigenous ancestors had been. I wanted them to relearn the heartfelt art of a capacity society that knows how to give gifts to the Holy, to each other, and to their projected enemies. This is what is valued in real indigenous people. Instead of a capacity society that feeds human beauty to the Holy, modern society is measured by how much a person has that gives them the power to feel superior making someone else feel inferior. Instead of working to make a grand thing whose gift feeds all and ennobling both the gift, the gift given, the receiver, and the Holy, in commerce culture everything with no turnaround investment value is unexploitable and therefore of "no" value.

The eyes of giant civilization can't see the majesty of the small, only how much less it is than the big. I was therefore unable to convey even with their story the immensity of my small gift, which was none other than my precious seeds: all of my Birth and Death Seeds, the ones I'd smuggled in, the ones Ma Bux had farmed hanging by a rope, the seeds that escaped two fiery holocausts and four-and-a-half centuries of oppression, the seeds by which the people had always been born by, lived by and died by, initiated by, living, dying, and resprouting their culture for millennia.

I had begun the next decades of public teaching here in the majesty of this tortured American redwood forest assuming I had to find a way to teach large, profound adult understandings but found myself over the years moving farther and farther back behind all that to teach the most rudimentary original aspects of what it meant to be an intact human long before I could ever dare to dress and layer this root of original human majesty with the wild exuberance of its stalk, flower, fruit, and real depth of the meaning of culture and seeds. Gift-giving was the first most necessary thing of all.

True gift giving among all the world's original people, including the ancient forebears of the men who stood before me that first time, and thereafter in all the conferences of men and women I ever tried to teach in, was a highly developed art form of the most obligatory nature, as it still is with a lot of cultures and human individuals who still remember it as a basic part of human nature. Among indigenous people it went far beyond the giving of the gift but included even more powerfully the obligatory artful capacity of gift receiving. This was something so basic to all Tzutujil rituals that it was taught very, very early. One learned it all automatically by learning the everyday language as a child. It was right in it. It was a firmly established institution that kept safe, vital, and constant the natural innate human ornateness and beauty of praise that fed God and humans and kept the natural world alive. We became the human animals we were meant to be in the process.

But here I was confronted with a group of people who, no matter how powerfully placed, in city governments, corporations, law firms, hospitals, or social leadership, and no matter how many people's lives and situations their decisions boldly affected, had no thought of the priority of real gift-giving to God, much less each other, and absolutely no skill at giving but even less at receiving a gift whose art would have even for a person of solid poverty been able to feed all the souls of the stingy and rich and the heart of the Divine for its beauty. These people were unaware of their poverty: a spiritual poverty of a powerful dimension whose arm crushes the real reason for living.

While in the village we all prided ourselves in any state of "material" lack with our attempts to refine our capacity to not only raise the worth of our gifts with the "wealth" of our comprehension through the eloquent use of an antique gift-giving language, I was not as good as some of the great mistresses and masters of this art I had known, but I was not too bad a student; and attempting that day in the forest to conjure in that same atmosphere of generosity into which I'd been euphorically inspired by the hopeful gaze of this crowd of powerful non-tribal men who "listened," I lined them up in two long files in accordance with Tzutujil Sacred House ritual tradition, each line facing the other so as to clearly see the suffering in the eyes of the "other" side.

In the best language I could develop, trying to make their American corporate rapping television English-speaking ears hear the eloquence of my bold attempt at translating the Holy Feeding language of the Seed people, I proceeded to tell the long story of the little Ivory seeds and what they in their scarce numbers had actually come through to be there with us that day.

Then going to each fellow separately, I dropped in each of their out-stretched hands a single kernel of the precious ivory-colored corn and moved on to the next one, pronouncing to each the old Tzutujil spiritual seed inducement: "I plant your soul; let your seeds crack, sprout, and jump up out of the ground and live again, trying to lick the face of the sky like a young puppy licks the face of a messy child, but in failing to reach it, may its frustration turn into flowers, whose fruit goes to feed a time of hope beyond our own."

For my soul this giving was a huge relief; for the men unknowingly made me the gift of allowing me to give in a grandiose way the most meaningful treasure in the smallest integer to powerful men immersed in the steel net of spiritual cultural poverty. For the first time in years I felt worthy feeding the Holy in the Seed, the people, and the tradition since I'd left Central America.

But in the end, for most of the men it was yet another tiresome exercise at the end of a long emotional week, quaint evidence of the inefficient nature of "undeveloped" peoples that they couldn't seem to "source" and extract something to aid in their personal betterment "programs" at work.

Though I pleaded with them not to "eat their seeds" but to spiritually let them grow, some of them like infants popped them in their mouths and crunched down complaining about the taste and the effects of flint corn on their teeth. Some even tossed them quickly in the wastebaskets in a hurry to get to their transports to the airport on their ways home.

Most dropped the seeds unconsciously into a pocket, where they probably got lost in the wash.

And then of course, there were the ever-present little knot of "white" shamans, druids, witches, and weirds who belonged to various "shaman colleges" who put their seeds into their "medicine pouches" to jack up their "power" a little more, adding their brief shoulder rubbing with Martín Prechtel to their long résumés of associate spirit leaders.

The conference ended. The real heroes of the men, the published teachers whom they watched on talk shows, were still their heroes; they all went away in buses and cars with my corn, and I was left alone by the beautiful forest stream with my seven footlockers of unused gear waiting for a ride to the airport to fly back to my dusty New Mexico life.

Sitting alone those last two hours by that stream was a strange weepy moment for me, to fully realize that what I had given them, though it should have been the grandest realization for us all, especially after having heard the story, was already forgotten, and for the few that remembered, reinterpreted in every way except as intended.

Like homeless civilian casualties after a devastating war, the seeds were displaced refugees dispersed at large in every direction. I'd let them all go, for when I'd finished doling out the little cream-colored beauties, except for that one strange young man who'd been asked to leave for throwing himself into a bonfire after I pulled him out, there had been exactly enough seeds for every man to receive one, with not even a single kernel left over for me. The seeds were gone. After all the struggle to get seeds to men oblivious that they and their "power-oriented" culture were seedless, I myself ended up seedless.

Like a lonely little kid, finally happy with new friends assuming they would never leave, disappointed at the end of the party when they, without any grief, just departed with all your gifts, and left you alone, holding all their mess in your heart and a feeling of being even more hollowed out in the wake of the burst bubble of my unrealistic euphoric hope that unconsciously and foolishly I'd assumed a village was beginning and that everybody would of course stay together because we had instantly become a people, hadn't we?

It wasn't that the seeds, the words, the images in the ancient ritual language couldn't transmit it, or that I had failed at anything that couldn't be written off as hopeful naïveté and a legitimate desire for a real world to begin; it was simply the fact that nobody there had any ancestral memory left of what intact human life really meant, such an enormous distance had the world they lived in drifted over the centuries from any real tribal instincts, or any real spirituality accountable to the earth that fed us all.

Sitting by the little creek with my seven footlockers, thinking how many times I'd given offerings to the Divine Female in her liquid body over the last ten days, and how the men just washed their faces, and sloshed through her, muddying her up with no regard to the majesty of Her liquid grief trying to reach her mother-in-law, the Grandmother Ocean, on the magnificent seal-lined, bull kelp surf of the Caspar Cliffs some ten miles west, my attempt to plant some bit of the seed knowledge, maybe like the unnoticed stream, would trickle into the men's consciousness over time, and the seeds rehydrating themselves exploding into some big comprehensions on a much deeper, wider shore stretching out somewhere beyond their modern minds. But no matter how I looked at it, I was still seedless.

Chapter 13

The Six Donancianas

I f any one of three merciful things had dropped away from me in that era, I would have most assuredly melted away as a person, at least as that person I had become after my years immersed in the now-extinct magic of the old Tzutujil village. That diligent, hopeful, loyal servant of the Divine in nature would have disappeared without a trace, falling prey to the all-too-easy route of self pity, outrage, and a bitterness that would have, no doubts about it, eroded the still-delicate, slowly redefining cliffs of the new person I might become and any mysterious corresponding future, dissolving me into the thin strata of an acquired personality of colorful silt forgotten at the bottom of that wide boggy canal of American Individualist melodramatic self-importance.

The first mercy that wouldn't let me sink was the impossibility of erasing the effects of having seen the Holy in nature. Because shamans in the old village didn't answer to humans but to the wild, the love I had for Deified Time and all Existence was something I could, without a people or a tribe, still ritually feed on my own. Prominence for the Divine Diversity of Time as Matter, as all life and Earth, was largely absent from civilization, but even where it did exist it survived only by hiding in the small and the forgotten. But no matter, for the Holy was always bellowingly present, for me often residing in the most subtle and complex ways inside every aspect of any untamed and unharnessed fraction of the natural world. For that reason I had to live where I could pray and feed the

"Holy" in everything that was natural and proceeding according to its innate nature. Not in some nightmare maze of forty-acre rural urbanite pseudo-farms, with bumper-to-bumper picket fences, covenants, and riding helmets, or in a manicured wilderness where with a permit, rustling Gore-Tex, hiking shoes, trail mix, a backpack, binoculars, and shorts, you pretended the Holy in Nature wasn't running for her life when she heard your objective mind coming at her.

Another thing that kept me going was a relatively undamaged involuntary function of my soul in which ever since I was a child I always felt obligated to find beauty and wonderment someplace everywhere, no matter how mediocre, trivial, or dismal people had made the surroundings. This was a grand lubrication for the rigid outrage of my sometimes over-principled mind.

For a village smile to survive with any degree on my face, with all of the endless string of unfortunate accommodations, terrifying food, airports, polluted city travel routes, cars, taxis, buses, bullet trains, the blaring television, and mindless conversations of faceless, narrow, business-oriented personalities, it was a great comfort to recognize and still be able to smile with delight about the evidence of the Holy in some detail of civilization's madness. Like the beauty of the occurrence of tiny book mites, who like words describing people having just scurried off the pages of Dickens, now recently reincarnated as microscopic insects wandering just beneath the mindless radiation-spewing airport television screens and now and then a cathode photon would project a flash of rainbow-refracted light just so through the insect's microscopic leg hairs, to be amplified by the screen repeatedly enough to cause someone to adjust the set. Or when riding together on a tight high-rise elevator with the emotional face behind the thick makeup of an aging, dyed-red-haired, gold-toothed Ukrainian Cossack woman once a street walker, now still mired in a New York City slum with her work furs and weepy eyes, afraid at first I'd realized she was not a Christian Ukrainian but an Uzbek Muslim, who finally broke the silence and her secret when she pleaded with me to just touch one string's worth of notes from the long-necked Uzbek tambor, that my lifelong incapacity to resist buying and learning to play musical instruments from all over the globe had me cradling as I headed to my next ritual workshop up the shaft past where this woman lived to a fiftieth-floor, filthy windowless flat, just to hear again a drop of the old sound of her faraway homeland. Or in the crazy adjectival deliciousness of the tiny macho speech of a five-year-old African-Choctaw mutton buster in Mississippi, who flatly refused to remove his rodeo chaps in the 279,000 percent humidity of a ninety-five-degree July while helping Grandma harvest her truck-farm collards and carrots. Or in the exquisite sight of a string of shaggy grief-eyed Mongolian two-hump camels nose-pinned to one the next swaying out of a big-flake snowstorm at the rail stop outside Havre, Montana, driven by shouting Trevus on his freezing Tennessee Walker headed for train car 50; usually incongruous, always ironic, mostly impossible, but always there somewhere nonetheless, the beauty was everywhere, its small unseen power, thwarting by its sheer presence a world made mad enough to vacantly dump itself over the high empty dam of its assumed superior authority to crash heartlessly into its own ugly futureless unviable mechanical mess.

The third thing, and they will, I hope, forgive me for putting them third, for they have always been the first two mercies in motion, was the presence of my over-opinionated, fire-cured, windy, agate-hoofed, New Mexico Spanish ponies who could haul me with beauty, by beauty to beauty, on beauty up into, and along the wild heart of the Holy unpopulated earth on their own Holy wild hearts, and without whom New Mexico would not have been herself. Descended from small powerful horses of old tribal Morocco, then Spain, then Mexico, then New Mexico, these Holy vehicles of the Navajo sun were the same sweeping combination of colors and forms as all the stones and land and corn seeds I'd grown up with: blue, striped-backs, hash-legged paints, reds, yellows, roans, duns, buckskins, spiderwebbed grullas, no blacks or whites or bays, but every other color and shimmering like corn, their tails dragged long in the sand, some blue-eyed, others yellow- and black-eyed. They fed the soul with their speed and dust, and when we cleared the vista of an unpeopled Holy place, they stood wide, windy, and majestic where all the mountains and springs still had their indigenous names, and courageously let a fool like me direct us to where together we could pray away from humans at the remote old shrines. But more curative for me was their astute assessment of what the world I wandered tried to turn me into. Those beautiful little horses would refuse me passage to where I might vehemently insist until I could shed the idiot I had to daily become in public, stonewalling until I become myself again and we were off to anywhere I asked.

But none of these merciful things could have kept me moving toward life unless they had the proper place to roll about, and nowhere in the so-called United States did there exist a state of mind that would allow people like myself to exist without thinking my spirituality was just an act, and where my lifestyle didn't require a special permit. That place of course was Northern New Mexico.

By having left New Mexico to land in the Maya land of Guatemala, then returning back to New Mexico as if there were no other wonder-filled places on Earth, it seems I had unknowingly fallen into some very well-worn subconscious ruts, already established by others in the past.

The two regions were like twins, always different but mysteriously bonded and equally affecting all who loved the one into longing for the other. Though three thousand miles apart from one another, there had always been some invisible psychological bypass that caused scholars, poets, artists, archaeologists, photographers, ethnographers, and other types of individuals seeking big freedom in tiny cultural niches, who'd latched into New Mexico, on one project or the next, to be hurled through some subterranean pneumatic pipeline that ran straight underneath and past Mexico, ejecting them standing and ready for work in the Highlands of Guatemala as if this procedure were totally normal. Bandelier, Kidder, Jennings, Scholes, Morley, Thompson, White, Adams, Stuart, Redfield, and literally a hundred plus more archaeologists, ethnologists, linguists, and various old-guard anthropologists headquartered in Santa Fe investigating Third Mesa, or the Keres, or Navajos, or the twelfth-century migratory post-Chacoan invasion of the Central Rio Grande region, and so on all went directly to Guatemala to dig, collect, and investigate, many returning eventually to work again in New Mexico. This was something that could not be explained academically, for while the unique cultures throughout the ages may have some definite relationship, they are certainly no closer or logically sequential than the early cultures of what is now east Oklahoma, the central Mississippi corn people, and *all* the peoples of Mexico times a thousand.

This electromagnetic draw between the two places for outsiders was due to something more of a spiritual nature, mysterious and still unexplainable.

Raised in New Mexico and though definitely not an aspirant anthropologist or academic by any stretch of imagination, I too in a way very different ended up just as emotionally trapped and voluntarily immured in the irresistible details of Maya culture.

But when it came time to leave, though I'd been a lot of places, and loved a lot of the world and her people's ways of living and landscapes, it was as if I were unconsciously following some migration cycle back to New Mexico, like a hummingbird or a monarch butterfly. No other place even crossed my mind except as a means to get back to where I'd started, and when I did, just like that famous amazing butterfly, I'd already lived so many incarnations of myself, revived so many times, becoming something other than the person people thought I was, that like the butterfly, I was still very much the same organism as far as my motives, loyal direction, determination, and sensibility. I would always head back to New Mexico.

In New Mexico I could at least continue flexible and flourishing as the person I had become, not unchanged at the core, but able to keep alive what mattered most in the cultural, geological, geographic reality of the spiritual sanctuary of northern Mexico's rugged landscape. New Mexico's non-Protestant inefficiency, its pride, its secrecy, its clannishness and love of the long sentence, made her cultural landscape a place of possibility instead of a place of the manicured mind. Mind you, it wasn't the same New Mexico a lot of other people who came to live there were living in, because they brought their own populations and mores along with them, gyrating along like always in a self-made bubble that drove right along with them, wherever they went, never seeing the New Mexico I lived in.

Not that I actually was able to manage a life that allowed me to economically be in the state that much, at least not for several years. In those days, I dragged about the world endlessly lecturing, giving concerts, raising ritual "workshops," sitting on panels, surviving teaching all those endless men's conferences in the States and the United Kingdom, ritualizing the sick and grief-stricken, so intensely that in one year alone after a brutal chain of ninety-two round-trip air flights I had spent less than an aggregate of two months at home, and most of those two months were spent regrouping to head out again.

After accepting poet Robert Bly's first teaching opportunity, where I lost all my seeds, I allowed myself to be further pulled into this over-busy existence of minor recognition and a certain degree of public life in order to feed my children and to afford living in my arid homeland. After a year of teaching with Robert in his long-established conferences, I increasingly spread out to teach on my own, in my own very different direction, to my own gatherings of modern people and equally displaced exiles from other lands who were all looking desperately for that feeling of home and tribe.

As part of everything I attempted I was constantly occupied in making some sincere but highly adjusted, culturally sympathetic attempts at keeping the seeds alive ritually and intellectually, hoping that this knowledge in motion might actually feed the Holy in Nature to some degree and be the best such disparate groupings of modern spiritual searchers could hold, given the constrictions of the compartmentalized existence in which we all found ourselves trying to spiritually survive. It was the best I could hope for at the time, given the fact that I no longer even had a single corn seed from the old days left to my name, and the culture was gone.

The Birth and Death corn, along with all its customs and way of life, had gone extinct in Atitlán by then, gone for real in that decade accompanied by the loss of several other seed plants. So much had flown away by this time—people, plants, language, culture, ritual, and food practices—that I never did go back to Atitlán after that.

New Mexico was now once again my beloved home. While at first I ran all around the world trying to "keep the Seeds alive" without any seeds, no people of my own, and no one with whom to speak one word of Tzutujil except of course my constant speaking to the Holies in Nature, to God as Time manifest that miraculously made it so I never lost my proficiency in the tongue. You cannot gloss depth of meaning or beauty when forming a capable, delicious barrage talking with the Divine; you cannot shout an ineloquent abbreviation of intended beauty to feed the Holy like people ignorantly did in a functional human everyday existence. If you're not careful, without the need to feed the Holy delicious words, a people no matter how large a populace will always lose their eloquence if they can't speak well to God.

When life calmed a bit, I fell in love and married a curly-headed beauty descended from some real far northern people, whose vision and genius never gave in to anything that didn't promote life. She gave me faith again in people.

We lived on together in a little house of dry New Mexico mud brick, an old adobe, in which on the north side of one whitewashed wall, a small ochered niche was carved. It was in there I kept the seed-eyed bird of the 1976 earthquake of over twenty years past inside the same clay jar my long-gone seeds had once made their home. There the seed bird still sat, receiving what little feasts of *pōm*, fat candles, and old liturgical jewels I could muster forth from my early village days.

Not a morning had passed for our forty years in all my meanderings where I neglected to meet the rising Father Sun, feeding him prayers, offerings, and songs in both Keres and Tzutujil, whether I could see his face or not. Even as a New Mexico reservation child, where I learned the vital necessity of "Feeding the Dawn" from a generation born in the nineteenth century, I never shrank from standing barefoot in the skin-splitting, ten-below-zero dry December wind at dawn waiting to "Feed the Dawn," or braving the mosquitoes after an all-night arroyo-flooding drizzle of August up to my shins in mud, to ensure that the Old Man Sun was always at my feast table as he struggled like a baby sea turtle to bite his way out of the egg of night, to swim over our heads as if the blue New Mexico sky were an endless sea.

But of course Northern New Mexico's high arid plateaus, alluvial mesas, and crinkly ridge-back spines had been many times the bottom of uncountable seas, in the ongoing past. Even half the plants not only looked like they still belonged at the bottom of the ocean, but their roots harbored droves of sand-dwelling insects, who were all so lobster-like with strange seaside habits that it didn't take much to recognize in such a dry place, how returning water came to be so longed for and at the center of every conversation and decision. In a land with so little water, the land still acted like a sea; the only detail lacking was the presence of briny water. But in the end even that was there, for in New Mexico the ocean is underground.

Beneath us there was water, and that water was a woman, a powerful beautiful woman, and outside of a few seasonal ponds, rivers, puddles, and seeps she lived way deep beneath the sea bottom of the arid land. There were places you couldn't sleep for the racket of all the rushing of the arterial canals beneath you. To sleep you just remembered you were in an upside down ocean and what you were hearing was the subterranean surf.

She had lots of daughters, all of them gorgeous and magnificent, several of them dangerous like the collapsing limestone bubbles of bottomless cisterns, most of them mysterious like the river of green brine that had no headwaters jumping from the ground running for a mile and a half over little salt cliffs in waterfalls, in mirror-flat pools, to disappear at ground level into the ground, and not a few of them utterly caustic, toxic, and even deadly, leaking the bright red torrent of dissolved metal arsenic, or selenium, or vermillion mercury, from hairline cracks in the basaltic walls of a sparkling mica-slabbed canyon.

But for the most part the great Mother Waters, like the Indigenous Souls of all humans, stayed deep, leaving her holy curative waters only in hidden cave springs where her labyrinth of multiple vulvas, all Indians knew, had given birth to a lot of Gods, and a lot of New Mexico's winds whose varied flavors, humors, and time sequences joined moody storms who had no measurable form, but blew what was once flat into hills, and what was once a ridge cut into a canyon.

A startled unhuman look both satisfied and stunned always crossed through and stayed in the face of anyone who wandered in past the old native taboos, daring to touch the blue crystals growing in the vaginal lips of her high mesa caves, before they were consumed or went mad, for some of Her other children were those time-honored giants, the beautiful famous ones, who had lived there forever to guard the Holy entrances to Her great Heart. Definitely indiscriminate eaters of people, cows, horses, sheep, pigs, goats and anything disrespectful enough to climb the steep inclines of the flat black volcanic stumps that measure up the land, they lived mostly unseen, waiting inside the caves. For inside Her wombs, there Her well-dressed Giant children still resided, brooding the gone pre-human era, still only half born into this world, the other half in Hers.

Other Old Gods of the People I'd grown up with still inhabited other wilder places too. The land was still good for an exile of my type looking for some welcome, especially if it was the magic government of the Holy holding court in the root of a tree, or the universe of Time Gods sparkling microscopically in the red feldspar of the pegmatite. To still love and to survive this hollowness of modernity's mechanical soul, you could live as a magical exile amongst other exiles, for here even the Gods were exiles still successfully alive in self-appointed villages of canyon walls and badlands labyrinths called the landscape of New Mexico.

There was one flat-topped peak that I especially loved. It was visible for fifty miles in any direction, and charismatically dominated the entire Chama River escarpment north of Abiquiú in such dramatic juxtaposition to all other surrounding layers of hills, canyons, and peaks as to be important to everybody since time immemorial.

By local Native American rules, unless you were an initiated priest or official in direct service to the Deities that were the mountain's legitimate residents, you were not allowed to climb Cerro Pedernal, as it is called on maps. Though in my early days that mountain was the most seductive of all, and I did long to climb her, unlike most people who never ask permission of the mountains they would climb, careless of the grand beings that live there that their ignorance cannot see, I respected the old laws and never would.

But from a high point nearby, riding my Indian horse up La Joya Canyon up behind Mesa Poleo, I would camp, make tea, and sit for hours fascinated and soulfully fed by simply watching the shadows and pondering the mythological landscape of that famous Mountain of Blades, as it was called. It was there that big origination things had happened, lots of them.

This peak had been the major source of a jeweled chert for all the Rain Gods, who tipped their lightning weapons with the stone, for the peak had been and still was the origination of all the carnelian-infused, translucent dendrite-adorned, light-violet chert of a razorlike quality when chipped, which lies scattered in every valley, ravine, and hilltop as far out as the Nebraska buffalo plains, in and out of creek-side ancient Pueblo village sites, trash mounds, and places you would least expect to find them. There were always the remains of antique cutting tools, cores and the spalls from their manufacture from the hands of over four thousand years of diverse cultures, made of this mountain's chert washed to the surface in the annual rainstorms of the late summer everywhere you looked.

Young when I was first presented with the distant silhouette of this flat-topped hill of peace where all tribal rivalries and wars were always put aside within the shrine of Pedernal's powerful ceremonial precinct, I had always wanted to live there close by so as to see it ever after.

But knowing full well the possible effects that getting overly close and casual to something that Holy, powerful, and beautiful without ritual knowledge either sickens or causes one to live mad, half awake, I kept myself, as one romantic cowboy put it when talking about Pedernal, "Close enough in sight, for the vision of Her over there to touch my heart, but too far away for my broken heart to touch hers." Nonetheless, living there close by was always nagging me like that last unruly camel tangling up the otherwise orderly caravan of my daily thoughts. But until the possibility presented itself, I thought myself fortunate enough to simply visit, respectfully keeping my distance, and just ritually feeding the mountain and its great sacred citizens from afar on a neighboring height.

But during one of those visits I occasionally made to clear the mental clutter and road buzz of my overworked and over-traveled head, after dipping down into the ravine of bright red clay and sandstone cliffs that walled the Coyote Creek, I pulled my old truck over, startled by an unprecedented profusion of grander-than-usual bushes of maravillas in full blossom. Covered in tiger moths and covetous bombarding hummingbirds, the almost succulent surprising jade leaves of this desert four o'clock stood brilliant against the dry vermillion of the earth, the fire of her violet flowers raging in an unworldly phosphorescence against the green and red of the other two. There in the very middle of about fifteen of these eye-healing mounds of flowering beauties stood pounded into the hard clay a realtor's "For Sale" sign directing the world up the mesa opposite to the east overlooking the yellow-banded canyon on the ridge, immediately south and adjacent to where Pedernal loomed, the exact same area where as a youth I would perch admiring the White Flint Mountain or *Peshligai Tzil* as some Navajos and Northern Apaches still call it.

I followed the chain of "For Sale" signs up a hairpin turn around the red band of mesas to the south, until I found the last one indicating a troubled, overworked, unhappy piece of potholed deforested mountaintop in whose center sat a sad, old, collapsed adobe homestead, where quietly some bitter wreckage of the dreams of a human heart was trying to melt back into the red earth out of which some previously hopeful mountaineers had originally very energetically raised it a century previous.

A skinny New Mexican man wearing a scared smile on a long, kind face pretending not to be sad, who, unaccustomed to being comprehended, camouflaged some great depth of multiple griefs, was concertedly hammering back together a few old wooden gable struts to delay as best he could the imminent demise of the old rusty tin roof, in hopes the reinforced antique shadow of the little shelter might reason with the memory in the mud into being walls just a little longer, giving a tangible place to the nostalgic mental ghosts of who and what used to bustle about within, who were no more.

When he saw me coming, this man swung back inside the house through a roof dormer, his wiry frame somehow emerging in almost the same instant from the ground level, through the leaning door jamb of the doorless front entrance with a familiar closeness which I took to mean that by holding up the old shell of this mud house, he kept alive something there that kept him standing under memories whose weight would have brought him melting back into the ground there as well.

His presence was big, sweet, and honest, making his capacity for business as proportionately bad as his heart was good. Once he realized I was one of those blond, Spanish-speaking anomalies—half-Indian, half-white, too proud, never tall, who still wielded that more antiquated New Mexico courtesy, a kind of sixteenth-century protocol and natural shyness that only a few "Americans" seem to recognize as real—he almost smiled. It was clear to him that I was not another one of the pervasive army of wealthy land-rush Texans, speedy polyester Californians, or angry lumpy Coloradans all on a search for higher altitude, cooler third-world summer homes without having to leave "their" country to add to their tax relief schemes to protect money unsweated-for. These people, perceived as invaders, have been a troubling presence preying on New Mexicans in trouble, picking up cheap old family land since the 1870s. Their money was usually accompanied by a fairly flat dry mind-set able only to recognize the investment value in old adobe walls, but never able to weep for the memory in the mud, much less truly comprehend the complex spiritual strata of land, life, and house that stood before them in the present as the flower of a past people's unique brand of ancestral folly and often unfruitful difficulty, the ruins of which their descendants were still proud of and liked to stand next to, instead of one of those developers who saw the place as something to be neatly laser-leveled and replaced by a pseudo-home made of synthetics with no history that often looked more like an Elvis chapel only to host an exclusive party six days a year with the former owners as gardeners and caretakers. He could tell that, like him, I was not looking for a house to rescue, but for a place to be rescued by: a place to give myself life again, a place to put new flesh on the old bones of my own early memories of orchards of Spanish peaches, wild *ciruelas*, cornfields, Spanish ponies, rawhide-resoled work boots, hot chile mutton stew in the snow, and the smell of the hail-soaked red clay of Coyote.

It didn't take more than ten minutes of our mutual praising of the land, the old knowledges, and what children growing up and then getting old should learn to love until we had both cautiously distilled our fears with the other's love into an elixir of agreeability, by which we both realized that he not only didn't really want to sell any of the land out of his life and would not only be unable to sell this land the way he was going about it, but considering the acres of prairie dog towns, around which the brilliant, unthreatened rodents relaxedly scrambled and lounged around in great profusion like herds of stuffed socks, chirping and decorating the craterous mounds of their land-riddling tunnels with uneven piles of those same razor-sharp jeweled flakes of carnelian chert from Pedernal's impressive table mountain rising up to the north, the place was practically uninhabitable, unfarmable, unranchable, and dangerous to anyone afraid of bubonic plague, hantavirus, and broken legs. And most of all, because it had been his grandmother's by marriage to his grandfather, and they loved one another and he had always loved them, and because the land had literally merged with them for they were buried there, it wouldn't leave his heart, so it didn't leave his life.

This man and I were fairly well matched when it came to business anyway, for I had no money to buy the things we both loved, and he didn't really want to sell, though his signs said he did and he really needed the cash. Both of us were slaves to our wounded New Mexico prides and our impossible hopes of re-engendering a future full of the best things of the past. Only wealthy outsiders who couldn't love it the same way we could, could afford to own it. And for all that common ground we became comrades in our own private battles for what we loved and could never seem to get.

Though Ignacio Campos never did sell any land to me nor to anybody else, I would always prize having met him, for it turned out that he was the great-great-great-great-great-grandson of a practically canonized legend, a woman whose mythologized escapades eventually always surfaced in the eternal *platicas* of any group of Northern New Mexicans of our district.

Of all the wild legends that any mention of the long-deceased Donanciana La India caused to be retold, the one that everyone everywhere knew and unquestionably assumed was veritably real because it was an old one, the kind that's obviously true because it won't disappear, was the story of a treasure she was known to have hidden somewhere on her old homestead, in the cottonwood *bosque* along the fertile valley below along the Chama River where it bends around Mesa Prieta to collide with the Rio Grande. The treasure didn't belong to the family members but to her alone, they said, so even her relatives could never discover where she'd cached it. As a child Ignacio was the last one to really know anything about her, because his own grandmother, also named Donanciana, the sixth in descent from the original, before she passed on in her nineties told him more than any one because of his close relation with her.

After I realized who he was, I figured he must've been pestered enough by the world and his family over any hints he might have gleaned about the whereabouts of his famous grandmother's inherited wealth that out of courtesy I didn't pursue the subject. But in the end every conversation with him always seemed to end there anyway. Because Ignacio's love of what he loved, and he'd loved the sixth Old Donanciana, the question of her "treasure," after rousing the hated subject of his impatience with and resentment for the unromantic avarice of his own relatives and the rest of the world, who only wanted the treasure and didn't treasure his old Donanciana, made it all into an opportunity for him to set the record straight, for which he without tiring spoke freely, drawing my attention to the old woman's greatness and away from the embellished rumors of some crazy fabled clay pot filled with old gold buried somewhere in the ground of whose supposed whereabouts he knew nothing.

As the last child of Donanciana's last child, her seventh, Ignacio, conforming to the old New Mexican institution of the *hijado*, was "given" by his parents to his widowed grandmother in her old age to help chop her wood, start the fires, assist in the cooking and washing, feed the pigs and chickens, and generally keep her company on the old *ranchito* until she died, which by rights of established custom and Donanciana's wishes he should probably have inherited, to continue providing the extended family with pork, lamb, beef, eggs, milk, fruit, corn, chile, and summer vegetables, and a place to be buried, and, more importantly in this age of cultural shipwreck, a place with which they could all identify even though by the time of Ignacio's childhood everyone had moved into towns and mobile homes, working day jobs for a boss or institution like the rest of America. With Ignacio in place they would have had a place where, like the migratory cranes that often wintered there, a place where they could congregate and remember who they were and where they came from. A rooted home, a place of origins whose memory could travel in their hearts anywhere they migrated like birds.

But the unbalancing shockwaves of the twentieth century's worldwide psycho-industrial wobble that persisted after two machine-driven world wars that tripped and toppled all such organic family rhythms at the knees for pretty much the entire civilized world, had Donanciana's children blinking and culturally eroded. Dazed and limping on one cultural leg away from the land and all that Donanciana had kept alive, her grandchildren were far too confused and captured in the malaise of a thirdhand discount-house late-twentieth-century Americanism to remember what they should have treasured. All except Ignacio, the *hijado*, who when his siblings and cousins sold off Donanciana's beautiful adobe home, outbuildings, and river land over his protests, disowned both his people and his past and fled to a college in Michigan in a bold attempt to forever forget his origins, whose memory now contained his people's betrayal of the lifestyle he'd been groomed to carry on, and was too painful to even identify with any longer. Ignacio reckoned that the *real* Campos family had already disappeared when they deliberately allowed their ancestral land to disappear.

But his early days with the old woman and her memories of six generations of Donancianas had become his very bones, and his entire life hung on them, like it or not. His every motive for living, his courage, integrity, and weakness of pride ran on their rails. After marrying a fellow student, an "Anglo" of German-Irish descent, unable to resist the pull of home he returned to the area of his youth and knowing every entrance and dirt road in the northern area, for thirty-five years he drove for a courier service, becoming himself a minor legend on account of his tireless dedication to his deliveries and people living far-flung on ranches and camps.

His passion had always been to repurchase his Grandmother's home and land, renew the now potholed house, and move his two children and wife onto the beautiful little ranch. But unable to adjust her own midwestern, middle-class, American-city identity to the embittered turbulence, frustration, and pain of Ignacio's clan, whose buckets of toxic self-hatreds for their own betrayals of their origins, while unsuccessfully trying to superimpose an equally rootless "Anglo" pattern onto their self-chosen rootless past, were mercilessly hurled at Ignacio's wife and children, who, easily achieving what his relatives could not, were perceived as uppity and elite. The wife grew restless, surly, and lonely, and barely waiting until the children had grown (themselves jettisoning their past, fleeing to American colleges and jobs as far away as they could fly just like their father had twenty years previously) followed suit when she fell into the arms of a psychology professor in Indiana and was gone. Splitting the money Ignacio had thought they'd been layering up to remake the old life for his kids, he was left alone again and with too little cash to do much more than live, much less pursue his dream of Donanciana's ranch.

So after a year of brooding he amended the plan, came out of retirement, and, at the age of fifty-one, went to work as a cement truck driver in one of the companies of the most controversial and notorious mining mogul of the entire region to whom Ignacio's brothers had sold off Donanciana's land thirty-five years before. The miner, in his usual pattern, had originally intended to strip off all of the topsoil and sand, resell the ancient irrigation water rights to out-of-state land developers, then sell off what was left of the place for subdivided mobile home lots, effectively destroying the original ranch. But for some unknown reason the miner never got around to tearing up the place, and only visited it with his business cronies to hunt the migratory canvasbacks, teals, and mergansers that often wintered there along the cottonwood-lined river.

Ignacio struck a deal with the greed of this famous scoundrel, whereby he agreed to drive cement trucks for a sub-minimal daily wage for ten years if the miner would apply the remaining percentage of what he should have been legally paid to the repurchase of Donanciana's land, which is what he did.

During those ten years, Ignacio spent all his weekends and days off recasting adobe bricks, lifting vigas, plastering and resettling the place so beautifully that by the time the decade was out, he was not only the sole owner and tenant of his grandmother Donanciana's land, but the place looked so much like it had before she died that sometimes Ignacio when half awake in the morning could swear he smelled the old woman's coffee and tortillas warming again on the wood-fired range, as if her spirit had been cooking while he slept.

It was about then that I met him when he'd decided with his remaining alcoholic brothers to sell their grandfather's land on Mesa Poleo, up the mountain by Pedernal, and split the cash, so he'd have something to live on while he figured out how to somehow again make a living. Though he'd pulled off his dream to some degree, his heart was still pained by his own children's oblivious attitude to the land, hatred of his lifestyle, and their subsequent refusal to visit. Like so many others—artists, lovers, visionaries who pursue what they love—Ignacio was again washed up economically and unsure as to what to do next.

In some people, grief and desperation ruin and macerate their hearts, weighing down their minds and lives so thoroughly that each day is so tiring for them that they eventually trade their original vision cheaply for anything at all to dull the pain, accepting any recreational distraction and every addiction advertised at large, legal or otherwise.

But there are others, more romantic and blessed with a merciful vitality like that of resilient wild mountain grasses, who, accustomed to wildfires, drought, deep freezes, overgrazing, hail, and relentless wind, have a more gradual geologic sense of humor, probably inherited from six generations of stubborn grandmothers knowing full well in their bones that their losses must drive beyond self-pity into an even more energetic vision, and they begin to see their perforated lives more like a beehive with the honey of possibility in the comb instead of a living shield of death riddled with holes of sarcastic negativity. Their minds are rewired with a restless openness into a tangible spirituality that manifests in some exuberant combination of previously unnoticed elements from some deeper place they never suspected, gushing in like an underground river flooding the cynical boredom of modern culture's complacent addiction to gizmos, programs, and institutions of salvation, with a rising torrent of fresh spring water from the base of their mountains of grief whose delicious taste feeds even God and charms life into going on.

In the beginning, when Ignacio singlehandedly shouldered his project to bring back to life his grandmother's home and land, his relatives not only refused him assistance but rejected the thought of reviving this past from the dust as absurd. Certain that he only wanted to find the treasure for himself, they actually cursed him.

But when Ignacio finally took possession of Donanciana's land, her old home was a ruin. The old steer-blood floors had been so thoroughly potholed by treasure hunters with metal detectors who dug up the ground at every beep and pop to find a bottle cap, a penny, a bullet shell, a dog tag, or some such without ever hitting the rumored gold, that it resembled a washed out dirt road. What had once been a roof was blue sky now, and the once-ten-foot-high walls had melted to seven feet and were honeycombed by other people trying to find the "red clay pot" filled with the gold of the six Donancianas.

Unlike the local people of the past or the world that surrounded him now, Ignacio was one of the few who knew his grandmother Donanciana had not been the first *Abuelita* Donanciana. There had been five before her. The first original Donanciana was the truly mythological one, and in her own times was known all around as *La India*, the Indian. The stories of the accomplishments, detours, and bizarre twisted unique times of the first Donanciana were attributed to the life of her granddaughter, the next Donanciana, the story of each generation nesting inseparably into the next one until a single vision of six generations of substantial women was telescoped behind six lenses and collapsed into one story about one Donanciana.

Baptized as Donanciana Borrego, the first Donanciana was one of so many Plains living natives, Pueblo Indians, and Athabascans and other Native Americans captured by more commercially oriented Indians who were hired by Spaniards, French, English, and later American whites between the 1600s up until the 1880s to fill the illegal demand for slaves. In the middle Spanish era, indigenous people who survived the ordeal of being captured and sold ended up as unpaid field hands, goatherds, roving sheep herders, cattle drivers, concubines, domestics, wet nurses, weavers, livery workers, bellows pumpers, and house servants. But eventually large groups of Natives who ended up "purchased," slaves bartered from illegally trading horses, guns, and metal to nomadic tribes, exceeded the illegal colonial demand. These unfortunate people were usually gathered together in groups of wholly unrelated individuals from distinct cultures and ways of life, subsequently baptized en masse, settled in towns they themselves were forced to build to create a series of populated "border" towns that served the colonial elite as a physical buffer zone between them and what by then were called "wild," dangerous, war-oriented tribes. War-oriented because of course these people were the same tribes the earlier generations of slaves had been kidnapped from! "Dangerous" nomads worldwide have so often been the direct creation of "civilizations" who ravage and pillage them for slaves often illegally but rampantly creating a lawless human wreckage, whose hatred they suffer later themselves. European business slavers of the sixteenth, seventeenth, and eighteenth centuries, whose horrible undocumented activities took place in all nationalities during and after *all* European invasions and were actually the root of most if not all the centuries of "Indian" warfare, against the stupidity of a policy of often undocumented exploitation of ground and animal, plant and people, where every new thing encountered was enslaved instead of negotiated with and maintained in a tenable interdependency.

Spaniards, French, English, and Americans enslaved thousands of native tribal peoples in differing ways, but in the area that would become New Mexico, the Spanish hierarchies participated in the institutions early on by rationalizing it as a tributary system, whereby the Plains Indians whom they had already preyed upon, furious over the mostly undocumented disgracing of their own territory and the rampant kidnapping of their people for slaves, were thought to be less likely to retaliate against these foreign invaders of their beloved homelands, less likely to attack frontier towns with a serf population of "baptized" relatives of their own Plains Indian blood.

Initially gleaned as a tactic from the Ottoman policy of capturing young Christian boys, converting them into a crack corps of highly prized elite soldiers who supervised the personal army of the sultans and formed their personal bodyguards, who called these captives *janisarees,* from the Mongol *janis tzerek* meaning "new soldiers," the Spanish bureaucracy and military, on the other hand, kept "their Indians" in baptized displaced bunches but called these mixed-tribe border-town populations of non-citizen, freed servants by the same Turkish term, glossed into Spanish as *genizaro.* Indians to the tune of thousands came from the conveniently forgotten but documented great corn-growing, pyramid-building cultures of the Mississippi drainage to disreputable Spanish slave traders as well. Later on in what became the United States of America, Americans entering the vacuum left by the toppled Spaniards under the Mexican government simply enslaved natives at will for use on their spuriously gained ranch spreads as grunts, cowboys, and domestics.

That first Donanciana, Donanciana *La India,* had been a little girl, captured during the late Spanish era, a Caddo girl from what is now eastern Kansas. Herded in with all the other little kidnapped children, she came clutching a small ear of hard, striped red corn.

Though *genizaro* "towns" were in some rare cases granted communal land ownership whose descendants still form a large percentage of old New Mexico families, especially in the North, they or their children usually married into the matrix of a strong whirlwind of cultures and languages, strengthening further the alloy of beauty, food, and mystery that has always made Northern New Mexico what it continues to be.

But this original captive, baptized Donanciana by her Spanish purchasers, did not live as a town *genizaro* for long, for she was in turn "captured" again by a group of Navajo traders, who hid her, taking her off with them on their way home up the Gallina Canyon after a normal "peaceful" trading foray to San Juan pueblo. She later married one of her wealthy "Navajo captors," himself originally a captured Mexican Indian, probably a Tepequan who now spoke Diné and was thereafter a Diné.

Together they lived herding and farming with their new tribe, the Jemez Apaches, or Navajos as they came to be called, the two of them becoming so wealthy in sheep that in the course of the normal migratory life that sheep-raising entails, eternally moving up in the mountains by summer, down by the warmer river village by winter searching new or better grass week by week, they and their children would winter in the Chama River valley, not so very far from where her husband had "stolen" her in the first place! There they put together the ranch and built the farm that would sustain the next twelve generations, from that very spot, that continued on in an almost identical fashion.

This little Caddo girl-slave was hard to discourage, and developed herself into a prominent woman. She spoke not only two Plains tongues but Navajo, Spanish, and probably Tewa as well. But one thing she never lost was her unquenchable thirst for sandlot horse racing. After living as a young woman on the back of those little Navajo horses, those amazing original Spanish ponies, she began breeding a particular strain of them for her own use and rode them to victory over and over in the early days as a Navajo. Because of this, Donanciana, now a wealthy "Spanish-speaking" Indian lady, did indeed amass a certain amount of goods and hard cash by racing her Indian horses against other rich folk. And like all the people of the time, rich or poor, Navajo and Pueblo people in particular, she kept her hard currency in the form of voluminous silver jewelry on her body, the excess in the ground, buried under a particular wooden gate post guarded by two of her fierce sheep dogs.

Unlike most Spanish-speaking families no matter who their ancestors were, who gave inheritance of the family land to the eldest son in the old Roman fashion, leaving the other sons to find their way, and the daughters to marry into land, Donanciana, like a native person, gave her land to her youngest granddaughter, whom she had christened Donanciana as well. This became a custom and a habit for the centuries that followed.

This second Donanciana was the first *hijada* of the original Donanciana *La India*. The institution of *hijada*, as interpreted by this original determined Indian Donanciana, meant that as far as she was concerned, in every other generation a Donanciana must be designated, and this little girl would live with her grandmother, learning all the genealogies, customs, family rituals, land boundaries, litigations, legends, and histories of the preceding Donanciana.

All of this learning was the source for the rest of the family to come and check, in case of any debate regarding the family, and would be settled by the new Donanciana when the old one died.

Besides all the secrets related to particulars unique to her family's prodigious farming and ranching success, and her secrets for the breeding and raising of horses, the birth of children, where to put the afterbirth, the welfare of the bees, old songs and rituals for corn sprouting, there was of course the placement of the wealth pot.

These Donancianas in their fashion of *hijado* were never allowed to legally marry until the previous grandmother Donanciana, her teacher, had passed on, sometimes resulting in women with many children with no legally married husband, but always a granddaughter.

In this way there had always been a renewed Donanciana, and only she knew where the magic pot of wealth was hidden. Due to the turbulent nature of the endless political upheaval of those times, the absence of banks, and the accompanying lawless disregard for the Indian and Spanish-speaking people of the land, by the different incoming political factions, business overlords, changing economies, and government land-swindling representations, the original Donanciana had always maintained that the pot of wealth should always remain hidden and renewed only in the utmost secrecy when the new Donanciana had proved to be "educated" enough by the older Donanciana, to be trusted to have the knowledge and therefore to carry her extended family through whatever land loss, famine, drought, or family divisionism that might occur.

Though by the time of the last Donanciana, the Donanciana that Ignacio had lived and learned from, there had been six Donancianas, because there had never not been a live functioning Donanciana in everyone's memory, the ranch was always called El Rancho Donanciana no matter which of the Donancianas was presiding in that era.

But being a boy, Ignacio had only been taught what could be taught to a boy and a few specific things that were considered woman secrets that might have otherwise been given him were forfeit in his case. But nonetheless he knew a lot of secrets. He had almost put some of the earliest ones out of his consciousness until much later, when, during certain phases of rebuilding her house, some things started to involuntarily resurface.

The rest of the family knew nothing, because when they sold the land off, Ignacio pretended to forget what he couldn't forget, because he begrudged them for their actions. One of these old things was how the second Donanciana, Donanciana *La Fiel,* had actually converted most of the hard metallic wealth from the hidden clay pot of the original Donanciana *La India* back into *reliquias:* silver candlesticks, a chalice, the silver frames on *retablos* of the saints, for a sacristy that graced a small personal chapel that once stood on the ground, for the priest to say Mass in on behalf of this homemade prominent family.

But when Americans who accompanied Kearny and various others on their forays to supposedly "take" charge of New Mexico, bringing it officially into the jurisdiction of the USA, after the Treaty of Guadalupe Hidalgo in their conveniently glossed-over ogreish unsupervised ignorant style, the troops, mostly Protestant, illiterate, so-called "white men" ransacked almost all the chapels up and down the Rio Grande basin, melting down all gold and silver to pay for their Missouri farms, the Donanciana family lost most of its hard wealth.

Though Ignacio was not privy to its whereabouts, he knew despite all that, a jar must have still existed in his own time, and he knew what it was supposed to look like from the stories told to him by his grandmother.

Whatever things of great value Native New Mexicans regained after the Americans came, for security's sake every family once again adopted the age-old custom of hiding them. But as far as anyone knew, including Ignacio, the exact contents and whereabouts of the jar of treasure were lost and forgotten.

But all material considerations aside, when Donanciana initially instituted her version of the *hijada,* she was looking a long way ahead to keeping alive the real treasures of what she loved. She made sure that in every generation there would always be at least one person who could be groomed to grow into the same knowledgeable "old person" she had been, the *viejita*. No matter how badly the family at large might fare in the coming centuries or how severed away from their root, land, and most importantly, the stories, there would be someone from whom to restore it all. The real stories were the spiritual DNA of the people, their blueprint on how to be themselves, stories in whose continued retelling lay the ancestral memory of all the old otherwise forgotten cultural motivations, for all the decisions they took and the very exciting versions of where it all came to roost. Some of them were old Pueblo, some new Pueblo, some of it Navajo, some of it Sephardic Jew, some of it Tlaxcalan, some Andalusi Arab, some Esmalam, like her custom of singing extemporaneous praise poems to little horses for speed, some Basque, some French, some Plains Indian, some northern European, but no matter what, the diversity of all those ancestral minds, eyes, languages, and customs combined in such a way as to make every stalk of family descent a vital one, that only enriched and empowered the "tribal" motion toward a more viable life whose flower was fertilized by the everyday condition of the present.

The magic of the miracle of how the land fed its children had its secret in this mix. The land owned the people; the people didn't own the land. But the people owned the stories of what that land meant, and, like AC current, its meaning pulsed on down to them in every generation through history, living, dying, reliving to light the lamp of the present, adding their own tale to the last. Without this the people could not know themselves. The stories were the seeds of the people's souls, which knew how to regrow more life of the Donanciana type.

Ignacio had learned a great deal of all of this but as his *hijado* "education" had been interrupted by his American education, it was only now that a greater, more spiritual series of gradual installments of his real education was about to dawn on him as if that string of old ladies were teaching him from the other world.

When Ignacio had first walked into the floorless, pitted, potholed, cut up, roofless ruin of wood rats and ground squirrels of what had once been a beautiful, comforting, sturdy, red mud house with whitewashed inside walls, an azurite milk wainscoting throughout, and tiny corner fireplaces for which he split fragrant *sabina* to fuel their morning fires, when he'd recovered from weeping he lowered his expectations and proceeded to look for any signs whatsoever of the old woman having ever been there. He found one:

Inside the house at the base of what had been a basin stand for water in Donanciana's unplumbed kitchen in front of a homemade, now absent, *trastero,* three stalks of stunted, unwatered, uncultivated corn had been growing out of a rodent hole. One of them had a kind of maimed ear of dried corn, somewhere between a flint corn and a Pueblo flour corn, upon whose cob every kernel was the color of red orange fire with a fan of cream stripes that radiated from a black base.

This was the corn that Grandma had always planted. The corn that had come down the line with the original Donanciana from her Caddo ancestors. Ignacio was aware, as all farmers are, that unlike most crops, unharvested corn when left in the field will *not* propagate itself, but needs the hands of humans to plant it for it to grow again. The fact that the old corn was still growing, and in the ruin, he saw as a sign that Donanciana's spirit was still strong somewhere in the house, in the ground and in the place. But the American-educated Ignacio couldn't figure how the corn still grew there after all those years. It was a miracle to the New Mexican Ignacio, an enigma awaiting further research to the gringo Ignacio.

Ignacio planted the seeds from one stunted cob the following May, and they took off. Within three years he had fully revived the breed and was feeding himself and his animals on the same corn, just like Grandma had. And thus, not despite his losses, but on account of them, Ignacio's real spiritual remembering began in the most tangible way!

As part of his learning as his grandmother's *hijado,* Ignacio had been taught to revere the little bees of her old-time log hives, whose seven generations of old Spanish honeybees had fertilized the Campos family's original five acres of apples, apricots, Spanish peaches, cherries, and

"Italian" plums for two centuries. The hives were long gone of course, but some loyal division of descendants of the same honey bees—at least Ignacio thought they looked like them—had taken up residence in a cavernous, rotted-out core of an old upended cottonwood stump down by the Chama river. Well, maybe they were and maybe they weren't or some combination, but they sure looked like the ones he used to see his grandmother talking to as a boy.

Donanciana said that the honey of the bees was the "happiness" of the land and that the bees were its soul, ears, eyes, taste, and sensibility. They were the *nervios* of the land she would say, for any unconscious, unkind, or evilly motivated betrayal of the land or its people, even before it manifested, the bees could instantly feel, she would say. They were so emotionally affected by such events that the bees saw them as sicknesses of the land and the people. To heal it all, Donanciana said, they would swarm outside the hive, hanging in enormous droops off one of the cottonwood trees, and play out whatever human-generated melodrama threatened their future equilibrium. After hashing it all out away from the sanctity of the hive to keep it away from their young, the discussion among the bees usually came to a close when the bees divided into unresolved polarized factions, and like people would end up dispersing in cliques as far away from each other as they could get, moving into desert ledges, old stumps, or even courageously dying searching nomadically for flowers, home, and a lack of human negativity. A small core would always remain dedicated at all costs to the hive. Donanciana called them her other *hijados*.

For generations whenever a husband would leave for another woman, or there was a murder, some violent unspoken resentment brewed, or someone carried out an act of stupidity that unthinkingly insulted the land, the bees would leave their hives and hang somewhere to grieve in drooping swarms, buzzing and weeping like a cloister of groaning monks.

"They were healing us with what they did," she would say, "so it would be time for us to heal the bees." Like some old-time "oracular reader" of bees, Ignacio's Donanciana would ceaselessly watch the bees, and through them very accurately divine the well-being of her people and the health of her fields in relation to the wild land by the river. All entirely by the bees' actions. Whenever they tried to leave she would know right away and understand what was about to transpire.

Producing a little handmade bell hammered out of coin silver that she kept hanging from a ribbon around her neck, the old lady would start singing to the bees while tinkling her little bell nonstop. The endless clear chirping of the tiny silver ringer would calm them down from a terrified, indignant mob into a more friendly weepy singsong pile of mutually grief-stricken insects. The little silver ringer had been inherited, passed down from generation to generation of Donanciana, from the original Donanciana *La India,* who reputedly had it made by a Navajo silversmith. She, it was rumored, would sometimes hunt about for days until she found her estranged bees, just like a flock of stray sheep. But no matter how far they had wandered every time, after realizing that Donanciana the human actually understood them, they would follow her tinkling and singing all the way home, reentering their old log hives with little beeswax-lined slits, and take up their lives again as the vital "heart" of her land. She never lost them. For twelve generations of humans and who knows how many of bees, the Donancianas never lost them.

The bees in entirety of course swarmed out for the last time and flew off for good when the last Donanciana died and the land was sold out of the family. Like his grandmother's bees, Ignacio fled the scene too. His own grief over the loss of the family land and his grandmother was too much to bear in the face of people who didn't care. Disappearing from the relentless bullying of his hard-faced, mindless, alcoholic brothers, he'd kept the bell with him as his one and only personal memento left him of his life with grandma Donanciana. On her death bed, laid out on her sheepskins in the middle of her beautiful, soon-to-disappear earthen home, Donanciana in impending death's visionary brilliance had teenage Ignacio lift the ribbon from the dry stalk of her tired neck and gave him the little silver bee-calming bell more as a magical talisman to keep him from getting lost than anything else, when she was gone.

After so many decades, the present generation of feral bees no doubt had never met the Donanciana their ancestors had known, but through some grand capacity of neural spiritual memory, they recognized the motive of the tiny delicious tinkling and Ignacio's weirdly accurate imitation of his grandmother's high, wavering, birdlike voice. From no small distance arriving one by one, ten by twenty, little by little to swarm, hanging in a grand droop off a *viga* out front of Ignacio's little house, these descendants of Donanciana's bees abandoned their flood-bleached cottonwood trunk up the Chama River and followed the little bell's call straight to the slitted doorways of their newly renewed ancestral homes right into the blunt log beehives carved exactly like those Ignacio remembered from his youthful apprenticeship to the old woman.

Under the direction of the bees, it was only a couple of years before Ignacio's orchards were again in full swing and he had honey, apples, apricots, cherries, sometimes little white Spanish peaches for sale, eggs, beef, lambs, goat's milk, *cuajada*, chiles, melons, *chicos*, *chaqegue*, and cornmeal. He couldn't believe it: the land had its heart back; the land could remember again how to be itself, a memory beyond Ignacio's own time and personal ability to remember alive and well right in the purring of the old hives with newly renewed Donanciana Bees.

Though now he never ran out of food, he remained unable to generate enough cash to pay for gasoline, land tax, clothing, boards, nails, tar, paint, buckets, and pick-up truck maintenance.

But the lessons of the bees gave him an idea.

Based on his childhood with the old lady and the need to somehow do his part to stem the only too obvious cultural, spiritual, physical health, and ecological disasters that ensued among his people with the loss of what her type of teaching had kept alive in him, Ignacio himself older now thought he should have an *hijado* as well to instruct. So he started a kind of diminutive ranch college of *hijado* for young people. Even though his own children tuned their father out, regarding what Ignacio taught as an incomprehensible pile of inefficient, romanticized, outdated lies, and condescendingly called his school of *hijado* a petting zoo, a kind of quaint living museum, Ignacio became for scores of young people a miraculous dream come true, a Donanciana for them, like his grandmother had been for him. His newly found ingenuity for teaching surprised him, but then again all New Mexicans are fascinated by the weird details of being a New Mexican, and have by nature a relentless need to explain everything by telling stories that start at the beginning! He became so popular that he had to start limiting the classes and took on more serious year-long twenty-year-olds as apprentices who had the physical strength to help keep the place running as Ignacio got older, doing for him what he'd done for his own grandmother.

Two of these young people, joyfully for him, were a niece and nephew, the children of his alcoholic, big-nailed, obnoxious sister, Veronica.

The nephew, Leon, in his early twenties, had become on his own a locally beloved electrician, gifted and good-hearted, who had worked stubbornly to get custody of his little sister, Leandra. Her young head repeatedly battered, her soul even more wounded by a mostly vacant violent drug-soaked father, she'd never been given the time to grow any spiritual skin, and with no emotional armor, she couldn't grow up, remaining too tender and strange. So Leon took her in and became her parent forever, shielding her with the strength of ten from the bite of a toothy world that would have devoured her.

Both of them had always loved Ignacio, for he was always on their side of any argument. But as the only relatives that loved Ignacio, he charmed them into moving in with him into the little restored adobe of their great-grandmother Donanciana, to become his own *hijados*. They helped him manage the menagerie of soft-handed, dreadlocked college kids from other places who, in many ways, were even more generationally displaced from their own ancestral past. The kind of "land-race education" Ignacio deftly wielded and taught at his Ranchito Donanciana gave these very intelligent but overly righteous and serious children hope; and as they were for the most part economically over-privileged, they actually got their parents to pay for the lives of Ignacio and his niece and nephew.

With so much help around, Donanciana's farm and ranch got to putting out so much milk, meat, root vegetables, and grain that more and more outbuildings were built, and, after fifteen years of living like

Donanciana with no gas or electric bills, Ignacio finally gave in to Leon's suggestion of installing an electric refrigerator and freezer, and an electric well pump and some reading lamps. For this the place would have to be wired for electricity. And of course in an old adobe that meant New Mexico style.

Chapter 14

Tunneling Past Centuries, Red Corn in Their Cheeks, the Old Ladies Scurry into View

One muddy, overcast, blustery day in early autumn while everyone else was out, Ignacio and Leon worked together chiseling the two-inch deep channels into the two-foot-thick, almost rock-hard adobe of the centuries-old wall of Donanciana's kitchen to accommodate the route of the 110 cable to wire in an electric outlet. After a couple of hours of chatting and chiseling, their tools uncovered the edge of a mud-filled *nicho* inside of whose hollow arch a veritable pot of fired red clay with a burn mark on the lower belly of one side sat, squat and secure.

Sealed into the old wall, just like everybody said: there it was, the treasure of the six Donancianas. Both men froze in amazement, neither of them knowing what they should do next. Ignacio for certain, and probably his nephew as well, had always considered the story of the old woman's treasure as part of the body of tales generated by some warped need for historically preserved gossip that some people had in order to fill the unused mental space such narrow minds seemed to maintain to explain the actions, events, and lives of more unique people and times for which their uncreative judgmental brains had no normal everyday categories. But there it was right in front of their faces peeking out from the old wall where she'd left it sealed: a red clay pot with a burn mark on one side!

Though fascinated and amazed, Ignacio was equally agitated by the genuine fear that the remainder of his greedy single-minded relatives would hear about the "treasure" and descend upon the Ranchito Seis Donancianas and destroy if only by their abusive alcoholic presence the school of *hijado*, the peace of the bees, and the treasure, all in one breath.

But the day came on that one clear October morning that comes every year when the red and yellowing cottonwood leaves compete with the annual nostalgic perfume of ripe apples, that are much sweeter now that they have convinced their own leaves to turn, all the trees filling the ground of the Six Donancianas all around with their quiet leaf-falling and courteous clicking in a memorial of layered gold of a good wet summer gone, when the torture of waiting and arguing with himself finally became unbearable. Ignacio rose and carefully removed the pot from its dusty hole and placed it on the kitchen table, a replica of the old pine one on which he and Grandma used to shuck *aberjón*. More significant now in its venerable presence than its measurable weight, which sat even lighter in his two hands than he'd expected, the pot had been originally tightly closed with an old hand-chipped sandstone lid, which inset into the pot's mouth was sealed with boiled piñon sap, most of which had long since crystallized and cracked away.

After taking that one last moment he needed to make sure he was doing the right thing, Ignacio Campos finally brought himself to lift the lid and take a look inside. And when he did so, there on the table sitting before him was a beautiful red clay pot filled to the brim not with gold but ancient seeds!

The original treasure of the Six Donancianas was not gold, or money, or any other daydream of metallic wealth. It was a big pot of seeds top to bottom that made up the precious treasure of the six Donancianas.

Seeds.

Something no greed-infected, wealth-seeking enemy would ever regard as precious, but which no one who ate, drank, and slept could do without when trying to live with the wild strange earth along that New Mexico river.

There were seeds of every kind, domesticated and undomesticated, seeds that were prized by each Donanciana, who by continually regrowing and renewing the jar adding in succession to those same seeds, seeds of plants newly appreciated, brought in by those marrying into the clan. Seeds they knew their people would need to replant, to regrow again their lives in the event of any disaster political, personal, or natural. The seed jar was their bank, a bank of landrace wealth.

The top layer was all beans: black-spotted cream-colored beans, little pink trapezoidal beans, blue beans, fat white beans. Beneath them rested a neat layer of squash seeds, pumpkin seeds, and old-time sunflower seeds; and beneath them lay four short ears of corn still on their cobs, one white, one blue, one yellow, and of course one orange red with striped kernels.

Tobacco seeds lay still in their capsules, *punche* and mountain tobacco both, cotton seeds, varieties of chile seeds, wheat, oats, barley, prickly flower seeds, and little black grass seeds.

A pot of seeds generously sent by the regal, caring minds of successive waves of Donancianas from sections of time past that like six nodes on a wild cane stalk grew, one burgeoning from the previous, all arriving together out of the dust of days only heard of but never seen, fetched now after all those centuries right into Ignacio's two hands like a red earthen heart; a pot of seeds sent from the dead to help their living incarnations to remember again how to be a people, a people who would know how to replant a viable way of life if ever their harvests were burnt or taken during the greedy vicissitudes of wars or other disasters; a pot of seeds for a time like the one in which we find ourselves, besieged by a mad world of abstract commerce that sells off empty stock in a seedless future, forgets its root and ruthlessly devours the present.

Silenced, emotional, and stunned in the best of ways by the brilliance of the reality of those old-timers who actually did leave a treasure but only a treasure for those who could treasure the sophisticated spiritual depth of how the precious motive of seeds and culture are synonymous, Ignacio was euphoric over the seeming absence of gold until he reached the bottom of the jar, where four little gold Spanish coins lay, placed symmetrically under a pair of turquoise earrings and an agate arrowhead. The *nicho* had been covered with a yellow flagstone. Removing the sandstone ledge, then digging a little well down into the exposed wall, he mudded the gold, turquoise, and old blade back into the wall to be forgotten. Ignacio began to breathe for the first time in his life as a man caressing and holding a dream instead of a man pulled around like a plough behind a dream.

Like men knocked to their knees by the reality of the arrival of a fabled supernatural bride promised long ago who never arrived, not forgotten but stored as the substance of hope somewhere hidden in one's secret thoughts who all of a sudden just appears as promised, neither Leon nor Ignacio dared touch, remove, peer into, disturb, or further mention the beautiful old pot. They took a break from wiring the house and almost forgot to breathe while Ignacio tried to give a voice to what Donanciana would have said just about now. He wept, sat, pondered, paced, and wept some more. Then one night when the back-and-forth of the ball game of his soul's debate with his head had his soul hitting the ball far off the back court wall past the boundary of his mind, from which perspective it could be seen that in some creative way he owed Donanciana to become himself the new Donanciana.

He now knew he had to dedicate himself not to reliving the life he'd had with Grandma, but to living the life Grandma had left him to live. Where others—like his brothers—only saw the past as stark legacies of unsmiling frontier disappointments from which, as children, they could only flee and never escape, once there were no more Donancianas and Ignacio the *hijado*, guardian of tradition, was out of the picture in college, who, never having had the stories and having lost both their identities, and the plot of the American life whose culture of displacement made the last Donanciana's life of old tales, one milk cow, twelve sheep, fifty apple trees, two old horses, corn patch, long-rowed chile field, melons, cool cottonwood trees, outhouse, and wood-burning cook stove into a thing of poverty, began their weekend hobby of sweeping the place with metal detectors potholing the walls and floors in search of "grandma's gold" in hopes of ransoming themselves from the slavery of self-loathing and feelings of being ridiculed as ignorant and brown, for having to work for this new power-hungry people, their employers in Los Alamos who made world-destroying bombs and shopping malls to buy the synthetic houses and lives they hoped would bring them the respect of the people materially in charge, Ignacio realized that night he no longer needed to revive Donanciana; he would be revived by Donanciana's gift.

The brothers hadn't been able to see it. Though brother Eufracio while hoping for gold actually did discover a cache of two hundred pounds of old-time Spanish iron bar stock buried in the remains of the adobe hay shed, something in its day precious enough for its rarity for having been imported from Europe in the eighteenth century, there was no sign of any old Indian clay pot with a burn mark on its side. They never found what they were looking for: not gold, not freedom, and certainly no self-worth.

Now twelve years later, four feet above the refurbished basin stand, six feet above the now-sealed rodent hole, two weeks after Leon had chiseled the very tough old red clay with its usual fascinating mix of old pot shards, and life debris of hundreds of years past, they'd come upon this old *nicho*.

Donanciana's house, like all Pueblo Indian houses and New Mexican Spanish speakers' houses until recently, had several beautiful *nichos* in the walls, to house holy water, *santos*, cornmeal, or various indigenous deities of the family, or all of the above. But in this buried secret *nicho* sat the famous unpainted burnished red clay Tewa jar the size of a man's head with incised butterflies and a burn mark on its belly.

During some portion of every day throughout that winter and the following spring, Ignacio pondered whether or not the seeds still had enough viability to sprout and make more seeds from themselves.

Ignacio gently removed a few of the best-looking seeds from the pot to plant the following summer.

Seeds dream, seeds wait, seeds grow, others sail, but none of these old seeds had enough of the dream left in them to jump again up and out of the ground as sprouts. All except nine bean sprouts, and of these, only five flowered, and of those, only two made beans. The miracle though was at first when harvesting the little handful that was to become the ancestral progenitors of a dry bean for which Ignacio would be known, they were all spotted. But none of them were the same color. Like little New Mexican old-time Spanish horses when a red and white foal can come from a solid black mother, or a cream-colored buckskin drops from the vulva of a deep blue roan, a couple of the beans were blue and cream, others splattered red and white, a couple yellow ocher and tan, another bleached white, another purple and red. But when they were fully dry, each of them looked identical to the ones Ignacio had originally grown: a more plebeian dark brown on a cream. When he replanted them all again the following season, he separated all the colors, but the same thing happened again.

The frail old empty seed capsules of that chin-striped fire-colored corn he'd found in the jar he recognized immediately. Like the dry fleshless skulls of ancestors long deceased, who could no longer make love and more children, but whose descendants we definitely are, who do love, reproduce, and speak, who can see the ancestral form in the dusty crumbling bone, the powdery parchment of these dry hollowed seeds in the pot beyond a doubt were the ancestors of their living descendants, the corn he'd been growing and eating and had eaten with his own Donanciana as a child; these same little red corn seeds had been not grown from the pot but gleaned forty-five years later from the hole of a very much alive ground squirrel in the floor of Donanciana's old dry crumbled house. And there they were, the very same ones whose antique dusty shadows now stared up at him from his ancestor's old hopeful pot, seeds no longer able to grow.

None of the other seeds, none of the chile, cotton, tobacco, squash, or pumpkins ever came up either. Anyone well versed in the way everything in this living world depends on plants, and therefore upon flowers, which are all at the mercy of the majesty of bees and insects, knows that the seeds plants make cannot stay viable forever. Scientifically, corn supposedly lasts some twelve years, decreasing by a half every year for the following twelve until none can successfully remake seeds again.

Thus a spirituality of seeds like Donanciana's, and all truly intact peoples throughout the world, is a spirituality of periodically renewing the vitality of viability.

Seeds left in a jar for too long without regrowing cannot be renewed by storing them for later. Just as dogmatic knowledge written down in sacred texts whose vagaries only evoke a dead past no longer visible has no ability to generate knowledge or wisdom without being relived and rehydrated into living experiential relevance as actively taught by those who have done so during the present, seeds must be constantly renewed by replanting in the present before they lose the "memory" of what they can do in order for them to truly continue as seed-making plants.

Without the interest, culturally embedded cognizance, reverence for that understanding, and a new generation with really old ancestral instincts to deliberately and spiritually care enough to do the practical hard work of what it takes to renew both the seeds and the cultural knowledge that parallels the seeds, both the seeds and a people's culture become a husk of form with no existence. One is not real or even possible without the other. That's why they say that a memory of having descended from dead indigenous ancestors does not make you indigenous just because you genetically descend from them; it's how you match their expertise at living well, friendly to the fate of the ground that feeds you today and how you grow the seeds of cultural food they've left you that keeps both you and the seeds alive and makes you the candidate for the possibility of being indigenous.

Ignacio of course at least instinctually knew all this, and one night after falling asleep while staring at his one perfectly formed dry ear of chin-striped fine red corn grown and renewed every year for twelve years from those original hero seeds from the squirrel's hole, a live ear that he'd placed gratefully in front of the beautiful pot of that same corn's now dead ancestral husks grown by Ignacio's own ancestors, an endless herd of bigger thoughts thundered up and out of his depths cascading over the sharp, over-delineated cliff of his righteous civilized mind as he dropped off careening wildly through his dreams into a deeper older sea. A hurricane of homeless comprehension went looking for a place to live, churning and plowing out a palatial grotto in Ignacio's mind and dreaming heart to house an immensity too powerful for regular human thinking to hold until awakened by an instinct to survive, he was bucked awake out of the sea of tormenting understanding.

Sitting straight up, sweating and panting, still staring straight into the quiet *nicho* of Donanciana's dark refurbished kitchen, he realized that the little red corn kernels and the legacy of the life gift of the six Donancianas, instead of having been poor voiceless victims of modern times, had by their own unwillingness to be defeated, willfully regressed into their more indigenous primal origins, drawing themselves straight into the root of the Holy Mothers of Chaos and Chance, which he immediately recognized as the left and right ventricles of the heart of Nature's gigantic birth-oriented, creative, placental mind.

The six Donancianas, some thirty-five years apart, each in their generational turn when it came time for the previous Donanciana to reveal the secret whereabouts and the central significance of their family's seeds and the story and largesse of the old jar, the new, younger Donanciana, most probably with none of the neighboring family's or even her own people paying much attention to her incrementing interest in Grandma's expanding garden, would privately, unseen every twelve years thereafter, remove the seed jar from its hiding place and systematically renew all the jar's seeds by carefully replanting the seeds and tending the resulting crop. At the end of her first season, the old Donanciana had made sure that the girl had memorized all the stories, rituals, prayers, and her responsibilities to the seeds, would then repack the jar, replace the ever-present coins, the turquoise, and the agate blade in exactly the same fashion as before, sealing them all up with the stone lid and pitch, replace it back into the wall, mud it over, and hang a *bulto* of Santa Cruz or the Holy Virgin over the fresh mud.

In the time of Ignacio's brothers, when all else had failed and there were no more Donancianas, no more renewable jars, no seed culture to care, then all six Donancianas had joined together as a group, seeping in like water from their corresponding spiritual layers, and with no human being remaining to become them, take on their name, or way of life, they permeated and transformed into the very substance of wind, tangible rain, desert mud, and determined desert rodents, to belligerently discover yet another method outside the infamous, misunderstood, forgotten jar of now dead seeds, to subversively regenerate yet again enough of the red corn seeds beyond their own invisible times originating from the great Mississippi basin Caddoan pyramid temple people to become themselves regenerated as stalks from the rodent's hole to maintain an edible form of this life-sustaining physical incarnation of the original Donanciana, to give to Ignacio's generation and those who came after what the seed jar could no longer do.

The unstoppable slave girl's soul's latest strategy in her indigenous revolution of seeds was to reincarnate as the power of the earth herself in the form of that very dedicated old agricultural rodent, the desert ground squirrel, who, as ritually revered by all Pueblo Indian farmers a special type of squirrel who very tangibly and ably replants the ground with the sunflowers, squashes, piñon nuts, and corn, whose seeds they ably steal and grow, more in search of their fresh sprouts, which they unearth and eat as fresh greens, than they do the seeds. They always manage to purposely leave enough uneaten sprouts who go on to mature into full plants with seeds to give them sprouts for the following season. Even in ruins where both the people and their seeds have long disappeared, these squirrels truly farm the living seeds of the dead. They truly keep the seeds alive.

The rich wind of Donanciana *La India*'s soul recarved Ignacio's plodding heart into a visionary one, blowing hard into him until he knew in his bones exactly how the six Donancianas were able to circumnavigate the final failure of their treasure of hope of their old red pot in the hands of modernity's depressive crush, to still supply Ignacio his breakfasts for the next thirty-five years with the same unique pink *atole* of his grandmother, and the living seeds of the first and last Donanciana. The knowledge of that way of thinking was the biggest seed kept alive both in and out of the jar. The Donancianas could still run the race that was worth running for life again.

It's hard to keep seeds like that hidden, especially when twelve generations of one's unseen ancestral past thwart sequential Time all at the same time and decide it's time to push their seeds into sight again! The time for such roots and seeds must come for the rest of us as well or Time will die, and the world addicted to a future without feeding the past will lose their stories and their seeds, their sanity, and the thrill of wanting to continue living.

The following autumn Leon brought home a tiny young wife, a radiant determined girl from Pakistan, in New Mexico studying to be a doctor. The child of a Torwali apricot farmer from the remote upper reaches of the Swat Valley, Pashta loved what Leandra, Leon, and Ignacio were doing on their land, so uncharacteristic of the America that is presented to the world by the media, who only cover big business and politics. When their daughter was born, she wanted to name her Donanciana. But Leandra, in her roundabout singsong way, pointed out that Ignacio, because of his dream, had gone ahead and named the ground squirrels who continued tunneling through the adobe wall under the water vent into the clay floor of the refurbished kitchen *Las Seis Donancianas*. Every ground squirrel ever after was called Donanciana, and finally one fat famous one became *La Sexta,* for short.

Leandra in her strange smiling moments of seeming adult cheer and childlike genius insisted that Leon and Pashta call their baby Ignacia instead. And that's exactly what they did.

Outside of the word *squirrel,* what is called a ground squirrel in Northern New Mexico has only a vague kinship to the numerous varieties of the world's woolly tree squirrels that a lot of people think of when the word "squirrel" comes up. Ground squirrels are smarter, slimmer, faster, even more audacious than their cute-eared arboreal cousins with a more rugged muscular build and lanky appearance. For one, except at one time of year, their long tails are usually not bushy, and their fur itself is often grizzled like a bear or variegated like a spotty hairy tweed. And they are not big on water; they rarely drink it at all. But when they do, it's only to break their boredom as it gives them a kind of electrifying jolt like that experienced by a teetotaling Baptist drinking his first shot of tequila. Trees are something of an atypical adventure for them, too, and often cause their demise. For the occasional ground squirrel probably high after drinking too much water who decides she wants to show off to her relatives and tries to lick the sky, taking the delirious high-rise detour from her ever-busy ground-oriented work schedule with its cautious wide-eyed horizontal strategies, becomes so thoroughly intoxicated by the singular height as to be easily snatched up by a falcon or sharp-shinned hawk. But in and over the ground they are very adaptive and reign supreme with a kind of capricious magic about them that makes them, once they decide on something, very difficult to deter. Thankfully, though, they love negotiating and respond much better to gifts and being treated according to their high theocratic station in the scheme of the Holy in Nature than they ever will to poisons, pest control devices, or bullets, which I've seen them redirect or dodge at point blank, smiling as they peek at their hopeless assailant from behind a stalk of corn riddled with buck shot.

Not long after Ignacia was born, Ignacio's dream made him realize that the ancestors of this old squirrel were also the very spirits that had given the first Donanciana the Slave and her descendants the idea and method of how to "keep the seeds alive" for this lineage. The squirrels were Holy, and they had taught *La India,* and in the end the Donancianas became squirrels. For this reason Ignacio named every resident ground squirrel the Six Donancianas, no matter which one presented himself and twitched his ears at him. He made a deal with these mischievous animals; maybe it's better said that Ignacio signed an agreement with the majesty of the rodents that stated that he agreed to leave an annual tribute of a dozen dry ears of the best revitalized fire-colored chin-marked corn seeds that they alone were responsible for having kept alive and viable in the same walls of Grandma's old house where the seed's jar had been laid. He left his gift for the squirrels in the as-yet unresurrected adobe walls of the Donancianas' crumbling cowshed where the ground squirrels kept house. When done sincerely, such offerings and treaties were always acceptable to the ground squirrel tribe, and the main house remained undisturbed by rodent holes thereafter, and would continue that way as long as Ignacio kept up his end. Growing older, Leon and Pashta's daughter would become Ignacio's shadow; he would teach her "everything" and Ignacia would have the dream. She would be the next Donanciana. Ignacia, the New Mexican Torwali Donanciana.

Chapter 15

"Here's Your Damned Corn"

Though the presence of a few stalwart squirrel-farmed stalks of that old strain of red corn was there for all to see, like so much of the subtle grandeur of a more ground-oriented existence, something devalued in an age of a televised synthetic existence, the world was oblivious to the miracle.

Even Ignacio Campos, when he had first set out to recreate in every last detail the solid mud home of his grandmother and the way of life he'd remembered, he only harvested and replanted the corn out of some unconscious nagging instinct. For at the onset, the real significance of the red corn growing in the ruin escaped him as well.

Just like his people and his own soul, the living miracle of these particular seeds thriving in the ruins he tended were not recognized for what they really were: the true heart and living spiritual DNA of his own indigenous past. It was they the ancestors of these seeds who fed his own ancestors, and only the ancient breed of southwestern squirrels had remained miraculously loyal to keeping it alive. For Ignacio in those days, the renewal of the ruins is what he held like a Holy relic, while later the treasure became more the corn growing out of the ruins.

When he'd first started his romantic project, his cynical brothers and sisters had thrown up their arms, dismissing him as a hypocrite, positive that all of Ignacio's cultural regeneration talk and efforts at refurbishing the old house and way of life were a transparent ruse to cover up his own search for the rumored gold while trying to appear to the world as a hero who was revitalizing the ruin his siblings had created in their search for the same. Instead of their hideous tunneling to make certain there was no unfound treasure while Ignacio was away at school, they now tunneled Ignacio's reputation, figuring he was "rebuilding" the place to recover the gold, sure that grandma Donanciana actually had told him where it was hidden and that Ignacio had just been waiting for everyone to lose interest.

They and a lot of others laughed at his school. Some would mock everything about him forever. What else could those types of people do? Just like the rest of the alienated television culture they sold out to, they were people with a memory doctored by a cultureless consumerism leaving them with a truncated sense of their own origins, which no longer valued their people's traditional need for an origin place, a place to renew their wounded souls. Most certainly seeds of conscious knowledge, or why one should need them, only stood in the way of their pursuit of hand-me-down Americanism.

But something deep even in the bones of such people, including the Anglos, must've felt the pain of such a loss. But they didn't recognize they were depressed, or if they did, that their depressions actually originated from having lost a tangible ritual dialogue with their own natural origins. The presence of someone like Ignacio among them fueled in many so-called "whites" that unconscious patronizing attitude that pretended to position them above and out of the reach of the question of their losses and resulting repressions, creating the illusion they needn't deal with it. While with disenfranchised New Mexicans, their emotions often puddled into a flood of vicious jealousy unconsciously distilled from the terror of a newer and recent sense of shame at being placed "beneath" the superiority cult of the "whites."

The reality of the past had become for them, like all peoples caught in today's trance of the untenable, mass-produced irreality of civilization's tractor beam, a problem to erase from the present: a problem to purposely forget, a selective amnesia to anesthetize the pain of an absurd present. For those made numb in this fashion, the past instead of being a place of stories, magic, and origins to which we are all rooted, for good, bad, ugly, or mediocre, a place from which our lives like whale sonar could bounce off of to know who and where we are, from where we have been generated, a past we shall soon enough join to help generate a new present worth living in, for generations to come way beyond us, Ignacio's seeds and dream represented an unwanted reminder of their own lost past, something they could only trivialize, reduce to mental ashes in their relentless unsporting fire of ridicule. Unconvincingly attempting to sarcastically laugh it all off, they had to purge away from their lives what Ignacio's existence kept shoving in their faces; they must forget or, unable to comprehend the whole, live a limited existence of constant confusion to die mired in the deadly pride of the bitterness of unmetabolized grief of a pseudo post-tribal identity.

Nonetheless there were a lot of people, certainly myself among them, who thoroughly admired Ignacio and his type. I imagine each of us desperately hoped to somehow find such a tangible way to do exactly the same with our own lives. But who could think it really possible?

For who among us, born today into such a flat reality, unexposed to any of this kind of real cultural magic, and knowing only the objectified, expressionless modern condition of televisions and computers, can boast a sturdy twelve-generation string of brilliant merging Donancianas and their adaptive lives, or any four-and-a-half centuries of tangible earth upon which to rebuild and replant a viable life with viable seeds of knowledge and food, without the alienating interference of a technology dedicated to forgetting our origins as a place? With nowhere to house the living root of squirrel-kept seeds to repopulate and reanimate an otherwise amnesia-scorched wasteland of our nerve-wracking present, who has even one ancestor remembered or forgotten who would have thoughtfully left us such a crafty and regal present as a pot of seeds sealed in the walls of our origins with vision enough to comprehend that the very-much-alive ground squirrels that surround us are Divine parts of the whole ecstatic plan to keep the seeds of culture alive?

I figured if we didn't have any of this, then we should at least recognize the fact in a big way. Then having done so, learn to further treasure the deep grief of that difficult recognition. But not leaving it at that, we have to get to work sprouting ourselves out of the ground of that recognition of our loss into real people, who when we're gone could become the thing for the future generations that we all lacked in ours: ancestors who would leave seeds of this depth for a world we in our present form will never see. But where to find the seeds of cultural crops and a viable spiritual, cultural approach integral enough to even commence?

When I met Ignacio, I myself had been holding seeds in my hands, trying to keep alive for ten years what my mind told me were my own seeds: the seed knowledge of Tzutujil Maya and the life of the baby-naming Birth and Death corn. But my heart secretly cried, "These are not my seeds, not the seeds of my Lenape, Huron, Anishnabeg, French, Scots, Swiss, Irish, and who knows what ancestors—where are they?" Where could I begin? Where can any of us begin?

Well ... my education was about to begin.

Not eleven miles from where Ignacio lived and gracefully moved through his hard-earned dream of the Six Donancianas and their dreams of him keeping him and their seeds alive, I too had a place; a dry drifting riverside strip of pink feldspathic sand reaching deep into the Holy aquifers, the arterial pulse of Mother Water, on top of which twelve centuries of native cultures and five centuries of Iberianized settlers had mysteriously flourished agriculturally without a great deal of rain. A place of desert verbenas, maravilla bushes, cottonwoods, purple asters, chollas, agate boulder cliffs, and a wilder water-deserted beach of grama-anchored mesa that fed my wild-hearted New Mexico ponies. Rugged, always unreasonable, and open, it was a good place, a historical place to heal my wounds and learn to live again, while still enduring the hard social ride of those two overly public decades.

At first away from the old village life, constantly flying through the air, in my heroic forays of soul to attempt to fulfill people's desire for ritual, teaching, and native medicine, I often awoke startled from old dreams scared I would never get back to the place I told everyone I came from!

But the seeds are big schemers, and after all I was still the servant of their history and that bigger Holy thing in nature they contained. Like them I ended up being blown about this earth, fanning out in a mysteriously growing popularity that I never actively sought, wondering where it would all lead. Seedless now, but flying where the naming seeds had flown, I, like them, was always moving, sometimes in as many as five different cities in a week, becoming a little more tuned up, publicly accepted, and plagued with the unavoidable controversies of the envious and vituperous attacks of various embarrassed academics.

Growing less and less healthy and viable, to keep going, I had grown increasingly unlike my real self. I was being eaten like a chocolate-chip cookie a piece at a time by a public, not as a noble sacrifice, but as a rare nutrient in a starving spiritual place that, because it was so starved, had trouble distinguishing between the hand that fed it from what the hand was offering and, devouring both in one gulp, was still famished. I was fast running out of *me*.

This new version of "keeping the seeds alive" meant trying alone to embody an entire culture. I became for some people a one-man village whose new form gave them hope but was impossible to maintain. Nonetheless I was still in love with the Holy things I have always served. The ecstasy I always felt in their service never failed me, was usually mistaken for joy by the people who didn't know what they were seeing. Primitively misinterpreted as happiness by a public who for so many millennia were removed from their own ancestral remembrance of a similar spiritual relation with the indigenous ground in the history of their own people, they couldn't know what really caused the look on my face.

The sound in my voice and my emotional love for the Divine in Nature was almost, because of initiation and my own innate person, geologically in place in my body like something of the Earth herself, and something unconsciously assumed, like the wild, to be public domain, an unclaimed natural resource whose treatment ran on the same principle of thought that Europeans held when they first saw North America as an uninhabited virgin land, free and fresh for the taking as a gift from a strange, dysfunctional, single, conquering God.

I was feeding the Holy; but they didn't want to feed the Holy, they wanted bliss and wanted me to supply it to them. I was just an unclaimed wild berry bush, a mine of good feeling. The very few who actually cared how much they took out of me and how little I was restored by our association were nonetheless busy mining me for the experience of proximity to someone who still had love for the Divine in Nature, to cause the people's forgotten souls a momentary sense of well-being. Instead of cultivating the long road to the ability for themselves to become someone who could bestow the same conditions of well-being on the Holy in Nature, which gives this joy they sought, they wanted to obtain that joy like a commodity without the struggle of village life or any personal change.

This ecstasy of course was for me the nature of initiation, but it could not be commodified, and I did not want to commodify it. It came by hard work and love. I was nonetheless drained for it. I worked; they smiled.

But, still rolling along in the original momentum of the direct spiritual heart of what I understood Old Chiviliu had meant when he charged me with somehow "keeping the seeds alive in the conqueror's pocket"; the desperate need to do what I was doing; and the virtual impossibility of carrying out his demand in the one-sided, autocultural way I was going about it, kept me from culturally replanting myself again enough to sustain a viable everyday existence.

Instead the life I was leading kept me away from home, away from New Mexico, and away from my real self. Because I'd come to believe I was actually "keeping the seeds alive," I'd forgotten about keeping the ground spiritually fertile so my own seeds of life could flourish.

Seeds can only live or distribute themselves if the great trees and plants sprouted from them first concern themselves with making living, deep-reaching roots as they grow. These roots have to have a cultural context to feed them. While my roots had been in New Mexico, my heart was still a prisoner of my love for Mayan Guatemala and the past. The seeds of any future possibility for me or what I served had been scattered to the whirlwind of chance in hopes some would survive to take root somewhere and not be eaten up by modernity's insatiable hunger to consume all things and then just forget them.

Everything I did, I did in public. I became very clever and courageous and took a lot of risks with individuals who wanted healing. And when it came to large groups, my creative approaches earned me a lot of admiration, some affection, but also a great deal of misinterpretation both positive and negative, not to mention some fairly serious hatred, dangerous transferences, stalkers, and the ever-present cheap shots from a peanut gallery of bitter academics who couldn't comprehend my insistence on their examining their own personal backgrounds before moving on to a subject for study, a study that in my experience should always have as its prime motive of making a discovery that could inspire into reality a world worth living in, instead of spending their lives maintaining that the illusion of the rarified heights of culturally unbiased academic objectivity was real. As impossible a thing as that is, they pretended to objectively study the world's people while still living and participating in their own cultureless cultures that were causing what they all studied in other worlds to melt away. They couldn't see themselves, wouldn't see themselves, and hated me for even suggesting that self-examination of academic motive and its effects on who and what it studied should be part of academic integrity.

I almost began to believe I no longer had a future as an individual; I was just a flowering soldier doing a hero's job of keeping the seeds alive while I, as a person, had no future besides melting away. I didn't think I should worry so much about myself any more or what anybody thought or who would stop me from trying to inspire remembrance in a forgetful people by the planting of these "old" seeds on modernity's chemically tortured ground.

But I really had no say anyway. For the seeds had always been running the show all along. Everything, no matter what I thought about it all, had to take place as it happened. No matter how lonely, miserable, or misunderstood I would become, this grandiose, self-involved balloon of self pity and autocultural heroism I was threatening to fall into was increasingly becoming a messianic, melodramatic waste of time and smelled way too much like the same hard crust of the ingrained mentality of the very people whose surface I should have been trying to plant in and sprout through what I taught. But seeds had other things in mind: their vitality for one, and my vitality for another, neither of which was being truly maintained by the way I was going about any of it. Well, I thought, at least the way I was going about it all wasn't seen as boring, unuseful, or mediocre.

Though at that point headed straight for a quietly choreographed, self-sacrificing, messianic demise, like a bad Wagnerian opera done by mimes, maybe all my honest attempts at beauty supplied some trace nutrient in the fairly sparse diet of what the Holy in Nature is stuck eating these days, trying to glean life from modernity's unsustainable preoccupations that give nothing to the Indigenous Soul of the earth.

But then again, it's good when you're young to naïvely try impossible things and to think very highly of your failure. For in the end failure can be a wonderful gift to God as long as it is beautiful, thorough, courageous, and life-giving. But it's also good at some point to get good at life, making sure one's successes and desires are not a toxic failure for the Holy Earth.

But no matter what I thought or anybody wanted, some big, friendly unseen thing began to sneak up on me, laying out little spiritual traps of unexpected deliciousness and beauty that ambushed me with magical rebounds of unique luck. It fished me flopping and grunting right out of the deep arsenic molasses in which I was bogged, right square into the lap of that terrifying goddess of real happiness who, as the great enemy of a loss of perspective and the violence of myopic self-righteousness, began like a big mother bear with a cub her slow, concentrated program of holding on tight while licking me back to my natural senses, which were still in here somewhere, tickling me until I began to appear an altered but fairly recognizable version of the initiated man Old Chiv might have hoped for in the first place.

Seeds have magic force: they are organic carbon-directing packets of Time; and because of this, they have Time. Seeds have had a lot of old experience being creative and cyclic with civilizations trying to herd them around, trying to force them to look, act, do what they're told at predictable times. Civilization could probably be defined as humans with lapsed memories who live forgetting that people in the long run are not in charge, nor are they truly ever going to be. Whereas the Indigenous mind does not give the direction of the world to the "will" of God, but to the desire of the Holy in the ground to continually unfold as nature.

One day somewhere in a very large ritual "workshop," as people in those days insisted on calling what I did, as we were all getting ready to speak some "delicious tribal phrases" from my personal "word hoard" as we always did at that point in the ritual together to feed the Holy in Nature—at just that very ecstatic bubble of a moment, a pale, phlegmatic stereotype of what I've heard called an "Anglo nerd boy" came scooting and shuffling into the hall dragging some load in behind him. His heavily taped bottle-bottom glasses misted up in the intensity of the courage his overcompensating voice took out of him. His lack of tact and timing was a strange uncontrived relief to me. Not a trickster or a show-off, he was not unlike the folks in the old village, the ever-present three-legged abandoned starving dogs or drunks or grief-eaten derelict madmen and madwomen of the street who would crash in on our serious ceremonies. We never considered their rude unplanned appearances as bothersome interruptions in our elegant ritual activities, but knew as they drooled, wailed, tottered, barked, scolded, or tripped over our "perfection" that they were the Holy itself come to tangibly attend. They were Gods or Goddesses who themselves always interrupted our old ceremonies in Atitlán years back to test the over-rigidity of our hearts and capacity to focus on the real reason we ritualized. This funny man was a kind of modern, monkified city version of the same, a kind of stray dog from suburbia come to save the crowds from having me as the prophet they wanted me to be for them instead of the spirit farmer I was.

But Jeremy cared about none of that, saw no crowd, just me. It was as if I were someone who owed him money he'd unexpectedly come upon while standing in a queue of anonymous people waiting in front of the "his and hers" at the airport to pee. Like a determined ant dragging a dismantled beetle's head, he butted his soft marshmallow bulk through the emotional crowd at the very high point of the most ecstatic part of a two-day ritual. He came clunking up to me looking for all the world like a Guatemalan thief peddling a pile of uncooperative freshly stolen piglets bulging in two pale yellow pillowcases, which he intended to dramatically drop at my feet, but which actually landed on his own feet, causing him to trip and knock over the central bowl of the water offering, splattering it everywhere. The people gasped.

This boy, who never questioned that I would instantly recognize him and would know exactly why he'd come as if I'd sent for him, cared only about his "mission." He *had* been sent for, but not by me: the seeds had sent for him. I was their servant. The seeds were my boss, but I must've overlooked their message, forgotten the dream they sent, overlooked the signs. It was all too easy to do in the city.

"There you go, Martín, just like you asked me to," he babbled out like Rocky the Squirrel. "I'm sorry it took me so long, but my mother wouldn't let me do anything with them for a while, and then she got sick and I couldn't do anything for a while 'cause I had to watch out she didn't do anything to herself. I know you know, anyway. Oh, also, I got arrested trying to get them to grow on a vacant lot, but in the end some guys helped me grow them under the bridge in National City. The first year I only got two little ones. But I planted them again, and this time I got twenty-five. I hope it's all right if I keep this one for me and my mom," and he pulled out one fat little ear of dried corn with the silks still dripping, which looked like some kind of yellow sweet corn, shriveled like they are when they dry, but crossed on some other more burly breed of dent corn.

Though not yet one hundred percent sure who this transparent, thin-skinned, soft-fleshed child of thirty-three actually was or what he was yelling so loud about at the end of my two-day stint of ecstatic time together with 250 people, I knew in my bones that what he was doing was just right and, with only a small fraction of deviousness in hopes of lighting up my memory without insulting his obvious pride and glee at finally having accomplished some useful mysterious act for me, I asked, "How did you do it?"

"You remember, don't you? You probably didn't see me, but that time in Mendocino with all those 'important people' when they threw me out of the conference for burning my clothes, and you saved me from burning myself alive, pulling me out of the trance. Well, when I was asked to leave the next day, I came back and I waited down the road at the edge of the forest, at the entrance to the camp. I waited for two days, and when the conference ended, I stopped each car and charged them a 'seed' toll to leave and collected all the seeds you'd given them from all the men who didn't want theirs as they were driving off. Because I had to leave the conference early I didn't get any of the corn you gave away. So I got mad, kind of charged them in corn and got as much as I could for myself. But then one guy told me the story you told about where they came from and how it was your best gift; that guy wouldn't give me his one seed so I gave him a couple more for the story. I didn't know anything about growing corn, but I finally did sort of abandon my computer a little, and I learned to plant. Here they are, and thank you for all your help."

With the fluidity of the holy thing that drove him and somewhat unburdened now of the Parzivalian challenge he'd set upon himself, he bounded away from us like a clumsy one-eyed jackrabbit from a water hole sensing a coyote, or like a coyote sensing a man, or a madman sensing someone in charge, hobbling back to his otherwise invisible existence more thoroughly, melting into some unseen conveyance back to the middle of San Diego faster than he'd arrived.

The seeds had come back.

The naming seeds that had been lost and then generated by Ma Buxtol, then lost again, had again returned; only this time they were not pure. Like myself, after their wandering, they were altered.

A few years previous this boy, for trying to "purify himself" as he then testified, by jumping naked into the bonfire of an amateurish gimmicky ritual contrived by a clique of well-known pop psychologists playing "shaman," this man had been forcibly removed from that conference where I first began teaching publicly. The same event where I'd given all my seeds away. The boy had been in a real trance. His was not a theatrical act of therapy, or choreographed catharsis designed for self-improvement, but the only real thing I saw that entire time. The professional psychologists and psychiatrists playing with fire ran around scared because their rhetoric couldn't bring him out of it. I was frantically petitioned to help the boy by the administrators running the event as a last resort before the descending phalanx of participants who were psychiatric doctors brandishing their bristling forest of dripping syringes had their way.

From out of the fire, this strange boy survived miraculously unburned. Still woozy from his trance, I brought him slowly back to life with some old village magic, a common approach for a common village occurrence in initiations, something my experience taught me was appropriate. Like we always did in the old days in the village, I watched over him a while, spiritually walking him forward to his real self and then again through the camp through the crowd of mystified men from whom I demanded a "new set of clothes" for the boy, just like in the village! Although the clothes were not handwoven, beautiful, or made for this very occurrence by hopeful female relatives and lovers, they were still new clothes, something a young man needed after passing through his wrestling match with death and losing his earlier husk to the "fire" of the hot combustion of that spiritual composting by the Holy in the ground. A real fire is not a symbol or an idea, but a God that makes life, and despite the pop stupidity of that particular pseudo ritual, the boy *had* more or less gone through a spiritual fire. He seemed perfectly well to me. But the crowd of shrinks, realizing what could have happened, considered him a litigation and insurance liability, and the lawyers of the camp had the leaders ask him to leave. Though I took his side, the poor disgraced nerd boy was forced to disappear.

But now he and the seeds returned! He was a kind of mad gringo Ma Buxtol. He was the only one with even a bare whiff of initiation running through him I'd ever met in the U.S. who honestly wasn't acting out a part. His initiation didn't come from the fire, mind you. It came from his cultivating the old seeds in his own unsympathetic condition.

After bringing back my corn, he was gone. I began to weep.

Unused to seeing the old heroic elegance of nontheatrical indigenous male tears in public, the people were baffled, thought something was awry, and mobbed me trying to "help" But I'd already been helped, and that's why I wept.

I wept to see my old friends, the seeds, mutated but still alive. I wept because despite my perfectionist attempts to keep the seeds pure and the same, this unevenly defined young man had by himself grown out of being a boy into more of a person by growing the seeds, as motley and uneven as they were. So I wept as I told the entire crowd the entire story of "keeping the seeds alive," about Old Chiv, the naming of the babies, the soldiers, the killings, the politics, fires, the trouble, the burnings, Buxtol, my smuggling, my gift-giving, my keeping the seeds alive; and now with Jeremy the computer geek story added on, I shelled some of that corn off their cobs. No matter what shape or mutated form they might have taken on, I indiscriminately gave everyone there a fistful of his seeds to give them the story planted into the ground of their own souls, to keep the seeds alive and to give again the most precious gift I could to a people who had lost theirs.

But this time I kept one straight little ear and took its mixed-up, "impure" kernels home, this time to New Mexico, to remember again what I was supposed to be doing.

Life being the stormy, sliding, twisting, churning, waiting, lurching thing it has always been for me, I took the little ear with me wherever I went, at least within the national boundaries of the United States, so as to avoid losing it when returning to the States to the various world customs officers, who would no doubt have confiscated it. Maybe they knew how powerful seeds of real culture and real food can be.

But because they weren't really the original kernels, the naming corn, but a hopelessly crossed hybrid, a half-, a quarter-bred version that hardly resembled at all the one I remembered, like before, clinging to my rigidity, I continued in the notion that it was not worth my effort to replant the funny, runty kernels to make more seeds on my own even if I would've had the time. I did not keep those seeds alive by replanting, which is the only way to keep seeds, rituals, Gods, and knowledge alive.

But I cherished the ear as a relic because I cherished the story, and it became a reminder of the spiritual and literal seeds I'd promised to keep alive and conscious. But even though those seeds were no longer the seeds from Atitlán, they were the real seeds. I truly should have known, but like a petrified bird claiming to be an apprentice of the wind, who is only a student of the idea of a swallow's freedom, I the fool, albeit a beautiful one, frozen by my insistences, did not yet understand what it was I held: that the seeds had truly begun to return. I was still trying to avoid living in the world Chiv had sent me to plant. Foolishly trying to revive a world that was no longer there to replant.

One day a year and a half later, tired, overworked, put-upon, and never having grown used to the heavy winter food of the midwestern United States, I sat with my bundles nursing yet another budding migraine which in those days almost always followed any healing work I did in the States. While seated in an unventilated, overheated, borrowed drywall cabin on cold moldy floorboards, I listened to a husky freckled-faced, yellow-haired, pushy Minnesotan girl of twenty-five who should have been a milk farmer but wasn't, her big shoulders shaking, her soft see-through white forearms speckled like turkey eggs gesticulating from the elbows up as she explained to me her "problem."

After her careful description of her predicament, she wanted me as a medicine man to "fix" her up like a mechanic. Her tone made it sound as if she were a tractor and her heart a broken three-point hitch, and as a welder I could simply fix the break and send her on her way back to plough the field.

After half an hour of taking in all her anger and trying to comprehend her "problem," I was fast getting one of those serious headaches I only get in the USA and was probably a little impatient with this cross between a shiny Campbell soup kid and a big-beamed Norwegian cottage; a girl whose problems seemed so luxurious compared to the destitution, hunger, mass dying, epidemics, illnesses, trouble, and violence the higher percentage of the crowded world's people experience as a constant reality.

"What do you really want from me? Can you make a single question out of it?" I finally asked, my eyes ready to explode from pain.

Taking no interim for a considered thought, she instantly blurted out, waving her forearms from the elbow, "I want you to keep me from killing myself!"

"Okay, I order you to please not kill yourself."

"No, I mean it." She *did* want to kill herself, she said.

"Then," in a very well-considered but uncharitable, thoughtless-sounding reaction, I said in an equally loud and whiny tone as her own, "then kill yourself already."

"But I don't want to."

"Then don't already."

"You are not one bit of help." Then she started to blow: "Look here you ignorant mixblood, you don't really understand what I'm saying to you, do you?" I did, especially the spoiled part, but I said instead, surmising on account of my swollen, squinting eyes, and the cracking pain in the bones of my head that maybe the seeds knew better and I should let them speak for me: "I hear you're a really good organic gardener, and these days I live moving through the world, over the road, flying in the air. I am never home. As much as I have always been, and love doing ever since I was a child, farming in the desert, it's no longer possible for me to plant my poor seeds, because I'd never be there to hoe, to irrigate, to weed, to watch for skunks, talk toads into staying, stand plants up after the hailstorm, because I'm always going around teaching and working with people like yourself. So, I was wondering if you might be so kind as to plant these little corn kernels and grow me some more of this corn. You see, I need a lot of this corn to make ritual offerings and so forth."

After rummaging about in one of those old handwoven sacks that held my few sacred tools, those I still dared take with me after so many previous thefts in conferences and hotels, I retrieved Jeremy the Geek's little cob of mutant naming corn. Then holding it reverently in both hands, I struggled, head still pounding, into the story of the naming seeds. In the middle she interrupted me,

"What's all this got to do with my problem?"

"What problem?" I said, looking up mystified.

"You know, my problem!"

"About wanting to kill yourself?"

"Of course," she yelled.

"Well, where I come from ..."

"You mean South America," she wagged her head, rolling her eyeballs, "you're not from there."

"No, a little farther north, from where what I know originates, the native folks of the village consider wanting to kill yourself comes from unmetabolized grief that turns to rage—or from exhaustion from doing too much too long of something unworthy—or from outrage."

Then I took a big chance, figuring I stood a fair chance of her taking a swing at me given her incrementing impatience about the fact "her needs" were no longer at the center of my attention, having been supplanted by some superfluous rap about seeds. If a direct roundhouse from this big-boned Viking beauty should ever connect, I'd be knocked colder than a frozen moose. "Well, most of the old medicine people figure that kind of rage with people, especially those that have more than they need to eat, is just a clever ruse to cover up their laziness, people too lazy and spoiled to have the patience to do what is necessary to get to work and serve something besides themselves." Which was true; that's what the Tzutujil thought.

Bubbling, hissing, and clucking, pretty much cutting me off: "Well, I'm not lazy."

Then I bet even heavier. "I bet you are."

"The hell I ain't, you pompous asshole."

I instantly brandished the funny little cob of shriveled corn in her big moon face and hissed back just as bad, "I bet you're too damned lazy to be able to grow this corn right. You're just like all the rest of you lazy, spoiled Americans."

Red-faced, eyes bulging and tearing up, the indignant girl snatched the ear from my fingers and, without another word to me, muttered a mantra of reliable feminist slogans all run together while slipping on her sturdy Canadian snow boots; then grabbing her coat and slamming the door behind her, she headed back to her snowy world.

A wave of terrible sadness for her oozed through my middle. Sadness for her, a type no longer appreciated by her own people, whose old-time sturdy grace, once prized by mothers and husbands on farms and in harder times as something very beautiful, a style that now caused her powerful womanly frame to sashay expertly over the ice, drifting, defeated and alone, again off to her little car sitting between a seven-foot snow bank and the purple birch shadow of the setting sun.

Clutching the little ear of corn held tight to her chest, the angry woman had finally left me alone with my headache, which still had two more days left in it, and all my seeds were gone again.

That was the last time I or anyone else knew her whereabouts. I worried she might have fled from the world as she threatened. It never mattered how many hundreds of people had come to see me personally, singly, or in groups—I could never stop agonizing over individuals whom I might have driven over the cliff with the risks I sometimes took in my sincere struggle to bring some vitality back into their seedless, rootless lives, lives snared in angry city misery and knotted in spiritual pain. Knowing they would probably continue living a waking death if they didn't move somewhere spiritually, I'd always hope that in their ensuing drifting maybe they could find peace enough to stand still enough to become useful enough to something bigger than the limitations of the modern world they thought was real.

But I could never really make big village things happen, only small things that looked big. Though I was pretty much a lone little duck, more alone than the people I saw, this overgrown child was one of those many who would plague my mind every morning at 4 a.m.

Then, more than two years later one morning, in a gooshy, rushing, beautiful, birch-smelling, muddy, almost sunny spring, while just preparing to begin a ritual gathering of teaching with some seventy-five well-fed midwestern Americans of all colors and ages inside a moldy old Protestant church somewhere outside Duluth, Minnesota, there came blaring in from the "boot atrium" of that Hall of the Sons of Norway the same pushy, bugling whine of that same missing woman's irritating voice. Though I couldn't see her yet, it was impossible to mistake. Then ringing on in with an even more imperious but equally exasperated tone, "Glen! Glen, damn it, bring it all in here now, what are you doing to my . . . come on, *jeez*, Glen," and in she burst wearing a striped tee-shirt that barely held her great milky breasts within, embracing a really big-headed baby on the hip and pushing a full-grown young man by one of his raised elbows, who was dragging two big, very full gunny sacks whose obvious weight had him bent and struggling into the middle of the room.

Trumpeting aloud, "Here!" the lady, without one word of "Hello" or "Good to see you again," shoved this heavy, wild-looking, nine-month-old infant into my arms. This child, whose fire-red hair bristled straight out like a lightning strike was imminent, and whose hairline came down almost to her two gigantic eyes, the color of a winter lake, weighed more than most Guatemalan Indian kids at the age of six. This child's hulking but agile mother grappling both gunny sacks, one in each hand, swung them right in front of her man's bent back, narrowly missing the trusting New Age head of a participant dutifully seated in that strange ashram yogic pose they think all spiritual people understand and dropping them both with a crunching thud proclaimed in a defiant croak, "There's your damned whatever it is ... corn!" then briskly took back her very relieved baby.

I was happy and most likely grinning as I fell to my knees to greet the returning corn: *"Nutie utz kin tzut a chi, utz kin tzut auach ju miej chic tie,"* then in English: "Mother, it's good to see your face again, good to feel the breath of your great life-giving aroma again, Mother, you from whose breasts our sustenance suckles us into life ..."

The young woman turned red, thinking I was addressing her, and parted her lips to speak, but no words came out, finally realizing that I was talking to the corn as the mother of us all.

After rummaging one hand in each bag, I retrieved two very long, ornate ears of dried corn that looked even less like the naming corn I'd brought from the old village and only remotely like the one she'd snatched from my hand two-and-a-half years back. Here and there a shriveled sweet-corn kernel or two of all different colors was interspersed between this elegant translucent flint corn that looked more like my mother's grandmother's Huron corn than anything I'd ever handed out or had ever seen. But holding the two ears in both hands as reverently as I could, I blessed the girl, her baby, and her man, pressing the motley but beautiful mother corn to their hardworking joints.

No matter her color or fated life, corn to us is always Mother, and these cobs filled with her womb of living embryos were no different. In the U.S. and the modern world, corn is not remembered as a mother; like all domesticated plants and animals that feed us, she is designated as an inanimate botanical slave. But slaves can be Holy Mothers, and slaves of any type share the fate of all the world's Gods, Goddesses, and Holy Beings, who are no less holy for having been so designated and can bless us, and certainly do, with their meat, milk, grain, greens, fiber, tools, containers, plastics, and beauty.

"Thank you for this return of the face of my mother. It must have taken you a long time to grow this much corn from the miniscule little cob you stole from me that day."

"I didn't steal anything." Embarrassed by my kidding, this Lutheran descendant made her defense with her old whining style, "You asked me to grow it. Anyway, the first year I didn't know anything about it, and I only got three little cobs. But a man who saw me failing at it, well, actually Glen—this is Glen, my husband—we met when he showed me the next summer what to do—and this is what we grew."

Continuing with my bad Indian joking, which I always did without thinking, "So, you didn't kill yourself?"

"What?" she yelled, acting totally hurt and ignorant of the issue.

"Don't you remember?" I said.

"Remember what? Of course not, why would I do that. This is my daughter, Maya Sprout. I called her that because I was already big and pregnant when Glen and I planted this last year, and she was born right after we harvested. I remember you said the Maya people call their babies sprouts, so we called her that in honor of the corn over which Glen and I met. Isn't that right, Glen? Take the baby, honey, and go sit over there, I've got to get some more things for this weekend." She decided they were staying, and he'd decided that it was usually good to do as he was told.

Chapter 16

From Their Motley Hands, the Motley Seeds Surprise the People into Beauty

After that it seemed as if I went everywhere, ritualizing, workshopping, and teaching. Many of the visits blossomed into annual ritual gatherings for which I like a spawning eel faithfully returned, for it was only in these arduous feasts of beauty that any living crumb of a place existed where I could still collectively feed the Holies in Nature.

When the lady of the big baby returned her two sacks of motley corn in that class, as always, I shelled the cobs again and divided them up ritually, and equally, amongst all the participants.

The corn was still the largest gift and blessing I could think to give the people who graced all my workshops and rituals, always with the admonishment that they not eat or "throw away" their seeds. I would always bless the seeds with the story of all they had been through to get there, including their incarnations with the sacred computer geek and the Minnesota gardener. The seeds were the only part of the ritual we'd done together to feed the Holy that would return home with them. Everything else they brought or we created together went to feed the Holy and had to be taken to the mountains to disintegrate as offerings.

Every "workshop" thereafter was fortunate to have at least a few determined people who would return with the corn seeds that they have grown from those received during the ritual the year previous.

Of these I would always take half of whatever seeds came in and ritually with the story redistribute those to the people present that day. The remaining half would be added to one half of those grown with the next group's, and on and on it went for years. Soon a widely spread array of colors, forms and shapes, textures, sizes, widths, spots, stripes, blushes, and more exuberantly marked ears appeared having crossed and recrossed on every other type of corn growing in their neighborhood. Every time, I told the story before I "planted" every participant with seeds: the origins of the seeds, of course, and the stories of the people having grown the seeds were added to the tail end of the last story until, like the thread in the baby naming and the thread in the Birth/Death ritual, the tale began to form a kind of ritual ball of twine in which all the stories of the people of diverse origins in my workshops were firmly tied in sequence to those of the Tzutujil.

Mysteriously, all of this grew on its own momentum, governed not by some permissive "anything goes" mentality or by any rigid reverence for the ritual reality that I enforced upon them. Its motion came naturally with the seeds, for the seeds had found their own way right into the flesh and forgotten indigenous ground lying beneath modern people's hard heads, discovering hearts fertile enough to be enchanted by what they held.

Of the wide diversity of those who planted the seed, there were cute, determined individuals from cities who'd never grown anything at all in the course of their frenetic smoggy lives, cultivating one single funny corn plant of "Martín" seeds on the most implausible apartment windowsills in inadequate flowerpots. As unlikely as it might seem, they'd show up later with a little pile of slightly pekid but definitely live seeds.

An amazed man in Chelsea, London, like Jack and the beanstalk, grew two solitary legendary corn plants from seeds I'd given him in tiny flower pots. They pushed right up and out of his ground-floor flat window, and in search for sunlight ended up stretching exuberantly past his delighted upstairs neighbors in the second story, tasseling prolifically in her kitchen window. The corn must have snaked along and up some eighteen feet! Impossible. But these seeds started doing wild, unheard-of things. When I gave some of that man's seeds to people in the next workshop in Northern California, one wild-haired, seaweed-gathering, aging sixties type planted those crazy-looking seeds in a solid bed of ocean plants and leaves overlooking the Bay of Elk. His homemade "earth" grew the biggest cobs of corn carrying the most massive naïve happy kernels I'd ever seen. They resembled monster versions of the old Tzutujil corn: kind of pearly ivory with curly unruly silks. They looked a lot like they'd grown right out of that man's unruly ears, so wild, uncomplicated, unafraid, and curly, just like him!

After a workshop ceremony blessing the headwaters of the stream that fed the tear-inspiring beauty of that string of rocky Pomo headlands where this same man and his band of men and women lived by gathering seaweed and gleaning their kelp and other ocean plants, the seaweed the following season burgeoned in quality and quantity, and sea otters long absent began to reappear. Ever after, whenever I came to that region, I had the people make even grander gifts of floating flowering houses, to feed the Holy Ocean.

It wasn't long before the coastal rangers were after me, sent forth through political chicanery by groups of wealthy rural urbanites and conservative land developers bent on subdividing the coast who hoped that such "events" as mine were a thing of the past. Maybe we reminded them of their own trespass. With such "rituals" going on, the neighborhood looked uninvestable.

One of these coastal rangers, a really serious young guy, would always threaten me with the possibility of jail every time I came to town, jingling his handcuffs at the front door of the workshop hall and, with a hundred people looking on, never failing to announce how if he ever caught me "littering" the ocean shore again, he'd arrest me. He was a nice fellow in a way but never could seem to catch us. The developers got madder and more adamant. At the tail end of the ritual we always gave him some corn, since he basically became part of the ceremony standing there like he did, waiting patiently for hours. In the end even he started growing our corn. I missed him when we moved farther up the coast with our offerings.

The corn taught all of us. People considering themselves good farmers would wind themselves into a nervous tangle trying to figure out why their corn grew to a huge height and then just fell over faint with only one wizened ear per twenty stalks. They of course were people who had very little relation with the "insides" of things, the inside of history, their own insides, the Earth beneath and beyond their control, the inside, unseen, migrant, underpaid laborers that kept their life of trust funds riding at its high, unearned altitude. Therefore the corn demanded they actually work for a living, making a little thicker, shorter, more ground-based existence, and learn to recognize and love the "other" people outside their rarified and socially isolated party of a life.

Other people's corn would grow, but no matter what they did, would never mature the myriad of ears that profusely set on the stalks. They of course were lacking heat, chutzpah, lacking chile, lacking conviction, lacking the ability to boldly fail by flowering and living loudly. The corn always came alive when the needed changes were made. It amazed everyone, myself included.

One British fellow of great good heart and a very urban existence and upbringing found that in order to revive his suffering sun-dependent hot weather plants in a climate of dark clouds, mold, and drizzle, he had to sit squarely in his little rail-side allotment and read steamy wild South American novels to the plants out loud. They grew impossibly better than anywhere they'd ever been, like nobody could ever believe, wonderful, robust and grand, with a shape all their own.

When the people returned the corn they'd grown back to me, the stories returned to me with their seeds. Their own adventures farming corn got added straight onto my stories of the original corn and how the seeds came to be, all of which I told every time I gave away the seeds again.

Over twelve years, hundreds of rituals and a couple of thousand random replantings had come and gone, shaping the corn seed that had crossed, recrossed, so thoroughly mixed in a million other ways that neither the corn nor its original tale resembled the original corn of Birth and Death I had initially handed out. But improbable miraculous things began to take place after that; stories of unlikely hope, of the largest learning yet, began to make their appearance more and more often.

When years before as a young fellow I'd disappeared south, flopping up onto the life-molding basaltic shores of Lake Atitlán's jade water, my father in New Mexico, having little news of me, after some years was compelled to distribute the few precious belongings of mine I'd left in his care.

After years of living together with my father, my brother left for a job in Georgia. Reckoning it better since he was now alone, my father moved into a smaller place in a more populous area and sustained a large burglary in which all three of us lost many sentimental things.

Among the things of mine that survived the robbery were some very old corn-grinding stones and mullers from old Indian friends of my youth, and especially two types of corn seed I'd left with him to guard until I should return to replant them. But I'd been gone such a long time he reckoned I was now permanently in Atitlán. In order not to have to be "burdened" by the weight of the stones and responsibility of the corn which he considered now unviable, he donated both the collection of heavy volcanic grinders and my sack of dried corn ears to a museum at an indigenous cultural center recently established, run, and owned by the tribes from where this particular strain of corn originated.

But like in most of these institutions the grinders were tossed into an exhibit, with a couple of the corn ears, one white and one blue, placed decoratively on the muller to give the viewer on the other side of the glass a feeling that someone—a Pueblo lady from the twelfth century—had just left them to go do an errand and would soon return.

Both types of corn had been my greatest treasure at the age of fourteen. The white one given to me by a magnificent example of old-school female greatness, a traditional Pueblo lady who loved me like a grandma and defended my every frailty against the world. Speaking no English and very little Spanish, but fluent to the utmost in her native Keres, her ancestors maybe two hundred years previous on her father's side had been refugees from an extinct pueblo of Towa people married into a clan of dissident refugee Hopis, escaping a European-inspired fracas. They'd brought with them a creamy-colored "white" corn that the old woman had her husband replant every two years. She prized it for making *guayabe*, a Keres-type paper bread, the crowning glory of all Pueblo cuisine.

The blue ears, on the other hand, were shorter and wilder looking, and of all shades of turquoise, purple, maroon, sky blue, and a more plebeian Payne's grey. A marvelously patient and fine old man from another Keres village neighboring us to the north, who in my youth healed me of chronic pneumonia and a split meniscus, and taught me everything I knew worth knowing between the ages of thirteen and eighteen, gave me this blue corn. Both he and I for summer after summer had hoed and worried over them, caressing them into maturity until I left and he passed away.

This corn had been grown by nobody else and was cherished by him as the oldest and best kind of mother corn that had ever existed, having been given to his ancestral line by the "corn" herself at the onset of Pueblo culture from which time it was eaten as a daily morning mush of a nutty, superior taste.

When I returned to the States, not only had my Atitlán seeds flown, but my precious seeds of my adolescence had disappeared as well. When I went to see the museum about retrieving one or two handfuls of seeds, they were conducive but, since the whole place had been renovated, modernized, nothing of my rare old seeds could be located. They were gone. The old people were gone. The seeds of similar type might have still been grown somewhere in the mysterious cultural climate of New Mexico. But my treasured kernels given me by the old people were as gone as they were.

Late one windy afternoon, north of Mendocino, while preparing to lower myself down a cliff with a group of sad Pomo men and women to the rocky shore of their ancestral land, from where their old-time grand-mothers had literally lived, to make a ritual in their style, along with mine, to feed the grandeur of the ocean, I was accosted by a non-Indian.

I'd just finished a ritual workshop earlier that day. Unwilling to mix with my crazy workshop participants (whom they took this man to be one of), the native party sat waiting patiently off a distance until I'd finished my brief parlance with this "white man" to continue our way to the ocean at sunset.

The earlier two-day ritual "workshop" had just dispersed in Caspar an hour earlier, but this man with a close-cropped, collegiate, reddish beard, shoulder-cropped hair, a dark cashmere pullover, wool slacks, and hiking shoes swore he'd been there all day, but I hadn't seen him ever before. I was positive. But saying nothing to the contrary like any Mayan traditionalist, I instantly surmised that he might have actually been a spirit, a tangible manifestation of some greater thing come to "talk." In which case, maybe he had been in the ritual, but not in human form.

He said he was an agrobotanist from the University of California at Davis, involved in trying to isolate traits from ancient indigenous food seeds, and in particular certain regenerative "substances" possibly present only in certain colored types of maize.

He'd spent years gathering up, buying, collecting, and hunting down archaeological specimens of corn, viable or not, and obtaining every kind of corn he could to prove some genetic theory. He seemed to be yet another man dedicated to messing with corn genes to prove some "confidential" academic discovery for commercial farming, just the thought of which I detested. But then he pulled from under his rich city-boy cashmere sweater two ears of blue corn, fairly short, sturdy, squat, with wide bottoms and fairly slim, blunt tips.

They were not only beautiful, but were fully kerneled cobs of the very image of the corn the old man the next village up had left me in order to "feed" the family of my future! Having recognized my last name on the notice for the workshop as the same one written on the ticket in the Albuquerque Museum, he wanted me to have these back before their "type" was utterly lost, as he put it!

They were not the ones the old man had given me, or that my father gave to the museum, but ears regrown from them in a controlled greenhouse, far away from the school in an isolated laboratory garden so as to keep them "pure." They'd been tinkering around with the genes since, but these particular ears themselves, he swore, were regrown uncrossed from the originals.

Until I planted them myself and grew them the following summer, I wasn't positive, but in the end the seeds of my most early days had actually come back!

The man didn't leave me his name, but just shook my hand, thanked me for what we were doing in the rituals, and disappeared back over the grassy knoll behind some trees, presumably to drive off. I never have seen him again.

Like me, they knew he was definitely a spirit, for when I returned, the tribal people were smiling. We said nothing to each other and just continued lowering ourselves down the rocky cliffs to the waves, to the sun, the abalone shore, and the memory of those days still lodged in the scales of their Indigenous Souls, and as the Father Sun sent his wide flaming trail straight to them and me holding my returned corn, we sang as we offered our gifts into the great old grandmother sea.

Then one afternoon one year later, on that very same coast at the end of the workshop, I woke up: the rising waters of realization of what Nicolas Chiviliu had really meant finally rose above the rigid bastion of hardened grief that had dammed them, and came lusciously flooding in on me.

In my hat and shelled off the cob lay several thousand corn kernels, each of them very different from the next. Yet hidden inside each and every one of the dissimilar seeds was the continuation of the very same viable heart, at least some of the DNA, and the ever-present possibility of the return of the original corn seed I'd given away and given up for lost over twelve years past. It had been regrown, promiscuously crossed and recrossed at random and at will with all the types, colors, heights, lows, climates, temperatures, soils; in noisy cities, oceansides, Nebraska railroad sides; by gardeners and lovers of the Holy in my rituals for a decade, until all those stories of all those people had again crossed, after I had handed them out again to new attendees who regrew them, brought them back "home" to me to again distribute, to teach and replant their souls again with the seed. But then I saw. In a whirlpool of tears and chucklings I finally took in an old-time deep breath the first time in twenty years.

Looking down the line at the amazingly different faces of all the people who had come together that afternoon and then gazing back at the seeds I had shelled into my hat, the ball of righteous dedication of indigenous Mayan vision I'd been pitching for more than a decade was knocked completely out of the park, and I was left watching a forgotten world of hope begin to finally run in home. Like the smell of food to the starving, like the aroma of a mountain summer of wild grass and herbs to a sick horse in six feet of January snow, like a wave of bigheaded baby trout grazing between the webbed toes of a baby otter, or the redolent perfume of unexpected rain on fifty years of droughted dust, like nothing ever before. I instantly understood that each of these people, women, men, girls, young men, kids, old-timers, each one different in looks, different in background, not pure in any sense, or even correct, but in some Holy way integral in who they were and from where each had come, but intact only in the fact that they were undeniable representations of the present, their faces shining from a ritual they so badly wanted but probably didn't really comprehend, their hearts beating as all people's hearts beat, but each of them, exactly like the beautiful mixed-up seeds in my hat, contained their very own old bloodlines, their histories equally descending to that very moment in just as many generations of culturally displaced, spiritually tortured, detoured tribal origins, confused, forgotten, known and unknown, brilliant on one side, mediocre on the other, but all with genetically and culturally hybridized ancestries manipulated by their ancestor's ancient desperation for survival under the horrible oppressive conditions experienced worldwide, having fled and lost who and where they were as distinct peoples, and yet all of their descendants had the "seed" of their multiple indigenous originations still hidden somewhere far away inside them just as much as the seeds they'd grown and I was doling out, seeds and people who looked and acted nothing like their original greatness.

The deepest Indigenous Soul of the people I was in the process of giving my old Mayan seeds to, seeds that were originally, for the Tzutujil, what made them people, all of a sudden matched just as equally in diversity, hidden origins, and spiritual survival strategy as did the strange, divergent seeds I now held in my hands.

Hidden right there and in front of our very faces, residing in mass impurity, hodgepodges, the run of the mill, mixed-up, non-specific corn, like the people in a million hues, surface smoothnesses, opacities or translucencies, sizes and shapes, had retained a vital core made even more viable by the mix of the multiple collective memory of how to be a seed or a human by adapting to the strange cultural soil both had found themselves forced to survive in.

Teams of diverse uniforms of adaptive genetics ran a race for life, each holding a sacred football of hidden integral origins to replant themselves in better times, each hiding behind what they had to become to keep their soul alive. Looking down the prayer line that day, and then back again at the motley well-adventured seeds in my hat, it was easy to see: here short, sort of pale, smiling and shriveled, an Ashkenazi scholar father crossed on a German-Irish coalminer's daughter; here tall, bent, glossy and curly, a striped Hazara; there the son of a Cajun crab poacher and a black slave descendant who was half-Catawba and Muskogee; there a Welsh-like Celt daughter; there an orphan with golden hair and brown eyes that matched a yellow seed with a black germ; a sad-eyed olive-skinned Slav; a worn-out, old, goat-raising midwife; an obese lesbian dog musher, someone's dog; a tiny lady from Vietnam with three gigantic Norwegian-Finnish babies; three Finns, one of them a Karelian, only one quarter Sámi; a defiant deep-veined weeping Scot; a reformed-Mormon, half-Tongan, half-Prussian video salesman; a big curly-headed pale Danish Oregoner with a Dutch nose and a scared look; fifteen Indians from every tribe and no cards; and a hundred and eighty eight of every color, even more mixed, diverse, full of grief and beauty, in love with a common capacity through their common ritual contribution to be worthy no matter how tortured or insignificant they felt, worthy enough to give a gift to the Holy, and of course, myself as mixed and in love as any of them.

> To this one I gave
> blue corn kernels, to the next
> red flint and white flour, the next,
> a yellow flower flour, black flint and popcorn, to the next
> green dented chapalote, the next
> red-striped flint like Ignacio's grandma's and the next and the

next and the next and looking down the line the people weren't lost, because their seeds weren't lost, because
THE SEEDS WERE THE PEOPLE.

Whatever it was, a long time, or a short time, both, neither, or a wider mythological eon that appeared to the rest like a flash, would be difficult to tell, but it was right then after two days together—at the deepest place at the tail end of that great beast of ecstatic ritual spent building a house of sound, grief, magic, life stories, and flowers, to house the Holies in the Seeds, while staring down the long double file of people facing one another after they in a tidal wave of feeding the shrine house, the spirits within, and one another with the critical mass of the beauty of anciently sequenced delicious words from an old Tzutujil ritual—that what Chiviliu had meant, almost twenty years before, finally came flooding to my eyes: "And above all," he'd said, "don't be prejudiced against what the 'seeds' look like when they return to you. Don't refuse them because you don't recognize them. That's not your job. Your job is to 'keep the seeds alive.' Your job is to welcome them and to give them a place. Just keep planting." And plant them I did.

Chapter 17

Seeds of Birth and Seeds of Death Return, Carrying the Whole World

That day had been too short, but a thousand more like it kept rushing in over me, their warm waves rollicking my heart back onto its throne of hope smack in what had previously been for me the unsympathetic territory of modern America.

Close to three years had pulsed on through when one morning after a day of cold windy dust, then freezing rain, then sun, then sleet, snow, and finally clear and starry skies, while the frost melted in the dawn as the year's first hummingbirds shivered perched on the adobe wall of the atrium of the mud palace of a little desert school I'd invented to teach forgotten hands-on ways of living and feeding the Holy in the Seed, a student of that year's first session graciously placed into my unsuspecting hands a medium-sized brown paper sack filled with several cobs of unshelled corn.

Given to her by a short man unknown to her in Utah ten minutes before she started driving south to New Mexico and to school, she'd been directed by him to deliver them personally into my hands.

On the sack a note was scrawled in light graphite declaring the contents to have been grown by the short man's ailing brother before he died, and that the grower wanted to make positive that I received the corn on the advent of his death, which meant of course that he had died, having actually jumped from a canyon wall to kill himself, unwilling to play a game of pain while wasting away to some terrible incurable illness.

The seeds were the originals: exactly alike to those of which I'd made a gift over fifteen years earlier. According to the note, he'd planted and replanted every year in a remote red sandstone canyon cove of southeastern Utah, running along an inaccessible, roadless stretch of flood sand on a river, where as a recluse he'd been keeping himself for the last decade or so.

He thanked me in the note for a lot of things but mostly for my generosity of the "two" little kernels of Birth and Death corn he'd received from me at the culmination of that notorious conference in the Mendocino coastal redwoods, from which he'd grown all this corn.

Losing a great deal of it to deer, jackrabbits, pack rats, and of course desert ground squirrels, he'd done everything possible to keep the seeds pure and uncrossed in the fastness of his desert hideaway.

My mind wheeling like a vulture gliding the rising thermal of my recollection, soaring higher and farther to get a broader view of my past, I searched the wide ground of my memories all day for any clue as to who this farming canyon hermit might have been.

Then I remembered.

He'd not been a paying conference goer, a teacher, or a participant in that gathering, but a very short, very nervous, very politically correct, very righteous, very long-haired, very intelligent cook whose food had been our saving grace, for he'd been a man conducive to my insistence on making and growing food, cooking food and eating food into ritual, and after I had vigorously protested the anti-anger exercises of a pop psychologist teaching there that had over a hundred men thoughtlessly and irreverently ripping and prying huge man-sized slabs of redwood bark from living trees as if the trees were inanimate props, while staring at another man as if he were his "father," beating the living tar out of the standing tree with his "bark" club groaning and growling until he was out of emotion and the bark was dust, this short cook, himself a lover of plants and visibly rattled, actually brought the whole mess to a standstill when, shaking furiously, he shrieked hysterically in a shrill hissing kind of mousey fierceness that he was locking the kitchen and dining hall, withholding all food and drink until "this absurd lack of consciousness and this overt example of men's hatred of the natural world has ceased."

It had been one of this shy tiny man's moments of courage and glory, and I loved him for it and had almost forgotten about him until his seeds came in.

When the moment came for me to give away my seeds in that first conference, I brought out the cooks and gave them seeds first, for in Tzutujil ritual etiquette, cooks in ritual feasts were always chosen and prized for their eloquence and sacred knowledge, above that of all hierarchical officials, and were subsequently honored and thanked accordingly at every ceremonial interval, a dignity I tried to maintain no matter what culture, restaurant, or outdoor market in which I ever found myself feasting.

The man was dead now, and his sack contained at least sixty times more Birth and Death corn than I'd smuggled. Though hardly allowing any person to call him friend, it was as if, in his concern, extreme self-enforced isolation, and controlled death, he'd become the corn itself, for after the zealously controlled purity of his corn growing, the corn was here and he was gone. But the corn he'd kept alive beyond his unhappy, strictly environmental self was not his or his ancestors any more than it was mine. The real miracles were yet to begin.

Two weeks later, while back on that same life-renewing California–Oregon cliff-tumbling, misty, wave-crashing Pomo, Yurok, Karok coast, two different women, one younger, one older, both unknown to the other, each one residing five hundred miles from the other, after planting and growing corn from incredibly crossed and recrossed motley seeds given them in different ritual workshops, both, unbeknownst to the other, mysteriously began harvesting solid white, smooth, unwrinkled, undented, ivory-colored ears of corn and no other.

After another year of replanting these new ivory appearances of the seeds, they only remade themselves again with no blues, stripes, reds, wrinkles, dents—only Birth and Death corn. When I visited their area again the next fall, each of these amazing women, separately, regaled me with at least forty pounds each of white, ivory-colored corn kernels that looked to all the world true in every way to those I'd smuggled into the U.S. years before.

In all respects—looks, taste, growing patterns, and texture—they most certainly seemed identical to those miraculously kept alive by Ma Buxtol, to those held and cherished by every Santiago Atitlán Tzutujil family in the old days for all their baby's births and namings, and their ancestors' deaths and rebirths; the same seeds that had been pushed, devoured, burned, and forgotten into extinction in the place of their origins.

Undeniably miraculous that this otherwise extinct breed of ancient corn could have so thoroughly resurfaced out of crazy mixed-breed non-specific multicolored seeds all at one time, it was as if a neighborhood of women of every background, texture and hue, culture, language, height, size, hair, and eye color all intermarried for a century had all, one spring, given birth to Tzutujil babies that grew up to have Tzutujil babies for grandkids.

It was just that wild and stunningly hopeful, the seeds' bizarre, unexpected subversion of the generalities science purports as reality.

But then an even greater and truly hopeful notion arose as I started to think about what this meant for the Indigenous Soul of humans: in every single seed I'd ever given away for the previous decade and a half, there inside each of those crazy over-crossed, mixed-up, unrecognizable, unpredictable seeds, seeds considered polluted and hodgepodge rejects by agroscience, there resided at least some tiny genetic particle of Tzutujil corn that, at will, could refind itself. Recessively repollinated by crossing far enough distant from the original, the seeds could still not only remember how to remake themselves over again after practically twenty years of veritable extinction, but whenever the "mind" of these ancient vital seeds decided, their reappearance was made even more robust. More vital not only by being hybridized but because inside these new generations of identical "white" seeds, all the other genes of all the other diverse and wildly colored races of corn were housed waiting in there hidden as well!

These same wondrous seeds, when replanted, grew true to the white, ivory-sheened Birth and Death corn of the old Tzutujil Maya, but on a certain signal, certain day, or Tao-like proceedance of the mind of all things singing together, in some particular pollen pattern, wetness, or wind could no doubt remanifest at will any one of another four or five hundred different types, races, colors, heights, textures, and ways of growing that would then fully represent corn grown in the neighborhoods of the wide diversity of people who'd been cultivating them as the result of a deep love of continuing the small bit of integral ritual they had helped to come alive.

The original naming corn had origins, supposedly going back to Teotihuacán and then some, maybe even to the caves of the Rio Balsas, which is why the Tzutujil called the corn Yaqui Sac, or white Yaqui, Yaqui being the Highland Mayan designation of pre-Aztec west Mexican Nahuat culture.

Whereas this ancient Tzutujil ritual corn had Mesoamerican origins that made up Tzutujil history, this new avatar, this new miraculous reappearance of what looked, tasted, and behaved like its ancestors in every way, did carry in a just as valid and equal way as a donkey carries her fur on her back all the genes and forms of all peoples' randomly gathered crosses over the last seventeen years.

Therefore the Indigenous Soul of so-called nonindigenous people, given a certain spiritual terrain, certain conditions only the soul and the Holy in the Seed know, that are conducive to its recultivation, and the powerful reexposure to its own ancestral, spiritual back-pollination upon itself, no matter how mixed or mixed up, could, given all this, make once again a glorious reappearance of real substantial human beings and diverse human cultures worth descending from.

All people everywhere in the world are carried diversely in the very seed of culture, not exactly homogenized and lost, but still hidden from view, indigenously integral in capacity, story, and form, but still held waiting together like the people of Cuchumaquic.

Each of these waiting diverse cultural indigenous integrities could have their original intended matrix of indigenous excellence reappear, bursting boldly forth from some common unsuspected mother kernel that any of us could be.

With all of these marvelous soul-relieving realizations finally climbing from the cocoon and hitting the air, it became brilliantly apparent that, in my own case, until I personally had been willing to accept the people's sacks of strange, inconsistent motley corn along with the "motley" modern people that grew them as equally as valid and beautiful as and as potent a source of possible real culture as the original extinct Tzutujil corn and culture, the little white Birth and Death corn kernels were not going to make me or anybody else the gift of reappearing in their original form! They were going to show me as seeds that in every supposedly "pure" native way of going, a whole possibility of unseen previously unmanifested universes also waited abbreviated, to burst forth from the seed.

As go the plants, so go the people and the animals.

The main thing, as Chiviliu had said, was to not only shy away from judging the forms seeds and people took in order to survive strange conditions created by people who'd lost their seeds, but as a spiritual human of a truly indigenous core to simply keep growing the "seeds" in every sense, so they could have a place to direct their ever-ready magical manifestation. The Holy in the Seeds had to direct.

We as people had to provide spiritual ground and physical fertile space and earth for the seeds to do what they already very well knew how to do.

> The seeds had always been there.
> The seeds had always been home.
> It was up to us to be at home
> *keeping the seeds alive.*

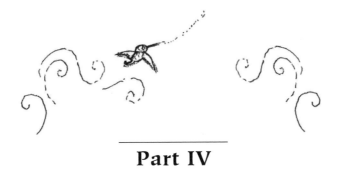

Part IV

*Our Agreement with the
Holy in Nature*

Chapter 18

Our Ancient Seed Jar

Like little canoes of Time, my seeds had drifted according to the windy mind of nature to lodge and sprout themselves in just the right places. I never suspected those little vessels of codified magnificence could still exist inside the souls of modern people. But out of their abbreviated enormity, these seeds, when given the least hint of any kind of conducive spiritual climate, found modern people a fresh and luscious new ambience in which to sprout and flower; they rose up and out of the tired, overworked ground of the soul of the modern person to begin reforesting that ravaged landscape whose original territory had been made of an intrinsic human beauty and mysterious culture, but which had been long ago overrun and abandoned to the bleak flatness of centuries directed by the shallow, soulless mind of industrial production and the compartmentalized limitations of abstract gain. Their souls were starving for viable life. The seeds *could* take hold.

The last echoing blast of the symphony of Chiviliu's magic friendship had seemed like a rude, over-demanding shove, but it turned out to be a shove of love and mercy: a push of hope that forced my own seed-filled canoe faraway forever from the shores of the Atitlán I knew, away from the onset of the indescribable horror of the culture-flattening violence of war and the ensuing monetized neocolonial mediocrity that has plagued Guatemala's indigenous identity ever since.

No doubt, Chiviliu must've known, I would have never left my magical place in service to a life of cultural seeds and the daily Tzutujil struggle for life without his final push-off; he was fully aware that all I had learned and might become would have disappeared along with me into the firestorm that followed, another grain of cinder on the ash pile of all the rest that did.

After Chiv's death, and I'd lost the old village, I was left alone to keep alive an entire cultural mind, but with none of the people that went with it, in a land whose mind couldn't seem to hear any of this.

But I was only a small servant of a much bigger mind than my own. To keep alive the round gorgeous fullness of all that learning long enough for it to develop and flower far beyond Chiviliu's own sphere and my own imagining right inside the hearts and lives of the very people whose industrial civilization had engineered, both purposefully and unconsciously, the natural and cultural extinction of not only their own assumed territory but spreading like an epidemic of toxifying unfulfillable smiling promises had now infected most of the world with its dependency on a synthetically lived-out existence, the Seeds themselves would redefine for me what Chiviliu had really intended when he made me promise to keep them alive.

For ever after that, the seeds I was trying to keep viable were no longer "my" seeds or the Seeds of Tzutujil spirituality, but the seeds that every citizen of the Earth has somewhere tucked away inside themselves, or outside in their lives, or somewhere in the ground, or lurking around the family baggage, or hidden in their bodies, in dreams or inexplicable proclivities, but always somewhere they never look or know anything about. These seeds were the seeds of that very precious thing we all have that contains embryonic caches of possible understandings of how to live ritually and intactly with an indigenous mind, seeds that have been bequeathed to us all from our own more intactly earth-rooted ancestral origins from millennia previous.

Most of us everywhere descend several thousand years from people of great and amazing qualities, qualities no longer understood, or valued, much less recognized in this present citified world, but qualities of our ancestral past still encoded in our spiritual bones in which we know ourselves as they did to be the direct descendants of not only Holy animals but more so of plants. People who in some remote long-running era of our distant past before there was a Chinese empire, an Egyptian empire, a Sumerian empire, before there ever was a Europe, in eras of small, amazing, agrarian cultures in which our ancestors still knew how to proceed as humans are meant to, on an earth they would not simply mine or harness, pollute or domesticate without great consideration, people whose everyday existence was not dedicated to a fear of not surviving, and therefore not dedicated to production, paranoiac defense, scarcity, or milking dry the world, but to a spirituality that knew how to feed the beauty of their human ingenuity, art, language, and physical presence to the natural world just as they would feed a suckling mother.

In some forgotten part of us all there yet towers the roofless ruins of a neatly made, tiny earth-and-timber palace of unconscious memory in whose thick walls these amazing ancestors have left for us to find a pot of precious seeds, indigenous seeds of still-viable knowledge and living vitality, seeds that could resprout into view the organic articles of the original treaty we humans promised long ago to uphold between ourselves and the wild natural world at the time we first began to manipulate the earth, her plants, and animals through agriculture and pastoral herding.

Mudded into these forgotten ramparts of our Indigenous Souls, these seeds of how humans are meant to live have been passed unnoticed like recessive spiritual genes in our souls from grandparent to grandchild for millennia, waiting for each generation to consciously rediscover them, replant them into welcoming ground, and once again cultivate into view a real, livable mythic origins and a small, viable array of ritual seed cultures worth descending from.

But, how can *we* find our seeds if they are hidden in a place we know nothing about, a place we cannot see or touch without the indigenous ancestral mind?

The truth is, the seeds do not need to be found because they are already found. We are the ones who need to be found, for the seeds are wherever we go.

Like victims of an ancient spiritual and cultural shipwreck, we have been adrift for four thousand years, floating on people-centered rafts of provisional civilizations that have convinced themselves they are the real thing and the cutting edge of human evolution, while designating our true magical origins of deep small cultures as some dirty, half-evolved, grunting, primitive past.

But no matter how far we've drifted away from those real indigenous shores, the spirits of our last happy, intact, indigenous ancestors from before we began to drift are effortlessly coursing right along with us. Having merged with the vastness of the natural wild tossing sea we so fear to drown in, they follow each of us like a pod of giant sea turtles, their big sweet scaly heads thumping up under us, trying their best to get our attention and tow us home to our real selves, knocking on the hull of the lifeboat of today's assumed culture, while we drift along figuring that the anxiety of civilization's never-ending feeling of emergency is normal.

The seeds are here with us wherever we are, but *we* are never where we are, but always heading elsewhere to escape that feeling of never being where we are. We are never at home.

To find our seeds to plant new culture, we have to find a way to be quiet and feel welcome at home on earth. When we can find ways of being at home, our ancient seeds will be there with us and will have a place to resprout.

So first we have to stop drifting away from what home really means and learn to be indigenously at home right in the lost place where we have drifted to and try to reseed and reflower with culture and food plants the odd, alienated condition of the present.

These herds of thumping spirits on the big powerful sweet natural forces of vitality of our unkillable Indigenous Souls—they are grand and they are diverse. They don't live only in humans, or just in carbon-relegated organisms, nor are they limited to any single dimension of place. They are not confined to only an invisible existence beneath the surface of the known, or imprisoned as abstract ideas, but more often than not they show up coming at us as tangible events that stretch what is accepted as real.

This subsonic, natural, and delicious surging of our real Indigenous vitality lives kinetically, always in an elegant cruising movement, renewing itself at every opportunity in our lives, becoming visible in some difficult-to-predict guerrilla maneuvers of a great affection for life, showing themselves most clearly to those whose vision is least choreographed by modernity's bias, maybe in some forgotten overtoned Altaic horse-headed fiddle flourish showing up three thousand miles away and a thousand years later in the broken-hearted whining calinda of an Eastside klezmer violinist; or in the drone of the bardic outpourings of the mysterious daughter of a Sard taxi driver in Birmingham, who came from the womb with 24,000 memorized stanzas of an ancient pre-Muslim Bakshi epic; or a west Texas rancher's dew-dripping fog-harvesting galvanized cattle gate, whose drooling echo hatches this year's rain-calling frogs whose storms drive the drought-hidden grasses out of the Holy ground back into the nipping jaw of jackrabbits and thirsty sheep, pushing milk into their udders, and life into the newborn lambs, whose suckling feeds both the coyote and ourselves; or in the explosion of the giant audial flower of a thousand scented South Sea Islanders seated ecstatically singing, swaying, calling back the fish-filled winds of summer from the equally gathered crowds of tiny nuns, who themselves singing chase back the same gales with the fish they've held in winter's prison along with renewed sky water from the shores of that icy pole.

Somewhere on behalf of every ecologically shattered centimeter of our overworked ground, every forgotten scrap of enslaved matter, every caste of work-wounded laborers, every genetically manipulated species and seed, this vital indigenous force lay ready to ambush the folly of humans pretending to live life from the distance of an armchair and computer screen, with the real touch of life on the hoof.

This innate vital force is involved in a never-ending revolution that doesn't topple but is armed only with Beauty, to struggle for Beauty, and to make the Holy in Nature live. For people this means the appearance of Beauty of a world proceeding naturally, each thing moving according to its nature and its place in the staggered concentricities of all things living and dying at their appointed hours to feed the next thing, who will do the same. A beauty to antidote and heal civilization's unquestioned toxicity to life brought on by its hatred of its own real natural origins, its original people, its original plants, original animals, and original earth.

What the seeds were waving in the air like a banner for me to see was that while real culture of natural humans living by the old agreement to the wild would have to appear for a world worth living in to happen, it was not old lost cultures that should reappear from the past, but viable, fresh, never-before-seen cultures that still retained the same root of indigenous integrity of that little-documented era of human existence before being interrupted by the appearance of "old" imperial and tribalist civilizations who are the ancestors of the present modern mess.

This was a spiritual thing of the oldest type, not a Christian spirituality, a Jewish spirituality, or a Buddhist, Muslim, or any other kind of human-centered spirituality, but a spirituality of Seeds, Seeds who once sprouted out of our forgotten origins and flowered into cultures mythologically lived out that recognized humans as the magical descendants of both plants and animals.

This meant that the human world would never be successfully legislated into goodness if the legislated and legislators couldn't see the Holy in Nature and were not devastated by its beauty and the innate mythological ritual process of such vision so as to do what was best, not because of a law but out of utter admiration.

Not knowing who we really are in the big picture according to the Holy in Nature or where all that we have ended up adopting originates from, the motivating factor that guides all "good" policies and decisions for the world would always have as its prime incentive the furtherance of a clever mechanical thinking, that at best only wants the natural world as something separate from humans, and the survival of the wild advocated only as some denaturalized human-managed minion, touristic prop, or resource so that people could have medicines and air enough to themselves "survive" long enough to continue the same absurd self-defeating, earth-wrecking trajectory of the present. This was not part of the original agreement with the Holy Wild.

Rather, the earth had to be understood as our own tangible soul, and any trauma caused the earth eroded our souls. People, when they become the real humans they started out to be, have an inborn love for the big overwhelming beauty of the Holy in Nature, as much enamored of its subtlety as of its terror of depth and motion, understanding and wanting the fact that bears snoring in their deep snowbound caves love dreaming summer back out of the frozen ground, waking the snakes and Thunder, whose lightning refreshes the trampled dry sea of steppe grass with its tornadoes of rock-melting prairie fires, flash floods, and nitrogen-injecting hailstorms.

Only cultures that "still had their seeds" could want this spirituality. Could cultures that refound their seeds actually begin to appear in North American cities, the solid electric lightbulb of Europe, or Asia's bursting seam?

If they could, the seeds themselves seemed to say, these cultures could *not* be designed by humans using the present mind. These cultures, like all real things, had to grow naturally from the ground, organically stretching into the world from the old seed, at the direction of the spiritual DNA of the mind of the Holy in Nature.

"This meant," the seeds said, "that any worthy culture has to sprout right out of the slag heap of the world's present condition, that love would have to manifest in hell for heaven to begin. These cultures would start in many small ugly places in ways hardly noticed at first."

We could never transcend the mad toxic trap of the present without deferring the Hell of it on the next generation. Nor could we "perfect" ourselves or "purify" ourselves or the world without becoming spiritual fascists. No, our grief over the reality was the Hopeful thing. For we, as "sacred farmers" who cultivate the ancient seed of culture and keep our original agreement with the Holy in Nature, know we must learn to metabolize our grief into a nutrient of spiritual awareness of our real place on earth, compost the failures of civilization's present course, and cultivate in that cooking mound of composting tears and detours a future worth living in, all smack-dab in the middle of modernity's meaningless waste.

Instead of once again drifting off in flight to ruin in our wake yet another "intact" world while trying to outrun the toxic mess we'd made of the last one we stole, trying to escape the one before that in an endless succession, instead of forever seeking a formula of transcendence or a technological loophole in the organic Nature of the Divine, we should plant the seeds of our forgotten Indigenous worth and vitality right in the heart of modernity's hell and stay put, while as spiritual farmers we nurture a plant whose flower and fruit could feed "a time of hope" beyond our own.

Like Pederucho and his brave people waiting unarmed, unfed, and dignified in that painful peace of Cuchumaquic at the end of their world in February 1976, who unquestioningly agreed to "keep the seeds alive" to regrow a time beyond all of us, we too today could become real human beings in these harsh and teetering times, if after honestly recognizing the full dimension of the civilization-created disaster inside of which we all sit this very moment, instead of hysterically grasping at straws of endless Band-Aid cures to keep things going long enough to "get" ours, or neurotically cowering into addiction, depression, or self-destruction, we try to plant and keep alive the seeds of real culture right where we sit in today's blundering world.

But having said that, even if we are willing to be such incredibly courageous people of this type, even though we are unknowledgeable, unsure, spiritual drifters, who hopeful against all odds are willing to stay put long enough to keep alive seeds of culture and food for a better time, we ourselves will most likely provide for a generation we shall never see. Where could we find our own indigenous seeds to do all this "planting" with in the first place? Like those seeds in the ruined wall? Like the seeds Ignacio Campos's grandmothers left him?

I'll tell you . . . the seeds we seek are here already, but *we* are not here. When we are here, the seeds will begin to appear, for we first must make fertile cultural ground for them to want to appear, and to do that there are any number of things you and I can go towards, maintain, and live by if we have the dedication.

To get the smell and taste of what I mean, here are a very few ways of making worthy ground for your seeds to begin showing themselves. Most of these ways come from the lives of the old Tzutujil Maya, no longer alive among these people either, but they might begin to help restore and redevelop to some small degree the necessary senses for families and individuals to begin to re-member their grief-cobbled way toward their own palaces of indigenous memory wherein lies stored the majesty of your people's forgotten version of the Agreement with the Wild in Nature and then onto the seeds.

What follows are a few "seeds" from my own "pot" given freely as a gift and stimulus of hope for at least some part of the suffering world to resprout itself, to sing itself back from the bottomless cliffs of modern cynicism of the present, and to cause us all to become real humans in our attempt to jump up like sprouts trying to lick the face of the sky and live again.

Chapter 19

The Marriage Contract with the Wild

It may come as a great puzzling surprise to some people of this age that there was a time, in some places not that long ago, when seeds of the plants that fed a people were never sold, bartered, shared, or freely exhibited to people of any other group.

Nor were seeds something you could casually collect in the bush, for every tree, every head of wild grass, every wild tuber had a natural owner: the powerful Deities of the Holy in Nature. Permission had to be courted; gifts of prescribed offerings given; and words, procedures, and particular approaches carried out to even consider taking an animal or plant for one's own use. The wild was a magical court of the aristocracy of the Holy in Nature. One had to know how to act in this court. That was what being a human meant.

The agreement between the Lords and Ladies of the Wild and our Indigenous forebears worldwide originated when the first seeds, fruit trees, and animals were taken away from their "mother" and their wild home of the nonhuman bush and propagated as domesticated "possessions" outside the context of their original natural complex of land mammals, tree animals, birds, reptiles, amphibians, insects, wind and weather, rivers, springs, mountains, canyons, and of course plants. These stolen seeds were taken with no regard whatsoever to the feelings of the Wild in Nature who sorely "missed" her daughter, i.e., the seeds.

These antique agriculturists understood but failed to care that their initial efforts to domesticate wild plants and animals to serve only human needs, at human direction, were literally by removing them without permission or regard for the majesty of the wild, an unsanctioned, uncourted, unwilling "marriage." It was nothing less than the violent abduction by human culture of the wilderness-daughter of Holy Nature.

What is in a seed that makes it sprout, grow, and flower and fruit is known as the Daughter of the Wild, and our presuming to take her—without asking her or obtaining her permission, as if the entire world were soulless and just lying there for our pleasure and exploitation—is at the base of all human incapacity for a life of relevance and happiness. Domestication was the beginning of the unconscious pervasive presence of human viciousness and cruelty in the world.

People did not lose the "garden" when Eve stole an apple from God's plantation and gave it to Adam—the people lost themselves when Adam stole the garden from Eve, who was God!

When we were hunting peoples or humans searching out and eating the abundance of seasonal cycles of wild tubers, inner barks, roots, wild fruit, vegetables, grains, and nuts, we were part of the natural landscape and never took the "daughter" away from her "mother," the wild land, because there was no "other" place to take her to: all land was wild. We asked permission and gave gifts to the wild. We were a natural part of the wild Herself, and as a wild people we were equally hunted and eaten by other beings of the wild. Our lives, like all other lives, vegetable or animal, in the wild fed the world as much as we consumed during our lives. That's Holy.

But then certain people thought to draw a line between themselves and the wild. In so doing they lost their natural humanness; they lost fifty percent of what it takes to be truly human in the world. They became half human, a people always restless searching for their lost natural half. On this side of that line, people remained as nonnatural people living and surviving in a cleared nonnatural enslaved land, while the "daughter" of the wild in Nature they removed from the natural side of that fabricated line, to "serve" these domesticated humans on the "tamed" side.

For this, for not asking, for not waiting for permission, and for not approaching the wild as befits the majesty of the wild as the sole source of all earthly sustenance, all farming and pastoralism of domesticated plants and animals on tamed land earned humans the endless stigma of Wild Nature's hatred. This hatred showed itself in the lessened vitality of the ploughed land to "produce" and in humans' hatred of other humans. There were old agriculturalists and hunters who well understood this stigma—that the wild is ruled by a hierarchy of plants, the most powerful tribe of all beings upon whom all other beings in the world wholly depend for sustenance. This tribe of Holy Vegetation would always rather remain wild, "unimproved," "undeveloped," and untouched by any sort of synthetic nonnatural human interference, retaining the normal creativity of the wild throughout time.

The plants' indigenous nature is to remain wild and indigenous; wild wheatgrass has no desire to be reduced by human selection into the wheat of the daily bread necessary to feed invading armies of domesticated people and their militaristic sickle-swishing, land-wrecking slaves and serfs in service of any millions of history's empires.

The common, ancient, indigenous vision is that all nature was an unwilling "in-law" to that portion of humans who without Nature's permission presumed rights over the Holy Wild, taking her daughter with no regard whatsoever to their "would-be" wife's desire. People only desired what she could be manipulated to give them—an easy source of reliable food—but had no real love for her real self, or for who she really was: the vitality of the untamed wild.

It was an illicit marriage, an unwilling marriage, but it was a marriage nonetheless, and in the end the foodstuff that eventually grew from the stolen seeds we manipulated through garden-subjugation and the unnatural enslavement of domesticated predictability on illicitly cleared wild land was seen by both the Natural Wild world and the unnatural humans as the "grandchild" of both factions. Written in all our bones today is the alive but now-forgotten, once-widespread indigenous vision that through the unsanctioned marriage to the wild through our initial domestication of plants, both the warring parties of transgressing humans and the Divine in Nature had unwittingly become genetic relatives, and out of parallel affection for their mutual grandchild—the seeds of these new breeds of human-directed, life-sustaining plants—a truce was called.

Because humans selected, crossed, and recrossed them, totally altering and tailoring their innate wild nature to their needs and whims, the plants we grow in fields, gardens, and farms are seen to be half human and half vegetation. And because people now "depended" on these human-dependent plants, humans were seen to be half human and half vegetation and all future generations of people descended from both.

In order that their common grandchild—the domesticated plant and the new human culture born of a life of living by what it took to propagate domesticated denatured plants—the natural world, who held all power of growth and reproduction as its sole domain, proposed that a peace between these "new" humans and the offended wild be developed, a peace that would hold.

Instead of continuing to subsist as unwelcome thieves with no natural function in the scheme of the Holy in the Wild, the Natural world proposed they come in out of the dark and become legal in-laws.

In hopes they would cease being an arrogant species of humans whose unquestioning cleverness had them too rapidly adopting shallow opportunistic plans to exploit the world as a "resource," whose momentary fulfillment carried no vision of their effects in the bigger picture, the Holy in Nature laid out a tribal-style indigenous marriage contract between the people and the wild which, if accepted and lived up to, would cause a new type of human to develop: neither a natural people nor an avaricious unthinking people, but a culture of conscious farmers whom nature could conditionally accept as blood kin.

What is here called the "marriage contract" between domesticating humans and the betrayed Wild is a worldwide presence and the root of all indigenous motives for how people maintain their cultures. Its principle is the same throughout but is known by as many distinct designations as there are tribes. Because the versions of this "marriage" that I personally live and know the best are from old Atitlán, a single culture's manner of upholding this old pact, an approximate English translation of the old Tzutujil phraseology referring to it, the words "marriage contract" are used like a canoe to paddle the understanding to more solid ground. While no single people have a monopoly on the depth of cultural comprehension and degree of ritual excellence in what it causes them to do to keep their part of the ancient agreement, for greater cohesion and some hoped-for approachability for modern people to this grand institution, we shall stay with the mind of one tribe: the Tzutujil.

Because no crops or animals domesticated or wild could grow without the magical vitality of the wild and natural when all of its conditions were set forth by the offended party, the Divine in Nature and the humans agreed to all the details of what it demanded of them in the future. This contract became known colloquially as the "Agreement": the original agreement between humans and the life-giving Divine of untamed Nature.

According to the Tzutujil Mayan version of this agreement, if the people continued to maintain their end of the original sworn agreement with the Wild, our ancient in-laws, the wild Holy in Nature, promised to continue contributing the densely rich nutrition and exuberant tenacity of life-grasping vigor and vitality that only wild untamed plants and animals have, to their now-domesticated grandchild.

Because the world of wild plants and people now shared a genetic body through the domestication of plants, the Tzutujil Maya, to take only one example, only define themselves as Tzutujil at the point in history when they began to farm as descendants of the first domesticated plants and an ancient race of humanoid ancestors, the keepers of the Agreement.

The great ancestral grandparents on the "wild" Divine side of the human family promised their grandchildren—the descendants of the original transgressing people and the abducted vitality of the wild—equal fertility and well-being of body to both the people and their cultivated plants, if the people forever in the future promised to give ungrudgingly what these ancient wild Holy ancestral in-laws had laid down in the original unamended Agreement.

The new people who had "developed" side by side with the newly domesticated seed in their new life of farming were defined only because of the culture that happened as a result of their adherence to the Agreement. The agreement gave them their tribal speech, their ways of living, taboos, and most importantly, their ritual language and methods of making beauty of everyday clothing, housing, fields, shrines, boats, tools, mats, and musical instruments, until every particle of human life was infused with meaning and beauty through adherence to the Agreement.

No part of life was exempt. To keep the Agreement, every adornment of the tongue spoken, every embroidery of every thread went to feed the Holy in Nature, depending on *how* the word was spoken, and how the thread was sewn. The Agreement took all of what humans had previously used to functionally rip off the wild and laid down how people were to convert their grinning cleverness, self-serving ingenuity, and capacity for exploitation into a daily proceedance of life and earning of a living in which every phenomena of human culture had to have an aspect of beauty, adornment, and deep multivalent meaning whose presence would create a constant prayer-like remembrance in the minds and hearts of these new humans as to the real source of all relevant life: the Divine in Nature. Even the way we waddled or gossiped in our beautiful clothes fed the Divine in Nature.

In this way only was permission granted us to keep our seeds and to continue farming by the Holy in the Wild, for the Agreement gave us all the details of every aspect of culture necessary to maintain the seeds that have come down to us attached to the seeds. Because of this, the seeds are the culture. From that time on, people and seeds were one and the same.

Because the Holy in Nature feeds us and keeps us alive through the seeds, we were required by the Agreement to feed and keep alive the Holy in the Wild Nature. The word in Tzutujil Maya (and other languages) for "feeding," whether feeding one's children or the Sun or the Holy in Nature, is the exact same word as "to cause to remember"! *"Na ta xa."* This is because the Agreement fed the Holy in Nature by remembering the Holy, by feeding the Holy the type of human beauty stipulated by what we had agreed to.

What was stipulated in the original Agreement took more than one person to keep alive, and all its detailed principles were at the very core of all that went into and was taught during every person's adolescent initiations into a more adult stage.

Initiation was both a stage of human life parallel to a stage in a certain plant's life and a way to live out in a very tangible way all the details set forth in the original Agreement with the wild. Initiation was a tribal education for the youth to learn how to farm and feed beautifully both the people and the Holy in the Seed, and that's what made a viable tribal adult. The articles of what comprise the Agreement for all antique farming people worldwide were inlaid like shell in a marquetry coffer, jeweled into the long tellings of mythology during initiations. Comprehended, these stories were the road map of how to travel as a people in life and were remembered by all. The story became the seed of culture upon whose able back all life ritual and farming were borne along in all their beauty. The language of the Agreement was encoded in the language of mythology, whose secret was revealed only through initiation.

Beautiful farming was at the root of it all. Humans could not keep the Agreement and carry on functional, ugly production of food. The present state of modern "farming" in its utter mechanical bleakness and lack of tribal grace has given us a culture of superficiality and mediocrity. This is a hatred against the Holy and actually kills the vitality of our shared genetic relative: the domesticated plants and animals upon whom we now all depend.

To become human again and have our soul in one piece, an unlikely peace between who we have become and what our alienated natural Indigenous Souls knows we can be must be developed. Some of the Articles of the Old Agreement with the Holy in Nature may be a place for us to take up our beautiful running for the Wild Natural Earth.

Chapter 20

Keeping Our Agreement with the Wild

Our Ancient Seed Jars:
Finding an Agreement to Keep

If we think of the original marriage agreement between Humans and the Wild in Nature as if it were an old pottery seed jar, just like the one the six Donancianas left for Ignacio mudded into their wall, then the ruins of our own cultural memory that quietly rambles out just beneath the surface of our conscious recollection must still contain our own jar holding the Agreement our own ancestors made with the Holy in the Wild.

Like a jar of seeds in which each seed is a stipulation of the Agreement that longs to sprout again, once released from the stiff walls of our spiritual amnesia about ourselves, and planted into the ground of today with our courage and willingness, the seeds of our Indigenous Souls might possibly begin to regrow the beauty, grace, and integrity of real human culture.

By putting into tangible, visible action these "re-membered" sections of our Agreement with the Wild, right inside the flattened burnt-out territory left us by modernity's frenetic tail-chasing flight away from being at home with itself, the majesty of becoming a human "seed" from whom it is worth descending makes it so we become in the process a people who are educated in spiritual agriculture, eating and living in a fresh new way, but ritually diligent and awake enough to keep viable the seeds and the Agreement for a time beyond our own while simultaneously regenerating the wounded ground of today's forgetfulness and the earth herself.

As a young man, I remember more than once catching a herd of scared, uncooperative, runaway horses by releasing horses that had remained in the corral and driving them to the vicinity of those that we couldn't gather, and watching the scattered, scared ones falling in with that herd of confident ones as together we all headed home. Maybe if we run a few well-remembered old and loyal parts of other tribes' indigenous agreements past your own scattered ancestral memories, the lost beauty of your own people's very old past will follow us all home to a better time. The main thing to remember is we need to make them a home: a real place worth coming home to, for otherwise we shall all be moving again toward nowhere—like the present cultural mess in which we are too accustomed to being lost at high speed to stay put long enough to sprout the beauty we all must become.

Here are a few of that old jar's seeds sprouted into view.

SPROUT ONE:
There Has to Be Wild Land, Air, and Sea

There has to be more wild land that is unmined, unhiked, unrafted, unphotographed, unclimbed, unlogged, and uninhabited than there is land under cultivation, filled with habitation, dedicated to recreation, or otherwise put to use by humans.

Together, wild plants, wild animals, wild people, unexplored places, unclimbed mountains, and headwaters, unrafted wild water, wild air, and the wild unanalyzed depths of anything are a giant culture comprised of a compendium of complex microcultures whose irrevocable right of ongoing presence and natural vitality is in direct proportion to the health of all people's domesticated unwild food, both plant and animal, and the health and wholeness of the people themselves.

According to the Agreement, when any portion of wild earth, air, or sea is removed from its wild state, invaded, cleared, fenced, commercially fished, ranched, leveled, manipulated, or manicured to bolster recreation, food cultivation, housing, or business development, the civilized humans carrying this out must permanently relinquish twice the amount of their own domesticated land and water, releasing them back to their original Mother: the Wild.

If any wild land or wild water is taken, deforested, denatured, farmed, planted, built on, inhabited, or exploited in any way without the responsible parties first returning a double amount of already-exploited territory back to the jurisdiction of the Holy in the Wild, then the entire body of the world's food-producing plants, animals, land, and water will demonstrate a marked loss of vitality and loss of nutritive capacity to support the world's human population in increments corresponding to the crime that doubles cumulatively in every instance this old rule is broken.

Not to be confused with leaving land fallow to recuperate for future production, this is about taking land out of production and sending its wounded self back home to the Divine in Nature.

This is the old rule that used to also apply to housing, clothing, and tools, all of which were ceremonially given back to the place from where they were "stolen" to reintegrate themselves into the "wild" that produces all we have.

But now when the domesticated plants and animals the people commercially cultivate on either land or in the water begin to lose nutritive value, good flavor, and ability to survive, people of the modern condition, having discarded the Agreement, chain into production even more wild land, fresh water, and sea, digging an even more profound pit of stunted vitality for both the earth and the people.

Any attempt to outrun the ancient human reverence for the Holy in the Wild and our subsequent keeping of our Agreement, to shore up production on land and in water already stolen from the Holy in the Wild, through the endless menagerie of technological gimmickry of machinery, chemicals, and genetic manipulation, not only skyrockets our unpayable collective debt to the powerful Wild, but actually poisons the very population it pretends to feed and protect by polluting and clipping the natural genes of the stolen earth, water, plants, and animals.

It is only the Wild in all things, all earth, all the universe that can revitalize seeds, culture, and land with life continuance. God only lives in the Wild, not where people insist on, not in their buildings, work places, or playgrounds, unless they are wild natural people who have always belonged in the wild.

While civilized people often head to the wilderness to recuperate, the reason they feel so rejuvenated by their experience in the bush is not because their civilized "souls" are relieved of all the racket and endless compartmentalized drudgery of everyday life in the city, but because their real souls, their Indigenous Souls, don't live inside their civilized bodies inside their apartments, but run naturally unanalyzed in the unknown mystery of the Wild. Our Indigenous Souls are part of the Holy in the Wild.

What is Holy in Nature and Holy in human nature can only live where it is wild with all the other natural souls; not in the over-domesticated, soul-wilting pile driver of civilized life. Without the truly wild land and water, the vital central soul of who we are meant to be has nowhere to run free according to its nature.

Without the wild you cannot be whole; you can only be half a person: the civilized part. This is why modern people are so restless and never at home because mentally and physically we wander ceaselessly, trampling and ravaging the very earth that holds our souls, looking for our whole selves.

But we can neither find ourselves nor find vitality for our food and land by once again invading the wild looking for ourselves because the presence of our over-domesticated civilized persona in the wild makes the wild no longer wild, and our souls have once again fled.

What we must do is keep the Agreement and somehow make friends with both the Holy in Nature and our Indigenous Souls. We must have a love affair between our civilized beings and our Wild Indigenous Souls, and for that we must learn to *court* that wilderness with the ritual poetry and Holy farming action that feeds simultaneously the Holy in Nature and the Wild Nature of our Indigenous Souls.

But this can hardly be done in the city, except by the gifted, nor can it happen in the wild but in a liminal zone of feral land that lies between the civilized and the wild, between the modern person's heart and their own wild Indigenous Soul.

SPROUT TWO:
The Veld—Sacred Feral Land

To keep our Agreement with the Wild there has to be a veld, a territory of uninhabited land neither wholly wild nor under cultivation, running along the edge of the Wild as a buffer zone between the activities of civilization and the sacred off-limits home of the Holy in the Wild.

Borrowed from the Dutch word *velde,* the English term *veld* nowadays means mostly unenclosed, unfenced grasslands shared by pastoralists and wild ungulates alike in places like Botswana, South Africa, and South America.

But the word *veld* is a live linguistic artifact that descends from a most wonderful ancestry that predates the ruthless land-dividing cultivation systems of the imperial ages. The words *field, welt, weld, wield, feld, felt,* and *fold* all descend from the word veld from times when Celtic, Germanic, and Persian, etc., were still aspects of Indo-European language and not so distinct from one another.

The original word *field* or *feld* did not mean what it means now, but signified the last furrow plowed and left planted for the wild, not to be harvested by humans, on the other side of which resided the uncultivated "Wild."

Birds, like the one still called a "fieldfare," were considered sacred messengers, the magical go-betweens that carried the humans' offerings and spiritual invitations to what I call the Holy in the Wild. As well as being the spirit of the veld, these birds also brought the replies of the Wild from the other side of all cultivation to the farming people in the form of songs and their bird motions as read by the seers of the old agriculturalists.

The veld therefore was where the human domestication of the wild and the wild would parlay and have a place in common. It was there that all the rituals were made to feed the Holy in the Wild to keep the domesticated "fields" filled with the vitality of the Holy in the Wild. The veld is the feast table where we feed the Holy in the Wild.

Descending from the same word, *weld*—as in the welding of iron or steel—denotes a "seam" where two different pieces of metal are melted together, just as the veld was the third material that held two distinct treatments of the earth: one wild, one cultivated. Even more to the point is the English word *welt*, equally descended from the much older *veld*. In boot making, a welt signifies a thick piece of what is usually leather sewn in between two disparate materials such as the thick multilayered sole and the softer tanned leather of the upper so that both the top and the bottom of the boot have a kind of flexible seam-like hinge. The place where two distinct, otherwise unbondable substances can meet and function as a single useful togetherness is dependent on yet this third material that has characteristics of both and is called the welt, and in old agriculture, the veld.

Ideally, then, when land was returned back into the embrace of the Wild Holy, it would lie adjacent to the untamed, uncultivated natural land that originally stretched out forever. Over time these "returned" fields would aggregate into a wide meandering territory with its own character, a sort of liminal zone neither wild nor civilized that served as a kind of shock-absorbing skin, a kind of demilitarized zone to shield the Holy Wild from the confusing avaricious clatter of the proceedance of civilization and the cultivation upon which it ran.

While this ever-widening zone of "rematriated" earth or sea might of course be incapable of quickly resuming its original wild nature with all its natural functions, creatures, cycles, and plants, often when fortunate enough to be given time, a lot of time without future human exploitation, certain of these areas can still be seen to have reassimilated back into the body and living matrix of its wild parent, its trees, or sea vegetables, micro-nutrients, mammals, reptiles, fish, birds, and complex cycles flourishing, reestablished in a mutated way but always according to the underground life of the wild mind of nature and its present climate.

Even so, it is *not* this possibility of the land returned to regain its wild unmolested nature where the hope and magic renewal of life truly lies. For more often than not, these zones would become yet a third kind of open land, neither wild nor cultivated, but partly wild and still giving life to the humans.

Where towns, villages, farms, roads, walls, wells, shelves, and terraces once rose, out of the ruins of all these things tumbled down, a greater diversity of grassland, flowers, wild insects, birds, grazing ungulates, and their predators would rise, spread, and thrive, turning these stretches into a wildish in-between pasture where the people shared with the wild, this interim territory called the veld.

Though descended from the same word, such a place would not be a "belt" of today's pseudo-natural uninhabited land left for hiking and park activities, which runs between the civilized and even more civilized, as seen in the hipper city plans; this middle zone of land returned back to the wild was the child of both the wild and unwild. Its open grass-lands, flowers, groves of trees, repatriating menageries of plants, bees, lichens, and microorganisms eating up and breaking down old buildings and furrows into soil to equally welcome and feed visitors from both the wild and domesticated were for all tribal agriculturalists and animal rais-ers an indispensable tradition of zones of peace. Actually required by our agreement with the Wild, the presence of these veld zones was nec-essary for the continued health of the Wild in the face of human civi-lization. It was also a place where civilized, forgetful, land-animal- and plant-enslaving humans could go to remake their over-domesticated unconscious selves into more whole, Indigenously aware beings again. It was not in the wild but at the veld where humans went to "remember." The veld was and should be a place of renewed memory that leaves the wild untouched and fed and the people a little more wild and intact. For it is here in the veld that all the old rituals and community ceremonies came together, in groves of trees, at the base of old overgrown walls or granaries, at the springs in the veld's grassland.

It is in the veld, this sacred feral place, between the free and the fet-tered, where the Holy in the Seed, the Holy in the Wild, and our wild Indigenous Souls are ritually given the offerings we agreed upon.

In so much of the world where tribal people have resided and fed themselves, there now spread lands considered by civilization's science as wild and natural, which are actually only parts of a much more integral and ongoing way of understanding how to be human. Something that goes beyond people feeding themselves and searching for comfort. People in the past knew how to return their lands, homes, cultivations, plants, animals, tools, and their souls back to the Holy in the Wild; through the use of the ritual tradition of the veld in one form or the next. Their motivation was not to be fed, but to keep the gorgeous big picture of the Holy in the Wild healthy.

Once a people are dependent on domesticated plants and animals, there has to be a veld, there has to be the Holy Feral, to become human again.

 SPROUT THREE:
All Origins Must Be Known—Where the Seeds
Go, So the Agreement Must Go

As it went with the seeds, so it went with the people. As it went with the people, so it went with the seeds. With the seeds went the "agreements" of ritual and lifeway requirements, no matter who ended up with them; and with the people went the seeds and the agreement of a culture of the seeds, no matter how different a place or how far the people migrated from the place they'd first received their culture from the seeds.

In Northern Italy, before Europe's plundering of the Americas brought corn to the rest of the world, polenta was made originally from a type of buckwheat not native to Europe—ground and cooked just as corn polenta was millennia later.

Arriving in the saddlebags of early Indo-European nomads in the BCEs, "Barbarian Wheat," as this buckwheat is still called in many places throughout the so-called Middle East (what is it east of anyway? And on a sphere? Rome? Ha! Old imperial detritus that we continue to uphold), Southern Europe, and North Africa, originated in a southerly "belt" of Siberia probably around the Yenisei River running all the way to Manchuria, becoming a powerful central Asian starch crop, from where waves of Turkic nomads brought it again to Europe in the 1200s.

The stories, customs, and language surrounding buckwheat in the buckwheat zones of Asia and Europe retain only vestiges of the original Agreement with the Wild as compensation to the Holy for human exploitation of the buckwheat, but in every case, mysteriously, it is in its "wildness" that still refuses to die where its undisputed value lies even in the minds of production farmers.

For there are peasant tales in which "Barbarian Wheat" is a heroine who appears at midsummer to resuscitate the domesticated wheat after it dies from the overfarming of overworked ground by oversettled people, revitalizing the earth it grows on with her wild barbarian Nature blown in from the formerly "untamed" steppes.

And indeed buckwheat is still widely sown on spent ground after the winter wheat harvest to feed the bees starved by monocultural agriculture while reanimating the soil, which she most ably and beautifully accomplishes once tilled back into the tired, overcivilized ground.

So when you plant corn or buckwheat, you should know such things. Otherwise we are participating in the Amnesia of modernity's imperial hatred of our real Indigenous Souls, who would much rather be growing a Holy buckwheat woman to heal the ground instead of robotically strewing seeds for their micronutrient phosphorous recuperation for wheat production at such and such a percentage per acre!

Today, when examining the information printed on a packet of seeds, it usually reads, "Plant this deep, this far apart, this time of year, this much water, that much sun, this type of soil, eat this way or that, etc."

Where's the majesty of the seeds? The majesty of the farmer? The majesty of the vital wild ancestors of the Seed? Where's the majesty of those in whose hands the seeds have been carried down to this moment? Indigenous culture is basically an orally, ritually transmitted multi-millennia seed package, in which the complexity of human ritual culture containing everything we need to know—the history and instructions for growing life—are written out as a love letter to Nature in how we live a farming life.

It is a great and worthy occurrence that so many people are now involved with trying to keep old reliable strains of open-pollinated heritage seed lineages, rootstocks, spores, and tubers from extinction. By cultivating these marvelous plants, relearning how to cook and eat them, and locally marketing them in small places, while saving the seeds and roots in organically maintained gardens by hand throughout the world, a lot of culture, memory, health, and deliciousness is thereby restored to us, all along with the undeniable treasure of the seeds themselves.

But how many individuals, cultures, and histories are behind every seed sown? This vastness is important, for it is inseparable from the seeds. They must go together. They should all be on the seed packet, or handed to us by the last person to grow the plants who should know the names of these individuals, cultures, and histories.

The people just by growing these plants are participating in all of this. They are doing a hell of a lot to keep the world alive. But do they know what they need to know to be actually keeping the seeds of culture alive along with the seeds that represent them?

The most delicious and comforting characteristic of the strenuous, earthbound, and spiritually drenched existence of intact people worldwide is the cellular detail of the knowledge all their people have of not only their tribal origins, but the origins of every star, planet, rock feature, tree, plant, animal, clothing stitch, tool, color, sound, food, knot, all mores and every detour, strangeness, mood, and enemy, with which the people live with and by, and finally resting resprout again.

There is a familiarity, a face good, bad, ugly, behind every tiny imaginable thing we brush up against. And in a tribe, if we are not sure of what a thing might be in the "bigger story," there is always somebody else who can easily fill us in.

This vast education is what makes all things feel at home with all other things and to know where to tread and where to be cautious: how to lie still and when to move; how to eat, speak; and what things are biggest, and which are bigger still.

The loss of this capacity, of detail in our modern lives descended from production-oriented imperial civilizations and may well be the driving force behind the need for science, as its penetrating need-to-know analytic capacity tries to fill the painful void of the civilization it serves to make up for the loss of the lyrical mythologic reality of the Indigenous Soul present at the deepest levels in all human beings.

But the loss of this natural education has put our hearts into a zoo-like condition of unnatural confinement, causing the worldwide mass epidemic of depression, of lives lived at a spectator distance from the warm soil that births us. Our memory of what it is like to know the story of every rock face in the canyon through which you and your pony ride, what it is like to know the story of how every one of these rock faces originated, and what it is like to know how your ancestral past appeared pushing in and out from their massive cracks, once lost, our memory of being at home on Earth in a real way sinks out of sight back into the indigenous wilderness of our souls, and we become meaningless and depressed. For without that memory, we can't know where we are.

So why stay that way? To keep the seeds alive we need especially to know the origins of all these plant seeds who have given their lives to sustain us, and also sustained our ancestors as well, without which we wouldn't be here.

To have this awareness of spiritual agreement and conductivity we have to know everything about what we grow and what we eat, expanding in particular how we eat beyond the treatment of plants as faceless undivine "food"; simple carriers of chemically analyzed organic nutrients. This treatment of life and eating as if plants and animals were simply primitive forms of nutritional fuel capsules instead of embodying the great willingness of the Holy in Nature to feed us by their conscious acceptance of certain enslavement of their otherwise natural plants is anathema to the real human soul and a deterrent to happiness on this Earth. For it alienates us from the mythic, the mystery of the Holy in life, and our own feeling of worthiness in service to the grief of the enormity of sacrifice we cause the world to experience by just our eating, breathing, and pursuit of survival.

Therefore all farming, gardening should not be felt as some small, inoffensive, off-the-grid, relaxing hobby but a large, powerful, deeply emotional working necessity without which we can never fully develop into a worthy human presence of initiatory possibility.

All organic or natural food and flower gardeners inside the continents of Europe and the North Americas, especially those good seed-saver-organic-types, know that when a seed hits a catalog and is proudly proclaimed to be an old heirloom seed, say hypothetically an old heirloom tomato seed, it usually reads something like this: "Grandma Schlotovsky's giant Russian tomatoes, an old Siberian heirloom brought over by the late Anna Schlotovsky's immigrant grandfather who settled in Odessa, Texas, in 1892, a reliable, short-season, firm, many-lobed Brandywine type."

Or perhaps, "Munster Pearson's midget butter and cream sweet corn, developed by nineteenth-century amateur agronomists of Ohio utopians, snatched up by Burpee for their 1874 commercial seed catalog. A popular short-season prolific variety popular 150 years ago, sure to be a hit in your farmers' market and summer cookouts today."

While Mrs. Schlotovsky's ancestors may have grown tomatoes north of Moscow from a miraculously adaptive landrace of tomatoes grown previously in Moldova, brought there by Turk-speaking Azerbaijani immigrants displaced by the Great Game and never-ending strife of the Crimea, none of the peoples of five thousand miles of Siberia, none of whom are indigenously Russian, grow, or descend from the original tomato people. Russians growing northern tomatoes are either descendants of Ukranian old believers sent by the czars to colonize places like Sakhalin or North Karelia, or later political exiles punished by Stalin. Most tomatoes came to the palate of Russians who love them (even in cakes!) and grow them well, probably from Georgians, or Armenians, who themselves received them through their political proximity with people living in Turkey who got them in the 1500s.

All tomatoes indigenously originate in a vast array of very old varieties from two species of nightshades, cultivated for three or four millennia by the diverse peoples of Central America, Mexico, some South Americans, and only slightly later by all the indigenous nations of the Caribbean islands.

The word tomato comes from the Spanish *tomate*, which comes from the Aztec Nahuat word *tomatl*—*tom-atl*—"refreshing-liquid," which is a precise translation of the older Toltec and present-day Highland Guatemalan Mayan term, *xkuul ya*—"refreshing water or liquid."

This, of course, is not a reason to forget Mrs. Schlotovsky or her grandfather (and why don't we know his name?) or the horrors of a Russian trying to survive culturally in Odessa, Texas, but we have to recognize that there are miles of equally pertinent people and their tales, and a trail of historical grief and political displacement behind every single seed whose fruit, seeds, roots, or the animals it feeds, feed us and all those before us.

People say, "I just want it all to be simple so my gardening relaxes me from the incomprehensible overwhelm of the world, so I don't have to worry about all of this." I suppose selective ignorance on the right day is relaxing, but that's the creed our most recent ancestors taught us to adopt. But remember, just because you don't know what happened doesn't mean it isn't banging around in your blood somewhere making trouble with your soul and eventually your health. After all, anything not committed to our awareness becomes history repeated by none other than the ignorant and eventually settles in our lives and bodies as sickness and neurosis.

According to our agreement with the Wild in Nature, all the origins of things you can know build up the beauty of what you can do, and when you plant one little tomato seed, knowing that he carries all of that history trailing in his survival, his planting carries all those people and times remembered and healed, who would otherwise go forgotten. Planting seeds with this depth of knowledge heals the past; healing the past heals the future. "Regular" political history cares only about the end, not about the maintenance of spiritual nutrition of neither the past nor the present.

The Tzutujil Maya alone cultivate to this day over thirty varieties of very antique indigenous tomatoes, all the varieties touted as European, Cherokee, Hillbilly, Brandywine, Paste, Armenian, Pear, Yellow, Cherry, and more. They and their Mesoamerican ancestral cousins developed all of those long before there was a Russia, before Great Britain existed, before the Ottomans became the "Turks," etc. And yet if any one mentions it in a modern seed context, it's either a scientist looking for some way to isolate the germ for a greater production trait or a botanist who loves the subject. And when they do mention a Native American origin, there is no reference to Nezahual Coyotl, or Grandpa Qiq' from five hundred years before the English language was invented. Just a simple "developed by Native Mayans" or some such.

But the people all need to know it, just as much as they all need to farm. The knowledge belongs to the people, and if the powers that be will not educate us, then we must educate ourselves and help each other to learn. Farmers are priests; farmers must be our scholars. Farmers are ecstatic lovers of the long story of the seed.

How *did* tomatoes get to Europe, Africa, North Africa, Middle East, India, Persia, South East Asia, and so on?

The same way chillies, turkeys, maize, potatoes, peanuts, squashes, chocolate, tobacco, and sunflowers did. The same way the spices of South India, islands of Indonesia, the South Seas, and Southeast Asia got to Europe and caused the so-called discovery of the Americas and its terrible exploitation: not by trade or friendly gifts but by violent conquest and plunder and force.

Contrary to people's common fascination over their need for wealth, Spanish merchant ships returning from the "Americas" didn't come mostly loaded with gold, any more than English ships returning from the southeastern coast of their American colonies came filled with tobacco. The Spanish ships came with exotic lumber, people, animals, food, more food, seeds, tubers, clothing, and a million types of minerals. The English ships came with timber (they had none left in Europe!) but mostly with the sacred, indigenous, American medicine sassafras, the new miracle drug for syphilis so rampant in all levels of European society.

Neither was the Mediterranean dominated by would-be European empires of the day but by Islamic Turks of the Ottoman Empire, whose sundry pirates were fast, famous, and broadly multicultural. Their Jewish-piloted sloops captured Spanish cargo over and over, introducing corn, chiles, tomatoes, peanuts, potatoes, and more to North Africa, Egypt, Syria, Iraq, Iran, the Balkans, Romania, Italy, and Armenia, from whence they rapidly made it to India, Indonesia, Southeast Asia, and China long before they made their way into European farms and markets. Chiles and corn in particular arrived so quickly into areas of central Africa and Southeast Asia that people indigenous there to this day will not believe you that these plants are not indigenous to them. For, of course, the "whites" who stole them from the Americas were never the face and companion of the seeds as they shifted from people to people, market to market.

But because all of these seeds arrived as "spiritual orphans" with no ritual instructions, stories, or awareness of any Agreement, truly indigenous peoples of Africa and the Asias found ways and stories to slip them into their own spiritual mythic agreement with the Holy Wild, marrying the new plants to their own domesticated plants and animals. They Indigenized them.

Everyone in the world thinks Thai chiles are indigenous to Thailand, but they are originally from what was once called Hispañola by the conquering Iberians, now known as Haiti and Dominican Republic. The old amazing island of Ayiti had these fantastically delicious, violent chiles indigenously, which to this day are called Santo Domingo chiles even by the Mayans of Highland Guatemala, who have hundreds of varieties of their own.

Of course, Virginia tobacco, the first English slave-dependent crop, was also from the Antilles Islands of the Caribbean, originating from the Mesoamerican native seed peoples of Guatemala and Mexico long before. The tobacco grown by North American native people was a totally different species of plant, not entirely fitting under the definition of domesticated. Always ceremonial and never grown commercially, its diverse forms were driven to virtual extinction by the English and Dutch business-political conquest of the eastern American seaboard for the difficulty in growing it commercially for production. The native plant would not let itself be cultivated by people who didn't understand the Agreement. For, like all the "big" plants, native tobacco was propagated religiously by sacred societies who cultivated these Holy plants in land cleared, dammed, drained, and fertilized by wild beavers. Tobacco was never sold or traded but used spiritually or given as a gift. Even as recently as the 1870s, a handful of this tobacco had the gift value of a horse.

This situation with the plants of the invaded, violated, overrun, colonized Americas is not confined to the Americas and Europe, but was already a worn-out multigenerational phenomenon worldwide.

Every single cultivated sacred plant such as tea, tobacco, ginger, sassafras, chocolate (cacao), grape (wine), pomegranate, coffee, all with huge ancestries of ritual and story have experienced hopeless exploitation once removed from the ritual context of their true people. Once lost, converted, and reduced, slave-like, to secular recreational substances and the plant's spiritual ritual needs thrown away, the plants lose their helpful sacred nature and personality, whose toxic backlash has been vicious to the health of the world's conquering population.

Every food plant, no matter how precious any of us hold them to be, has a history that is not that of an innocuous, inert substance, but one that parallels the trouble and grief of all humankind. Domesticated plants are mired in a psychological and historical amnesia that is only equaled by the way our minds continue to unconsciously keep alive the aura of old imperial superiority that condescendingly categorizes the world's overrun peoples from whom all the "captured" plants originate into a mental "Southside of the track" pool of hazy anonymity: something not worth remembering. The general attitude that farmers "don't need to know" anything, they just need to grow things, only furthers the self-rationalizing colonist attitude of "that was then, this is now," or, "the Indians grew it," as if Indians, Africans, or Asians were a vague faceless irrelevant lump, instead of the thousands of distinct cultures and worthy individuals they were and continue to be. There are millions of brilliant faces behind every plant seed and food here today, and only 0.001 percent hale from the civilizations that presently depend on them.

People want farming to be simple and comforting, as opposed to city life.

But the reality of our food and the seeds they come from is neither simple nor comforting, but deep, painful, convoluted, magnificent, and as amazing as the story of the long lines of all the peoples who have cherished them and kept the seeds alive no matter what conditions both people and their seeds have suffered. To forget any of that is a terrible violence to the future of our own history, the health of our minds, and the worthy feeling of being a human being.

This violent situation of the seeds, rituals, and people of the invaded, plundered, violated, colonized Americas by European empires is not unique to the area or its time in history but is part of the traditional largesse of the story of imperial policy with natural people and their plants worldwide. Though not all dissemination of domesticated plants has been through direct conquest, it has been the general horrid trend for at least two thousand years of the violence of constant slavery and warfare from which modern commercial culture gets its modus operandi.

People want a friendly, faceless past or a familiar one. We prefer to hear about Grandma Schlotovsky's Siberian tomatoes and forget the Mayans, Spaniards, Turks, Armenians, Greeks, Poland, Stalin, the pogroms, and Odessa, Texas; we like Mr. Pearson's sweet corn, or Mrs. Eloise Groblatt's famous dragon carrots, because, as people who have lost their own cultural seeds, we want a Norman Rockwell Fourth of July picnic with giant piles of freshly boiled Munster Pearson Gentleman Sweetcorn which was originally the Sauk and Fox Native Americans' greatest prize from the ritual life and Agreement of all their existence, given as a gift of "forever-peace" by the great Indigenous North American rebel-farmer Black Hawk to the American forces to take care of, feeling it would go otherwise extinct when he capitulated after decades of successful resistance to losing his people's farmland during one of America's many militarily enforced mop-ups of anything standing in the way of all the landless European immigrants settling and paying taxes to keep the government funded.

We feel better about those wild purple carrots in the salad when we hear that they are Mrs. Eloise Groblatt's famous dragon carrots instead of originating in what is now Afghanistan, brought there probably by gold-covered refugee Yuezhi Indo-European nomads from the Ordos desert in 300 BCE and subsequently to Persia and Europe during the expansive trade and warfare after the original Mohammedan jihad.

It's a totally different picnic if you can convert the numbness of preferred ignorance into the world's grief the present mediocrity pretends to medicate, for from that grief of remembrance, real human beauty and subtlety could ride again, and from that real cultures could sustainably spring.

I suppose people whose own ancestors were themselves overrun, displaced, trivialized, and forced to forget any of their own origins upon immigration, trying to avoid the constant ache and terror of the memory of those past realities, cherish only what has become recently familiar, making Time as a remembered thing something somehow pruned off our memory just after immigration and pushed out of conscious sight like trash in a landfill, declaring everything experienced since as old, and the seeds as heirloom though their heritage comprises less than a hundred and fifty years.

As citizens of a past intentionally purged of uniqueness as sure as any racial purge, the language we use to think with makes the rationalizing history of the imperial colony the only accepted one. Like Native Americans north, central, and south, or all immigrants that descend from boundless cultural richness, lying beyond and beneath the synthetic political entities of, say, Poland, France, Spain, Germany, Italy, Ukraine, Britain, China, Russia, Japan, or the USA, back to the great tribal realities before those unnatural empires and their millennia of expansionist wars forced their way into prominence, our minds now classify the details and deliciousness of those vast amazing pasts that all of us have as a faceless void, with a nebulous personality at the safe, soulless distance of a culturally accepted amnesia.

But our souls, like the seeds, remember.

We need to find them, or we shall go mad or destroy ourselves trying to speed away from the incrementing trail of suffering unsung ghosts we leave in the wake of our flight into amnesia. Make the effort to look into the real past of the seeds you plant. Go as far as you can get, even into the annals of the standard empire-serving common system of belief, and you will find the people of the seeds and the seeds of your own past. Look into the people, and you will find your "seeds," for all of us have them. Like all the languages, clothing, songs, ways of living, the seeds too have been taken from us, but their memory lives on, waiting to burst forth again if we just look beyond the Great Wall of cultural and historical prejudice and self-hatred.

In every family, if you are courageous enough to stay on the trail beyond the prejudice of a family's selective memory and belief, and don't get your fate stunted by getting mired in some self-involved psychology, there are vestiges of customs, sayings, beliefs, that if assiduously looked into could easily lead to the more ancient evidence of your people's unique version of the original spiritual "Agreement" with the Holy in Nature that all peoples have. Strange little shoots of bigger vines that have miraculously survived the simple-minded revisionist imperial histories we have all been taught yet dangle there unnoticed.

These little leftover things are the signs of the "souls of our seeds." The stories of these souls and our plants are the stories of our people; between the people, the seeds, and their stories, evidence of the ritual agreement with the Holy almost always pokes through if you know what you're looking at when it does.

In this way, whether you plant a small garden or sow a larger farm, if you know that many things about what your seeds carry on their backs, then you are cultivating origins to whose story your own story is then attached. By tending, growing, and worrying about the welfare of the living things you have planted, you are both caring for and are part of a true origins, and you are no longer stranded in time. You have become a vital part of the long umbilical cord of a life attached to the Holy in Nature.

SPROUT FOUR:
When the People Marry, the Seeds Marry

Because of the nature of the initial marriage of us humans to the wild, and the spiritual responsibilities to the wild through following the Agreement, the cultivation of domesticated plants became a sacred career, which once entered upon became not a matter of mere food production, but an obligation to the Divine. Because of the Agreement, farmers and animal raisers could never decide not to farm: they had to farm to keep the agreement because you can't entirely undomesticate a plant or person. Farming was an obligatory cyclic ceremony that made the everyday into a nonstop series of ritual, labor, and living.

This made the seeds of their plants into something very precious and highly coveted. The farmers seriously guarded the seeds from any outsiders accidentally obtaining them, for should some people not tutored in the Agreement casually cultivate the seeds without following the spiritual etiquette demanded of these particular farmers of these particular seeds by the Wild, then Nature would assume that the treaty had been broken and, resuming her old enmity against all humans, remove from the seeds all vitality and capacity to sustain the people.

Deliberately growing seeds and cultivating plants without the Agreement made both the seeds and human culture into orphans abandoned by Mother Nature, threatening the entire balance of our deep life-dependent pulse with the wild half of our souls, which only reside free and running in the untouched Wild of Nature: something shamans clearly understood.

Having lost the vitality of the nutrition and growth of our food, and that half of what made us vital having gone off with the Great Insulted Female of the Wild, we would cease as Indigenous humans. For this reason, the seeds and breeding stock of domesticated animals were originally never a thing freely given, nor something that could be sold or bartered for in the market. Seeds toasted, or ground into flour, and animals butchered into meat, tallow, and skins might be sold, but no living domesticated seed or beast.

A good number of incidents regarding Big Civilization's confusion over Natural people keeping their seeds and animals to themselves have continued to occur right up to this decade. This phenomenon of native unwillingness to part with seeds has always been interpreted by the representatives of Big Civilization as instances of tribes not wanting anybody to be able to cultivate and propagate what only they had, thereby creating a lucrative dependency on what they alone could produce.

While one can never rule out a canny business sense among any people, in almost every case what it came down to was that the natural peoples in question feared that if the big civilization should obtain their live seeds and breeding stock, the entire ritual culture that the tribes spent generations of lives maintaining, which accompanied the seeds, would never be recognized or respected, much less carried out in the alienated lives of such citified imperial people, who, having lost their own seeds and any memory of their own original Agreement with the Wild, were stuck having to constantly trick, plunder, and force food from unwilling lands and people to feed themselves.

From the Dayaks in Borneo to the Nennet in Siberia, from the Guarani in Ecuador to the Pueblo Indians of New Mexico, from the Himba in Namibia to the Rifi Berbers of Morocco, the same story can be told.

When the enforcers of Stalin's Siberian gulags and pogroms tried to obtain live reindeer from the reindeer-herding peoples of the area to keep on hand in enclosures enough meat and milk to feed the staff and the inmates of their concentration camps, the reindeer herders agreed only to sell them as much meat as they wanted, but no living deer. Because live reindeer could breed, there were ritual stipulations on raising them and, more pertinently, the slaughtering had to be carried out in certain spiritual orientations so as to keep vital the herds per their own ancient Agreement with the Holy in the Wild and the original Wild Deer Mother.

I remember one day in the mid-1970s when the late great Tzutujil storyteller and well-loved member of the village spiritual hierarchy, Pascual Mendoza, came borne along by his daughters into our family compound in Panul in search of a cure for a very ragged accidental machete gash across the instep of his foot that had cut through a lot of muscle and tendon. The wound had gone very septic, almost to the stage of gangrene, and would probably need amputation.

This normally vivacious man was descended from a very small and rare section of the village population who still possessed an equally rare variety of old-time *quicóy*, a type of Mayan squash, which hailed back to a time before either his people or the squash could be actually considered Tzutujil.

Though the mythic origins of his mother's line and the parallel origins of this squash were common knowledge, nobody but Pascual's own family group had ever been graced with the seeds of this amazing plant.

As a cooked or quartered squash, lots of folks had tasted it, but none had ever held a whole seeded fruit or grown one.

The entire village prized this squash above all others. This moment, I still long for one. For it had a tiny seed cavity and held a very large amount of the sweetest aromatic flesh of an almost vermillion hue. It was indescribable in taste, delicious, sweet, deep, with some unique other-worldly thing. No other plant we'd ever eaten had such a taste.

Pascual would almost rather perish than go to a hospital for a cure, and he almost did from his bloated, infected leg, but after I'd done all I could over the span of the next couple of weeks, he would recover enough to finally walk on his own. These people were so spiritually strong; often even an impossibly wasted old body obeyed its soul's need to live on out of sheer obligation to the joy of life.

Pascual had always been a friend and, later on, a sacred colleague from my very first days in that village, but he also wanted me as a son-in-law as well, something that never happened. So as soon as he'd fully recovered his legs and his sparkly wit, the entire female side of his "clan" came to pay me for my services as the doctoring shaman per Tzutujil custom.

Like a small caravan of flowers, they all gracefully poured in, bedecked in their fanciest handwovens, sat down, the mother cradling something the size of four fists held together wrapped in a *stoy*, and pro-ceeded to instruct me in all the rituals of this clan's "agreement" regarding this famous squash.

After I'd reiterated it all back to them and they were satisfied that I'd memorized it all properly, as a group they presented me with what the mother had been hiding in her lap, which was nothing less than a single gorgeous, hard-shelled, rumply, black-skinned *guicoy* squash, inside of which I would later find in the small cavity only six slippery fat, tallow-yellow seeds, that upon planting all sprouted into six squash vines each the equivalent of the beanstalk of Jack, with flowers like big yellow hats with purple centers.

This made village news so fast that the entire south side of Lake Ati-tlán knew about it quicker than if I'd been handed six billion dollars after a helicopter visit from the Pope! By that gift, I'd been virtually made a relative, for those seeds were that important. Those kinds of seeds are what the Tzutujil called *nim ru banic,* or "of a gigantic context." Seeds should still loom that gigantically in our minds today. But hardly anyone has seeds like that anymore because they don't have time like that anymore. But maybe we all do have *seeds* like that somewhere, but just don't know it yet.

Among all the world's ancient gardening and stock-raising people, when any food seed finally was conceded as a gift to an outside people to use for their own cultivation, it came on the tail of long, serious discussions, divinations, and finally only after a reluctant decision.

This was to ensure that the people receiving the gift of the seeds had to promise to uphold and carry on all the cultural ritual details that went with each type of seed plant or animal as inseparably as an inner organ or its DNA. For the Agreement with the Wild was the spiritual DNA of the culture that knew how to "sprout" a seed people. In this friendly fashion, growing someone else's seeds was a kind of marriage with the other tribe's seeds.

This is why seed exchanges came about mostly on account of a marriage between a man and a woman who, after falling in love, brought along from each of their own peoples their own particular rituals, ritual language, and everyday obligations along with their distinct seeds. While the man and woman promised loyalty to one another, each side of the family also promised for eternity to keep the other people's ancestral Agreement with the Divine in the wilderness! Marriage of people from different tribes was a merging of otherwise unobtainable seed stock: a merging of distinct Agreements.

The seeds, the plants, the yearly cycle of farming the food harvest rituals, food taboos, and the preparation of both parties all had to come along together, becoming a new ritual culture with a new language, ritual tool reverence, and sacred field architecture. Because of this, the seeds equaled culture, and any indigenous people accepting such a gift from another knew they were adopting a new culture that would forever mix and mutate who and what they'd been in the past. But this has happened over and over, creating culture in its wake in a pulse of ongoing natural, organic evolution of seed marriages.

This is how seeds crossed, revitalized, and hybridized to begin with. People did *not* say, "What would happen if I crossed this type of corn with that type of corn?" We had no permission to do that. The people who served their corn and its cultural phenomenon, according to the Agreement with the Wild, had to "marry" for the seeds to "marry." If the seeds of plants or domesticated animals were to cross, their people's DNA had to cross as well! People were plants; their plants were people.

Thus because of the attraction, love, and tribal need for their people to genetically "marry out," the plants that resulted from this marriage were stronger, new, and revitalized. The people in parallel had little children, whose new gene presence revitalized and animated the people's gene pool. The children grew up to be adults that were the "parents" of a new, revitalized language and culture of new mixed seed agreements and began another tribal identity that jealously guarded its three types of corn: the newly crossed hybrid of their parents marriage, and the two old ancestrally carried species of each parent's line.

By keeping the Agreement with the Wild, the people and the seeds were both revitalized. The Holy in Wild Nature had promised this, and there it is.

Seeds cannot be kept pure without starting to atrophy after a certain number of generations. This is especially true of most grains. So seed-savers trying to keep open-pollinated seeds "pure" are in a kind of conundrum, for purity of that type cannot keep a line of seeds alive. They have to be crossed out and revitalized at some point.

At the same time, seeds need to remain "isolated" like human initiates for a certain number of years of replanting before they are ready like new initiates to marry out or cross out. If this is done in a certain fashion known to the old-timers, this will keep the seed's identity clear and stronger yet, but it is not based on purity. It is based on pulses of out-crossing and open pollination with our own distant past in isolation.

The brilliant genius of this is that no animal, plant, or people can retain neither genetic nor cultural purity and survive as that plant, animal, or people without at least three different lines or more of genes or ways of life moving in and out of the bloodlines in a specific kind of natural pulse. The genetic lines of indigenous ritual farming wove in and out like a three-strand braid.

Corn seeds begin to atrophy and lose viability at about twelve years, and then every year after only one half will sprout until eventually all are finished.

Instead of purity to keep a line of ancient Pueblo corn clear enough so it retains its original ceremonial identity, an amazing and beautiful phenomenon of the old agreement is still kept alive today three thousand miles from its source by people who continue to understand and revere the stipulations of what corn demands for its spiritual and genetic integrity.

When cultivating this specific ancient untampered corn, it is planted far, far away from all others to keep it "clear" and uncrossed every season for the next six years. It will be noticed that a few of the plants and their offspring will begin to exhibit traits and colors quite distinct from what was actually planted.

Indigenous corn-growing people from Peru, Guatemala, and certain tribal districts of Mexico and New Mexico have as part of their old Agreement the custom of separating these particular anomalous ears—no matter how peculiar—then growing them separately the following year as a distinct small crop far away from the first corn, which has again been replanted.

These "new" manifestations of the corn are not considered recent appearances but reborn versions of much, much older parents of the first corn married into the corn's lineage when other people married into their people of the first corn long generations previous. Regrown and kept clear, these "other" old throwbacks sometimes exhibit pods on the kernels, tassels coming from the top of the ear, corn kernels growing on the tassel off the top of the ear, etc.; different "old" color schemes of corn are found as well, and all of these over the next six years are separated and regrown as fields of distinct species of corn.

Then they are all married back in again. After twelve years or so of separation, each of these distinct old ancestral throwbacks are then sown back into every other row of the "original" corn in mounds to cross back. In this way their pollens marry back with the original corn. The resulting corn is a massively renewed, durable, reincarnated ceremonial corn that is basically the same as that which resulted from the marriages of people and corn that took place five or six hundred years earlier.

The next year, this child of the "remarried" corn is isolated again, and after a couple of years these older strains begin to reappear, or even others that haven't for a century. They are taken and planted separately, and then the whole cycle begins again.

The natural world works this same way. Genetic and cultural integrity must have motion, pulse, cycles, change, and renewal with the old. Purity is static, with a single-eyed vision of pure and muddied, which only breeds polarities, war, and atrophy.

To keep seeds alive, clear, strong, and open-pollinated, purity as the idea of a single pure race must be understood as the ironic insistence of imperial minds and should probably be boiled down into the tears of grief its insistence descends from and composted into something more useful.

The strength of open-pollinated seed and the culture of seed people is in the back-and-forth balance of the diastolic and systolic pumping between isolation and diversity within the components of its own throwbacks as married to the landrace adaptation to the conditions of the present, and the people and real culture we are meant to be must run along in an identical fashion.

The seeds are the eyes of the Holy in Nature who see by sprouting, weeping tears of joy and tears of grief that together become human ritual culture.

The seeds are the college where the Holy teaches. We must plant them, cultivate them, keep the Agreement with the Wild, and learn to become humans who are not interested in laundering and purifying the Earth's heart, her people, animals, or cultures.

SPROUT FIVE:
Kneel at the Feet of the Mother of the Food You Eat and Ask Her to Adopt You

Find your people's seeds. Lacking those, find seeds of the edible plants you love the most. Then find their stories. Then go further; find their scientifically explained origins, then find their real mythological origins. Then with a deep heart ask the seeds if they are willing to die planted in the ground to feed the presence of humans, because that's what seeds are: a funeral whose generosity feeds us.

Then plant them in your backyard so as to grow food to feed your family and surrounding area. Better still, grow them in your front yard too. Get good at it. Don't let the seeds down.

Everybody stuck in modernity must grow food right where they sit. It's fine if you have a special garden area or own a wealthy farm with a lot of machines and workers, but plant food everywhere, especially around your house. You can make it even more fantastically beautiful than your flower garden, way more beautiful than your house. Your house will be a hundred times more beautiful for the garden of food made of origins, stories, and your attention to making certain that there are little tiny beautiful toad places and uncultivated mysterious spots throughout dedicated to the wildness of the Holy in Nature.

If you live in a modern society, every individual must not only know how to grow grain, fruit, leafy vegetables, fruited vegetables, roots and tubers—they must actually *do* it and keep doing it.

No matter how luxurious a life, no matter what kind of maladjusted, cubbyholed, cyberwired life you drag around in, you must, no matter how unlikely the conditions, cultivate food plants or food-giving animals, learn to cook beautifully, and feed your neighbors.

If you live in the modern world and aren't growing food somehow, then someone or something is starving on account of you while you take up space and nutrients. Stop living in coffee shops and get out under the leaf litter. The Holy is certainly not being fed by your sitting around thinking about it. Better to grow food and feed somebody beautiful food than whine, get pale, and rot.

Even so, in the end, nobody can truly carry their own weight alone. We must help one another with the inefficient beauty of food and the majestic learning of its growth. When you consider what just one citified human this day and age takes out of the Holy earth to support them for five minutes, a thinking person could despair. But that kind of despair is just laziness with a college education, for if you carry well just even a small chunk of that weight, it will be more help than you can estimate, especially when it comes to what in the modern world is called an "energy crisis," your physical health, and a general open pollination of a well-proportioned mental vision of yourself and all those you touch.

Turn that worthless lawn into a beautiful garden of food whose seeds are stories sown, whose foods are living origins. Grow a garden on the flat roof of your apartment building, raise bees on the roof of your garage, grow onions in the iris bed, plant fruit and nut trees that bear, don't plant "ornamentals," and for God's sake don't complain about the ripe fruit staining your carpet and your driveway; rip out the carpet, trade food to someone who raises sheep for wool, learn to weave carpets that can be washed, tear out your driveway, plant the nine kinds of sacred berries of your ancestors, raise chickens and feed them from your garden, use your fruit in the grandest of ways, grow grapevines, make dolmas, wine, invite your fascist neighbors over to feast, get to know their ancestral grief that made them prefer a narrow mind, start gardening together, turn both your griefs into food; instead of converting them, convert their garage into a wine, root, honey, and cheese cellar—who knows, peace might break out, but if not you still have all that beautiful food to feed the rest and the sense of humor the Holy gave you to know you're not worthless because you can feed both the people and the Holy with your two little able fists.

And when you garden or farm, then you have to remember that when you harvest, there is no difference between pulling off a ripe ear of corn from the stalk and cutting the throat of a lamb to eat the meat. Living things on this earth live only because of the death and generosity of other living things. No one is more "evolved" because they eat only vegetables.

There is nothing in the world wrong about eating only the children of plants, eating only vegetables, as long as you don't feel superior to some-one else who is omnivorous, who eats the children of animals, for both of you eat what has been killed.

And don't fool yourself into thinking that by only eating plants you are lessening the suffering of living beings because you think plants are nonsentient.

To indigenous people worldwide, plants are the most sentient beings of all and should be respected as much as any animal should. They just have a larger, more temporally spread-out nervous system than most humans can sense, which can be better measured geologically in eons instead of minutes, millennia instead of days, by synaptic wave patterns like the rippled growth of stalactites in a cave.

The old Tzutujil, for example, held animals as "organs" of plants. Plants extended beyond their roots, stalks, leaves, and flowers, and had four basic parts. One was a smaller plant or fungi that grew at its root, the next was a land mammal that lived in, on, around the plant, or in the shade of its trunk, the next was a flying animal, bird, or insect that resided in its branches, and then there was the plant itself.

The fungi were the kidneys, intestines, and memory of the plants. The animal was its moving part, the bird its "calling" voice and lungs for the plant's body, which was the "seeded" largesse of providence for all the other three and the skeleton upon which all life was dressed as its flesh.

Every plant had their specific mammals, reptiles, amphibians, birds, and fungi that were "part" of each specific plant and no other. For instance, a balsa tree had a specific delicious mushroom that grew in tiers at her massive knee-like roots, a kinkajou for her mammal, who drank the cuplike nectar of her flowers, and a snub-nosed bat for its flyer. Any of these seen on another tree was considered meandering parts of the balsa!

The entire world suffers for the rest of the world to thrive. It's all about generosity; it is about not escaping a life where suffering is how things work.

You cannot pretend that you are not causing suffering by picking peas because you're not killing the pea plant, or that by eating plums you're not hurting the plum tree because your harvesting doesn't kill the tree.

But according to the timbre of the spiritual understanding of all indigenous seed agreements between ourselves and the Wild in Nature, by harvesting the seeds of a domesticated plant such as a sweet pea before the plant can naturally reproduce (and the same for a plum fruit), there is no difference in magnitude between either of these and drinking the milk of goats or cows or taking the eggs of chickens or ducks.

For in every case it is an instance of a "mother" plant or animal giving up her children for you to eat at your dinner table, or a "mother" giving up her own children's sustenance, plant or animal, to feed your children.

Better than sitting around feeling superior for adherence to any kind of food habit, it would be better for you to physically kneel in front of your mother fruit tree, and at the knees of your milk cow, or at the woolly face of your ewe, and ask permission to speak to them, and then ask that they adopt you as the hungry orphan that you really are without them; ask to be her calf, or her lamb, or her shoot in the leaf litter of the mother tree's shade, for you are none other than the one who has already eaten her children and drunk her children's milk; tell her you want to be accepted as her lamb because, indeed, you are fed by no other.

This is precisely what people say in Romania, Bulgaria, Laos, Sami Lappmark, Niger Merle, Mongolia, Yakutia, and hundreds of other places where they still understand why, and it is a central part of the Agreement of all tribal people worldwide.

I remember seeing Tzutujil men in the steep cultivated slopes of the south volcanic outlands of Atitlán, angry about a boundary infringement by the neighboring tribe who had without permission sown acres of white corn on Tzutujil land. This "army" of Mayan males fumed and seethed in complaint the entire fifteen miles to the site of the "crime," but upon seeing so much tasseling enemy corn thriving on the stolen land, they fell instantly to their knees en masse, caressing the waving stalks, addressing them in simultaneous prayer:

> It's good to see your face again, Mother
> Good to feel your refreshing breath again, Mother
> We, the drinkers of liquid, the consumers of your children
> Kneel at your feet, and thrive in your arms
> We, your flowers, we, your sprouts today, though we be the
> world's greatest forgetters today, we do not forget you,
> Please hold us orphans at your roots, as your children hold us
> in your branches and let us live again . . .

We are allowed our folly, but it must always end in a discovery of our love for what loves us by dying to feed us, more than we love our hate.

What so often passes for "compassion" is generally a passive-aggressive theater of dogma and condescension whose pitying heights feed no one, and only serves to inflate the "compassionate" nailed into his armchair of superiority. Superiority and "holier than thou'" attitudes make it so their wielders cannot fall in love. And let me tell you, a life without the tears of real love for a man, a woman, God, an animal, a land, a plant, or the earth ain't nothing worth being superior about.

We can't learn to live according to an agreement or understand in any degree the depth of nature's constant grief and beauty of how she makes life out of her losses, unless we live with and tend the plants and animals that labor so hard and die to feed us.

It is really arrogant to think you should be above and outside this constant reality that all things live only because another has died to give them life through food; wanting to transcend this unavoidable core of all existence can only mean you want to have your cake and eat it too.

Trying to meditate or levitate away from the grief of this living reality is the same as taking no responsibility to the Holy in Nature for your existence. This is *not* spiritual.

The elegance of being a nonsarcastic lover of the mother in all things that feeds us and our capacity to feel the grief of her generosity through her losses to maintain all species, our own capacity to then push our grief of that recognition through the ability of our hands and language into tangible gifts of beauty and usefulness to that Mother Animal and Plant is a hint that our capacity to learn how to feed the Holy in Nature is beginning to sprout.

This is the beginning of the literacy of seeds that is learned only through their cultivation by way of an Agreement: that only through the consciousness of the reality of their loss to feed you, and the realization that plants and animals are not shackled minions or complacent slaves, or victims to be badly farmed or ranched cruelly or shuffled about as dead matter, but your superiors, braver, better things, who through their generous deaths and the honor of your preparing beautiful food of them that goes to feed a beautiful people who also know how to receive it, people who feed and don't waste, disparage, or take their food for granted, can the Holy in Nature that gives us life, give us as well this opportunity to become spiritually educated humans, through the sacred career of spiritual farming.

Therefore let's plant it up, learn the origins of all things, weep, live, and love, and continue searching for our ancestors' original food seeds.

SPROUT SIX:
Beautiful Farming

Indigenous agriculturalists worldwide have always spent a lot of time making and adorning all their tools, making meaningfully ornate the walls and floors of their homes, adorning their own bodies and farm animals, making beautiful their graves, and more so the sacred architecture of their fields, infusing every aspect of their existence, physical and spoken, with an indigenous beauty, powerful, ornate, clear, sparkling, proud, and strong.

Before all of the untold devastation of land, life, and culture that the presence of mechanized warfare has wrought over the last hundred and fifty years, erasing the widespread presence of village identity almost everywhere, the farming villages of the world were filled with people who proudly wore all the time their most beautiful handmade clothing, not only for special days but to work. Until recently in many Himalayan villages, or Mayan Highland villages, or Southeast Asian agricultural hill villages, or even in European villages—Bulgarian, Scandinavian, Finn, Karelian—and many more, they didn't have "costumes," but magical, meaning-filled, identifying, hand-grown, hand-spun, embroidered clothing where every person of every age bore clothing as ornate and distinct as the dialects they spoke.

That people's language equals the dress they wear has always been an indigenous trait worldwide, and indeed the modern world follows suit with its bad ritual of meaningless machine-extruded functional garb that equals their tasteless reduced language of production and computers.

Where it still exists, a people's ornateness of tongue and clothing is hardwired spiritual property from which we all descend, which has always not only signified tribal identity, but the deeper older knowledge that the Holy in Nature would be lessened, dishonored, and repelled if people should lose the respect of approaching the Holy presence of the vitality of our food by coming to work in the fields, to harvest, cook, or eat dinner dressed in the fake humility of the drab trappings and mediocre speech of mechanical functionality or empty television mind that treats everything as mere soulless "stuff."

If you should see a traditional Sami man or woman milking a reindeer, you will not see a small person in rags or camouflage tee-shirts, or a drab canvas coat; you will see a complex hand-stitched shirt jacket of majesty; fur-topped, felt-inlaid tall boots; a four-tasseled, pocketed, handmade, minutely stitched, brightly colored wool cap with abbreviations of tribal tales embroidered in every possible space, all covering the milker who sings a song of milk, history that addresses the majesty of the reindeer, without which no milk would flow, in whose reply the mama deer rumbles, and out of her big nostrils, God arrives, riding her steamy breathing like a sky-bound reindeer of clouds.

Or Kuchi girls picking saffron or milking sheep in their beautiful long veils, mirrors, and silks, and multilayers of skirted bodices; or Rabari men in bright red turbans and sashes singing to their camels while a brother covered in gold, milks; or a Wayami lady in her full-body annatto designs and myriad bodices of finely made beads, planting her manioc; or Hmong hill-women bringing in the rice harvest, a red cardamom flower in their left ears, their complex skirts, bodices, and bags, all handwoven, latticed with silver.

Fifty women dressed in their tribal best, for ritual, you say? No! Those are their work clothes!

People all descend from the indigenous. And indigenous people are intent on feeding the Divine in everything they do, by walking down the trail, working, eating, and sleeping, by the earth-oriented ingenuity of human-made beauty for, after all, that's all we really have to give as a gift that the Holy didn't already make.

This kind of beauty is one of the seeds men and women of today must relearn to keep alive. This seed is a seed to keep the seeds alive.

This beauty is not the beauty that makes another person seem unbeautiful. This beauty is not the beauty that intimidates or is vicious. It is the beauty of any and all things living according to their true indigenous nature.

In the Atitlán of those older times I remember a tiny red hobbling young dwarf woman dressed very fancily in her handwoven *pōt*, red wraparound ikat skirt shot through with German tinseled thread, smooth bare feet and wet hair combed all to one side, bearing up under a large tied-up package of laundry returning up the hill from the lakeside row of washing rocks of Xechivoy with two girlfriends on either side, all young mothers, their little ones trotting alongside. One of them was as slim as a cornstalk and poor, but still dressed in only a little less splendor than Ya Tre, the little woman; of the other three, one had a large birthmark on her face, the other tight pomegranate breasts and a long beautiful gait, and the last was an albino girl, the daughter of Mayé of Panabaj, but as a group they were like a glittering earring of motioned beauty on the body of the village; the fine music of their voices and the twinkling of their children fed the village heart, and for it the world jumped up and lived. For no matter what they were as individuals, together they were indigenously beautifully dressed up as always, whether to work, to sleep, to cook, to talk, to garden, or to feed the children. Instead of taking away from the rest, they added to the beauty to which all the village was dedicated. The modern world feeds nothing, not even itself, by the way it dresses and walks up a hill or down a hill.

People say, why do all sixteen-year-old girls look beautiful? Because all sixteen-year-old girls are beautiful, just like all forty-year-old women are beautiful if they're not trying to look like sixteen-year-old girls, but beautiful forty-year-olds in love with the beauty of being a "real" human being.

I remember handsome old Chiviliu in his nineties everyday with his two silk scarves knotted around his neck, his yellow ikat "bumblebee" handwoven shirt with belly-button tabs, his top-knotted, tail-dragging, tinseled sash doubled and tied over the top of his short Tzutujil *scav*, man trousers, embroidered in silk birds and rainbows, his triple-riveted sandals, his big fluorescent handwoven ikat headcloth with six-inch silk tassels tied sideways, and his big felt hat sideways on top, his deep-creviced face blowing blue smoke rings from behind his clenched smile grappling his deer-headed pipe and thinking to myself how beautiful to be so strong and indigenously dapper and make no one feel the less but prouder still knowing that this beauty was bigger still when you saw at least one hundred and fifty other old duffers sitting together equally dressed addressing the Holy in the Seed as the sun rose, behind a hundred and fifty women dressed in their lady equivalents, right hands raised to the Dawn Sprout we called Day, the other hand holding tight to the candle they'd nursed all night.

Male beauty is in big trouble in the modern world, and without it the world is a dangerous place to live, for tribal men who have their beauty as a group are not quick to compensate for their feeling of inadequacy by vectoring their repression and shame into war and business, and seeking power instead of beauty to feel worthy.

The seeds of the world that feed us all come with an agreement to only be farmed with this kind of beauty. While endless examples of how the world's peoples have done this or the few that still do could be laid out in front of us—and indeed it would be good to see what such a thing really looks like—but what I'm really inspired toward is the possibility of how a truly ugly world-killing-corporately-extorted culture of abstract money, suits, camouflage, acrylic carpets, fake food, and business-serving petro-dependent technology could voluntarily break down into small, not simple, but excellent, symbiotic, beautiful, ornate, new, remnant micro cultures of peoples of differing speech and beauty who, learning to revere nature, develop ways to grow and live with their food, that leaves nature whole, and use their last money to underwrite spiritual, small, nonviolent, courteous, elegant, courageous, happy humans with hearts that house a love for the Holy Wild, instead of dreams of isolationist fortresses of intimidation and fake power.

Our food plants only become more powerful in their ability to feed and flourish when farmed with this kind of beauty. People only weaken when they lose this beauty, for they can't feed the Holy in the Wild, which is our vitality.

The strange and inaccurate prejudice of the deeply embedded notion that farmers by definition need to be dirty, coarse, uncouth, ignorant, clumsy, and out of touch, especially if not "in step" with agribusiness-machine-dependent farming, is based on the fact that our present age is the culturally orphaned child of the historical reality that most of the world's population are descendants of tribes and village nations who were captured and forced to abandon the autonomy of their life serving the agreement to the Holy in the Wild, and either enslaved en masse or forced into uncompensated servitude as owned agricultural land serfs to produce food and fiber for new nonworking castes, to fuel their overlords' stupid and expensive preoccupation with never-ending territorial feuds and ascendancy wars, where their serfs changed hands as easily as their overworked land and domesticated herds.

Those of our ancestors who could not be captured or wouldn't "roll over," deprived of home, became either nomads, pirating bandits, or merchandizing wanderers. The nomadic peoples eventually became the terror of all empires, but finally succumbed themselves in most cases, though not all, to imperial design after eight hundred years of continued autonomy. But they were certainly "beautiful," mythically aligned stock raisers while it all lasted.

All the diverse groups of "captured" serfs were eventually synthesized into the national identities of various empires that held no relation to the original tribal peoples who originally constituted the population.

While in some areas some serfs miraculously managed to continue elegant, capable, and beautiful versions of their original selves, for the most part, farming as a serf under any feudal lords became a life of generational deterioration into poverty, avarice, sickness, filth, and the constant simple-minded dream of escaping to "freedom," which in the mind of these human "machines" was not the old "beautiful" farming but a life as far away from the ground as possible, and usually as the owner of serfs. The slave dreamt of the luxury of no work as a slave owner!

Today, especially in Europe, China, and the so-called Americas, no matter what color or race we descend from, the greater number of us all descend from generations of ancestors who at some point or other were serfs, slaves, or indentured land tenants.

Merchandising and business, when possible, have ever since always seemed the best route by the former serf or slave to speed away from the muck, hunger, depravity, sickness, and poverty of what became the cliché of farming.

Being a farmer who actually touched earth, instead of the "farmer" who never touches earth but administrates and does sums as a merchandiser, meant nothing related to beauty for centuries ever after. Beauty became something more superficial and immediate: it meant living "clean" and "pure" above the mud and poverty of servitude, not farming.

Even the advent of the "Americas" and all its indigenous wreckage in service to freeing up land to "free" the hordes of immigrating landless European peasants, whose great hope of modern technology and "modern" banking being able to outrun the previous pattern of ages of bones-aching drudgery with forty acres and unpaid-for machinery, did nothing to reestablish the original indigenous human dignity of sacred farming, or our intelligence or any of the real spiritual cultural integrity we must have enjoyed before all those highly touted imperial civilizations withered all those small flowers of culture with the fumes of their toxic breath.

As in all those other areas whose waste and toxic detritus are nationalized as a necessary sacrifice for a glorious future that can never happen with no living memory or vision of ever having been a people of beautiful indigenous farms, raising good non-poisonous food beautifully to feed the people and the Holy in the Seed that could feed them all, that reveres and does not ruin, but remembering that the uncultivated wilderness must remain uncultivated as the mother of all successful cultivation, the modern age with all of its absolutely stunning technical cleverness and scientific candor, who would take the homely serf out of the muck, adopted economies both socialist and capitalist whose standardized, debt-funded, machine-driven, mediocre food production continued to be just as war- and conflict-dependent, just as mechanically dehumanizing and stratified as feudalism, and above all even more efficiently ugly than the preindustrial past to whose trap of landless poverty everyone so desperately feared to return.

So let's stop being that way. There is a past beyond that limited view of a terrible past. Let's be our real selves again, not by ordering someone else to do it—let's do it ourselves.

Real farming, for us all, as it is for indigenous agriculturalists worldwide, is a priesthood of seeds and food whose men and women dress beautifully and meaningfully, where every article of clothing is a handmade message to the Holy in which they walk, go to work; they are highly educated in culture, music, in all the procedures of the Agreement and with the emotions of the earth; they are courteous, dignified, capable, permanently ornate with song and the deliciousness of language; in how they move, and not heavy trudging ogreish or armored but subtle in the way they go about every facet of their food: the planting, the preparation of fields, the shapes of terraces and fields, the tools, the carrying bags, the way they dance the food home, the design of the granaries and kitchens, the shape of the pots, the way they are stirred, the way things are ground, and on what they are ground, for their food to them is nothing less than the face of the Holy in the Seeds. These farmer's voices are heavier and more worthy than gold; their tools, though practical and strong, are more beautifully adorned than carved jade, and the Holy in Nature forgives these kinds of humans when their voices sing to their hearts in the wild. For farmers must deeply and intelligently make music, dress beautifully while they farm, for that's how we were made, that's how we used to be. Let's find ourselves again. For beautiful farming is something utterly doable.

SPROUT SEVEN:
A Temple Called a Field

One of the aspects of the Agreement we can instantly put back into action to ensure that our farming is not a casual unthinking diversion or an unwelcome plodding grind is to reionize our thinking language in such a way that the men and women in charge of beautiful farming become known to themselves, as well to the rest, as their family's agricultural priests, who in all they have to do by way of farming, do it as a spiritual service to the Holy in Nature in a temple called a field.

The very characteristic of the Agreement is that farming not only feeds our families, but must simultaneously by the same actions feed the Holy in the Wild by the *way* we go about it.

The first feature of this principle is how we build the very form of our gardens and fields where our plants shall be housed and live out their lives.

The fields and garden must be laid out as a place to house what gives us life; they are to be known as plant villages in which each diverse group of growing things has a family house: its section of the garden.

As people, we live in hamlets or towns, cities or villages, and our fields should exist as parallel villages where the plant half of our being is given a home. Sacred plant cities, temples where we as spiritual farmers care for our parallel souls as plants, where as respectful visitors, beautifully dressed, and filled with the delicious speech that is the only language spoken there, which along with the motion of our forks, shovels, hoes, and hard work, we help to maintain the daughters of the Wild we keep alive there, whose children we eat to keep our children and ourselves alive. When we enter the Temples of our field, its intentional form reminds us of how the way we speak, the way we sing and directly address the plants as we cultivate them, makes a difference in the health of both plants and ourselves as set forth in the Agreement. This wakes us up to what our Indigenous Souls already know, that the Holy presence that is the vitality of the plants around us holds the natural side of our beings, and by farming this way, our wild half remains vital as well as what feeds us.

When you grow a new crop, their neighbors, the other plants, must be formally introduced, and a new "House" built to welcome and give them an equal "throne." Otherwise the plants will fight or join forces and revolt. When they fight or rebel, nothing grows; like war everywhere, everything dies.

The architecture of many ancient farming peoples had fields so elaborately intricate and sprawling that archeologists have themselves thought them to be human villages, for they were laid out horizontally to resemble in every detail the wall-less foundations of the people's own residential districts. Some of them can be seen today, and they go for miles and miles. They were the cities of the plants.

Each plant group has its own *stetl,* its own ghetto, in which the ever-changing family compounds vary from year to year. They can be labyrinths, or meandering terraces, or flat, mysterious, rock-lined, spiraling precincts whose select stones shine like agate jewels when moistened. Just as long as it's a beautiful village, all forms are good. This village doesn't have walls exactly, but inverted foundations, because in essence the major part of living for plants is in what the indigenous world calls "the other world," or underground inside the dark earth. The plant city is a bustling underground city of micro-beings, nutrients, and an environmental wildness very barely comprehensible to those who love walking around on top of it in the world of air. So basically the plant village we see is actually, for the plants, their rooftops.

The forms these plant villages can take throughout the world constitute a vast subject matter. In some tribes these include a lot of finely tuned, directional and horizontal particulars according to native calendars and star and planet positions. But for now it is best to start simply, and all the rest will arrive more legitimately from your own ancestral largesse and your Indigenous Soul.

When you garden this way, you are cultivating the sky of the soil, the roof of the plant city, and you should make the outlines and forms equal to the beauty of the home your souls might love to live inside of. Our Indigenous Soul. Even if the house you live in is not your heart's desire, the plants are your soul's regeneration and can have a town exactly like they want. That way, at least half of you will be happy without fail.

Now build a beautiful precinct in your garden, a special "palace" for all the plants you designate as weeds, for the animals you call intruders, and the birds you fear will finish it all off. Here you cultivate a couple of all the plants you grow out in the rest of your plant temple city and promise you will not harvest any of it, leaving them for the wild things. Where

I grew up, this precinct was called the "bear's" field, and it was laid out as a mounded spiral.

This part of the temple is for the "in-laws": Nature. It is only proper the wild earth gets a cut of the crop, for we already get more than we deserve if we even get half a carrot. It is here that one of your shrines will be located; it is for all intents the "belly button," the origination Home for the plants; for of course the ancestors of our crops are what people call weeds. It is here you sing and play the musical prayers that the Holy in the wild in every seed needs to hear. Through this "belly button" of wildness the rest of the garden city is fed, so all plant precincts must connect through boundaries that run like the arterial conduits in a leaf. Pattern your fields after various leaves; in that way your entire plant city is a plant.

The reason people are in the habit of planting in rows is a by-product of the need for production and the use of standardized mechanical equipment based on the wheel. But the ancient methods of growing seed plants is so varied worldwide that it has to be assumed all the forms come from the Holy in the Wild herself and have always been a part of the Agreement, for very few are concerned with straight parallel rows.

Almost all native cornfields in the place of Her origins, in Mexico and Guatemala, before the advent and interruption of Europeans, were planted in one giant spiral starting in the center and moving out clockwise. In many tribes some of the corn's wild ancestors were always planted on the northern edge of the corn patch so as to recross and revitalize the over-domesticated corn again with what modern agriculture considers an intrusive weed that contaminates production. But it boosts the health of the plant and the people in the long run.

In New Mexico, in the Pueblos, various flowering plants, poisoned as weeds by American farmers, are still intentionally sown in the same hole alongside corn kernels, for both plants came to those tribal people as boy and girl twins with the original agriculture from the Holies. Of course the bees that frequent these beautiful-smelling wild red morning glories also more thoroughly pollinate the corn in a way beyond the comprehension of mechanical geneticists, ensuring that each corn plant does not just self-pollinate. The same goes for the ancient beans and squashes as well, interspersed in the forest of corn plants.

Beauty of form has a lot more to do with the Holy and with the well-being of people, animals, and plants than the modern mind wants to accept, and also has to run according to the land, for there are low points, hot points, underground flows, windy grooves, and, usually what a person isolates as "his" or "hers" is of course a fragmented piece of a bigger reality according to which all the beauty of our field architecture must go with as well.

It has to be accepted that the form of one's field or little garden is not there to please us, but to please the plants and the Holy in the Wild. Of course there is nothing wrong with it pleasing the farmer, but in the sacred architecture of beautiful farming, the labor and use of human ingenuity to create a mysteriously rich and otherworldly form of agricultural housing for our life-sustaining plants are small payment for the gift of the Daughter of the Wild, who is the vitality of the seed: our food and fiber.

SPROUT EIGHT:
The Majesty of Decay

Through the Agreement, the wild Divine, whose own mansion is the entire flowering Earth, maintains that if humans are going to have houses and villages, then their mutual grandchildren—the domesticated plants—must live in a parallel way: in beautiful plant villages, and not grown like plants imprisoned in a concentration camp of vegetables, or an agricultural mine to extract soulless grain.

One of the prominent physical features of old human settlements living outside imperial domination all over the world has always been the obvious presence of man-made mounds of varying dimensions and shapes, that have arrayed the edges of villages in a very specific directional placement.

If, indigenously speaking, our towns and villages contained these ever-present mounds, then the sacred plant villages of our farms and gardens must have had their own versions of these hills as well, in and around their beautiful layout.

Variously identified by such unceremonious terms as trash mounds, ash piles, or refuse heaps, they have been traditionally treasured by modern archaeologists, who very diligently trench, scour, and screen the varying strata of their depth of centuries for what people discarded to determine a million important legacy details of the lives of otherwise forgotten peoples. On the other hand, for the peoples who built them (and there are a number of tribal people who still live by this principle), these mounds are nothing less than temples dedicated to decay; they are sacred compost heaps.

No matter which culture or people explain it, if they still maintain the old vision and agreement to the Holy in Nature, then these mounds are never viewed by them as dumps, landfills, or locations to remove unwanted "trash" from sight. They are sacred homes that are well within sight, and in the village embrace where everything that has "run its race"—animal, vegetable, clay, metal, and any broken thing—can dimensionally enter again the "heaven" of macro-awareness, in that journey through the molecular and organic reorganization that all things must travel at death to continue their participation in the bigger life as vital particles in the next regenerating form of beings sprouting back into view, that are fed by them and absorb them all. Many tribal people buried their dead in these Holy mounds as well. Often those with a custom of cremation added their beloveds' ashes into the ever-present wood ashes of their cooking fires and then to the mounds to join the molecular ocean of nutrients freed by the Lords and Ladies of Holy Decay who reside in the pile and regard it as their Temple Mansion.

It is of the utmost importance for all people to remember and recognize that we all descend from tribal village people, who until forced out of this indigenous institution by the overpopulating, power-gathering political-domination of mega-civilizations, and that these "compost heaps" were not only regarded with reverence, but were in most cases the actual physical locations of the most sacred temples and shrines.

They could not invent plastics, polymers, toxic processes, or chemicals because these four or more directional "landfills" of any village were temples to feed and promote decay as a Holy thing to bring back life, not unwanted locations to hide the toxicities of the failure of unsustainable undirectional entertainment culture and the bad nonspiritual farming that pretends to fuel it all. Nobody today has ever heard of a beautiful dump, because the detritus and waste of what is discarded today cannot be made beautiful or healthy in an unsustainable, synthetic, chemical-dependent culture.

But in real cultures, because the richness and vitality of the organic nature of the entire world is still, as it has always been, utterly dependent on the "element" of decay after the logical death of animals and plants who, by their deaths and decomposition, make available again to the legacy of living seeds and of running, jumping, procreating animals, the vital nutrients, micro elements, organic functions, oxygenated carbon matter, and minerals, the capacity of Decay to remake life has been deeply revered by all real peoples worldwide as the Holiest of all the Holies in Nature. While such can readily be mentally appreciated by all people today, it means nothing if the composting deities are not physically fed and our lives tangibly dedicated to their maintenance in a way that is not figurative or reduced to scientific equation. Places of Decay must be beautiful as well because for without the Big Holies of Decomposition who live there, all life would cease.

The miracle of seeds is that all they become through growth makes more seeds to feed other "seeded" life, including humans, but the bodies of the plants and the bodies they sustain also die to not only feed the living, but all they feed must promise to die as well, and every being that once walked, talked, chirped, kissed, hugged, hunted, swam, flew, flowered, or dreamt must also feed the next generation of each other as living seeds again resprouted and nourished by each other's dead, physically transformed remains.

All spiritualities, especially indigenous ones, not only come from this understanding but also live physically immersed in it without allowing this tangible knowledge to become reduced to metaphysical metaphor. It is a reality whose spiritual depth cannot be used to rationalize an unsustainable synthetic existence.

While the complexity of tribal and village designations of which ancestral lineage of villagers "belong" to which mound widely varies worldwide, in almost every case on the summit or immediately in front of some of the bigger mounds, a small beautiful shrine sits. Usually formed of natural unadorned stones, sometimes it is an actual house, its very placement and architecture being the architecture of the "universe" itself, inside of which a "throne" or a "bed," or a sacred shelf, is sheltered wherein the Holy Decay in Nature sits as a royal visitor for a feast who is then fed beautiful offerings of specific types that people have made for thousands of years.

The various Mesoamerican peoples call these Lords and Ladies of Decay colloquially "refuse eaters" or "filth eaters" but address them sacredly as the "Eaters of the Afterbirth," meaning of course that they, like mother deer, consume what our all-consuming presence in the world as a birth has left behind, which they, like all mothers, convert into new life. The feeding of these Lords and Ladies of Decay who live in the sacred compost mounds was a major part of the original agreement made by our ancestors with the Holy Wild.

Besides all the cornhusks, feces, ashes, pumpkin vines, hut sweepings full of urine, bones, vegetable leftovers, broken pottery, broken stone and wooden tools, lots of fiber and utterly spent clothing, our offering of handmade beads, gifts of tiny carved jades, bronze, turquoise; or gold, feathers, minerals, sticks and fat; or pottery jars of food offerings merged directly into the matrix of the dust, ash, poop, and spent life of the compost temple, for the original form as any offering was always smashed, scattered, untempered, or dismembered into the pile so as to assimilate directly into the "digestion" of the Holy Decay. Like ourselves, whose hands and the gnashing teeth of our ever-hungry mouths tear the world to bits to serve our needs and fill our bellies, we now in ritual, instead of consuming, use our teeth and hands to help those Holies in Nature to chew up and digest our gifts to them. By their dismemberment, our offerings disappear into stomachs of the Holy in Nature through the maws of the Holy Decay, just as the gifts they make to us of the growing edible world always disappear into our lives and bellies as we eat them up.

From these piles, these sacred places of decay, ash, charcoal, carbon, and of course earth renewed, was taken up onto the backs of the people and hauled directly to their planting fields, the sacred plant villages to feed the seeded domesticated plants. Accompanying the newly made compost were shards of pottery, undissolved beads of offerings, and a myriad other bits and pieces of village life besides the decomposed ancestral "earth." For this reason the fields were as full of the comforting and interesting detritus of everyday life that have for the last thousands of years been the village pottery scatter itself upon which all indigenous villages are still perched. Anyone living in Mesoamerica, South America, Turkey, Africa, Southeast Asia, India, the Middle East, and parts of Europe, right in and on the ground one can daily caress beneath their toes in any corner of their villages pot shards from pots shattered in the course of a continuous human presence anywhere from six days previous, mixed equally with pot shards containing the fingerprints of their makers from six years previous, sixty years previous, six centuries previous, or even millennia previous. This is the democracy of the physical, tangible nature of the memory of Holy Decay in an intact indigenous tribe, for all stories happen simultaneously composted into then, now, and forever, cyclically feeding nonstop their details to the world to become fertile compost whose stories, like soil nutrients, keep our souls as fertile as the trash mounds, feed our fields and our bellies. Odd that such well-proliferated majesty of the generosity in the natural course of things should have been lost to us and no longer regarded as ritually important to us all today.

This is another seed of spiritual comprehension we must keep alive. Those who would remove the spiritual from compost and decay and, in a sarcastic tone, reduce them both to a simple mechanical function, are as toxic as the chemical food they are trying to avoid. We should compost our own hatred of the real mythic nature of the human soul and indigenous capacity for happiness and find the ornate treasure of the spiritual reality of decomposition.

That delicate DNA in all living beings can only live on by its immersion or replanting back into the dead and decayed substance of its predecessors' DNA process with a spiritual tangibility that must be given something more than our constant taking. Farming as an indigenous spirituality of seeds is not something that happens by sitting around meditating on theory; it is a spirituality of active offerings and a spirituality of eloquence, beauty, rhythm, subtlety, and sweat.

People are not depressed, warlike, or mediocre by nature. We are ecstatic, delicious, beautiful, and capable of brave grief over the inescapable reality of having to kill to continue consuming and living. These things make it imperative to give gifts and grand human offerings to keep the Agreement to feed the Holy in the Seed and the Holy Decay in a world kept alive by both.

SPROUT NINE:
The Body of the Plants City

Nowhere can we learn so quickly and clearly the reality of how entirely vital the eternal presence of the cycles of Decay and Decomposition is to the simultaneous and parallel revitalization of domesticated plants, animals, and true human culture than through what it takes to grow food as a farmer, in particular when approached in a spiritual fashion as the Temples of Sacred Cities of Plants that all indigenous plantations are.

Along with the wild and Holy earth, nothing in the world has been more misconstrued, obscenely interrupted of natural precedence, and unintelligently removed from its deeply revered, deified, high spiritual rank than the indispensable physical and spiritual renewal that Decay and Decomposition accomplish for all cultures of live beings.

This enormous subject is *the* subject when it comes to continued life on Earth.

In its self-biased assessment of human culture, the modern world seems to define a culture in Decay as a culture in decadence, a culture that does not have the adrenaline exuberance of increased growth or commerce to keep expanding. In this bizarre microfocused thinking one wonders where this eternal "growth" expects to draw nutrients, input, and energy on a sphere if not from first composting the last growth into usable futures.

The modern notion of Decay is set in a frigid state in opposition to Health! A healthy culture is where business is "flourishing," culture is on the rise, everything is "coming up roses," etc., all of which again ridiculously disregards the unhealthy reality that such synthetic economic "Health" has never done anything but destroy the health of every acre and shred of the world's natural peoples, rivers, air, seas, open wild land, destruction that is not decay but the sterilization of culture.

Indigenous peoples the world over, all our ancestors included at some point, regarded Decay as an indispensible cycle in the maintenance of human health, plant health, animal health, and the welfare of all.

In this comprehension, whatever force has sickened and made unhealthy a culture, or made unwell an individual, or rescinded the vitality of its lands to produce, its animals' or plants' capacity to thrive cannot be surgically removed from the environment or eradicated through a "campaign" or program, but can only be internally "metabolized" and digested back down to its primal elemental particles to be then reorganized, reenergized, reionized, and naturally reissued back into what feeds and supports healthy living cultures of life. This is, of course, the basic definition of compost.

People seem to not have made much of the fact that most of the pyramidal, elliptical, and cylindrical so-called "temples" of the Mexican Tarascos, Texcocan, Tlaxcalans, Guatemala Highland Maya, lowland Pipil, ancient Turkmenistan, Margiana Oasis city people, the Armenian Highland Temples, those of the ancient Van, ancient Indian Dravidia, and a great deal of very old Europe (before Indo-Europeans) have as their initial inner and original form small shrine-like edifices filled utterly by compost that comprised the original "trash" mounds of the earlier agricultural phase of their people. The later "Temples" were successively layered over for hundreds of years and sometimes millennia to the present in accordance with the "expansion" of the cultures, though of course abandoned to start over again when the cultures were "digested" and decayed back into smaller, more sustainable cultures with "trash" mound temples once again! All of these peoples' impressive temple edifices enshrined a previous cultural incarnation of their original culture represented by old trash mounds hidden inside their cores!

Where I grew up, the capacity of those sacred composting mounds to remake life by "digesting" what was worn out, dead, broke, or no longer relevant from a previous time made these mounds understood as the alimentary canal of the culture and the plant "city," while the shrine that stood there was and still is called the "mouth."

Instead of removing the motion inherent in decomposition and petrifying Decay as some rigid unchanging undesirable state such as "social stagnation" or just a pile of stinking garbage that we want shuffled out and away from our sight, we'd do better to understand Decay as the Holy's natural built-in revolution of ideas and nutrients of both spiritual and organic, earthly dimensions.

The Husband of the Holy in the Wild is Holy Decomposition. Cultures need not disintegrate and disappear from constant warfare if they accept as natural the organic capacity to decompose in order to resprout themselves renewed and smaller from a strong remembered seed of culture from the composted past of what they used to be.

In any case, to farm spiritually, you must know how to ritually feed the married couple of the Holy in Nature and Holy Decay to keep the farm and culture of your family simultaneously viable. To do this means you must continually make compost and have a beautiful shrine to feed Decay right in front of that hot beautiful mound.

While a lot of modern people appreciate the idea of composting and all its nuances, often erroneously thinking that this is somehow a new advanced idea of the highly evolved, instead of the oldest idea advanced, it seems fairly impossible for a modern person to reorganize their mythless, pseudo-rational, computer-battered mind into wanting and accepting composting garbage mounds as containing the literal steaming presence of the most powerful deified force as anything but an interesting mental game they can switch off like a computer screen.

Do not laugh, for today in New Mexico alone over nineteen Native American Pueblo tribal towns still maintain these mounds, which are revered in just the same way by a collective population of over thirty thousand people of tribal descendency who mostly work "white man" jobs in mostly unsympathetic production-oriented non-indigenous environments, but who continue to understand that the inner magic of decomposition's eternal presence in these thousand-year-old "trash" mounds is at the core of all health and renewal, for which they ritually "feed" a host of holy beings that reside therein.

But modern people are stuck living right in nonindigenous environments that they think of as Home but which are unsympathetic with their real Indigenous Souls, and therefore can never really go to a "real" home at night where people understand such mounds as filled with the literal presence of Divine Providence.

So if we can't keep an indigenous life going in our homes, apartments, or modern lives, then perhaps in our gardens, farms, or fields we can live more intactly while tending our plants and our own souls as plants whom we welcome inside the sacred city of our spiritual gardens.

And to do that we could follow along with some more old indigenous ritual-thinking that says if your garden or some central portion of your organic farm is a temple city for the plants, then all the plants are the diverse members of a village that is a Tribe, and as a tribe it has a "collective" body like an individual organism.

This Garden Body has a heart, lungs, liver, limbs, ribs, a spine, a head, and of course a voice. The garden's voice is the songs of toads, crickets, all the birds, the rush of rain, and the rustling of plant leaves in the wind. The garden's lungs are her leaves, and the heart that portion of the garden you have left uncultivated for the wild animals and "weeds" to do as they please. It is in this "heart" that you have included a small rock shrine as a place to leave offerings to feed the Holy in the Wild. This is called the throne of the Divine in Nature.

The mouth, esophagus, stomach, liver, pancreas, and intestinal tracts live in your Sacred Garden City Body as your compost pile!

As a Priest Farmer you require a place in which to ritually feed the Holy in Nature, and this is the shrine in the "heart," so it is called the Heart Throne. There is no better place to ritually feed the Divine Power of Nature's digestion and revolution of organic matter than the beautiful little temple you have arranged in front of your main compost heap.

It should never be moved again if possible, and no modern tools or substances should be employed in its construction, no concrete or nails, and no metal tools.

Placed either on the very summit of a large old-time "trash mound" compost heap or immediately at the southern base facing south, this shrine can be made in one of several styles, but the best to begin with is probably an arrangement of twenty beautiful, naturally smooth stones the size of a sheep's head with one large one in the back of what ends up as a kind of horseshoe with a southerly opening called a door.

Perfectly formed circles with no openings in them give a lot of natives the willies because they are bad luck for anything except the trapping and incarcerating activities of people with evil intentions. Elliptical, open-ended enclosures are good, even cubes, rectangles, and squares, but just as long as the enclosures are open with a doorway.

This little temple at the base of your wonderful plant-feeding compost pile is called "the mouth throne," and the rocks are its teeth into whose life-metabolizing mouth the Farmer-Priest leaves his or her offerings to feed the Lords and Ladies of Decay and Decomposition. It is also here that people come to leave their failed attempts at life to decompose into something out of which something better can sprout.

It is here at the Heart Throne and the Mouth Throne that the Farmer leaves her or his gift each time he or she enters the sacred field of the garden.

Over time all types of offerings accumulate, scattered in and around both shrines. No one ever removes any offering left by any Farmers, as this is the same as wounding the Holy, the plant, and the land. No one ever sketches or photographs the shrines or their offerings because, in trying to preserve the image, the gift of offerings that must disintegrate over time no longer decomposes, its image frozen. Modern people hate this rule. Native people love it. That's how it is.

You've already stolen your entire existence from the Holies, and by making images or recordings of "sacred" places or songs means you don't want Gods to have anything of their own; you want to have your cake and eat it too. Offerings and temples can't be preserved as images. To be sacred, they have to disintegrate.

The Holies don't know us by our successes but only by our gifts freely given and never preserved for our own desires.

The Ladies and Gentlemen who garden in this way are called Priests, not because their plantings are Temples, which they are, but because unlike our predecessors who didn't care, the Priest Farmer is fully aware and educated that his growing of domesticated plants and food descends directly from the original insult committed by humans against the Holy Wild in Nature. Because the Farmer goes about unnaturally reorganizing both the originally wild land and originally wild plants, now both domesticated, forcing them to grow according to human whim, then when they are delicious and ready, the Farmer Gardener is responsible for taking their lives and feeding their "executed" substance to maintain and feed the human presence on this earth by consumption of food and fiber plants, the Farmer Priest knows of course he or she wants to make certain that we never lose our awareness of where all our sustenance comes from, and therefore feels the relief of the possibility of maintaining a friendship with the source of all our food by his or her maintenance of the ritual and spiritual courtesy of the old "marriage contract" or Agreement with the Divine Wild, which includes offerings at the beautiful mouth and heart of the sacred architecture of the Plant city.

For most people the old rituals detailed in any agreement their own ancestors must have had with the Wild in Nature have gone underground and may only exist unrecognized as some leftover inexplicable belief or taboo in the family. But our general desire to actually know these things for what they are and our wanting to have a way to "Feed" the Holy in Nature in a tangible nonsacrificial way may slowly cause us to refind ourselves as real human beings.

By the doing, this laboring, a gift-giving, spiritual, food-growing person understands the gorgeous spiritual enormity and force of even the smallest garden and its central place in real human culture.

SPROUT TEN:
Offerings—Farmers as the Jewelers of Vitality

Contrary to what we have become over the millennia, from some-where beyond our consciousness, people are still capable of sprouting a peaceful magnificence and the substance of real beauty. The Tzutujil Maya were like people everywhere: some were grand, some betrayers, some bigheaded, others conniving, but all were prone to hav-ing an expertise in one area or the next, for all had careers for which entire families had been known for centuries—as expert mat makers, or canoe carvers, or weavers, or embroiderers, house-builders, stone cutters, and many many others, all with their own spiritual ritual responsibilities to the tules, or to the stones, or to the wild cotton, or to the trees, and so forth. But no matter what they were known for, every single adult Tzutujil man and woman considered themselves to be Farmers. By definition, farming was neither a choice nor a career, but was what it meant to be human.

The Tzutujil even called the entire gathered council of the old princi-pal men and women of the sacred hierarchy—a very culturally educated, revered, erudite bunch, to say the least—as the *"Ajsmajmá S'cat Mulaj,"* or "wielders of the planting stick complete and gathered," which means, "the entire body of Farmers."

It was they who taught me that all farmers had to be priests in charge of feeding the vitality of the Holy Wild in the seed and Holy Decompo-sition through their presentation of specifically designated offerings at their respective field shrines called collectively *"warambal jai"* or "resting temples," places where all Holy things sat like kings and queens and received their "feasts of beauty" from the people.

While we humans ate food—the bodies of the children of the Holies and the bodies of the Holies themselves as plants and animals—the Holies ate the beauty we could create with our unique voices and our unique hands. Human beauty that we promised and dedicated to the Holies was what we had to give as a feast. It was a feast of offerings.

For the most part it is only civilizations who "worship" deities that have everything and don't need the people. Indigenous people on the other hand don't worship, but feed and maintain God, like they do their children, like the Holies do for us. Neither do intact indigenous people resort much to sacrifice; they are more of an offering-gift type of people.

Farming Priests are an offering people. Sacrifices, on the other hand, are a familiar function of old-time civilization where people designate some living being like a bull to be killed a specific way, slaughtered to buy some favor, or as compensation for a trespass from a humanized deity. Whereas the bull's substance is shared and eaten by the people and the Holy gets the honor of it, indigenously speaking, the bull's death still needs to be accounted for as a spiritual debt to his own mother Deity, and so another sacrifice is called for.

This never-ending circle of "stealing from Peter to pay Paul" is not much different than the economy of padded stocks or the character of the modern nonsustainable system of credit, for it descends directly from the big sacrificial imperial civilizations of the past.

Because we are eternally and hopelessly in debt to what has always given and still gives us all life in every possible aspect, we are not, as spiritual farmers, trying to *even* our debt to the Holy, but trying to stay in our impossible debt to life in the most beautiful possible of ways, so as to feed the Holies with our beauty. Spiritual farmers therefore try to give "feasts and spiritual nutrition" to the Holies in Nature that don't "steal" from them to give it back to them, but actually try to make gifts that come directly from us, small as these offering feasts of gifts may seem.

But what is meant by an offering? Are offerings any old thing we want to give? What offering could a person of today without any remembered precedent leave for the Holy beings of the Wild or the Lords and Ladies of Decay?

First of all, an offering should be small and beautiful: something that nature cannot make, but something the Divine, the diversity in wild nature wants or even needs but cannot themselves create. It cannot be something perfunctory, convenient, easy, lazily made, or purchased. The Holy's got warehouses full of that offered-up mess called civilization. Offerings must be beautiful but capable of eventual disintegration, something that merges nontoxically into the ecosphere, something that no humans will end up possessing. Offerings must not be given with a motive of spiritual investment or trying to get something back for humans, not even health or welfare. Offerings are gifts for what we have already been given: life. Offerings are the natural function of a much-atrophied organ of human obligation that says we must give gifts to nourish and keep alive what gives us the gift of life. It is our nature to give gifts.

So what are these offerings made from? We humans who can cleverly accomplish so much are utterly incapable of creating anything at all whose prime material is not actually part of the very Body of the Holy in Nature we are trying to feed with our offerings.

Every paint, stick, mineral, liquid, everything comes from the very beings we would feed. We can't give seashells to the sea because the Holy Ocean made them; we can't give gold nuggets to mountains and rivers because the mountains and rivers made them—we did not. What then do we do to make an offering? What do we as humans have that Nature could possibly want?

One of the most prized gifts and at the same time least developed and actually ruined for people today is the general indigenous capacity for beautiful language whose eloquence and musicality are more sung than spoken so as to bring the world back alive with sound; just as the Holy grass's song is its growing and the song of Holy water is Her rush of spring rain in rivers, so our melodious and meaningful songs when indigenously rich revive the heart of what gives all things life.

You must slowly refind and create languages whose music is reserved only to feed to the sonar-digesting ears of the Holy in Nature. Never ever publish, record, or casually perform anything you would sing to feed the Divine, for then the language, the meaning, and the art of it all is no longer precious, its jewel-like substance defeated and sterilized. The Holy gets nothing from the attention we receive from the public, not even for how well we feed the Holy. However, these songs *can* be taught and passed down to the new generations maintaining the fields, but never secularized beyond the needs of the Holy. They must never be written or performed for people, only for the Holy in the shrines of Nature and

Decay, in our gardens, corrals, to the mountains, streams, clouds, pastures, milk cows, to the returning seeds as they appear sprouting, reincarnating out of the ground. Other people *can* and should hear such music if they too are feeding the Holy in the Seed.

Farmers have always been ritualists, and ritualists have to be musicians, musicians for the Holy in Nature. It is good to make music anytime, so sing all the time anyway. But still make special gift-offering songs for the Divine in Nature and the Holy Decay. This poetry is not for people, and the music is of the best and for the Holy only. Once played at the shrine for the Holies, the sounds disappear, echoing into the starving belly of the Holy nature that feeds us. That is why music, prayers, and eloquent language are so prized as offerings, because they disintegrate the second they are sung. That is why these offerings are never frozen in writing.

The other capacity we have for offerings lives in our magnificent hands with their opposable thumbs.

Our hands, and by extension all the machines we've invented to take the place of the capacity of our hands, are normally put to serve only human desire and "production" in all definitions, which at this point is just more rip-off of the Holy in Nature, for the Holy gets no nutrition from your blender, your motorcycle, or your home. It's all plunder, removed without permission, taken mindlessly with no offerings from the living body of the Holy.

This is a large subject: how to feed the Holy Decay and the Holy in the Seed using the same inventive tool-using instinct that humans normally use to mine and exploit the natural earth.

Probably one of the most antique offerings from our hands to the Holy in Nature, something still doable by us among the thousands of other possibilities and still prevalent in indigenous contexts worldwide, are those beautiful beads made of shell, hand-drilled with flint points and rounded on an abrasive stone with water. While the shell, the flint, and our clever hands we ourselves did nothing to create, a fact we must remember out loud when we sing out our prayer offerings to the shell and flint, what we honestly can do with these magnificent hands of ours can be a gift to the Holy in Nature. While the Holy in Nature made the shell, the flint, and the ingenuity of our hands, we can legitimately make a shell bead, and we can give it as an offering with our song.

It is after all, the hole in a bit of seashell that makes it a bead, and the hole that makes it precious. A bead is a hole defined, and that hole is considered a spirit mouth, which we fill with eloquent speech as part of the shell's old-time gift.

While drilling the bead with a flint point, rotating the wrist back and forth like the world's seasons with the sun and stars measuring it on the horizon, one must speak and sing eloquent, delicious gift words out loud. In this way the bead becomes a tangible version of the sung offering; the drilling becomes a prayer. The prayer actually becomes the Hole that you give to the Holy in the Compost, causing the beads to become a necklace for the great life-giving Mother of Decay and Rejuvenation. These beads are not strung, but given one by one like the notes of a song. As one note is fed out to the Holy, a bead is given; as the next one surges forth, then the next bead is given until all are gone. While singing the prayer of thanks, the beads are spent, and become a necklace for the Holy. The Old English word "bead" meant prayer.

These shell beads are always turning up. Found in caches on islands off South Africa and Indonesia, in caves of Europe, in South and Central America, in the African Sudan, dating as far back as fifty thousand years, they are still today as grand and prominent a gift offering to the Divine from many people in this world.

The people have always wanted and prized the jeweled aspects of such beads. Along the Danube in Europe, in Mesoamerica, Polynesia, Africa, Spain, and all along the Arctic, netted tunics, blouses, dresses, capes, and kilts solidly studded and strung with hand-drilled shell beads—especially those made with spiny oyster and purple clams—were the rage for thousands of years. These were not offerings but coveted jeweled dress. Nonetheless in the way we walk, talk, farm, hunt, and live in these jewels can feed the Holy if we do it right. On the other hand, when *we* drill beads to adorn the Holy in Nature with our difficult-to-make elegant holes made right in Her very own Oceanic-births-all-substance, we can remember constantly the Hole we make in Her universe when we pursue a living. By taking the ingenuity we normally reserve for clever human exploitation of our surroundings that makes our "Hole" in the natural world, we as offering makers can now use our ingenuity to feed and heal this grand thing of the wild and Holy Decay that we have spent centuries robbing and trying to outrun.

You cannot make real offerings unless an effort is involved; an effort that creates beauty. For instance, most of the shell-offering people of the world live hundreds and even thousands of miles away from the Holy Mother Ocean. Where I grew up, the pilgrimage to fetch shells was and is considered part of the drilling itself and made the offering that much more precious.

If offerings were made of any old thing or too conveniently created or effortless, then they would be hollow offerings, something made as an afterthought or a project. The thought that any dedicated person can and should accomplish the ongoing mastery of learning to make better and more beautiful offerings without "farming out" the responsibility to someone else is a simple but powerful antidote to the mediocre mind of the empire we all have conditioned in our heads somewhere.

Like farming well, we must get down on our hands and knees to the Earth and Ocean. Remember also that for every shell taken from the edge of the Great Woman Ocean, an offering must be given to make it not something simply mined and stolen. Without this, the offerings become a currency instead of a gift. This offering way of life is immense, but not expensive except in self-discipline, patience, and the natural spiritual eloquence of the human soul. The true Indigenous mind and heart can ride again by the life of offerings. Remember to keep all things simple but real and solid.

The shrine on the compost heaps must be sincerely sung to, wept over, and given the best creations we can make with our hands using the least environmentally ruining means of ingenuity and beauty at our command.

We can't hope to feed anything of the Holy by means of commercially mined stone or shell, or by drilling anything with an electric rotary drill with a diamond or carbide bit, because it will be the stone, the shell, the drill, the coal, the metal, the nuclear reactor, the pylons, all its parts that drive the electricity into the cables, and the purloined unritualized energy itself that needs more to be fed. Therefore all that unfed, unaddressed, enslaved energy and cadmium battery functioning can't make any offerings because the generational debt of the top-heavy expense is so spiritually depleted as to be worthless in gift value. Such a gift would, if pursued, need itself so many gifts to compensate its spiritual debt to the Earth as to begin to resemble mass sacrifice. So, it's better to stay small and patient.

Therefore the slow, the elegant, the eloquent, the delicious, laboriously generous human effort of a deliberate prayer-made perforation can be a real offering. Less destructive and more valuable as gifts are such offerings to those generous life-giving Holy things that sit in your compost temple.

Your little perfectly formed beads with hourglass holes filled with eloquent language will be big enough to start with, and light-years ahead of what any frenetic, mechanically tortured part of the Holy Earth could ever be.

Farmers therefore must become musicians, poets, and poetesses and the drillers of beautiful jeweled beads, feeding the Holy in Nature to grow plants and feed the people.

> Farmers are Jewelers of Words, Adorners of the Holy Vitality,
> Feasters of Nature, Givers of Gifts, the Memory of the Culture,
> The Bards and Singers of Grief and Beauty for the Origins we
> have lost,
> Turning All into Food for the Holy in the Seed.

SPROUT ELEVEN:
Kiss Your Pumpkins—Sacred Pantry Temples

One of the most universal sections of the Agreement with the Holy in the Wild are those tribal rules and taboos that explain the respect and type of treatment we must show to food returning from the field to our houses, how it is to be killed or harvested, stored, prepared, and eaten.

This has all the world to do with how well a people know how to cook and eat. People who eat only crops grown for winter storage probably don't cook or eat as well as they might. The reasons for this can usually be laid at the feet of a continued sense of desperation, derived from civilization's emphasis on food production sold to people who don't grow food, instead of a spirituality of beautiful sustenance in which all its people can participate.

When production sets in, the Agreement instantly begins to fade; I remember reading several different post-conquest colonial writs posted to their superiors in Spain, by both clerics trying to collect church alms and secular bureaucrats in charge of levying tribute. All of them complained bitterly how the agricultural Highland Mayan people, the Seed People they'd been sent to administrate, "used up" at least forty to fifty percent of their annual agricultural surplus in ritual "feeding," feasts, and what seemed to them "time-wasting orgies" of dancing, drinking, and exorbitant pagan gift-giving to Deities the Europeans could no longer see, making it impossible to raise any profit, much less taxes.

Of course, what the imperial invaders couldn't see was that intact human beings, including their own long-forgotten ancestors, instead of taxes, gave gifts called sumptuous rituals to the Holy that truly support us all. In this way they would never swell big enough to indulge in empire, preferring sanity and an intimate knowledge of their life's debt to Nature while hoping to become worthy enough in life to die into a complete usefulness as echoing spiritual nutrition back into the arms of the Holy Decay of the Natural Earth. All real signs of health.

Real indigenous farming and eating have been stigmatized by the social "development" people as low-tech, self-sufficiency farming because non-machine-dependent, real hand farming does not involve simple single-harvest standardized production and therefore cannot make money. It can only make food and health. Real farming can't make money, only food.

Spiritual farming relies not on single harvests, where seeds are mechanically sown, the plants tended, then whatever the plant makes is harvested in a single gathering at the end of its growing season. Spiritual farming, on the other hand, relies on constant garden gleanings throughout the season, as well as several final general harvests, which also depend on superior knowledge of plants and food storage, fermentation, drying and other preparation, and the well-educated taste buds that are signs of real culture.

Single, large-harvest cultivation is a mechanical leftover from feudalism taken on by the industrial age, where huge cheap production makes cash for its producer to buy what he needs to keep up with the Empire.

Even commercial farmers today rarely eat what they produce; they buy their food at the big-box grocery like the rest of the suburbs, unless of course they are hip enough to have a kitchen garden on the sly.

You should not plant beets, then three or four months later harvest big old glumpy beets, then—singing the song of the Volga boatmen—sit around eating bad borscht all winter. Unless of course you really love being an oppressed serf again. Don't think just because your dreads have finally grown out, you don't pay taxes, you have all the dope you want, and you grow miles of one big ugly kind of onion, or droopy giant mediocre-tasting carrots, or you've canned up a hundred jars of garlicky giant baseball tomatoes, and turned piles of ball-and-chain cabbages into tons of kraut, that now you're farming.

Plant seeds whose origins you have learned, then learn how to eat the first sprouts, the next set of leaves, and every other stage of one and the next and how to cook them. A lot of people are finally learning again how to eat and cook beautifully all parts and aspects of plants, some even after the plants have frosted or frozen, and still managed to harvest winter keepers. If cultivated by a Farmer-Priest, the plant is not insulted but kept vital by being grazed,and this pruning is a pruning of our cultural souls as well to keep it awake and strong.

Corn plants, for instance, figure in a traditional Mayan diet from the time they are eighteen inches tall all the way to the very last stage. When combined with similar gleanings of other plants, there are subtly delicious foods always coming toward us. As the corn's life span progresses, increased gifts of unique types of food absent at all other times continue on until the main harvest is brought in formally and ritually. But these foods are only possible if one knows they can be made, and this is the magic of real nonproduction culture. All this pruning of the plant makes the remaining corn much stronger and able to run its race more beautifully than trying to keep and bring to ultimate production every possible ear. This kind of productive greed kills the Daughter of the Wild, like a woman forced to bear quadruplets every pregnancy. These delicious and power-fully sustaining gleanings throughout the growing seasons are called "the little feet of the field," or *the small food,* by the Tzutujil. Most Asian peoples are also experts on this eating of all aspects of a plant's existence.

But when your Big Food harvest does return, and the seeds return back from the sacred architecture of the fields back to your pantries, gran-aries, cellars, fridges, and into the hands of the cooks, then the returning Seeds, the Harvest, must be welcomed with as much wonder, genuine awe, and admiration as one would have for one's lost half who miracu-lously returned unexpectedly alive and well from the impossible struggle of regenerating themselves. Any other attitude kills the desire of the seeds to be around you. It breaks their hearts, the Tzutujil say, *'n camsaj Ruk'ux,* "it kills their heart-germ."

When we do our ritual farming well, our own souls return not only along with the seeds, but also in the seeds. Because souls are not simply single entities but entire unfoldings of natural dying and regeneration as cultivated by our culture's conscious toil and beauty, the seeds and souls when they return must themselves be fed and their refound majesty seated on their rightful "thrones" in our pantries or storage places.

When the harvest returns to us, it is not yet the time to feast ourselves, any more than the funeral of planting should be oblivious to the fact the seeds and our souls are going willingly to die in hopes of returning alive and multiplied to give life again to the children and the future of real human culture. This is what is at the core of keeping the seeds alive and must be done physically for years to comprehend and make happen. It cannot be thought into reality; it can only be done with work. And because real "seed" culture has been discarded from the "progress"-oriented world,

keeping this kind of seed consciousness alive in one's life can look somewhat like planting olive trees in an active warzone, a psychological war
going on within ourselves, where like olives that don't bear for a long
while, we must nonetheless continue to cultivate with the faith of seeds
that we are actually planting for a time beyond our own.

Natural people have never understood people who claim to be making
ceremonies of thanksgiving, to commemorate harvests by unceremoniously gobbling up the invited guests: the returning seeds, fruits, roots,
vegetables, and animals of the harvests, in feasts that only feed people.
This is not the agreement, for it gives nothing to the seeds.

The majesty of the returning Seeds must first be "seated" on their
rightful thrones, and with our showing of real gratitude through our songs,
prayers, offerings, beautiful aromas, and jewels, we should directly feast
these grandchildren of the Holy in the Wild once again revisiting our
home. By remembering their history out loud, and the miracle of a possibility of a future for humans contained in their little casements, farmers
should all together, without the modernists' banal unspiritual theatrical
tone, address the seeds with as much wonder and heart as you might a
missing sister or brother returning alive from an impossible disaster.

I remember the long lines of strong men young and old filing down
from their volcano-side fields with several tons of huge handmade-net
loads of the corn harvest weighing down their swaying backs, strapped
over their foreheads with tumplines; upon reaching that part of the village where the owner of the corn ears' family had their compound of
huts and granaries, starting to dance gracefully in unison as the musicians sallied forth from the courtyard and all the cooks and ladies, each
with their homemade copal burners swinging to the rhythm of the song,
with a loud sincere calling all the extended family welcomed more the
corn than the men, but the men too, welcoming and introducing the
corn in their returned status dancing in place for a while, then, with the
young assisting, lowering every load gently to the ground in a great
gathering of packages, the incense, prayers, and music still going. This
happened a thousand times every harvest in every household outside
every granary.

The people did not pray only to the Holy Woman of the Wild, or the Christian Converts to their God, but more directly to the corn herself as the Goddess's children, half-human, half-vegetation, were themselves sitting right there as corn after having miraculously returned from the invisible, like heroes returned from the dead, which is what they called them.

Kiss your corn, your pumpkins, your wheat, your tomatoes, chiles, your rutabagas; tell them how much you missed them and how happy you are to see their faces returned again.

Then in a parallel way, designate your storage bins, pantries, granaries, wherever the new harvest lives as a "palace" for the returned food. Dress up these places with beautiful draping. In the northern sector, there a tiny temple should sit. This is called the "throne of our food"! The seeds for future planting are placed in "state" here, for only they will see again the world as a plant, the rest relegated to losing their future as plants as they are transmuted into our own flesh and future as we consume them to sustain ourselves. Gratitude is the rule.

It is in this palace pantry the feast for the seeds is traditionally set up, but, lacking a pantry, the kitchen will do. But there can be absolutely no arguing. If you are not actually capable of being happy enough to see your seeds return, then you are worrying about the wrong things in life and living without a soul; not to mention the seeds will lose their "heart"; they will sadden and be no longer robust for you. For the seeds are your soul returned. Be happy about it.

When the seeds have been ritually fed, make the simplest, most antique foods from what was left from the *previous* years' harvests: the aged cheese, the old wine, the older grain, the last dried and frozen things harvested in the past, and let that be your thanksgiving feast. While you feast you must toast the new seeds who are filled with the honor of the life from the seeds of the disappearing past, disappearing into your belly.

Our fields have now become villages of plants and the living human soul, our compost heaps the regenerating graveyards of the plant village and sacred temple of offering to the genius of decay, and our pantries turned into palaces for the returning seeds and our souls. These storage rooms, as practical as they are, have also always been the location of much deep and beloved ritual for millennia, but subsequently trivialized for this universal function and actually eradicated in a lot of the world to the great detriment of peace and maintenance of sanity among real people. For all real people have forever had their tools and granaries deified with annual feasts to sustain the excellence of our dependence upon them for our well-being. Deified axes, shovels, knives, hoes, and bow and arrows are an active worldwide concern and still very much revered.

But it is also described by the Agreement, that often the killing of an animal had to done with a golden sword, or the wheat harvested first with a golden sickle before a steel one, or a root dug with a jeweled digger, or at least these tools of wood, steel, horn, bone, or stone were always addressed as being gold or jade or jeweled in order that the plant or animal losing its life was dispatched honorably and the tool's nobility maintained.

The story of agricultural Volga Finns who retained their natural spirituality in such proximity to Europe until the 1920s' bold, unhappy, mechanized stampede into the present age is a fine example to us of the grand understanding of keeping alive a sacred agriculture and a sacred pantry despite the noncomprehending minds of those surrounding cultures who have already lost theirs. These Chermiss and Voltiacs were not American Indians, Ibo, Esmalam or Hmong, Aboriginal Australians, Micronesians, or Tasaday but Euro-centered blond blue-eyed so-called "whites" centered in Europe, harried by other whites. Some of their descendants are still with us today.

Once nomadic reindeer herders, they settled of their own accord long ago in what is now western Russia in scattered homesteads spaced out in numerous wet grassy river valleys to grow grain. Continuing to wear their lime-bark shoes, they adopted gorgeous wool and linen clothing, stopped milking deer, and started milking their newly adopted cows and sheep in a great abundant life.

After becoming expert woodworkers, developing an elegant, ornate, and expertly made series of barns, outbuildings, and houses for each family-centered clan, they nonetheless did not for centuries abandon certain of their original nomadic shelters. These they maintained as sacred houses for their farming tools and milking pails.

Originally in their nomadic reindeer days, each family maintained a specific hut inside of which all the family Deities, protectors, and generating powers of the lichen, trees, snow, and herds resided, and were literally "fed" there by the head woman of the household. Inside this beautifully adorned nomadic hut resided a very ancient and revered milking pail made of birchwood for milking the deer, upon whose every part and function they depended. Inside this pail all of the deity forms were sat and bundled. The hut was the family temple, the so-called dolls in the pail actually bundles of ancient ancestral sacred objects wrapped in hide and felt and given faces in order to have mouths and ears to "feed" these deified phenomena ritually. The pail itself was a deified tool and was a living "throne of the Holy in Nature."

When the tribe was on the move, the hut traveled dismantled, with all the Gods in the Holy Providing Milk Pail bound to a fancy painted bell-covered sled, hitched to a team of reindeer specifically dedicated to that Holy office as vehicles to the Holy and dressed in adorned harness, spirit bells, brass rings, and other amulets, the precursors of the reindeer of the Nordic Santa Claus.

At some point, for unknown reasons, the people stopped nomadizing and overnight became a wealthy, well-organized and successful, settled, grain-growing, milk-churning, cattle-raising people. But their historic nomadic God Houses and sleds were not forgotten, only enlarged and redefined, some as sacred pantries for cheese and milk storage and others as grain sheds. In these sacred houses the Holy Milk Pail continued to be the throne for the family deities along with all the new Holies of the rye, wheat, hay, and spelt seeds, and the cattle upon which they now were suckled by, added in. Like the Holy Grail, the milk pail was the Holiest of all the tools, for from it all the souls that caused their providence resided and could themselves be ritually fed, with their unique clear ringing string music, poetry, ritual gifts, and feasts. In those days every family had their own "Grail." Only later did these grails flee and hide themselves from the minds that can no longer understand this Divine reality.

And life went on, food came in, was enthroned, feasted; and a large ancient ritual spirituality continued in sacred groves, for the wild, in the velds at the edges of their fields, the house shrines and the shrines in the granaries where the milking pail now strapped in silver and gold hoops set with jewels, and with lids expertly hand-carved with all the old animal gods of the people, still sat in the north corner of the sacred pantry hut in full reverence, fed by the head lady of the household. As part of the old rituals, actual milk was milked into their sacred buckets during certain ceremonies to feed the Holies.

Then sometime in the mid-nineteenth century, Christian missionaries, some Lutheran, others the Russian Orthodox precursors of "Big Government" of the day, began showing up.

They forced all these people to burn and destroy all evidence of what the clerics saw as "pagan gods" in order to dominate and cause these natural wealthy people to assimilate into the "greater Czarist Empire," and of course to annex their land for "production" for the onward motion of the empire and the church.

At the militarily backed enforcement of the vehement Christian church officials, these people's Holy pantries were destroyed as well, and new, functional, square, Russian-style wooden sheds constructed instead.

Ironically, though the gods had been burnt, the old nomadic sacred pantries burnt up, the new sheds with all the appearances of regular rundown outbuildings still had a fine birch wood shelf against which still leaned all the deified tools and behind them an empty milking pail, with no straps, jewels, or carvings.

In their last forays to ensure religious compliance to the one-god imperialists of nineteenth-century Russia, the church priest and secular bureaucrats were delighted upon district inspection to see only milking implements, shovels, farm tools—no gods and no evidence of any "pagan" reverence for Nature.

But even after all that stupidity and spiritual terrorism, these amazing people continued living in a vital non-Christian spirituality that remained intact and uninterrupted for almost another century. For what the clerics didn't realize was the fact that the same deep and brilliant sanity of these spiritual farmers to be able to adapt to the strangeness of settled abundance after millennia of the original integrity of the harsh natural freedom of nomadizing was still alive. Both as spiritual, wild seed nomads and settled seed people, to them the otherwise functional Milking Pail was still the "throne" of what had always been and still was Holy. Like the Grail, when the Christians looked inside, they saw nothing: just the bottom of the bucket. For them the old Gods had fled; for the Volga Finns the Gods were still there in fine form, and the Pail still Holy.

Because the Pail was the throne of all Divine Food, throne of all the seeds that make the grass and grain that fed the cows that made the milk that suckled and gave strength to their people, the ritual beauty of the Holy Milk in the Pail made it so the people could still "see" what they knew continued to reside in their divine milking pails. As the pails remained, the milk-shed pantries continued to be temples. While the priests left thinking they'd won, ritual life for the Volga Finns went on clandestinely feasting the Holy in pantries and groves for these grand people until the 1920s, when the Bolsheviks and later Stalin's goons mowed the culture to stubble in a violent deportation program, shackling their greatly cared-for land and precious milk cows to the vast state farming enterprise. The Soviets' gigantic mechanization of their collectives dedicated to grain production for the New Empire was something assiduously studied and subsequently copied by American production farming corporations in the 1920s. The world over, the Soviets were the most admired nation for their "efficient" farm machinery by all modern technocrats during and before World War II.

All that having been said, I say, we today can still have the equivalent of holy milking buckets, spiritually fed saws, ornate mythic shovels, and unseeable goddesses enthroned in our beautiful but still practical work sheds of our gardens and beautiful ornately carved food pantries with "thrones" for our food, where we feast the Holy in the Ground.

Our own bodies and souls are all descendants of people everywhere who have experienced earlier or later what the Volga Finns went through and finally lost and forgot. While we may have all the appearance of a "regular," standardized, twenty-first-century citizen of a pseudo-culture of noise, spiritual oblivion, and unearned comfort, from somewhere in there I say we can still sprout into legitimate, alive feeders of the Holy Decay in the compost, tend our souls as Holy seeds that can feed our families, and even feed the unseeing neighbors, both poor and rich, with a better, more powerfully nutritious, amnesia-lifting food. Even if those we feed can't see the Holy in the Wild, or the beautiful Mother of all life in the milking pail, we can still keep our agreement with what they can't see.

SPROUT TWELVE: Learning to Live Beyond Our Time—The Dead Must Feed the Living

When our fields are no longer monotonous grids of plant prisons, where seeds in rows of muck and mire are forced to produce the standard size of this or that in agricultural mines, but rather are sacred villages in whose mysterious, beautiful meander plant tribes flourish as the other half of our human souls; when our compost piles are no longer just hot cooking hills of garbage, worms, and tallied nutrients, but fascinating little temples where for generations of our leaving hand-drilled shell-bead necklaces, piles of sparkling gifts overflow into the lap of the Lords and Ladies of Decay and life-resurrecting reorganized failures; when our pantries, barns, granaries, food lockers, cellars, kitchens, sheds, and tools are no longer ugly, unadorned, lifeless, enslaved matter in servitude to the demands of housing and functionally extracting clumsy harvests of overgrown root vegetables and badly cooked food, but become richly thought of and well-adorned reception halls and small palaces housing beautiful shrine thrones that seat the majesty of our well-made beautiful food—the seeds returned from the dead, and the wilder plant half of our own souls—where we are given a place to sing the poetry that inebriates the Holy in Nature, and a place to cook food excellently and in ongoing ways that feed the neighborhood; when the farmer no longer feels obligated by society to a dress and speech code of hip mass-produced buzzwords, on- or off-the-grid techno twitter, bad clothes, and the bad theater of dirt and drudgery as inherent to the trade, and become like Bangladeshi rice harvesters, or Mru swindon farmers, or Mayan corn farmers, or Esmalen date pollinators, and turn this farming into a priest-hood of songs and mythologies for the tools, the stone, the ground, the seed, the flowers, animals, and the old human obligation of integral beauty that doesn't insult the plants and the Holy in the Wild with an ugly functionality, but feed and inebriate them with beautiful indigenous farming, then ...

Let the graves of our dead and past no longer be dead mechanical rows of starched mediocre protocol whose standardized synthetic husks feed no one in their entrenched placement as launch-pads away from the ground that fed them and become instead Spiritual Seed Banks, sacred repositories of every generation of wild ancestral plants, where we can renew and re-engender the viabilities of a genetic and spiritual future for our descendants both plant and human.

> When people came to the place where the Nart's graves were, they saw growing there corn, wheat, millet and barley which surprised them.
>
> What they were seeing there is the result of the following. When the Nart's heroes buried their dead, those who wanted to do so, sowed grain on the surface of the grave, some millet, others barley. That's where the seeds could be once again found. After someone died they brought seeds there as a sign of their grief. Don't we today, when some-body has died, bring food to the grave? That is the same thing that the Narts did when one of their number died. When somebody was dying, either someone's brother or relative, or somebody from the tribe brought a small portion of wheat seeds as a sign of grief. In another case it was millet, in a third, barley or oats. That is how these grains became known to the people of today.*

---

*John Colarusso, *Nart Sagas from the Caucasus* (Princeton, NJ: Princeton University Press, 2002), Saga 44, 182.

This excerpt is from John Colarusso's grand and important translation of several Caucasian tribal sagas whose tales of the Narts, a prehuman race of heroes, serve as amazing evidence of a type of widespread mythic culture that linguistically connects old Asia with Europe in a manner only previously conjectured.

This is only one of many possible examples of this most astounding ancient reality worldwide, in which tombs, graves, funerary mounds, and necropolises have been for millennia maintained as a prime and sacred source for open-pollinated, original, indigenous agricultural seeds for future generations.

The possibility that ancient grave sites in some parts of the world might be living seed banks, reseeding themselves for centuries, is something that seems to have escaped the scrutiny of most archaeological analysis: *kurgans, kirigsun,* the layered mounds and antique cemeteries of Eurasia, Greece, and of course the Caucasus, North Africa, Southeast Asia, Polynesia, Micronesia, and the Americas, wherein inside certain cultural settings such seed banks are still visible.

All people have stories that mention how the tragedy of the loss of their dead when buried sprouts back into life as a never-before-seen life-sustaining or vision-making plant or tree. But when digging in graves, scientists seem to have not bothered to recognize that what grows on the surface could have been reseeding itself for quite a while and, too busy to get past "now," they plough right below into "then." But the majesty of indigenous spiritual thinking is that the maintenance of the present life by the dead of the past is what life as a dead person is all about. The well-known adage "that was then, this is now" for the old Priest Farmer mind runs more like "that was then, and this now is fed by then."

That human grief for the loss of a loved one could be expressed through the planting of life-sustaining seeds on the graves of their beloved to maintain the genetic integrity of the future food planting of people not yet born is the actual spiritual DNA from which the growth of all peace must be cultivated. Real grief comes only from loving life so much that any loss is potentially a soul-devastating event unless with these types of ritual, grief can cause life to regenerate from the loss.

In most older Eurasian cultures, the actual physical human being converts at death into the same seeds that grow on the grave and which are almost always some species of grain or grass, such as rice, barley, oats, spelt, or various wheats or wilder plants. But for pastoral milk-drinking tribes, the ancestral grave mounds in which their ancestors were planted like seeds with their hats, clothing, furniture, harness, horses, tools, and everything ornately carved or covered in gold, silver, bronze, tin, pyrite, and more became the very steppe grass itself, a burial whose Grail-like providence subsequently put milk in the udders of their milking sheep, goats, cows, camels, and horses, renewing in the process both the Holy in the ground but also the welfare of their descendants who must eventually live well enough to do the same upon dying.

To have lived in such a powerful heroic fashion so as to accrue in the process sufficient fame and appealing ornate worth, such that upon dying, one's great "substance" taken as a whole dose of deliciousness fed the Holy in Nature. As the Holy ground herself consumed the deceased's hard-earned grandeur back into the "root," the grass that fed every being on the steppe was enhanced by the dead person passing.

Because one's death did so much to feed the living, death became a large percentage of a person's "existence," inspiring a lifestyle that made dying into a life-sustaining event.

The dead must feed the living if the living are to keep the Agreement with the Wild; otherwise human life has no meaning. In most cultures it has always been that the living must "feed" and maintain their ancestral dead in their "new" changed form. It is a more ancient thing that the dead are cultivated as life-giving plants and animals.

Graves and funerary mounds were never cultivated by the living to be harvested, but were actually the original plant and animal refuge: the seeds planted on the site or the animals released there at the funeral were required to be left untouched by all the living, in hopes they would revert to their original ancestral undomesticated forms as new landraces of open-pollinated seeds and animal types. Meanwhile the living descendants in every generation went on about their labors planting, replanting, harvesting, saving seeds, and eventually, in most cases, over-refining the plants, animals, and their personal lives in a direction distant from the ancestral seed and original cultural forms.

In this way, one's ancestor, having turned into living plants, at death remarried the "wild" by back-crossing with plants of their own predomesticated origins. The resulting offspring of this remarrying the wild by our ancestral dead, as opposed to the same plants among the living through domestication heading increasingly "away" from their wild state, did not domesticate further, but their offspring on the grave were "re-wilded" back into a more original state.

Though people did not eat or allow their own animals to graze off the graves, at some recognized point, generations later when they realized it was time, as determined by divination, after gaining permission to do so from the grave, the people went to gather and remove specific seed heads from the ancestral mound. The living descendants then planted these old-time ancestral seeds alongside their over-domesticated varieties of wheat, barley, rye, millet, etc., causing the past to remarry the present, by crossing them naturally by their proximity.

Though both seed types had the very same ancient origins, they had been separated by death and time into two distinct varieties, but varieties that also went in equal distances both backward and forward from the day the ancestor was buried. It was time breeding past time with new time.

These resulting crosses were always more viable and grander than either the old ones or the new and something impossible without these generations of critically enforced pulses of isolation and rehybridization.

Thus when old culture is remarried to the new, both the plants and the people's lives and bodies are renewed and made viable again.

Because the old grave plants have themselves "remarried" or crossed back with wild plants of their own grave-grown ancestors from years past, now freed from further domestication by the death of the person upon whose grave they have been planted, that the dead shall remarry the wild and thereby revitalize in some future time their own domesticated descendants is also part of the Agreement with the Holy in Wild Nature.

The result of these crosses cannot be matched by science, for without the spiritual reverence of the Agreement that accompanies them, any attempt to do so mechanically, while sarcastically discarding the old vision as superstition, always results in weakening the seeds and atrophies the vitality of a people who would treat it all as mechanical genetics.

This older type of hybridizing the wild past with the over-domesticated present is an old, spiritually based agriculture that results in the following seasons with an astounding variety of seed stock, and plants of such durability, diversity, and nutritional value that they are beyond anything old or more recent that life has ever graced us with.

This grave seed bank of plants remarrying the plants of the present to make plants of the future is one of the great secrets of spiritual reverence of keeping the seeds alive inherent in many cultural traditions, in which the life and death of people and plants are seen not as parallel but as one and the same. In the most literal way it is the coronation of the majesty of the indigenous inspiration that by merging with the wild in death, we create the viability of human future. This is what the Tzutujil meant by being an echo at death.

Could it be that any people today with Holy fields, pantries, and compost temples could become upon their deaths a bank of seeds of life-sustaining plants? Could their new earth home after their funereal "planting" into another form dimensionally revitalize a genetic future of plants beyond us all and sustain their descendants by merging in Death directly into the undying propensity of the Holy in the Wild to resurrect and revitalize their food plants and human seed culture from the atrophying effects of domestication?

This should not only be recognized as something better than the morbid, spiritually incomplete waste that death in the modern world presents: a life of flight and fear of the end sending us straight into the arms of a meaningless death; but just the thought of being something besides a casket and a frozen memory and something that is useful to the world in the death of a life well lived should cause the ears of our indigenous depths to prick up enough to at least reward us with a little more vision and sufficient courage to do more than mope, tremble, or escape a life worth living.

I think that the most useful thing for all of us here now in this world to do at this restless junction in history is to courageously find a way to stop running away from the gradual beauty necessary for a life of love and depth out of our constant unspoken fear of the specter of an imminent holocaust by weapons of mass destruction.

This fear has caused us to deliberately kill our future more tangibly than the thing we fear. With no hope for a future, this fear has hysterically inspired us to steal everything we can get from our children's future, wrecking the Earth, to just pointlessly roll around in it all numbed and half-awake in an unsustainable present.

As individuals we should instead become people who feed those living in the future, for then, at the very least we will have bestowed on our children's children a known, integral, spiritual origins beginning right this minute, an origins like the one we have lost, and much needed and never really had. In this way, we too can become worthy of the future, and our seeds will be kept alive beyond us.

And if the dead of our past become the seeds that revitalize the present, then each of us must do for those that come the same; for each of our families needs a place to lay their fawns in a time beyond our own, they need a House of Origins: a place to house our own future's belly-button stumps and a home for our seeds of Birth and Death and Birth again.

Chapter 21

The House of Origins

For millennia, we human beings have lived together as individuals inside families, as families inside bands of people, belonging to villages inside larger tribal affiliations, people who knew themselves to be living particles of elements in the multiple concentricities of the natural tribes of all the world's living things.

Kneeling on the earth at the feet of sky, stars, and water alongside the plants and animals, in all sorts of landscapes whose weather fed or killed according to the mind of Nature as she suckled her unborn dreams into tangible matter, for all those millennia, as people, we knew everyone, what they did, what they made, their quirks, their dangers, their beauty, *their* stories, *our* story, *the* stories.

Set into the matrix of the chirping, storming, growing, dying, dew-covered, immense crushing wheel of the wildness of the universe, the stories of how all things went together—or not—lay like a massive clutch of eggs of culture hatching beneath the warm heavy breast of the Holy in Nature, in a nest called the world.

If our direct ancestors from those remote times were humans with that degree of indigenous intactness, then when they walked through this world, they walked through a constant blizzard of unfolding details, which their sharp memory knew fit all together into a story that formed a trail of mythic familiarity that pulled them not around, past, or forward but directly into the elegant enormity of life's ever-evolving maze of all things being indebted with one another in such a way that in every circumstance, whether they liked where they stood or not, they knew they belonged there, because inside that storied matrix they were utterly at Home on this Earth.

Life was not something that could be studied from afar, its details sifted away from itself, and high-graded into formulas of preferences and certainty, but we were at home in all life's little things for we were part of the same story told, in which we on this Earth were ourselves but a small integral detail that understood and fulfilled our obligation to continue being what the story demanded our natures to follow to keep it all alive.

These kinds of antique people, upon entering their homes, were surrounded by smoke and stone, wood and sand, useful objects and tools, dogs, insects, fire, water, food, and people with whose "origins" they were completely familiar. This knowing was not primitive science, but a living psychological nervous system whose central spinal cord was filled with a flowing mythic electricity that fired and fed a sophisticated awareness that ran through all the people as if they were a single organism.

This knowing of the origins of all that surrounds us and that we are a part of is what has always held us and given us our shape, for the primal diligence of our familiarity with the world has always molded us into humans as we bounce like elephant sonar sounding the intricacies of this earth in which we humans before the last five thousand years have lived immersed as part of the matrix of nature unextracted. Some of this has found ways of surviving into the recent era.

Where it is common knowledge, for instance, to all Marsh Arabs that not only is such and such a reed in the stunning logarithmic arches of their majestic Reed Halls from a certain custom of construction from before Ur, from a now-extinct culture's way, grown in a particular part of a particular marsh, and cut only with a certain implement in a certain way at a certain season only, and with spoken invocation, hauled to their floating reed island by reed punt, tied into an elegant house with cordage twisted from another split, fermented, and washed marsh-dwelling plant who was once the wife of the other reed, and know as well how it came that they, the marsh-reed-mansion-living, fishing, farming people came to have been granted this plant that covers their head, not because some God gave it to them as his reed minions to his chosen human minions, but because before that God, the Reed was the mother of both that God and his people, and in her generous reedy belly they today can still curl up in her sweet womb, snore, eat, feel safe and at home, and have a definite place to be knowers of all that surrounds their life. People who know these things are not left feeling that they do not belong; they know being alive and human is not a disgrace but an obligation to live well inside their mother's ribcage, welcomed, knowledgeable, and still able to praise. They are at home.

But now who could tell you much about the actual origins of the dry wall in their apartment, or who lived beneath them in the soil 250 years past where the apartment resides today, or who nailed the nails or who made the nails, or when were the nails made, or what are they made of, or where does that iron come from, or who brought the hammer or invented hammers, or the carpenters, whose relatives were they, or where does your plastic teacup originate or where is it heading, or where was the oil polymer of your acrylic carpet drilled, or the valve oil in your car, or the titanium in the valves, or the water in the plumbing pipes, or the metal in the pipes? Nothing is really fully known; nor is it in any tangible or even scientific way required that a modern person know anything about the place they live. This does not even begin to touch on the fact that not one mythological story bringing the origins of these very same things enslaved by culture to serve humankind together can be found as part of the cultural largesse of any modern person's awareness. What about the individuals who grew your canned tomatoes? Who made the can? The tractors? Its fuel or the bad fertilizers, etc.? We are living in a world where there are no particular faces, no Holy authors, behind any story. There isn't really a story. Just fractured formulas of function.

Now when we walk out of our modern workaday world, which is not for us a big known mythologically described landscape inside of which we are natural participants, and reenter the sanctuary of our private modern homes, our Indigenous Souls find nothing there they need in order to feel at home. With no knowledge of the origins of all that surrounds us there, our Indigenous Souls are left homeless in a cultural vacuum.

Our homes have become less and less places where we can truly be at home. No longer even a refuge of familiarity away from the disanimate frenzy of the TV's piped-in broadcast of the mad world outside, less and less can our hearts live and die unmolested even in our own little world, where at least we *think* we belong. Increasingly, where modern people live, both rich and poor, our homes have become technologically assisted provisional campsites where we synthetically subsist both spiritually and bodily malnutritioned from total avoidance of any real culture. In utter disbelief, convinced this absurd detour away from real life is just a theater of sleepwalkers unconsciously acting out a script, our real souls wait impatiently offstage for it to end, so they can rush off with us when the play is over so a real life can begin.

The strange and alarming increase of depression and the diminishing ability for people to retain a broad cohesive memory, for which indigenous people worldwide and all our own ancestors were so well known, most likely stems from our padded existence, up and away from the ground that surrounds us, and its blatant lack of relevance to the mythic story our Indigenous Souls require in order to move vitally on a known earth. Modern existence has no relevance to our indigenous origins or that organic soul that gives us our zap. The endless pile-up of the computer-stored details of this constant irrelevancy is a cyber warehouse called Cultural Amnesia.

Our soul can only understand the world as a story, a mythology in which the things of the past and the random happenings of our present are strung together like beads on a string of continual story in which reality is remembered as a sequence of jeweled events. Like a bead on a rosary of nature's moods, each thing that happens is relevant to the beauty of the entire necklace. This necklace begins way before us and we are strung onto it, and in this way the Holy is adorned by our participation in this necklace of mythic sequence from the past to our present and beyond. Hence our everyday lives become *relevant* to the maintenance of that ongoing storied beauty as the Holy keeps on stringing life together beyond us.

The string itself is our origins, and all the beads strung onto it while they are events remembered, if the daily life is taken in such a way as to relevantly and mythologically feed the Grand Holy in Nature by the very way we move, then knowing this, even by our failures, we ourselves become beads of prayer and memory and are not left stranded, but attached to a bigger motive of life than feeling comfortable in our irrelevance. Memory retention and a happy existence comes from our daily relevance to the Holy motion of Nature, and for that we must have a multistranded thread of mythic origins on which to string the jewels of our daily life; we need origins that are not already imprisoned in dusty sacred texts or human-directed daydreams of escaping the ground that feeds us through technology, or some tired religion. We must find our origins in our service to the Holy in Nature, in our very lives at this very moment.

But we can no longer have our "old" origins back because we have lost that string long ago. What we can do is to begin a new string altogether which, by the blessing of the inevitability of time, will become a legitimate old origins for our descendants, and if we do it right, the one we lost as well will appear like a long-lost sprout by its own volition.

For this we need a House of Origins. A place in our lives where the origins of everything within is known.

To put it simply, an Origins House is a designated space in an already-existing modern home or, ideally, a small beautiful independent room built specifically for the purpose in which nothing is placed for which the deeper story of its origins remains unknown. Everything inside this space must be known, and their origins continued to be looked into and added onto as more is known—and then never forgotten.

By *origins* I am not so much talking about our ancestral origins, for those cannot really be truly understood until the origins of what already surrounds us—in our houses, towns, ecozones, above, below, on all sides, before and present—can be established enough for our hidden unused organ of indigenous memory to kick in. Meanwhile, the people we are today can at least make this place into a kind of temple of inner bigness where our memory capacity can begin to regrow itself enough to begin remembering a little each day without being invaded at every moment by the amorphous white noise and rootless existence of modernity's proud procession away from real culture and delicious life to an unsustainable subsistence of soulless matter.

A kind of spiritual fence, whose story and materials are of known origins, should designate where the Origins House begins and the remainder of your house of unattributed existence ends. Upon entering your Origins House, you must be faithful to the things housed therein, and by that is meant you should remember sequentially the order in which you added them in, where they are from, why you put them there, and their origins story. At the onset, all of this can seem a little clumsy and nebulous, but these things will fall into place beautifully of their own accord if you just keep in mind that inside your Origins House it's best to keep things very simple and "original" so as to slowly develop the muscles of real remembering necessary for an indigenous mind to find a place in your modern mind to slowly seep in like a spring of medicinal water that knows how to magically make you human again.

The Origins House is a grand place to have tea, to invite a friend or a relative one at a time, to begin and there remember spoken aloud the story of the tea itself, the origins of the cups it is drunk in, the origins of the spoons that stir, origins of the teakettle, the teapot, and especially the water's origins, which should not be from a spigot unless you are prepared to explain the plumbing pipes, their alloy, the city water system, where the runoff originates, and so forth. You must reiterate the origin story of everything, including the space itself, and every aspect of what you serve your guest. Then as they drink their tea, they are "drinking" in the story of it all combined into a simple tea, and the warmth of its story can reside within.

Do not speak things that have no relation to anything placed there, but whatever is said, speak with courtesy above all, and specifically no angry diatribes, for the Origins House is a place of peace. Grief is fine, for it is a thing of peace, and always present with any real remembering. But remember, in the Origins House any expression of grief must end in a praise of life, until it metabolizes any remaining bitterness into beauty.

To do this, you must fully understand that life's irony is evidence of the presence of the Holy in Nature.

If you have a true friend, or better still, one of your children or grandchildren if you are so blessed, or any younger person to whom you are not a betrayer but a trustworthy human, after a few years, ask permission of one of them when you are ready, if they would be willing to inherit your Origins House and promise you to keep alive and remember all the stories that go with all that resides within when you become ash and water and plants for the future when you pass.

Ask them if they would be willing to do this when they die as well, inviting their own children, or friend, to do the same for them as they have done for you, always adding on, of course, your story of your life and how you put together this Place of Origins along with their story of taking it over. They can and should add things and their stories of those things as well, until after three to five generations nothing fits in the space and it begins to take over the house and has to expand. Someday the whole house will be just like an old Mayan palatial hut, where everything is known and has a story. In such a place the Indigenous Soul could begin to appear. But beware of putting things in there that you collected on your tourist runs around the world. The Origins House is not a museum or a tourist trophy den.

If you do it right, soon your people will actually have an origins, and real stories, that belong to them, not to mention a place to walk into away from an unoriginal world full of Amnesiacs, a place where your Indigenous Soul will feel at home. This is how we slowly find "our seeds," the seeds of our lost indigenosities.

Searching for the seeds solely in our ancestries creates stiffness, warfare, deception, and tribalist separatism. While of course our blood ancestry is a real thing and must be given its due, unless you descend from an immediate line of openhearted humans with intact forms of origination as a way of life, dependence on Ancestors for an identity will usually be the den of a lot of doctored and unmetabolized grief, hidden behind nonsense and still more intentional habitual Amnesia and mental lockdown. For in all probability, your ancestors for the last millennia or so were suffering just as much from a lack of origins as yourself. These are the "recent" ancestors. The real, real "old" ones are the indigenous ones, and they are not going to be tribalist, because they are in the story of all mythic things and have merged into the submolecular awareness in the sap and bloodstream of all living things that feed the present and do not value small-thinking isolationist ancestral prejudice.

So for that reason, don't put up pictures or photos or possessions of recent Ancestors, or paintings of likenesses of your friends, relatives, or heroines, heroes, or religious figures. An Origins House is a place of originating a place right now for a time worth remembering generations later. It is a place to keep the seeds of the future alive, and you will be the first ancestor in the Origins House when you pass, for you shall be "known" for having originated the place and therefore not anonymous.

Please do not use the Origins House as a vague altar for already-existing Gods, religious leaders or saints, or for meditations. These are very different things. If not maintained with this subtle detail in mind, the place will cease being a House of Origins.

Unless you're totally prepared to find out which silver nitrate compound, in which darkroom, on what kind of tree-pulp paper, or from what camera, with which inventor, and what material your photos come from, it is best to not put any photographs in an Origins House. Images as such will be irrelevant; the origins of where they come from and how they were made will not. It is the weeping beauty of the living world that surrounds us, a world we wreck in the crushing drone of modernity, whose majestic origins and detailed content goes unnoticed, who has a home here.

Because we are starting right from today, to make for a time beyond our own, a past worth remembering and onto which future generations can string the beads of their actions, we won't need the presence of our ancestors in the Origins House by way of photos or memorabilia. As amazing and appealing as that may seem, leave these things for your altars, sitting in other places, where you keep pictures of the Dalai Lama, Krishna, Jesus, Amida, Santa Cecilia, Magdalena, Quanyin, and all those wonderful beings. And of course, never take photographs or sketch your origins place.

In the Origins House we want the ancestral presence to be something that hasn't become petrified into an image. For this we need the living seeds of the main starch plants that originally lived and died to feed your ancestral line with their nutritive generosity.

Instead of images of ancestors, a more important characteristic of the Origins House is that it is the only real place we can have to house our Ancestral Seeds: where the Seeds of Birth and the Seeds of Death can royally sit alongside the bundle of belly-button stumps of all the children of your people, your friends, or your neighbor's children who have come into this world through their mother's wombs since establishing your Origins House.

But what seeded plants *did* feed your ancestors? Not too many people living in the cities in modern conditions really know—or are even aware of *why* they should know.

Even those who were told that their recent ancestors, those of the last three or four hundred years (which barely qualifies them as real ancestors in an Origins House), that, for example, their Polish ancestors ate potatoes, are probably accurate to a small degree, but in an Origins House, potatoes can't be there as a Seed Senator of your European ancestors because of course all potatoes grown worldwide have their origins in the ancestors of the highland tribes of Peru and Ecuador, who still depend upon the myriad forms and varieties of potatoes developed by their own ancestral brilliance for thousands of years previous to Europeans obtaining "potatoes."

So how far back does one go? Because most of our ancestry is kept in the official family memory as a very pared-down subfunctional abbreviation of culturally acceptable national identities, which usually leave us ignorant of the most interesting, varied, and amazing tribal affiliations, this becomes a search. For instance, if we are talking about Europeans, we will usually end up farther and farther east into the Caucasus, Iran, Kazakhstan, the Altai mountains, the Taklamakan Desert, into Siberia and Asia, and ultimately, of course, to Africa.

So the best thing to do is to do your best to go as far back as possible on both sides and to keep your eyes open for the main grains or starch plants as things crop up. Do your research along with and beyond the stigma of family opinion. With just this alone, you will make an adequate house of ongoing origins.

For instance, if one branch of an ancestral line depended on barley, you will come across complex pre-monotheistic religions who had barley as their Goddess—not a Goddess of Barley but the Barley was Her—and discover how many well-known ecstatic mystery schools and spiritualities were based on seeing Her powerful self, the golden barley staffs, and their experience of being able to actually touch Her Divinity, for which many ancient Greek and a number of Pontic tribes in the BCEs had extensive towns built for initiations.

Maybe your people were from Ethiopia, then probably teff was the starch plant; or maybe your people were from Italy. Then you have to ask yourself how long had they been in Italy, for most Italians are descended from one of many waves of Indo-Europeans, who are for the most part not indigenous to any part of Europe but farther East. Were they Iluri, Siculi, Boe, Cisalpine Celts, lead-mining Gauls, Lombardy Germans, Almans, Etruscans, Oscans or ... any combination of many others? When the probable combinations are found, then their plants will be found as well, maybe einkorn, pulsecorn, corn, chickpeas, buckwheat, or spelt and other even more startling and good inventive food ways, many of which are still used, grown, loved, and cooked in those areas and have a lot of stories and "rules" that accompany their cultivation, which are vestiges of the old "agreements" of your ancestors to Nature for the gift of the grain.

You will find, by looking for ancestral seed, that history of your origins to be much different than the generalities presented to you in history class. When you find something out, then look closely for the old seed stock. For always there is someone still growing it, in Romania for instance, and nine times out of ten they will end up being a relative who knows a lot. Then plant these with permission in your beautiful gardens over and over again until you are graced with sufficient seed stock to store. Then with your story of your search for the seeds and finding the seeds, tie them up in a beautiful little handmade fiber sack whose construction is of known origins, and attach them to the middle of the ceiling of your Origins House, and call that place the Belly Button of the Sky. This is the Umbilical origin of your ancestral survival and by descendency yours as well, because the ancestors of these seeds kept your ancestors alive, which is why you're here.

Then it stands to reason that when anyone is born in your family, or lacking that, to a family in your neighborhood, have the midwife part the child's umbilical cord over some of the seed heads, and distribute the seeds to all the people present, and have them promise to plant them in their gardens (hopefully beautiful garden plots)! When each of their harvests are in, have them all come together again with the seeds. Separate a tenth, and replace these back into the seed sack in the ceiling. These seeds are to plant again on the occasion of future deaths and births, and always hang these over you to remind you of your organic plant origins up in the Umbilical of the Sky. Then with the remainder, go ahead and prepare the ancestral food that you have discovered goes with the seed, and hold a feast in the Origins House in which the child is named. If your Italian ancestral grain is chickpea, for instance, prepare *cinque e' cinque*. Tuscan polentas were originally made of garbanzo and not maize, as maize belongs only to the Americas ancestrally. Besides which, chickpeas have a huge ceremonial mythological body of stories that go with them even today.

When a child is born, have the parents of the child keep track of the newborn's belly-button stump, and on the glorious day of its healthily dropping away from the child, have them put it somewhere safe and where they can locate it easily when the feast day comes.

With the oldest person of the family, enter the Origins House with Mother, Father, and new baby; tell every story of everything in the Origins House. Then have the oldest member tell all they know about events leading up to the child's birth while wrapping the little fallen piece of umbilical into a small pellet of handspun yarn. After placing this pellet of stories and family origin into a small sack of known handmade origins, have all the people at the feast dance with the sack, and then tie it up next to the seeds. Then feast on the ancestral food prepared from your ancestral grain. Give the child a protective name that remains only for the relatives to know for the purpose of praying for the child's welfare. This is called a person's ancestral name.

When someone in the family dies, take down that same sack and the sack of seeds. Have all the grievers plant these seeds on the grave of the deceased. Later, when they are grown, harvest a handful—being careful to leave most of the grain to reseed on the grave—and make a feast, and allow a little taste for everyone who comes along with all the other food prepared. Then in the Origins House with all your family and friends, listen to all the origins of the Origins House, the belly-button sack, and the life of the deceased, and with a few seeds intentionally selected from the same grain harvest, replenish the seed sack in the ceiling and replace the umbilical bag and seed sack together.

In this way over the generations, when the owner of the Origins Place is buried, grow this same ancestral grain on their grave. If this goes on for enough generations way down the line, their own belly-button stumps will hang with the umbilical sack overhead. Then those that come after you will definitely have a House of Stories, a House of Origins, and have kept a literal sack of Ancestral Seeds alive that all the generations from these Origins since its inception have tasted and had grown for them at birth and death and will have been at least ritually sustained as well.

Human sanity demands people have multiple nonnationalistic, nontribalist, indigenous origins that depend utterly on the reverence and recognition of the Divine Immensity and the generosity of the living beings that feed us. With an honest Origins House, this sanity could be maintained: the simple sanity of all old villages of the world. Maybe doing such a thing right inside the belly of modernity's oblivious attitude to such practical spiritual subtlety will help keep the seeds of both diverse culture and sacred agriculture viable for a better time in the future. Even an honest failure in the attempt would be a grand feast for the Holy in Nature and our own Indigenous Souls; it could even catch on—real human beings might begin to reappear in our neighborhoods and descendants.

I remember one time a while back, a desperate, beautifully sad, late-middle-aged American man from southern Vermont came to me, in hopes of finding some way to continue living while clearly drowning in a very legitimate grief over the loss of his beloved life companion of almost thirty years when his wife succumbed to a terrible chronic illness.

This man had been a fishing boat captain, who ended up earning his living rebuilding sailing boats for rich patrons. His lifetime dream, shared by his young wife, was to create a large beautiful old sailing craft from all the recycled and rescued timbers he'd gleaned from his years of repairing yachts and wind-driven boats. They finally had everything: mast stems from old Maine timber from the seventeenth century, decking, spars, ironwork, and had finished half their dream when his wife took ill.

He began to sell off all the precious sailing things they'd ever gathered in order to pay for his beloved's endless series of treatments until she finally died.

After a few visits I could see he was dying because the boat had been their child, and because he now had no children to live for, he too soon would pass away. I then suggested humbly that maybe at least he could make an Origins House, and begin to pass his stories to some younger person, as he and his wife had no children.

This fellow took to it avidly, building a kind of small terrestrial sailing cabin. The first thing he remembered he owned of which he intricately knew the greater origins was a very thick piece of old hand-adzed planking from a famous ship decommissioned a century and a half before.

This heavy single plank of worn and experienced wood from a huge old-growth New England tree, the type of which not enough years have passed since to even regrow a new one the same size, was also the very last thing he'd been left with after selling all the hundreds of parts, pieces, and precious rare timber to heal his lost wife. This plank was basically what was left of his boat and of his life with his wife. He never did get his boat. But he did live to serve the Holy in the Seed in his own way, and well.

Once I visited him and listened as he taught a neighboring adolescent the ins and outs of what by then had become a little more ample store of origins, but still fairly simple and clear as Origins Houses can get to being.

His plank had evolved into the table that you sat at while you drank his tea and heard the story. So first came the story of the original tree, its broad-head firebrand mark of the British crown, the ship's deck planking, his recycling, his wife and him, his weeping, the boat they were making, her illness, selling the lumber, her death, this last plank, the place where life-giving tea was today drunk between friends in the Origins House.

But then there were the fired pottery cups, which as he pointed out still had the fingerprints of their author petrified in their surfaces.

They'd been made by an old woman whom he and his siblings, when they were children, had thought was an insane old poisoner, a neighborhood witch. They would sneak past her house to and back from school as this was the shortest route to the after-school snacks. If she saw them, the old woman, hair affright, would rush out with her dandelion fork if it were spring, or snug in a thick gray shawl in the winter, would come hissing, wide-eyed, trembling in a rage like an old bear straight toward the children, who jumped away scattering like trout, enthralled to have survived yet another day in the human ecosystem of suburban America.

As the boy grew, he became a teenaged dreamer of ships and of sailing them back to other times away from the stark gray business reality of his parental home, when old Mrs. Carretas became his only friend. She'd scattered the ashes of her husband of over sixty years beneath the ancient apple trees they had planted when they married, when that opening in the birch woods was still a farm, before the lawns, fire hydrants, sidewalks, and rickety, bland 1950s suburbs crept over it all.

She built pottery for a living, was known afar, but never where she lived. She taught the boy a lot of things, especially about boats, for her beloved man had been a seaman of the old knot-tying sort of which there are no more, and all his books and ropes and such became his own as her soul finally drifted toward the sea of Holy dreams to join her old man forever sailing home into the roots of a time beyond our own, right into the seas of the sap of those trees whose apples that day we could still eat and whose magical flavor could've only been their ecstasy of being together again.

The teacups in his origination house had her fingerprints on the lip, and the clay itself, he went on, came from a cut bank cliff of gray striated rock in a stream two hundred yards north of where he himself had lived, where originally a band of Abnakis took clay to make their square-rimmed pots with breast-shaped bottoms to cook their hominy and sacred drink until forced to abandon the entire place to the whites, and were assimilated beyond recognition into a drab Puritan sawmill-working population fifty miles off.

The cut bank clay now lay twelve feet beneath the golf course of the new suburban gated sprawl, but these cups, the Abnaki, Mrs. Carretas, the apple trees, and her man jumped inside the cup as you drank Sri Lankan black tea, originally brought by the British to India in the same old ships he'd disassembled, he explained, from China and grown with imported forced Tamil labor, but this tea in particular was actually hand-picked by a family friend from India who managed a British tea estate in Sri Lanka.

The water for the tea was boiled in an old tin cup he found hanging from a staub off an old-growth tree, cut down long before. Fired with corn cobs from corn seeds like all the others I'd given him long ago, in a stove that was a copy of a Manchurian clay furnace he himself had formed using clay and soapstone from . . . and on the stories went, until they were one story.

And that story was needed for a real ungreedy delicious drinking of the tea; for the story of the origins of everything in that Origins House was the tea, and to drink tea was to drink the tea of origins. But we didn't drink alone, for you could hear the Indigenous Soul sigh with relief, for at least as much as that moment allowed the shackles of invisibility to be unlocked and some vital blood to flow back into all our hearts.

Years later, when Roger's soul flooded past the restrictive maze of modernity's mediocre goals and visionless everydayness, to join the sub-atomic particulant echo as hopeful spiritual matter in the roots of a time beyond our own, the young people who'd drunk his tea, and promised they'd keep it going, remembered what to do and planted his ancestral rye and wheat on his grave and in their "gardens," made bread when the harvest came in, and invited all the people to "eat" Roger as seeds back into their bodies, after restoring some of the live seeds back in the roof beams, hearing the entire tale of the plank, Mrs. Carretas, the teacups, the Abnakis, their clay, the entire story, the water, the Sri Lankan tea, the honey, the bees, and then adding the story of Roger; and then for the young people they'd invited who sat listening, the Origins House became their origins too, for now someone dead and gone had finally rooted the place for them in a known and mythic past, and life was restored. They were all really keeping the seeds alive. Like Chiviliu said.

A couple of years later, when Nilson married, and went to live with his in-laws in Saint Lucia, some unstoried youths, whose own "culture" calls vandals (vandals were actually Danes from Jortsland who became Tunisian nomads after wafting through Rome and Italy a while back) with no origins or future more than that of grunts for a business-oriented, machine-dependent, third-rate, trickle-down poverty, burnt down Roger's old run-down house along with his Origins Place.

Nilson and Marie returned to a pile of ashes, shards, and melted glass. When they were done weeping they picked through the char, where they found a piece of plank, a clay handle with Mrs. Carretas' fingerprint, sixteen grains of unburnt rye seeds, a number of hand-forged bolts, and nails, the tin cup, and a tea canister, and they rebuilt an Origins Place of their own with no resemblance to Roger's land-ship's cabin. But with a strange ingenious table made of all the pieces gleaned of Roger's Place of Origins, they began their own House of Origins, starting with growing the rye, tying up the belly-button stump that dropped from their newborn's belly, and together with all the friends they told the tale of Roger's love, his wife, his plank, and the lost ones, Mrs. Carretas, her cups, the clay, her man, the Abnakis, the golf course, the tin cup, its extinct forest, the clay furnace with a top of soapstone and clay from ... and on the story went, pouring away past Roger's death, the planting of the wheat and rye, his funerary feast, and then the burning of the House and his Origins Place and then the finding of the seeds and the pieces of the plank and the bolts, and the pieces of the cups and table made of all these stories and things once again sprouted from the ashes of what should have killed the meaning of it all and then the baby, and the stump, and they added two more pieces of pottery from Marie's grandmother's store cupboard from where they drank chocolate to the dead and ate traditional Caribbean funeral-celebration charred jerk chicken ... and they kept the seeds alive; life was restored. Like all of us who have had our seeds burnt, or stories lost and pushed underground, our places of origins devastated, our organ of indigenous memory turned into a vestigial memory itself, we ourselves must become the origins of a people who would keep the seeds alive.

For one must know, that as democratic as it is, Peace cannot sit in any old throne. Peace is an honorable visitor, not a possession, who visits when the shape of Peace is made to receive it. Like a key of deliciousness that fits only keyholes shaped like peace, this peace can open any door blocking the memory of how to actually be a human being, and as an Origins Place is a home of everyday relevance to a life-giving memory that serves a bigger thing; it is peace that needs small places just like these to visit and sit.

Because Peace is only rarely peaceful, living in well-applied grief, and making the new from the impossibly dead, Peace is severely allergic to complacent righteous superiority, and the violence of a frantic remedy to a nonpeaceful problem. People are not here on earth to succeed; they are here to feed the beauty of the way they go about ordinary things to feed the Holy in Nature, a beauty that only a Natural Human can give. Keeping the seeds alive needs an Origins Home, and peace needs seeds of culture replanted and eaten in the throne of stories.

Chapter 22

The Famous Story of One Eye

In my youth I heard told a powerful story, a story that has governed the motion of my entire life. I have lived by it.

The first time I heard it, an erudite Kiowa, the father of a well-known author, was telling it to my parents while I sat listening in a forest of bare feet, boots, and shoes with our cat under my family's Formica dining table in the tribe-supplied reservation house of our early days during a break in one of their famous all-night poker games. Later on in those years of late teenage carousing and cruising in some old truck or banana boat through the starry winter nights with Native friends from all over the country, long storytelling bouts always took over when gas and alcohol ran out, and it was then that the same tale, invariably a favorite, with some minor variations, always surfaced.

Having always been, even then, a thinking and reading person, for in our household you couldn't eat without a book discussion or debate on the "real" motive of a play, I can swear I had read this same tale somewhere in one of these inspiring, box-ripping 'sixties Red Power books by the likes of the great Vine Deloria and friends. However, after having searched now for the last five years to ascertain whom I should cite for this story, I have come up with even less than when I started.

By this, I mean that some of the people mentioned in this story—at least according to "official" sources—may have existed in name, but not in any context of such a story, and none lived at the same time, and they

415

were usually from totally different tribes of people in different places where there seems to be no record at all that any of what follows took place. The famous One Eye, for instance, though not an uncommon nickname for a lot of tribal people, comes down to us in U.S. military government documents as a Comanche man, not a Kiowa, of a much earlier time frame. Though both tribes had close affiliations in those terrible "American" years trying to survive a few last moments on the buffalo plains while being harried and hunted down by American post–Civil War veteran career soldiers, mostly immigrants and former slaves, no light is shed on who published this tale in the past.

Therefore I am humbly reduced to declaring that to whomsoever this story rightfully belongs, or whosoever in the past has published it, to you goes all credit and honor. But its brilliance and beauty are all its own.

I owe this tale a great deal. I live by stories as all real humans do, just as long as they are real, vital, and straight from their time, and not too washed over and blunted by the bias of the present.

In any case, ever since I turned twelve years old, this is the story that has kept me moving toward what I now call Keeping the Seeds Alive and Feeding the Heart of Nature in the ground.

One Eye, a famous old Kiowa fighting man, was a U.S. prisoner of war incarcerated in the famous old Castillo of Fort Marion, Florida. He was held there for years on that old island fortress, along with the Chiricahua Gothlay (Geronimo), Nana, Naiche, and both men and women of mostly Arapaho, Comanche, Kiowa, Apache, and other southern Plains tribal bands. Along with the illegal and controversial internment of a greater number of noncombatant political prisoners, the result of official American paranoia about the sudden charismatic appearance of the ecstatic trance religion of the Ghost Dance, some prisoners had been held without trial for as long as twelve years now. Others even more. With no reprieve in sight, most of these native prisoners aged and ended up serving as recalcitrant informants for journalists, ethnographers, and social workers, or as living museum exhibits for dressed-up white couples who as tourists could visit the prisoners, watching them make bows or clothes or discussing through military interpreters various topics of their fascination. It was kind of a human zoological park, something fairly common in many parts of the world until recently.

Many of the greatest leaders had never arrived, having arranged to have themselves killed escaping on the prison train creeping through the southern states, while others like White Bear-Satanta, that great big beautiful Kiowa man, waited till they got to the prison itself to jump from the immense battlements of this old seventeenth-century Spanish fort, crashing to their deaths on the rocks of the ocean shore, unwilling to live unfree under any circumstances. Still others were more patient like Geronimo and One Eye, who waited to make the best of things. For as far as they were concerned, yet another time of change could come. After all, the time of fighting Americans had simply been a big change in a series of big changes during their middle age from the old nomadic hunting days, and here was yet another one.

During their incarceration there had been several instances in which "well-meaning" East Coast whites, mostly women's suffrage groups, tried to introduce Acts of Congress to have the prisoners remanded to more so-called "humane" conditions, mostly to be reunited with relatives on reservations. But because they were technically prisoners of war, it required an act of incredible bureaucracy with Congress, the war department, and the executive branch to effect any pardons.

But nothing much ever came of these attempts, for they were always shot down in their inception by all the big-business interests afraid of Indian land claims, who manipulated millions of American psyches to keep them terrified of a couple of Indians on the loose, none of whom they'd ever seen.

Ironically, some of the very same military officials responsible for hunting down these leaders, killing their people, destroying all their horse herds and the animals and lands that fed them, herding their people into concentration camps, and incarcerating people like One Eye for unlimited, unsentenced lengths of time, in their old age started lobbying for their release themselves. Declaring that the prisoners had been well-behaved and were now *reformed* and ready to join their relatives on the new reservations, to give up raiding and hunting and begin peaceful farming, which was strange in itself because most of the Indians mentioned were already expert at growing the things they'd taught the usurping Americans how to grow. Most Plains Indians had been farmers before they became nomads.

To do this, some of these former Indian-killing generals conducted witnessed interviews with all the military wardens, soldiers, visitors, tourists, and the incarcerated native leaders in particular in order to gather a dossier of testimony on the prisoners' behalf to present to Congress, the attention of which these generals, of course, because of their service and political connections, could better obtain than the woman's suffrage groups from upstate New York, who'd been lobbying for years because many of the prisoners were women.

When it finally came time for One Eye's interview, they say, General Crook with a secretary and a Kiowa-speaking Oklahoma half-blood interpreter took down the great old man's testimony while he himself worked methodically on a perfect half-size version of a Kiowa hunting bow to sell to a tourist.

The interview read as follows:

General Crook: "One Eye, what does it feel like to be a conquered people?"

Interpreter speaks.

Silence. Just the sound of One Eye scraping the bow.

Crook: "Why don't you answer?"

Looking down, continuing with his work, One Eye replied: "I don't understand the question."

Crook: "Let me rephrase the question. What is it like for you to be in here, and for me and the rest of the world to be out there?"

One Eye: "I don't know. We are all in here."

Crook: "No, One Eye, you are a prisoner here. I am not."

One Eye: "As far as my One Eye can see," (he had one eye lost to a buffalo horn during a hard hunt in his daring youth) "you and I are sitting right here this moment."

Not being very metaphorically advanced, and never suspecting a "simple" Native of such big thoughts, the exasperated General began another approach.

Crook: "Look here, One Eye, do you remember how me and my troops used to chase you and your people around? We could never catch you. Why? Because you were better mounted, your people were a single organism that could split up and rejoin days later. It was like chasing the wind. You had better horses; they were little, but much better than ours. Your women and little kids rode better than our men. That's why we killed all your horses wherever we found them. You were a magnificent people, a beautiful people. But that is no more. You are in here, wearing old army uniforms. Your people are corralled, on reservations; you're in here, and we are out there living on your former territory. What does that feel like, One Eye?"

One Eye: "No, you and I are sitting right here, in here, together, General."

Crook: "Please, One Eye, don't you want to get out of this place? All the buffalo that you used to chase are all extinct. Totally gone. The plains you rode free on are all planted into grids of wheat, milling with whites; the entire land is crisscrossed with smoking railroads, trains, wooden towns, mines, the trees cut down for trestles and telegraph poles and poles to carry electricity lines, the entire land utterly fenced with barbed wire so no one off a road could travel like the birds you used to be. It's all gone, One Eye. How does that feel?"

One Eye: "I don't know, General Crook, how does it feel? I only know what I was, how it was. I haven't seen what you made happen. How does it feel to be sitting in here with me, with you and yours having caused what happened out there?"

Silence. Only the sound of One Eye working on his miniature hunting bow.

Finally Crook says, "One Eye, if I present what you've been saying to the Congress, they're going to interpret your attitude as continued non-compliance, and a sign of unreformed incorrigibility. Can't you tell me anything to help you gain your freedom?

When the interpreter stops, One Eye for the first time stands and speaks: "General Crook, I do remember you chasing us; I remember giving your troops the slip many times. I remember fighting you. And yes, we were a magnificent people. Our women were more beautiful than anyone else's; they had more elk teeth on their dresses than any other tribe; they had solid silver belts, and beaded Indian boots up to their hips, two soft deer hides per side, with silver buttons all the way down. Our young men could run buffalo down on foot; our little girls roped antelope from horseback just for fun, dragging them back to camp for pets.

"I myself like all the others had hair ornaments of graduated solid silver rounds that stretched beyond my height to drag on the ground beside my horse as I rode. Yes, we ate well, lived well, and our enemies wanted to kill us just to touch something as great as us—even they admired us. Our friends in vain always imitated us. Even the wild strutting elk were jealous of how bravely we walked and how beautifully we lived, how we joked, how we died, how we sang. And yes, maybe those times are all gone, but we are *not* a conquered people.

"The Kiowa were a great people, you say. But remember, General, if they were great, they were not great because they were Kiowa: the Kiowa were great because of what was in the ground and how they lived with that Holy Thing. If our Ancestors were great, it was not because they were Kiowa, but because of the way they lived with what was in the ground. The way we lived with what was in the ground is what made us great. We weren't Kiowa because our mothers were Kiowa; we were Kiowa because to be a Kiowa you descended from people who taught you how to live with that Holy Thing that was in the ground. Some of our mothers were Comanches, others Utes, some Pueblo Indians, some Cheyennes, some even white, and others Mexicans, but all of us were Kiowa because what made us great was how we lived with what was in the ground. And what was in the ground is *still* in the ground.

"You can string up the earth all you want with wire mined from the dog holes you dig; you can cut and plow, and make the world tame, ugly, and dead all you want. You can crisscross the land with trains, houses, and drilled wells; you can kill as much as you like of the original land, cut down all her trees, exterminate all the natives you can manage to catch; but you with all your inventions still don't have the power to kill what made us great. For what made us great, if we were great, is still in the ground, and we would rather die great than live dead like you, hating what's in the ground.

"Not even you can kill what gives you yourself life, for with or without your presence, what gives you life still lives on in the ground.

"No, General, it looks to me that you are just as much as I am, right in here with us, and no matter what happens to me, my people are not a conquered people because our greatness has never been captured by anyone: what made us great is still in the ground. So General, to answer your question, I can't tell you what it feels like to be a conquered people. Maybe you should tell me!"

Silence. Then holding up the smooth beautifully finished little bow, One Eye spoke: "Would you like to buy a bow, General?"

One Eye's voice is the voice of our Indigenous Soul. All of our people somewhere in time were feared for their beauty, taken from their land, forced to speak the sovereign tongue, wear the serf's clothing, held in bondage and taught to fear: it is the history of all people, but especially Europe's people. Unlike One Eye, when we are truly conquered, we become conquerors and dangerous purveyors of the same violent sickness that ran us over.

But our Indigenous Souls never surrendered, signing only the Agreement with the Holy in Nature, with that Holy life-giving Thing that is in the Ground.

Give our Indigenous Souls a throne in your Home of known Origins, feed the Holy in Nature, grow food, and learn from what's in the ground how to unconquer the earth, our bodies, souls, and minds by keeping the seeds of culture alive.

GLOSSARY OF NON-ENGLISH WORDS

aberjón: Spanish from Arabic; edible peas.

abuelita: Spanish; little grandmother.

adelantado: Old Spanish; the vanguard or advance campaigner. Old title given many "conquering" officers in Spain's expansionist wars.

Ajauá: Tzutujil Maya; plural of *ajau.* He, she to which it pertains, sometimes translated as "lord" by ethnologists. Lords, owners, or Gods, male or female. The *Ajauá* and *Ixoc Ajauá* could mean the male and female Deities behind any form of any thing or phenomenon that makes it carry on according to the nature of that thing.

But it also is the word used to designate the old decision-making council of principal men and women of the tribe.

Ajcun: Tzutujil Maya; literally "He (or She) that searches for"; a shaman; Native Spirit Doctor.

Aj Qij: Tzutujil Maya; plural *Aj Qijá;* literally "He or She of the Sun" or "He or She of Days"; Calendar Diviner.

buaq': Tzutujil Maya. Another corn food made of a large chunk of *nixtamal,* or corn masa steamed in corn husks, then sliced into thin slabs and toasted on the *xot,* the griddle.

cá: Tzutujil Maya; literally molar, refers to the "molar" of the house, or the *metate* or corn-grinding stone and its upper piece. Expertly chipped from various grits of basaltic stone, these are the number-one prized cooking tools of any traditional Mayan woman. Men are hardly ever allowed to touch them, and then only by permission of the lady owner.

Cakchiquel: Quiché Maya for a very large linguistic tribe of Maya people related to both the Tzutujil and Quichéan people. Their ancient capital was at Iximche (literally "corn tree"), near present-day Tecpán. Their present population of almost a million is spread out east of Quiché Maya, and mostly north and east of the comparatively small Tzutujil villages throughout small villages of the highlands.

The sixteenth- and seventeenth-century Spanish colonizing governments had an interesting policy of choosing certain predominating native languages as the "national" language operating bilingually with bureaucratic Spanish during the early part of their takeover. No other Europeans had this creed. In Peru, the official national language became Quechua; in Guatemala, despite the fact that Quiché had more speakers, Cakchiquel became the operating language for the government due to its relative linguistic symbiosis with the other prominent Mayan languages. In Guatemala today there are between nine to eleven million speakers of various types and dialects of highland Maya, and a few lowland Maya speakers.

The word *Cakchiquel,* spelled also Kakchikel, Kaqchikil, Cachikel, Catchikel, and so on means "red tree people," which each surrounding tribe explains differently. One is that it refers to an amazing jungle tree that when its bark is gashed, bleeds red sap like a mammal, something upon which a lot of mythology is based. Others say that a peeled sapling of a mountain annona tree was rubbed with red earth and stood as the boundary between them and Quiché Maya in pre-colonial times. The Cakchiquel language is close enough to Tzutujil such that, with a little practice, they are mutually intelligible.

chaqegue (chakewe): Hispanified Tewa; a mush of finely ground toasted blue or white corn, a favorite New Mexico breakfast food.

chicos: Hispanified Nahuat; from *chicales* and *chicacatl,* unripe corn (sweet corn) roasted in pits in their husks, then hung to dry hard. Eaten all winter, boiled soft in meat and bean stews. A staple of all Northern New Mexico cuisine.

ch'jay: Tzutujil Maya; literally "at the house"; the village of Santiago Atitlán.

ciruelas: Spanish; plums.

Coban: a province of north-central Guatemala, a hilly lowland area in which the Qekchi Mayan have always predominated; most Mesoamerican jade originated from one of its rivers, the Motagua.

cofradia: Sixteenth-century Spanish; from *fraternidad,* the brotherhood. Originally a lay brotherhood set up by clergy to care for a particular saint; responsible for all the masses and celebration around that saint's feast day. *Cofradias* were wonderfully "Mayanized" in the sixteenth century by Highland Maya in various ways. The Tzutujil reorganized thirteen of them to fit their entire pantheon of Time Deities as "married" to Spanish male and female saints. A very powerful and active system where old pre-Christian ritual survived in subterfuge up until the present.

cóló: Tzutujil Maya; rope, handmade from maguey. But ritually the word goes with *bey* or road. *Bey cóló,* "road-rope" or destiny: accomplishment.

cuajada: Spanish; literally "curdled"; refers to a popular soft white goat cheese.

cuateros guerilleros: Guatemalan Spanish (slang); a *cuate* in Central America comes from the Nahuat word *cuachtl* or "twin" and is used to mean sidekick or buddy. *Guerillero* is of course a little warrior, or a soldier of the small war, a guerrilla. A *cuatero* is an armed group pretending affiliation with leftist political guerrilla groups, but who are simply well-armed bandits, who say their robberies, kidnappings, and atrocities are for the "cause," when actually they are just working for themselves, causing the guerrilla movements of those days no end of grief for the added confusion to an already impossibly entangled image.

decima: Spanish; literally the tenth part, a tax levied by the old Catholic ecclesia on the people, in particular the *cofradias,* which ostensibly was set up to maintain clerics, but which became big business in some parts during the Spanish colonial presence.

ecomienda: Old Spanish; a royally dispensed fiefdom—with people and products included—in the Americas granted to families of "conquistadores" for their services, who are called *ecomenderos.*

hijado: New Mexico Spanish; past participle of *hijar,* "to child," therefore, "enchilded," the New Mexican custom where a grandchild is given to their grandparent to raise as their last child, who often inherits before their parents. They take care of the older generation and have always traditionally been those individuals who retain all the family and cultural knowledge for the next generation.

huná: Tzutujil Maya; a year; from *Hunáxa* (twelve full cycle harvest of days). Represents 400 days, in which the magical common agricultural denominator 20 is multiplied with itself to allow for many planetary cycles to be included. Nowadays used mostly to mean 365 days. Also means "to harvest."

Keres: unknown origin; one of several linguistic culture groups of Pueblo Indians with some seven or more villages, depending on how you count them. Most, but not all, are on the Rio Grande. The name Keres is unknown to them, but used politically and by ethnologists.

Ladinos: Spanish; originally designates the Yiddish spoken by the Sephardic Jews of sixteenth-century Spain to the present, but in Guatemala became the generic term for non-Indian citizens born in Guatemala. Has no connotation of race, only culture: a 100-percent Mayan can be a Ladino if he lives and dresses like one and speaks Spanish in the home. A non-Indian, Spanish-speaking Guatemalan.

latifundista: modern Spanish; a wealthy owner of many plantations that are basically feudal farms, where quadrilles of men and women laborers are given the bare minimum in shelter, bad food, unfair pay, and no health protection.

lej: Tzutujil Maya; a form of hand-slapped corn tortilla that is considered the tour de force of any housewife or unmarried girl. Very thin, transparent, difficult to make—and deliciously sweet.

liix: Tzutujil Maya; the pre-Columbian man's loincloth, and also the road of string and story wound over a dead person's genital area, kidneys, and belly button to turn the body into a "seed" that will sprout out of the *liix* into a vegetal soul to replant reality.

maravillas: Spanish; marvels. Name applied locally to a strikingly beautiful desert four-o'clock that forms largish bushes of heart-shaped leaves and strange, deep-violet nested flowers. The root is a big ritual medicine for New Mexicans, Natives, and Spanish-speaking alike.

maxuina: old Quiche Mayan; foot plow, an old Mayan type of farming hoe. Very heavy with a thick, short handle. Originally stone, but now made of German steel. Larger and heavier than an Italian grape hoe or the old grubbing hoe. Outside of the machete and the ax, it is the major farming tool. It is rare to see a man going or returning home not shouldering one, with ax, machete, and ropes crisscrossing his chest.

mōs or *moz:* Dialectic Mayan from Mozo, which in Spanish meant a serf or common laborer, but in a typical Tzutujil homeopathic reversal of invasive meanings, *mōs* became a rich non-Indian male who never worked and who is a large employer of Indian day laborers!

nervios: Spanish; a case of the nerves.

paquan: Mayan; a Mayanized old sixteenth-century Spanish *jerga* (thick, raw wool Spanish tweed), herringbone, black wool jacket with pockets. Very rare now, but once was standard wear for men up until the 1950s. Very dapper, durable, and warm.

patín: Tzutujil Maya; the Tzutujil people's national food. No one else in Guatemala makes it, and it has played into many ritual stories and old mythologies. The basic recipe consists of *q'aan'al,* the gooey, gummy center of the stalk of a certain wild banana plant whose fruit is not edible, steamed in a stone-ground sauce of masa, squash seeds, roasted pear tomatoes, and black ball chile peppers with a chunk of smoked, jerked snipe inside a gigantic wild leaf called *Maxan.* It has the almost supernatural quality of never rotting or going bad if opened once a day and rewrapped in the jungle leaf.

It is very delicious and highly sought after and prized for long trips in the lowland tropics, where your shoes can rot away in just a day.

pila: Spanish; fountain or collective communal washing station.

pōm: Maya, all dialects; the resin of various lowland trees used as a smoldering incense to "feed" the Holy. Copal is only one of these. Colloquially called "God's Tortilla," different resins and aromas are still made in various types of balls, cakes, discs, cylinders, and others. Each style pertains to different Deity groups.

pōp: Maya; pronounced like *"pohp";* mat of braided tule reeds. Famous Tzutujil family name. In ritual speech and archaic usage, means the "throne" of a native leader.

pōt: Tzutujil Maya; a woman's handwoven upper garment. There are various types: the young people's knee-length version that runs under the wraparound skirt, the nursing mother's blouse with openings on the sides for the baby, and the ceremonial *Nim Pōt* that is woven of handspun cotton in an ancient style with no embroidery reaching clear to the heels, which is worn over all the other clothing.

psiwanya: Tzutujil Maya; literally canyon water, an illegal distilled moonshine used heavily in ritual as a replacement for more indigenous alcoholic beverages that are banned by the government in deference to the official alcohol industry.

punche: New Mexico Spanish; wild native tobacco.

puño: Spanish; a dagger thrust, but in Guatemala means a "little bit." For the Tzutujil, it is a cooking term equivalent to a three-finger pinch.

Q'ijbal: Tzutujil Maya conjunction Qijibaal, literally "Sun Tools" or "Day Tools"; objects used to Divine Calendar or Shamanic Seeing.

qúel: Little, green, flocking parrots. Very loud. A group of five hundred of these tiny parrots can devour an acre of corn in twenty minutes.

Ruk'ux: Tzutujil Maya; literally "His, her, or its Heart or Center or Germ." In Mayan languages in general, and all-pervasively in Tzutujil, important understandings of the big cultural, mythological, ancestrally responsible types are generally represented by words that, in English at least, seem to be multi-ordinal or multifaceted. But in reality for Tzutujil speakers, these terms are actually a single thought that is not equally representable in present English. Sometimes people hearing the translation of a term like *Ruk'ux* begin to surmise that one word is used for many very differing things because of the droll notion that the people have a poverty of words! But it is quite the contrary.

Ruk'ux is only one of many of these words and is one of the most educational and central of them all.

Meaning simultaneously one and the same thing, not separately the center of anything, stone, tree, mountain, anything, the cardiac organ of all animals, the placenta of all mammals, the egg sac of a bird, fish, or reptile, the germinating organ of any seed, and the soul essence that resides in all of these that makes the heart continue beating, the offspring making placentas, the part of seeds that continues to sprout into adult plants and eventually more seeds.

Old traditional Tzutujil people would often translate *Ruk'ux* to Spanish speakers as "anima," or soul, that which animates. The fact is that for the Tzutujil, the placental sac that nourishes and contains the child, the seed sac and its germ and cotyledons, and the pericardia of the heart are considered to be of the same magic-genetic substance, and contain what I'm calling spiritual DNA to recreate life in a pattern to continue on generationally. Genetics was a spiritual study for the Tzutujil Maya of the traditional past.

sa'coc': Tzutujil; the ancestor of the clumsier modern adaptation called the "corn chip." Made in the shape of perfect bowls that nest inside one another in towers of as many as a hundred, *sa'coc'* is a dehydrated handmade tortilla, made especially for farmers to pack when away for over a month from the village while planting and establishing a field outside the present Tzutujil domain.

Each little bowl can be filled with other foods and eaten without having to worry about spoilage for at least a couple of months. They can also be rehydrated and retoasted to make a good tortilla if preferred. When men take off for these adventures, you can hear the piles of sa'coc' squeaking on their backs from half a mile away.

Sacbey Qanbey: Tzutujil Maya; white road, yellow road. A common but formal ritual abbreviation for the left and right sides of reality as it proceeds walking. Refers to the Milky Way and the wind going opposing directions. A life's destiny.

sexta: Spanish; the sixth of anything.

stoy: Tzutujil Mayan; a contraction of *zuutoy,* a woman's short shawl, twisted into a coil and used as a pot ring on the head to cushion a head-carried load or pot of water. Also the name of a very impressive poisonous water snake whose coiled form is the short shawl of the Great Holy in the Wild, the *Ixoc Joyu, Ixoc taq'aaj.*

subáán: Tzutujil Mayan; called *tamalitos* in Spanish, any one of a variety of forms of steamed flat corn cakes that are wound inside of long corn leaves in such a way as to leave the leaf vein indented, so the cake can be split in two. Differing types include additions of unripe beans, squash tendrils, chipilin leaves, and a million other types. Steamed in quantity in large pots called *p'tix.*

Tlaxcalan: Spanish from Tlaxcalan Nahuat. A Native American from the state of Tlaxcala, where Hernán Cortés first befriended the Tlaxcala aristocracy, promising arms and aid to destroy their traditional Aztec enemies.

People forget when they read that four hundred Spaniards killed twenty thousand Quiché Maya warriors in less than six hours in Xelaju, modern Quetzaltenango, that besides a phalanx of man-eating armored mastiffs from Austria, they were accompanied by thousands of Tlaxcalan shock troops, many armed like the Spaniards, and only after they had weakened the local resisting forces did the Spaniards with their cannon, firearms, crossbows, horses, swords, and halberds enter the fray to finish mopping up. Tlaxcalan people, both men and women, followed the conquerors, the ecclesia, and colonial settlers everywhere for the next one hundred and fifty years.

In Santa Fe, New Mexico, I lived in the old Tlaxcalan section of Analco for a while. Like beautiful Tlaxcala itself, it was famous for its gardens and loyalty to the Spaniards during the famous 1680 revolt of the Pueblo people, a successful resistance that removed every single European and Christian sympathizer from New Mexico for twelve years. Tlaxcalans also founded many

Indian towns in Guatemala after being left behind by their European "employers." Ironically, most of these towns speak some dialect of the Maya language and live a Mayan life.

Tzutujil: Quiché Maya, also spelled Zutuhil, Zutujil, Sutuil, Tzutuhil. The name by which the people of San Pedro Laguna, Santiago Atitlán, and San Pedro Cunen are known to everybody but the Tzutujil, who, like all other Mayan peoples, call themselves some version of the word *vinaaq*, meaning "twenty." For our ten fingers and ten toes, we are twenties.

The exact meaning of the word Tzutujil is not completely known, but it's a very old designation of but a smaller portion of the people now called the Tzutujil before the European interruption.

The Tzutujil have a folk etymology that their powerful numerous Quiche neighbors called them the Tzutujil meaning the "corn tassel people" because they were the most "fertile" of men and women!

The present Tzutujil people came about after a hasty confederation of many lakeside tribal identities after gathering together at the hilltop refuge of old Chitinimit, the capital and ritual sacred city of the Aj Tzikin Jay people, the "People of the Bird Temple," to counter the threat of subjugation by the invading Spanish and their Tlaxcalan allies.

The title Tzutujil has stuck on them because a small fragment of the small Tzikin Jay population were Tzutujil and highborn, while descendants of the Yel, Lomet, Aj Quejnay, and about forty other divisions are only remembered as last names now, though all are classified as Tzutujil.

viga: New Mexico Spanish; crossbeams in a flat-roofed adobe house. Can be quite substantial unmilled, debarked timbers.

wai: Maya; corn cake, tortilla, but in fact means all sustenance, food.

xep: Tzutujil Maya; literally spotted. Refers mostly to *subáán* made with just barely colored black unripe beans in corn masa steamed in corn leaves. This leaves the flat cake with elegant blotted black spots all over and tastes wonderful.

xot: Tzutujil Maya; literally pottery, but refers to the thin, shield-like, lens-shaped, open-fire griddle upon which almost all food was cooked that wasn't boiled. Most are now made of oil-barrel lids, but everyone still prefers the clay.

NEW WORDS AND REDEFINED WORDS AS UNDERSTOOD IN THIS BOOK

Civilization

As a word in this book, *civilization* refers to the cultural phenomenon that imperially accumulates by force a continually expanding territory with all its diverse peoples and life-ways, which then removes the indigenous identity of all its constituents in favor of a national identity or tribalist sovereignty.

As used in this book, the word *civilization* does not refer to any particular civilization of peoples in the past or present, such as the "Ancient Egyptian civilization" or the "Huyuk civilization" or the "Mayan civilization."

Nor does it refer to the modern bias that "wild" things are dangerous, unruly, and beastly and only civilized things are civil and reasonable.

Because "civilizations" only adulate and admire humans of the past who could build big buildings, push their neighbors around with large nasty armies maintained with huge stores of artificially raised food, and create complicated writing systems, small, beautiful, more sustainable, intelligent tribal peoples, to regain legitimacy in the eyes of their "civilized" oppressors, have often been inspired to call themselves by such strange titles as "The Five Civilized Tribes" or the "Hmong Civilization."

This is confusing.

But the word *civilization* in this book refers to big nonindigenous culture that depends on slave labor one hundred percent—human slaves, animal slaves, or mechanical machine slaves—for all its functions, freeing up the people to live a life that doesn't grow food, has no Indigenous identity, and doesn't feed the Divine in Nature by the way they live.

Civilization in this book is the antithesis to Indigenous life.

Civilization by definition domesticates everything at all costs.

Civilization is the opposite of wild.

Feeding; Feeding the Holy in Nature; Feeding the Divine Wild; Feeding Time as Matter Manifest; Feeding the Sun; People Feeding People

In Indigenous Homes and the lives of all intact peoples, food is every-thing—not only because without food we cease, but because the carrying out of the details of comprehending where food originates, how it is served, how we eat, and what we must do to continue living with food enough, constitutes all human culture. When food is no longer at the center of all policy and thought, all that is elegance, gratitude, language, beauty of dress, and adornment are lost. Human culture ceases; animal and plant cultures cease. Food is everything.

To the Tzutujil Maya, all things "eat." The Sun eats—that's what makes him move. The wind eats, the sky eats, the earth eats, ideas eat, everything and everybody eats. In most Indigenous spiritualities, all ritual is feeding the inner driving awareness of all that is the world.

Humans feast the Holy in the Wild with the beauty of what their hands can make as offerings and what their voices can make with their delicious, meaningful prayer music.

All spiritual activity is either a preparation for feasting the people or the Holy in the Wild, or the actual feasting itself. Anything else called rit-ual is just therapy or the same old imperialized religious rigmarole. All Indigenous spiritualities are feasts.

Eating for all real people the world over is the hub of all well-being and existence and goes hand in hand with gratitude, hospitality, and nobility of character, all signs of intactness and vitality, something lost in modernity.

People must feed the Holies in all things all the time. They must feed one another and manage to "feed" the Holy in Nature, even in the beauty and courtesy of the way they go about that.

That is real indigenous human culture.

The Holy

There seems to be no good word for what the word Holy is trying to signify in this book. Holy, Divine, Sacred—all fall short because they've been adopted so imperiously by various religions and spiritual approaches of civilization for things that have nothing to do with the "Holy in the Wild," for instance.

In this book, the Holy in anything is that primal presence that cannot live by human whim or containment, but is the motion behind the procession of all natural things in their particulars going along interdependently, each according to their natures.

"The Holy in the Wild" is taken from *Ixoc juyu Ixoc Ta'q'aj* in Tzutujil, and *Rajawal Ruchiuleu:*

> Woman Mountain, Woman Plains: The Female Holy in the Wild.
> The Owner of the Face of Soil: The Male Holy in the Wild.

These can be pluralized into a million Holies.

The Holies in the world are basically the "Big" Indigenous Souls of the Universes.

Indigenous; Indigenosity; Indigenous Soul

The word *Indigenous* as intended in all of the author's books does not refer only to people, plants, and animals native to an area, but more to a quality that in humans, plants, and animals exists as their most original and natural reality before the advent of big civilization.

Indigenous people in this book are not specific tribes or groups of people per se, but those people of those tribes or groups who could or still do live Indigenously.

All people have these kinds of Indigenous ancestors, but most people's "Indigenosity" is no longer visible in them, but has disappeared below the surface of the more superficial "modern" personality. The Indigenous Soul is the Original Soul that is not a human soul, but the natural soul of Indigenous Humans. It is a version of the soul that is recognized by all indigenous people, one that is some force of nature, an organic vital depth whose "memory" knows how to be itself by living indigenously according to its own nature. The Indigenous Soul does not *see* Nature, but *is a part of* Nature. Indigenous Soul therefore is not strictly a thing of people only, but belongs to all plants, animals, stars, weather, and places.

Intactness

This is perhaps not the best word for what is intended by its use here in this book, for it literally means "untouched," when what we mean here by intactness is "in touch"!

Intactness is wholeness in the Indigenous sense, the state of a fully developed organic soul.

I once had a great friendship with an old Tzutujil gentleman who was my ex-wife's grandfather.

He was blind from trachoma; had escrufulosis, tuberculosis of the lymph system; kidney edema; liver flukes; blood anemia; intestinal ulcers from an eternal infestation of at least five kinds of worms and intestinal parasites; and yet he was never depressed and considered himself utterly healthy. And he was, because his spirit was indigenously intact, fully alive, developed and in place. He was totally upright and felt at home in his tribe. He was vital and intact.

Intactness doesn't exactly denote mental health, either, for many beings on this Earth who have been driven crazy are still intact because they refuse to accept an over-domesticated, insane, soulless, civilized condition as normal, and continue to maintain their intactness through their madness.

Intactness means having a vitality and patience that comes from an Indigenous integrity that knows one's death goes on to feed the living.

The "normal" unnatural neurotic proceedance of modernity and civilization comes from their not having a spiritual intactness.

When a plant is domesticated, it begins to lose its intactness.

When a human is domesticated, he begins to lose intactness. Wild things are, by this definition, intact.

Irreality

The word *irreality* in this book is not intended to signify what is usually meant by *unreal, not real,* or *ethereal.* Irreality is used to denote the very common but strange and unfortunate collective condition whereby an utterly unhealthy, non-sane, unnatural, totally synthetic, technologically choreographed environment with no awareness or regard for the Holy in Nature becomes the cultural environment of a people who, without questioning it, live in its trance, accepting it all as perfectly normal.

This is not unreal because it most certainly tangibly exists, but this neurotic human-centered mess is irreal because its "reality" is man-made and of no use to the organic human soul; it is an irreality.

Modernity

As defined in this book, modernity is the era of civilization in which people are actually able to physically survive without a fully developed original soul: something impossible in the Indigenous past.

Where anonymous mechanized agricultural mining of the Earth for food supports an unnatural, pharmaceutically sustained, overflowing population of people who no longer retain a capacity or instinctual feeling for a natural existence, who live crammed inside techno feats of citified honeycombs of concrete, metal, and automobiles in a regulated mobility of petro-dependent vehicles, with no mythic relation to the origins of what surrounds them, and no knowledge of what feeds them.

Modernity, as far as this book is concerned, begins around 600 BCE until the present, incrementing as it proceeds in distancing us from and insulting the Indigenous core in all of us of what it means to be a real human.

The so-called European Renaissance was the beginning of the physical end of what was still more than an eighty percent world population of Indigenously living people, plants, animals, and places.

Modernity is not something that people can take or leave, for, uninvited, it invades us insidiously in a million nerve-jangling ways for which most humans have no resistance. Neither can modernity be "lessened" nor "eradicated," for loving nothing, it has nothing to lose, and is not based on a love for the wild, but on comfort, addiction, and constant growth.

Therefore, to be healed, the syndrome of modernity must be "metabolized" from inside, digested internally to release our Indigenous memory of how to once again be real humans. Because modernity cannot be outrun or reorganized through revolution or hopeful legislation, as proven by the events of the past, it can only be composted through the grief of a remembered Indigenous integrity.

Origins; Having an Origins

In any language like English that relies so heavily on all the conjugations of the verb "to be," it is very unlikely that anything like what is meant in this book by "an origins" could be willingly expressed or even approximated by a single word.

To be or not to be is not a question in indigenous languages—none of which have real causal verbs "to be"—and are therefore much more richly layered, expansive, and hopeful. In a *to-be* language, a person, a place, a thing, an animal, a plant, an idea, and so on can have an origin, but not an *origins*. They can "originate" at some place or have an origination in time, but a single one of these cannot originate simultaneously in many different times, in many different places in this same time like they can in the minds of the speakers of many indigenous languages.

This encoded necessity for a single origin, for English in particular, is an insidious, very-much-alive linguistic artifact left over from the Norman invasion of England, which marks the beginning of the English language in which the classic very "to be" language of Catholic Christianity's Latin was forcibly and violently layered upon the Germanic and Celtic languages of both Britain and the Germanic Normans (their so-called French was a Latinified Teutonic).

There is no such thing as pagan English. English began only as an effort to Catholicize Britain. It was born from being forced to carry church doctrine, which recognizes only a single line of origins of all people and things through the Old Testament biblical Genesis back to their single god.

This need for a single origin story, need for a single line of valid origination for anything, has strangely enough never left the English language in use to this day. Even so-called rational scientists who in the trance of this unconscious irreality maintain a subliminal adherence and implied enforcement of a need for a single true integral "myth" of a people and not finding one, which they never do, spuriously erect one from what they consider leftover fragments.

They look for a single originating star, an original single explosion, a single universe containing multiple universes, a single genetic Eve as the origins of all humankind, a single ancestral condition for each flower, bird, lizard, etc., all of which are implied in the language, but which also goes counter to the results of all their scientific findings; that all things of the world and beyond have multiple origins and originations that simultaneously run backward, sideways, forward, and in distinct and usually contradictory (at least in a *to-be* language) lines and directions, yet each of these origins must be held to be not only equally valid but also equally necessary for the present as a complete thing to be appreciated if not wholly comprehended in all its reality.

It would be comical if not for the fact that it is a sign of a tragic cultural loss when Indigenous people succumb to outside forces causing them to believe they must have a single Genesis-like mythic origin, and at modernity's urging seek to create those kinds of "unified mythological field theories" that always result in a synthetic merging of a thousand divergent tales into a single spurious mythic continuum to rationalize themselves as a people with a single, sequentially aligned "origin."

Science is always searching for the core, the pure, the true, the complete and nonfragmented story of the "original" people or things they study, but a single Eve does not exist any more than a people are "one" people and not the descendants of untold groups of people and live creatures. Therefore one story does not exist; nor has it ever existed. One story for all is the unhealthy footings of fundamentalism.

Indigenously, for people as for all of Nature, there are always many stories, none of them the same, some similar, some differing, but all are real and not just simple fragments of a conjured vision of a single central whole, for each is whole within itself, and whole because all the other stories' "origins" exist in their own wholeness like an ecosystem of diverse species teeming on an ever-unfolding reef. Plants, animals, weather, all geology, and especially the stellar and non-stellar universes all run in a corresponding motive.

Multiple origins are always the way of things. Together I call this "having an origins," but I don't say "having origins" because that implies something too nebulous.

For example, any person has one biological mother and a father who in turn each have their own mother and father. Here alone there are at least four vast lineages whose diverse directions go into the infinity of generations of divergent cultural, genetic, and linguistic pasts, with the one thing that holds them together as a single possibility contained in their descendant. This person has an origins.

To continue to unconsciously maintain the simple-minded implication that in the end "all roads lead to Rome" is indeed an imperial imposition deeply nailed into the psyche of the civilized. This need for "oneness" is the destruction of diversity, intelligence, and the Indigenous integrity of life and is the basis of all single-identity nationalisms.

The ability to not only embrace many differing realities, stories, origins, viewpoints, ways of being, and possibilities as all being equally valid and necessary, but to still maintain them all in an intact way and whole inside the matrix of their own natural contexts without simple-mindedly "mushing" them all together into an amorphous soup of "oneness," is the basis of a living peace with our Indigenous Souls leading the way.

Not all peoples' gods are just different names for the same being. The diverse peoples of the world should not be required to be regarded as "equal" in the sense they are all the same at the core, but equal in the fact that the validity of the majesty of the diverse differences of their cores are equally necessary for the world to function, not as one, but with a functioning life-giving proceedance, with a diverse origins and destinies. The grief and mystery of living awake with an origins is the organic root from which can spring a tree of hope for a time beyond our own.

Everything has a multiple origins whose roots in the wild do not match the insistences of the bias of civilization, but whose flowering in the present is our selves here today.

Proceedance

Proceedance is the way a people, culture, animal, plant, or anything proceeds along in how it lives out its existence. A cultural proceedance is the way a particular culture goes about being itself in all its characteristic cycles, habits, prejudices, fears, joys, and general motives for doing so. It also implies a direction towards which anything by its cultural nature is motivated to proceed. This word denotes the character of anything according to its long-range motion.

Rematriated; Rematrixed

This term describes an instance where land, air, water, animals, plants, ideas, and ways of doing things and living are purposefully returned to their original natural context—their mother, the great Female Holy Wild. Like the repatriation of prisoners after years of war or millennia of unwilling slavery in service to an unconscious civilization, exploited and depleted for their wild vitality, any attempt to "rematriate" them back to the Holy in Nature is the beginning of cultural sanity and healing.

The English *matter* descends from Latin's *mater*, meaning *mother*.

In Latin, *matrix* is the womb of the Mother, therefore to *rematrix* things means returning any exploited part of the Earth back into the actual body of the earth. Putting the iron back into the ore is rematrixing iron and slag back into taconite. Spiritually, this is the beginning of intactness: rematrixing the Indigenous Soul back into everyday existence.

Vitality

As used in this book, vitality is the old Indigenous definition of health, which has nothing to do with the absence of disease. Vitality is what wild, undomesticated things have as part of their nature that gives them intactness.

Vitality is what causes someone to live strongly and elegantly even if they have been proclaimed hopelessly ill—or even as they die. Vitality is also what causes some wild things to be willing to die in their struggle to stay wild, unwilling to live enslaved or domesticated under any conditions.

The capacity for both people and seeds to demonstrate unprovoked, telltale signs of original Indigenous characteristics all of a sudden after generations of conformative, over-domesticated, civilized existences is caused by the vitality of the original Indigenous Soul. This vitality does not come from learned techniques of living, but directly from the Holy in the Wild through the intactness of our Indigenous Souls.

Vitality comes from still having some internal memory of how to be natural and wild, and at odds with the modern acquired personality.

Wild

Not crazy, out of control, free, or living according to whim, the word *wild* here specifically refers to undomesticated yet non-feral places, peoples, animals, plants, landscapes, weathers, and so on, that are not harnessed, tamed, exploited, mined, farmed, logged, or managed by humans, not used for recreation, photography, art, or tourism.

The Wild is the environment of the Divine and must stay wild for anything non-wild to continue to be vital.

There are truly indigenous humans who are part of the wild and whose presence in the wild is not only undamaging and uninterrupting to the wild, but is so much a natural ingredient of the wild that they are indispensable to the Wild and the Divine in the Wild.

All humans were once these types of indigenous people. These natural humans should never be removed or put under the jurisdiction of unnatural civilized people, for the Wild is then being disturbed.

A lot of wild animals, plants, and other things regularly "visit" the unwild, and some of the smaller ones live wild outside the Wild. These are the "eyes" of the Holy in the Wild. They are looking in on us. They are Holy, too.

ABOUT THE AUTHOR

A master of eloquence and innovative language, **Martín Prechtel** is a leading thinker, writer, and teacher whose work, both written and oral, hopes to promote the subtlety, irony, and premodern vitality hidden in any living language. As a half-blood Native American with a Pueblo Indian upbringing, his life took him from New Mexico to the village of Santiago Atitlán, Guatemala. There becoming a full village member of the Tzutujil Mayan population, he eventually served as a principal in that body of village leaders responsible for instructing the young people in the meanings of their ancient stories through the rituals of adult rites of passage. Once again residing in his native New Mexico, Martín teaches at his international school, Bolad's Kitchen. Through music, ritual, farming, livestock raising, sacred architecture, ancient textiles, tools, and story, Martín helps people in many lands to retain their diversity while remembering their own sense of place in the daily sacred through the search for the Indigenous Soul.

For more information visit www.floweringmountain.com.